ISBN: 9781313156943

Published by:
HardPress Publishing
8345 NW 66TH ST #2561
MIAMI FL 33166-2626

Email: info@hardpress.net
Web: http://www.hardpress.net

6921
B869
R14

CORNELL
UNIVERSITY
LIBRARY

FINE ARTS LIBRARY

Cornell University Library
N 6921.B69R14

The women artists of Bologna /

3 1924 020 692 624

THE WOMEN ARTISTS
OF BOLOGNA

THE APPEARANCE OF THE INFANT CHRIST TO S. ANTHONY OF PADUA
PINACOTECA, BOLOGNA. SALA DI GUIDO

THE WOMEN ARTISTS
OF BOLOGNA

BY

LAURA M. RAGG

MEDALLIST OF THE ROYAL HISTORICAL SOCIETY 1900

WITH TWENTY ILLUSTRATIONS

METHUEN & CO.
36 ESSEX STREET W.C.
LONDON

First Published in 1907

TO
MY HUSBAND
LONSDALE RAGG
IN MEMORY
OF MANY PEACEFUL HOURS
SPENT TOGETHER IN THE LIBRARIES
OF BOLOGNA

CONTENTS

	PAGE
PREFACE	xi
INTRODUCTION	1

CATERINA DEI VIGRI
THE NUN
1413–1463

	SANTA CATERINA DA BOLOGNA	11
I.	CATERINA'S CHILDHOOD	13
II.	CATERINA AT THE COURT OF FERRARA . . .	24
III.	CATERINA'S NOVICIATE	46
IV.	CATERINA THE PROFESSED "CLARISSA" . . .	67
V.	THE NEW COLONY	103
VI.	THE DEATH OF THE RIGHTEOUS	126
VII.	CATERINA'S POST-MORTEM HISTORY . . .	136
VIII.	CATERINA THE ARTIST	150
	AUTHORITIES	158
	APPENDIX A	160
	APPENDIX B	163

PROPERZIA DE' ROSSI
THE SCULPTOR
1500 (?)–1530

PROPERZIA DE' ROSSI	167
AUTHORITIES	187
APPENDIX	188

x   THE WOMEN ARTISTS OF BOLOGNA

	PAGE
THE MEETING OF EMPEROR CHARLES V WITH POPE CLEMENT VII IN BOLOGNA, 1529	184
Detail of picture by Marco Vecellio in the Hall of the Council of Ten, Ducal Palace, Venice	
PORTRAIT OF LAVINIA FONTANA PAINTED BY HERSELF	193
Uffizi Gallery, Florence	
From a Photograph by Signor G. Brogi, Florence	
THE GOZZADINI FAMILY	208
Gozzadini Palace, Via Santo Stephano, Bologna	
From a Photograph by Signore Rambaldi	
THE INFANT FRANCIS I OF FRANCE, PRESENTED BY HIS MOTHER, LOUISE DE SAVOIE, FOR THE BLESSING OF S. FRANCESCO DI PAOLA	214
Pinacoteca, Bologna. Sala del Tiarini	
From a Photograph by Signor P. Poppi, Bologna	
PORTRAIT OF ELISABETTA SIRANI PAINTED BY HERSELF	229
Pinacoteca, Bologna	
From a Photograph by Signor P. Poppi, Bologna	
CARICATURE OF THE OLD MAN RIALI	274
From a tracing made by the author of the copy preserved with the MS. of the Processo in the Archivio di Stato, Bologna	
THE BAPTISM OF CHRIST	294
The Certosa, Bologna	
From a Photograph by Signor P. Poppi, Bologna	
THE CHRIST-CHILD ON THE GLOBE	296
Pinacoteca, Bologna	
From a Photograph by Signor P. Poppi, Bologna	
THE CONVERSION OF ST. EUSTACHE	304
From an engraving in the possession of the author	
MAP OF BOLOGNA	*At End*

PREFACE

THIS book came into being almost against the will of its author. Other work had been conceived and was taking shape, when Fate decreed a long residence in Italy, and then making her commands more definite, unexpectedly enjoined an eight months' sojourn in Bologna. There the libraries and the environment offered but scant encouragement for a study of Napoleonic France, while the opportunity of learning something of the history of one of the most interesting and less known of Italian cities was too precious to be neglected. Desultory reading in the Archiginnasio was begun, and then ceased to be desultory. By degrees facts were strung on golden threads of biography: soon the distinction and achievements of Bologna's women were noted as a characteristic of the city's history. Eager inquiries elicited the ignorance of the cultured many, and the very partial knowledge of the learned few. Curiosity was piqued; the obscurity of the subject enhanced its fascination; its elusiveness increased the ardour of pursuit. Little by little the conviction gained ground that the lives of the women artists and the *bas bleus* of Bologna might well be brought before the notice of English readers.

That the task has been accomplished, however unsatisfactorily, is largely due to the encouragement and help of friends and counsellors to whom the author would take this opportunity of returning heart-felt thanks. Chief among these are: the sisters of the Convent of Corpus Domini in Bologna; the illustrious Corrado Ricci and Ispettore Ferri in Florence; Cav. Livi, head of the Archivio in Bologna; Professor Albano Sorbelli and his colleagues in the Archiginnasio; Dottori Ludovico Frati of the University Library; and Herr Frank, the genial Padrone of the Hotel Brun.

L. M. R.

BELLUNO, *December, 1906*

THE WOMEN ARTISTS OF BOLOGNA

INTRODUCTION

FROM the days of the shadowy precursors of Accursius down to the modern times of Carducci, Trombetti, and Marconi, Bologna has shown herself the mother and nurse of genius. Nor has she reserved her maternal tenderness exclusively for her male nurslings. No city in the world has produced more women of distinguished talent; none has been more prompt to further their achievements, more generous in crowning their success. We are not speaking, moreover, of ladies of exalted birth and exceptional opportunity, such as those who graced many of the Italian courts of the fifteenth and sixteenth centuries, and who, betrothed in childhood, owed alike their unusual education and their subsequent influence to their husbands' power and position; but of women belonging to obscure and sometimes to poor families, who achieved a name and fame by their own exertions, before or independently of marriage.

Conspicuous among these are the women directly connected with the University. In the fourteenth century there is the romantic figure of Novella Andrea, outlined for us, alas! as vaguely as for her students, from whom, on account of her perturbing personal attractions, she was screened while lecturing by a curtain; while towards the end of the eighteenth and beginning of the nineteenth century we meet three deeply-learned ladies crowned with every possible University distinction—Laura Bassi, Clotilda Tambroni, and Anna Morandi. Next to this triad of *bas bleus*, and between them and the veiled lecturer in point of time, are several ladies remarkable for culture and philanthropy, while the four artists whose lives are sketched in these pages form a third category of distinguished Bolognese women.

Every biography is like a coin with two faces. The one is stamped with an image and superscription, the other with a coat-of-arms, a device, an allegory. The one relates to the individual, the other to his environment. Sometimes the obverse, sometimes the reverse is the clearer and more interesting. Sometimes both are blurred, and can be deciphered only by comparison with other coins of the period.

In the first of these four sketches the personal interest predominates. The likeness of the woman is clear: her surroundings are misty and undetermined. She was a cloistered nun, who saw the world without only *per speculum in enigmate*, as the Lady of Shalott saw the life and stir and pomp and toil of the high road to Arthur's capital—but without observing it so closely. Her book of religious instructions, with its innumerable fine autobiographical touches, gives us a picture not of the times, but of the inner, nay the inmost, life of a fifteenth-century religious. It takes us into the secret places of a soul, and we know the "Santa" of Bologna as we know few of our friends—perhaps as we only now and then know ourselves. And while her own writings make us see her from her own standpoint, the memoir written by her loved companion, Suor Illuminata Bembo, enables us to view her from without, critically, at the distance from which we contemplate our acquaintance. We recognize that she was a nun first, by natural fitness, by heart-whole profession, and only secondarily a painter; but the artistic level to which, even under these conditions, she attained, her administrative ability —often only another manifestation of creative talent— her faculties of observation, shown in her knowledge of character and the tactful management of her nuns, her faculty of expression in words, and her generally cultivated mind, may well lead us to believe that under other circumstances, in another age, Caterina dei Vigri would have been a greater artist than any of her three successors.

In the life of the sculptress, Properzia dei Rossi, it is the picturesque and external aspect of biography which predominates. In spite of the bas-relief in the Museum of S. Petronio, which is said to be the revelation and the monument of her love and her despair, we never really come close to her. But the story of her unhappy passion, the superficial classicality and intense individualism of her work; the boldness, the graceful self-possession, the lack of self-consciousness with which she ventures into paths hitherto untrodden by her sex; the spontaneous and unstinted appreciation of her fellow-citizens—all are typical and redolent of the age to which she belonged. Her death, too, is inextricably associated with one of the most picturesque and eventful episodes in the history of Bologna—the coronation of the Emperor Charles V by the Pope Clement VII.

The period between the death of Caterina dei Vigri and the childhood of Properzia dei Rossi coincided with the brilliant but insecure rule of Giovanni Bentivoglio II, whose life has somehow escaped the attention which Englishmen have bestowed so abundantly on other Italian tyrants. That rule ended in 1506, and the gorgeous ceremony in S. Petronio in the year 1530 seemed the outward visible sign of Bologna's willing submission to the papal government—a government which lasted from that time onwards to the day when the city became part of the "Kingdom of Italy" as the "Department of the Reno." It was the signal also of the advancing wave of the Catholic reaction, destined before long to sweep away all the aspirations and tendencies and many of the achievements of the period which had produced and inspired a Properzia dei Rossi.

By the time Lavinia Fontana had begun to paint, the pendulum had swung backwards to its limit. The childlike spirit of fearless curiosity, which was the peculiar charm and peril of the men and women of the renaissance, had been chastened into conventional correctness. Orthodoxy triumphed all along the line—making its own even the pagan culture and worship of antiquity which had consumed an earlier generation, everywhere erecting sign-posts and fences for the guidance and restraint of the human spirit, and, to some extent, strengthening and restoring the moral boundaries overthrown by the intense desire for self-realization and self-development.

Three events which occurred during Lavinia's lifetime, and within the range of her immediate cognizance, give us the measure of the social conditions of her day. They were: (1) The execution of Giordano Bruno as a heretic (1600); (2) the death of Tasso in the Convent of St. Onofrio in Rome (1597), a weary, disappointed craven, fearful lest the Holy Office should censure his Gerusalumme Liberata; (3) the publication and enormous success of Marini's "Adonis." Scientific inquiry and free discussion are prohibited; true poetry is suffocated in an atmosphere from which the oxygen of the renaissance has been exhausted; and as a substitute for it Italian society is supplied with a *soufflé* of preposterous metaphors and frothy hyperboles creamy with facile imagination, unsalted by genius, devoid of a particle of spiritual nourishment, but served with a sauce of piquant lasciviousness.

Lavinia Fontana's life and works reflect for good and evil, the evil and good of her day. An excellent daughter, wife and mother, exemplary and regular in conduct, tranquil, popular, and prosperous, she is a complete and significant contrast to the brilliant, beautiful Properzia, with her tragic, shamelessly proclaimed passions, and her miserable, untimely death.

As an artist Lavinia was successful in her day, and remains admirable, chiefly because of her limitations, and the good sense which made her recognize them. Portrait painting does not demand—and perhaps cannot express—the very highest gifts of imagination, while it gives unlimited scope to technical skill and the colour sense. When Lavinia accepted commissions for religious or historical pictures, she remained a portrait painter. Her well-known picture in the gallery of Bologna, representing S. Francesco di Paolo blessing the infant Francis I of France, is merely an interesting and highly decorative portrait group. More historical imagination is shown in the "Multiplication of the Loaves and Fishes" in the church of S. Maria della Pieta; but while all Properzia's pseudo-classicism of treatment has disappeared, and the old forms of religious art have been restored, the breath of life no longer animates them. Lavinia's Madonnas do not inspire, and were not inspired by devotion.

In the days of Elisabetta Sirani we see the received types growing more stereotyped, while a certain meretricious sentimentality differentiates them strangely from their *Quattrocento* prototypes. This sentimentality, artificial though it be, is the genuine expression of the *Zeitgeist* of the seventeenth century, and has its counterpart in the dress, the furniture, the manners of the period. It is sufficiently marked in the work of Guido Reni, the master of Elisabetta's father and her own exemplar, and is still more accentuated in her sweet-faced Virgins and graceful Holy Families.

Her story is full both of personal and social interest. It exhibits most picturesquely the conditions of domestic service, the medical ignorance, the legal procedure, the pompous funeral ceremonies of the time, while its central feature is that horrible characteristic of the *Seicento*, the prevalence and constant dread of secret poisoning.

The trial of the maidservant who was supposed to be the instrument of Elisabetta's death is as much within the MS. of the Processo in the Archivio of Bologna "and nowhere out of it," as the trial of Pompilia's murderers was in that "square old yellow book" which Browning picked up for a *lira* from a stall in the square of San Lorenzo. There we find the deposition of witnesses —made in no open court, but taken down separately and privately by the Sub-Auditor of the Torrone; there, too, are the pleadings of the lawyers, the Sirani's friend Bianchini, counsel for the prosecution, and Niccolò de Lemmi, acting for the Committee for the Defence of the Poor. And these *interrogatorii* and these orations give us not only a clear understanding of the conduct of a criminal case in the seventeenth century, but also a strangely intimate knowledge of Elisabetta's rather dreary working life, and of her last hideous sufferings.

She was younger than Properzia dei Rossi when she died, having only attained the age of twenty-seven; but in a short time truly she had fulfilled a long time. Her own, by no means exhaustive, catalogue of finished work reveals an almost incredible amount of activity and accomplishment.

CATERINA DEI VIGRI

THE NUN

(SANTA CATERINA DA BOLOGNA)

b. 1413. *d.* 1463.

THE FIGURE OF THE SANTA SEATED IN HER CHAPEL
CHURCH OF CORPUS DOMINI, BOLOGNA

SANTA CATERINA DA BOLOGNA

THE enormous quadrangle of blank brick wall, representing to the world outside it the Convent of Corpus Domini in Bologna, is broken in the Via Tagliapietre by a portal of singular beauty. This lovely door with its terra-cotta mouldings, the work of the medallist Sperandio, is all that remains of the original[1] outer church, which, less than twenty years after her death, the pious Bolognese erected in memory of the first abbess. The fifteenth-century portal gives access to a *barocco* temple, well proportioned and richly decorated, which is, however, only the ante-chamber to a small cell, entered from the second chapel on the left. In this cell beneath a gorgeous canopy the " Santa " sits enthroned, to receive the homage of the faithful.

The body is unsupported; the posture is natural; the skin on hands and feet and face is perfect, uncorrupted, it is said flexible. Yet no grinning skeleton or ghostly corpse could be more unlifelike than this small erect figure, whose discoloured wizened face is thrown into hideous relief by the splendour of silk and gems and cloth of gold. A splendid diadem glitters above the black veil; the brown habit of the Poor Clare is replaced by a regal mantle; there is a written notice in

[1] Built in 1481 by the architects Marchione da Faenza and Bartolomeo da Dozza.

the cell that priests are permitted to kiss the Santa's hands.

That the woman who yearned for strict seclusion and shunned observation, who in early youth fled from the pomps and vanities of a court, and who loved poverty as whole-heartedly as her master St. Francis that this humble, sensitive, reserved gentlewoman should be thus arrayed in garish splendour, and exposed to the gaze of the curious, seems the irony of a satiric fate.

We turn with relief to the relics disposed on the walls of the cell. There, in a locked glass case, is one of the many breviaries copied and illuminated by the Saint, for the use of the community. There hangs a picture, unsigned, but attributed by constant tradition to Caterina, the lovely Madonna of the Apple. There, most interesting of all, is the little viol on which the dying Abbess played to the wonder and admiration of her flock. With these objects, not the bedizened husk of her gracious spirit, in our minds, let us try to trace the history of this gentle follower of St. Francis, who, long before her canonization, was to Bologna what Anthony was to Padua,—*The Saint.*

CHAPTER I

CATERINA'S CHILDHOOD

> A child most infantine,
> Yet wandering far beyond that innocent age
> In all but its sweet looks and mien divine;
> Even then, methought, with the world's tyrant rage
> A patient warfare thy young heart did wage.
>
> SHELLEY, *Revolt of Islam*

"CATERINA 'poverella,' Bolognese, that is in Bologna begotten, born and bred, and in Ferrara by Christ espoused." Thus Caterina dei Vigri, as though foreseeing the subsequent competition between Ferrara and Bologna for the possession of a new saint, defined with legal precision her position in respect to both cities.

She died in the city where she first saw the light, and, though professed in Ferrara, her life as abbess was passed in Bologna. The Ferrarese had, however, this much in their favour—the Vigri family was wholly theirs. Girolamo Baruffaldi, an industrious Ferrarese writer of the eighteenth century, gives the family tree as follows:—

Vigrio, lived in Ferrara in 1307.

Ventura.

Zaccaro Capitano.

Nascimpace, Doctor of Law.

Bonaventura.

Count Alberto. Died 1470; buried in church of Ognisanti Ferrara, in the chapel of St. Ives. His descendants became extinct in 1619.

Giovanni, Doctor of Law. Died 1426.

Santa Caterina da Bologna.

The family was certainly an honourable one. Some authorities declare that it was connected with the ruling house of Este, while Caterina's friend, successor, and biographer, Illuminata Bembo—herself a Venetian patrician—naively informs us that the Vigri were "visited by all people of consequence in Ferrara," and that Giovanni was "a man of substance and came of a good house, nor had he ever exercised any trade (arte) nor knew how to do so, but was a good scholar, and a doctor, and many important offices were given to him."

It is unfortunate that Sister Illuminata does not tell us where the father of her friend studied and took his degree. In the eighteenth century, at the time of her formal beatification, the good citizens of Ferrara maintained with much plausibility that if "La Santa's" family were Ferrarese she herself could not be Bolognese.[1]

[1] "Memorie della Lite e Pretensione de Ferraresi che la nostra B. Caterina da Bologna si dovesse chiamare da Ferrara. Unpublished MS. Archivio Arcivescovile, Bologna."

"For," said their advocates, "when embassies and affairs of state take men with their families for many years away from their native country, it must needs happen that they have children born in foreign parts," but these children belong legally " not to the country of their birth, but to that of their family." To this the lawyers of Bologna answered that Doctor Giovanni dei Vigri having taken his degree in civil law in Bologna became according to the law of the city a Bolognese citizen. A Bolognese citizen, he married a Bolognese lady, and of this marriage Caterina was born—a Bolognese.

The fundamental assertion of the Bolognese lawyers cannot now be verified, the University registers for the opening years of the fifteenth century having been destroyed by fire. But the fact that Giovanni dei Vigri took his degree in Bologna never seems to have been disputed by the Ferrarese, though they may have scorned the inferences drawn from it; and it is unhesitatingly accepted by the Jesuit Father Grassetti, who, in 1653, wrote what may be called the authorized life of the Saint.

Nothing, indeed, could have been more natural than that a Ferrarese youth of parts, with a distinguished lawyer for his grandfather and an elder brother destined for a military career, should have been sent to study law in the famous neighbouring University of Bologna, nor could a youth of character and parts intending to serve his country as a diplomat have had a better training than that afforded by the life of a medieval student.

It was a many-tinted, eventful existence, demanding and enforcing self-reliance, courage, and address, and ensuring an acquaintance with many foreign tongues and modes of thought. At an age when a modern boy is surrounded by teachers and governors at school, the fifteenth-century undergraduate selected his own teachers, course of study, and lodging, making his own contract with his host, and living practically without control. In Bologna the bell of S. Petronio summoned the students every morning to common worship, after which they went their several ways to the private houses or class-rooms (*scuole*) of their chosen teachers, who lectured between nine a.m. and midday and between three p.m. and six, for at least one hour at a time. Giovanni dei Vigri being a student of civil law would have directed his steps to the legal quarter of the city, the district in the neighbourhood of Via S. Mammolo (now Via d' Azeglio). In the *scuole* he would have mingled with boys of all nations, kindreds, and tongues—students from England, Germany, and France, from Spain and Portugal, from Sclavonia and the Indies, and from every part of Italy—a cosmopolitan audience which was not always patient or courteous.

Even in the seventeenth century, when the University organization was more centralized and defined, we learn from the letter[1] of a Bohemian student that the lecture-room of an unpopular teacher was the scene of outrageous disorder. "When a doctor does not please in his lecture," wrote the young Bohemian, "they clap their hands and stamp their feet in order to compel him to quit the chair. Swords on such occasions are some-

[1] Martin Horky to Kepler. Published by A. Favaro. *Atti e Memorie Dep. Storia Patria*, per le Prov. di Rom. Vol. X. Further he declares: "Vita dissoluta. Fui Bononiae per sexannos lunares, gladios vagina vacuos magis quam millies vidi."

A LECTURER AND SCHOLARS IN FIFTEENTH CENTURY BOLOGNA
FROM A FIFTEENTH CENTURY MANUSCRIPT

times drawn. Vidi et saepe video." Sometimes unpopular teachers were attacked in other ways. In 1414, for example, Doctor Jacopo dei Vinidani was insulted by a law-student of Lucca, who placarded libels against him in two different places in the city. More frequently still they were robbed, the objects stolen being generally books.[1] It is fair to the offenders to remember that the poor scholar could seldom afford books of his own, and was terribly hindered by the lack of them. Sometimes he stipulated with his host for the use of a very limited library together with board and lodging; sometimes he borrowed at a fixed rate from stationers and lecturers—practices affording ample scope for bibliophilic dishonesty. He suffered also from lack of privacy. Frequently he shared his mean room with a student as poor as himself, and used the streets as his study and parlour; so that a modern Bolognese writer [2] believes that the existence of the porticoes which are such characteristic features of Bologna and Padua may be largely attributed to "the immense number of scholars who were obliged to pass great part of the day and evening in the streets," and for whom a shelter from winter storms and summer sun was imperative. Such a practice, given the extreme youth of the students and the mixture of nationalities, was of course not favourable to the quiet and order of the city. Brawls and quarrels, often ending in bloodshed,[3] were of frequent occurrence

[1] The records of the actions for theft are interesting in that they furnish us with the names and values of the books used by the teachers of the day and coveted by their scholars.
[2] L. Frati, *Vita Privata di Bologna*.
[3] The quarrel was sometimes carried into the lecture-room. Giovanni dei Vigri was probably a "fresher" at Bologna when a Genoese, by name

among these "Cervelli turbidi ed ingegni storti," as a chronicler of the fifteenth century calls the undergraduates of his own and Giovanni's day.

No student could be a candidate for the *laurea dottorale* till he had completed the twentieth year of his age and an eight years course of study; nor, we may add, unless he were what Illuminata Bembo explicitly affirms Giovanni to have been—"a man of substance."

The closing act of the scholar's career was performed with costly pomp and circumstance. In the case of a youth of good family belonging to the city it was celebrated like the coming of age of a modern son and heir. Thus when Taddeo Pepoli took his doctor's degree, his father, Romeo, presented all the city guilds with sumptuous liveries, and kept open house to the entire populace of Bologna. Humbler or more obscure individuals entertained in a less extensive but sufficiently liberal manner; the newly-made doctor being expected to provide a banquet for the troop of comrades[1] and well-wishers who accompanied him from the cathedral, where the degree was conferred, back to his own house. Besides these supplementary expenses there were various fixed dues and unfixed "tips"; fees to the Archdeacon, Vicar, and notaries; payments to beadles, bell-ringers, and musicians; oblations of wine and sweetmeats to

Gabriele Giustiniani, was assaulted during lecture by a scholar from Lucca, who entered the *scuola* with a knife, and would have killed his man, had not the other students rallied to his defence.

[1] On the way *to* the cathedral the student was accompanied by his relatives and by "not more than ten" of his fellow-students, together with the two doctors who presented him to the Archdeacon and certified that they had examined him privately and were satisfied as to his capacity.

the Archdeacon; of a ring, cap, and pair of gloves to the Prior, and of eight "braccia" of fine cloth to each of the "presentors."

There is a tradition, made use of by the Bolognese lawyers in 1704, that Giovanni dei Vigri, after receiving his doctor's degree, remained in Bologna as a lecturer. The tradition is not disproved by the absence of his name from the lists[1] of professors of the studio receiving stipends from the commune; for on the one hand the lists are imperfect, and on the other there were many teachers outside them whose payment was a matter of private contract between themselves and their scholars. It is, moreover, supported by the fact of his marriage with a Bolognese lady of good family, whose attractions may well have increased the disinclination felt by many a graduate since Giovanni's time to leave a spot endeared by countless romantic and intellectual associations.

We unfortunately know nothing of the wooing and wedding of this lady, who bore the sweet Italian name of Benvenuta—a name surely full of suggestiveness to a lover's ear. She came of the family of Mamolini, who in the year 1465 certainly possessed houses[2] in the Via dei Toschi, and who were presumably there fifty years previously. One of these houses, recently destroyed to make room for the new General Post Office, was marked by a tablet declaring it to be the birthplace of Santa Caterina da Bologna; but the Bolognese tradition that this house was her home till her eleventh year cannot be proved or disproved by documentary

[1] Mandati di Pagamenti. Archiv. di Bologna.
[2] See Guidicini, 1463. Via dei Toschi.

evidence. The wording of Caterina's auto-description, "in Bologna acquistata nata ed allevata," appears to favour the Bolognese pretensions, but *allevata* may only mean that she remained in Bologna till she was weaned; and the Ferrarese maintain that Benvenuta merely went to her parents' home for her confinement.

On one point all authorities are agreed—namely, that Giovanni was at Padua, on the business of his master, the Marchese Niccolò, when Caterina came into the world. This fact afforded scope for the introduction of one of the supernatural incidents indispensable to the infancy of a child destined to attain sanctity, or even conspicuous mundane celebrity. The absent Giovanni's thoughts continually turned homewards to the wife he had left enceinte and the child who was coming; till at length on the night of September the seventh, he dreamed that Benvenuta was safely delivered of a daughter, and that she was destined to be no common child. Little by little this most natural vision of a young father was improved on, till at length Caterina's birth was said to have been announced by the Virgin Mother herself, who declared that the newly-born infant would be "a clear light to the world." In a curious hymn in Caterina's honour, printed less than forty years after her death, we see the legend growing :—

> Quando nascisti virgine beata
> il padre tuo a padua era andato
> la tua nativita li fu annunciata
> per visione e per divino trovato
> dicto li fu che fosse ritornata
> a la sua patria che tropo era stato
> per questo ritorno poi lui a bologna

CATERINA'S CHILDHOOD

> quello che dicto li fu non fu menzogna.
> *Non so che annunciasse questi al padre.*
> *Credo che fusse la divina madre.*[1]

Another of the hymns puts the incident more briefly and adds a fresh touch.

> Trovo che a padoa fusti revelata
> *Da feminil roce* a tuo par dicendo
> Va a bologna chuna putta te nata.[2]

The new-born infant's placid disposition and low vitality furnished in retrospect additional indications of the Divine calling and election. To quote again from the quaint hymn in her honour. The father on his return from Padua—

> Ritrovo nato quello olente fiore
> Che per tre zorni lacte non gustava
> nutrita ella era del divino amore
> e come agnello mansueta stava
> non piangeva ne monstrava alchun dolore
> tanta alegreza Deo nel core li dava.[3]

[1] When thou wast born, blessed virgin,
Thy father to Padua had gone.
Thy birth to him was announced
By vision and divine discovery;
It was told him he must needs return
Unto his country, that too long he had tarried.
Therefore returned he forthwith to Bologna.
That which had been told him was no lie;
I know not who announced this to the father,
But I believe it must have been the Divine Mother.

[2] I find that at Padua thou wast revealed
By feminine voice to thy father, saying,
Go to Bologna for a baby-girl is born to thee.

[3] Found born that fragrant flower,
Who for three days tasted no milk;

Caterina's equanimity of temper and preternatural gravity outlasted her swaddling clothes. She was never naughty and never played like other children; was quick at her lessons, and eager to imitate and aid her mother in devotional exercises and works of charity. And, since the fifteenth century for good and evil know nothing of "child-study" and "the principles of education," the precocious piety and learning of the sickly, intelligent, sweet-natured only daughter of Giovanni and Benvenuta were encouraged, forced, and applauded by admiring relatives and friends.

The fond father continually employed on affairs of state, undoubtedly talked proudly of the infant prodigy to his master, in whom paternal affection was also a strong feature. Its objects in the case of the Marchese d'Este were unfortunately not born in wedlock. It is possible that had the childless Gigliola da Carrara—the bride given to Niccolò III when a mere boy of fourteen —been able to hold him by the ties which in the case of others he acknowledged readily and loyally, he would never have formed the licentious habits which increasingly disfigured his strong, vigorous, and enlightened character. It is certain that many of his natural children enjoyed not only a princely state, but a liberal education and a careful upbringing, such as was received by few of the ruling families of the day.

One of these children, a daughter named Margherita, was a few months older than Giovanni's little girl, who

> Nourished she was by divine love.
> And like a gentle lamb she lay,
> Nor wept, nor manifested any pain;
> Such joy God gave her in her heart.

was possibly a distant kinsman of the Marchese, and was obviously what would be considered a desirable companion. Thus it came to pass that at the age of eleven Caterina, doubtless to her own great benefit, became a member of the Este household and found a friend and mistress in the " Principessa Margherita."

CHAPTER II

CATERINA AT THE COURT OF FERRARA

> Come
> Ne le scendente spire de la conchiglia un eco
> d' antichi pianti, un suono di lungo sospiro profondo
> dal grande oceano ond' ella strappata fu permane
> cosi per le tue piazze dilette dal sole, O Ferrara,
> il nuovo peregrino tende le orecchie e ode
> da' marmorei palagi sul Po discendere lenta
> processione e canto d' un fantastico epos.
> CARDUCCI, *Alla Città di Ferrara*

A GREAT part of the charm which the smaller and less progressive cities of Italy possess for the traveller lies in the fact that in them he temporarily forgets the haste and vulgarity of modern life, and realizes with intense vividness the days of their former splendour, so that the present grows remote for him, and the past becomes present.

Ferrara, for example, except on market-day, is what a great modern poet has called it, a " città di silenzio." The men and women who glide down the long vistas of deserted streets seem less substantial than the ghosts which throng the sunny squares " where no footfall violates the luminous mysteries." Beautiful "in splendid April hours," indescribably mournful when wrapped in autumn mists, icily calm amid the snows of winter, the Lady of the Po, as Tasso called her, sits benumbed and apathetic, high and dry above the water floods, dreaming of the long past days when she and the river were young and vigorous together.

But the decay of Ferrara's prosperity was due to something more than changes in the physical configuration of her territory. Her life was derived not only from her river, but from her rulers. When the fecund strength of both was drained away, her active career was over. With his singular power of enunciating profound truths and compressing large tracts of history in a single dramatic episode, the late Mr. Shorthouse described, by means of a brief conversation between John Inglesant and a Ferrarese beggar, the disastrous effects of the extinction of the house of Este, and of the Papal government which followed. Inglèsant, leaving his companions after dinner, wanders forth to take the air, and enters into conversation with divers priests and loiterers. Some of the latter, perceiving that he was a foreigner, and ignorant that he was riding in the train of a Cardinal, begin to whisper of Papal severity, exactions, and confiscations which "had doomed many of the principal inhabitants of the city." "They talk of the bad air," said one of these men to Inglesant; "the air was the same a century ago, when this city was flourishing under its own princes—princes of so eminent a virtue, of so heroical a nobleness that they were really Fathers of their country. Nothing," he continued, with a mute gesture of the hands, "can be imagined more changed than this is now."

Mr. Shorthouse's Ferrarese beggar speaks with the appropriate exaggeration of a man who remembers "happier days." With the exception of Niccolò III's son, Leonello, whose charming personality typifies all that was good and gracious in the early *Quattrocento*, the princes of the house of Este were not paragons of "heroical nobleness," nor were they actively and consciously Fathers of their country. They had the faults common to the Italian despot of the time but they had them in diminished strength; they had the numerous and brilliant facets, the intense vitality, the genuine humanism characteristic even of some of the worst rulers of their age, and they had them in an intense degree. They were cruel and lustful, but they were always men with passions controlled by reason, not madmen at large, monsters in human form, incarnate fiends, like Sigismundo Malatesta, Galeazzo Maria Sforza, or Ferrante of Aragon. They were tyrannical; but like our own Tudor sovereigns they had a knack of feeling the popular pulse, and of winning popular applause, and their heavily taxed subjects were proud of their magnificence. Most of them had a singular genius for diplomacy, a singular personal charm, and a real regard for art and letters. Under them Ferrara became one of the most ardent foci of intellectual life in the peninsula, a magnet attracting "whoe'er in Italy is known to fame."

This brilliant epoch was inaugurated by Giovanni dei Vigri's sovereign and employer. Niccolò III, and the young wife whom he wedded in 1418, stand with their backs turned to the dark, rude epoch of war, and their faces lighted by the dawn of the renaissance. Parisina da Malatesta, with her æsthetic instincts, her capacity for organization, her radiant vitality, reminds us not a little of her husband's granddaughter, the "incomparable lady" who summed up and expressed all the charm of her family and of renaissance womanhood. Like Isabella d'Este, the Marchesana Parisina was an "errant princess," wandering continually from one summer palace to another. Like her she played and sang, and delighted in all sorts of music. Like her, she had a fine taste in the adornment of her rooms and her person. Painters decorated her oratory and her household furniture, while the merchants of Venice supplied her with finely wrought combs and delicate perfumes. She was less highly educated than the pupil of Jacopo Gallino, her reading consisting chiefly of French romances—"istorie francesi"; and she was much more of a sportswoman, caring greatly for her dogs and falcons, entering her horses not only for the races of Ferrara, but for the *palii* of other cities, and sharing her prizes with her jockeys. Pleasure-loving, artistic, athletic, she was none the less an excellent and industrious housekeeper. Her husband's heterogeneous family found in her a kind stepmother. She trained her twelve maidens in housewifely skill, found them husbands, supplied their dowries, and filled their marriage chests. She was responsible too for the clothing of the entire household, from her stepsons' tutor to the meanest kitchen-boy.

The little Caterina dei Vigri had been a member of that household only a few months when its fair and brilliant mistress was suddenly removed. After 21 May, 1425, the name of Parisina appears no more in the annals of the house of Este.

The story of the guilty love of the young Marchesana with Ugo Aldrobandini, Niccolò's first-born son, is obscured by the reticence of contemporaries and the embellishments of poets. The disgrace of an illustrious house was decently covered, and all that we know with certainty from original sources is that on the night of 21 May, in that part of Niccolò's great red-brick castello called "The Tower of the Lions," Parisina and Ugo expiated their sin, and that with them [1] "was beheaded one Aldrovandino di Rangoni of the same family as the aforesaid lord because he had been the occasion of this ill." The contemporary Bolognese chronicler Griffoni adds that two of the Lady Parisina's women were also executed, and that [2] "all the people of Ferrara lamented greatly at the death of the aforesaid Ugo, for that he was an honest, fair, and good youth, and much beloved of the people of Ferrara."

We do not know what impression the fate of the Marchesana made upon her heterogeneous family. Leonello,[3] who was shortly afterwards legitimated as heir-apparent by Pope Martin V, benefited by his brother's fate; but, gentle and gracious spirit that he was, we can hardly suppose that he rejoiced at it. Borso,[4] at the time a boy of twelve, long afterwards, when he had succeeded to his father's and his brother's place, spoke with approval of Niccolò's terrible act of vengeance. The girls, to whatever extent they mourned her, must have been disagreeably affected by the loss of a woman's care. The household was without a mistress: the court was under a cloud. Of one thing we may

[1] Diario Ferrarese, *Muratori*, Vol. XXIV.
[2] Matthaeus de Griffonibus, *Muratori*, Vol. XVIII, pt. ii. Edt. 1902.
[3] Leonello was seventeen when his brother was executed.
[4] Borso was born in 1413; he was therefore the same age as Caterina.

feel certain, Margherita and her young companion were assuredly not ignorant of the details and import of the tragedy. It was an age of plain speaking and brief childhood, and the composition of the household, Margherita's own position, the French romances read aloud by Parisina's maidens, together with the sermons of the day, must already have enlightened the two children as to the meaning of the seventh commandment and the frequency of its infraction. On a sensitive and precocious girl like Caterina dei Vigri the awful fate of a kind mistress and a gay and gallant acquaintance cannot but have produced a horrible and permanent impression. The sting of love and sin and retribution must have left a painful mark upon her mind, originating, or increasing, the distaste for the life of the world which she very early evinced.

This distaste certainly did not spring from pique, disappointment or sense of failure. Caterina's life at court seems to have been successful and serene. Her young mistress loved her with a tender and enduring affection; and in spite of the marked favour shown her, she met with no unkindness. A woman's superiority of intellect and character rarely provokes jealousy unless she be beautiful, witty, or conceited. Caterina was plain, a fragile brown-skinned creature, whose only remarkable feature was a pair of large expressive eyes. She talked little, but her voice was sweet. She was modest and unassuming, grave and discreet beyond her years, seeking not her own, shunning rather than courting admiration. She was, in fact, one of those retiring, reliable, gentle natures who " wear well "; who are not exactly popular with either sex, but whom women seek as confidantes and men as wives.

Of suitors, and that when still what we should call a mere child, Caterina had no lack. She had more than her amiability of character to recommend her. The only child of a wealthy man whom Niccolò III delighted to honour, she was distinctly a good match; and possibly she had something of the heiress's natural distrust of fortune-hunters. Certainly she was averse to matrimony, and her indulgent and well-beloved father put no pressure on her.

We have no direct information as to the education of the " Princess " Margherita and her young companion, but Caterina's writings and the relics in the chapel of the Santa at Bologna prove that she was an apt pupil, and indicate the range of her studies.

Little more than a hundred years before, Paolo da Certaldo[1] in his advice to parents had declared that "if the child be a girl she should be put to sew and not to read, for it is not good that a woman should know how to read." The parents of Margherita and Caterina evidently thought that a girl should be taught not only to read but to read Latin; not only to read Latin but to "write fair"; not only to write but to illuminate, to paint, to play on an instrument, and to sing. This is a liberal education not calculated to form women of the patient Griselda type, and far beyond the requirements of the mere housekeeper and child-bearer. The ideals of the thirteenth century are visibly fading before the advance of the new learning.

[1] *Breve Consiglio di Paolo da Certaldo*, published by S. Morpengo. Florence, 1872.

Caterina's book, *Le Sette Arme Necessarie alla Battaglia Spirituale*, mystical and *Trecentisti* as it is in sentiment, is essentially a product of the new feminism. It was written when she was only twenty-five, but it bears no traces of timidity or immaturity. It contains many expressions of deep humility—expressions which in Caterina's case were certainly more than conventional—but these are not incompatible with a note of dignity and authority. The young authoress speaks with the poise and conscious competency of a highly educated woman.

The work is worthy of attention from several points of view: it was a new departure; it is practically an autobiography; it has real literary merit.

The woman who wrote at all in the early fifteenth century had something of the temper of an adventurer—she who ventured into the region of theology had the boldness of an explorer. In the "dark ages" female education, in so far as it existed at all, was found in the shelter of the cloister. Even Paolo da Certaldo was willing that a girl should be taught to read if she were destined for a nunnery (se la vuole fare monacha), adding that in that case she should be sent young to the convent and should learn there. There had been highly cultured and even literary nuns before Caterina's day. Learned Benedictines were occupied in transcription, and produced MSS. far surpassing in beauty Caterina's comparatively simple breviary. Saint Radegonda in the sixth century had obliged her sisters at Poitiers to devote two hours a day to reading. Saint Lioba, the associate of Boniface and Walburga, and the honoured friend of Charlemagne, was a poetess and introduced the study of the Fathers and of the Canon Law into the teaching of her convent and its school. Cecilia, daughter of William the Conqueror and Abbess of Caen, was remarkable for her knowledge of grammar and philosophy. Hroswitha of Gandersheim had written dramas for performance in the convent. None of these ladies, however, had attempted to deal with the subjects which presumably chiefly occupied their time and thoughts. It was reserved for Caterina dei Vigri to write of the difficulties and progress of the spiritual life as lived within the walls of a convent.

She conceives that life as a combat for which the Christian who would follow the banner of his Lord " who died upon the battle-field " must duly arm himself. "The first weapon is Diligence; the second is Distrust of Self; the third is Confidence in God; the fourth is the thought of Christ's Passion; the fifth is the thought of Death; the sixth is the thought of God's Glory; the seventh is the Authority of Holy Scripture."

This arrangement of the spiritual armoury—an arrangement which seems to be original and arbitrary —determines the division of the book into seven chapters and an introduction. In the martial spirit which inspires the scheme and which breathes through all the autobiographical passages, we may perhaps trace the early influence of Caterina's paternal uncle, "Comes et Miles," while in the systematic arrangement of her material, a tendency to scholastic subtlety, and a marked accuracy of definition, we may see marks of her legal ancestry. As one example out of many of her careful reasoning, and of what we may call the legal quality of her mind, we may quote a little passage dealing with Christ's capacity as man to suffer the extremity of spiritual distress. Her theme is the third weapon—Confidence in God—who, she declares, will never abandon those who trust in Him. "Albeit by his permission the Handmaiden and Bride of Christ is sometimes placed in such severe and painful conflict that she cries from her heart towards Heaven, saying: My God, forsake me not: yet then, when she most fears that she is abandoned, is she lifted closest by a divine and occult mystery to the highest perfection of God. And of this we have an example in his only Son, who, being at the point of a most bitter and painful death, cried, saying: 'Pater, ut quid me dereliquisti?' Yet we know that at that moment Christ, true Son of God, triumphed in complete and true perfection in the fulfilment of obedience to the Eternal Father, with whom he was perfectly united, although at that time, in so much as he was man, susceptible to pain and death, he said: 'My God, why hast thou forsaken Me?' But this was because the Divinity inseparably united to Him left the human and sensitive part of his nature: and this justice demanded, that the painful obedience of the same Christ might cancel the pleasurable disobedience of our first father.

"Now returning to our proposition, the Handmaiden of Christ fears not to be forsaken, though sometimes she may seem to be: for she knows that the Eternal Father will not let that befall her which did not befall his own Son: thus when she finds herself in great straits and tribulation, she has confidence in the Divine succour, mindful of the sweet promise made by Him, when He said by the mouth of the

Prophet: *Cum ipso sum in tribulatione, eripiam eum, et glorificabo eum.*"

It is noteworthy that of Caterina's direct quotations from the Vulgate, seven are from the Psalms and Prophets. The same number are from the Gospels; there are three from Saint Paul's Epistles, one from that of Saint James, and one from the Apocalypse. She quotes also from "that most glorious doctor of the ancient fathers, Saint Anthony of Vienna," from "the most venerable Saint Augustine," and from Saint Bernard, and is familiar with the sayings of "Frate Bernardino," "Frate Egidio," and above all "il Padre rustro S. Francesco." But there is absolutely no trace in her little book of any knowledge of the classics, an absence which perhaps supports, but quite as possibly originated, Father Grassetti's assertion that she resolutely closed her eyes to the antique world, and refused to read any Pagan authors.

Perchance if Guerino, that most famous of renaissance scholars, had reached Ferrara a few years earlier, and Margherita had shared the lessons given to her brothers, or if Caterina had remained in the world a few years longer, and begun to feel the power and spirit of the new learning, as it penetrated from literature to thought, from thought to life, softening customs and disciplining manners, perhaps Ferrara would have gained a scholar and a poet, and Bologna would have lost a saint. As it was, the rising tide of humanism barely touched the maiden's feet, and she recoiled from it.

In spirit Caterina belonged to an epoch earlier or later than her own. She might have foregathered with the Desert Cenobites of the third century—and indeed the life of a hermit had a peculiar attraction for her—or have given her testimony in the meeting-house of some devoted, obscure, sixteenth-century English Puritans : and in either company she would have been more at home than in the fifteenth-century Court of Ferrara. She entirely lacked the *joie de vivre* of typical renaissance womanhood ; she had none of the delight in physical loveliness, the faculty for existing beautifully, the knack of gliding easily over the surface of life, which were beginning to be cultivated and displayed by her contemporaries.

Her paintings are archaic, conventional, Byzantine in character. They somehow remind us of Illuminata's testimony concerning her :—

"And this I say in commendation of her purity and *cleanliness of body* (mondezza di corpo) and mind that I, and others living here, heard her say these words, that never, never, never, had she looked upon her own body."

And if her paintings show no trace of the new conception that the human frame is worthy of patient and reverent study, still less do her writings indicate any loving observation of natural phenomena or of animal or plant life. The world which to Leonello and his nieces, Isabella and Beatrice d'Este, was truly a garden of delight, was to Caterina only a place of exile and repentance. Men were to be strangers and pilgrims, travelling unobservant and self-absorbed as Saint Bernard on his Swiss tour, not like Chaucer's sociable caravan, nor like the companions of Saint Francis, noting the ways of beast and bird and the humours of the road. The power to appreciate the latter was apparently quite absent from Caterina's composition. And if it be urged that a book of spiritual instructions offers but little scope for the display of such a faculty, we would ask the reader to turn to the sermons of her contemporary, S. Bernardino—whom she greatly admired—to see how even direct religious teaching may be salted with humour. Moreover, while Sister Illuminata tells of her friend's kindness, industry, obedience, prayerfulness, and other qualities, she relates no incidents which indicate that Caterina had any sense of fun. On the other hand, she does dwell on what we may call her Puritan seriousness, which refused to take delight in arts or crafts for their own sake. " During the day," says Illuminata, " she was never seen to stand idle for a moment, because she held time so precious that she did not want to spend an ounce of it without profit, saying : How great is human blindness ! For time is given us as the greatest treasure we can possess, and we are so mad as not to consider that in its use lies our salvation or damnation." " And holidays and work-days she was never idle, having a cultured mind and skilful fingers. Yet would she never occupy her time with those things which seemed to her merely curious and vain, such as fine stitching or writing and ornamentation, saying that time given to such things was ill-spent. But she made an exception for the adornment of breviaries, saying that these should be used reverently, as one would use a chalice, out of respect to the holy words which minister to God's praise. But she did not like flowers and branches and borders even then, saying that they only served to dissipate the mind. And thus she wrote her own breviary with great simplicity " ; and often while

MADONNA AND CHILD
CONVENT OF CORPUS DOMINI, BOLOGNA

writing, carried away by the words she was transcribing, she would rise "with her eyes full of tears," and then "extending her arms she said the Pater Noster, and then began to write again."

Caterina's ethical theories were in conflict with her æsthetic sensibilities. She had to excuse and explain to herself her persistent delight in music, painting, and literature; and, thus with the peculiar mingling of humility and sublime presumption characteristic of the mystics of all creeds, she attributes her various accomplishments to direct Divine inspiration. Sick unto death, she plays upon the viol, deaf to all other sounds, unmindful of those around her; but her melody, she declares, is but a repetition of strains heard in dreams of the celestial choir. She paints the Holy Child[1] "for many places in the monastery of Ferrara and in little for the books"; but she claims that her model was no earthly child but a reproduction of a vision granted to her one blessed Christmas night. She writes her spiritual instructions; and in her preface she affirms that the "piccola operetta" is composed with the Divine aid and by Divine compulsion.

The Seven Weapons, by reason of its style and scope, its mysticism and poetry, necessarily challenges comparison with the writings of S. Teresa. But as we should expect from its earlier date, the work of Caterina is slighter, fresher and more spontaneous than that of the Carmelite. The Northern Italian was less complex, less emotional, less intellectually powerful, but more original and robust than the famous Spaniard. Her mysticism had not the same Oriental tinge; her

[1] Illuminata's *Specchio d' Illuminatione.*

reserve was greater; and her autobiography, instead of being written deliberately and at the prompting of her spiritual advisers like that of Teresa, must be read between the lines of her instructions, which were penned in secret and seen by no one in her lifetime. She draws upon her personal experiences merely by way of illustration, warning or consolation,—fearing, as she solemnly declares, " The Divine reproval should I keep silence about that which might help others." She must needs deliver her testimony, and to do so is her single aim. Thus her confidences are singularly intimate, spontaneous, and sincere; and, supplemented as they are by Illuminata's recollections, they make us extraordinarily well acquainted with the inner life of a fifteenth-century nun.

But albeit *The Seven Weapons* is interesting to the modern reader chiefly as a human document, it is by no means despicable as a specimen of fifteenth-century Italian. Caterina's style is unstudied, but her *naïveté*, her intense earnestness, and her vivid imagination sometimes produce the effect of great art. Her sentences are occasionally as long as those of seventeenth- and eighteenth-century authors; but their length is due not to verbosity, but to a kind of breathless eagerness or to complicated and sustained thought. Like S. Teresa she was something of a poetess, writing devotional sonnets and canticles; while the distinguished Italian writer, Marco Minghetti, has remarked that her prose is always musical, and that her more ecstatic passages might be broken up into blank verse. He instances the opening of *The Seven Weapons* :—

" In nome sia dell' Eterno Padre, e del suo Unigenito

Figliuolo Cristo Gesù splendore di essa paterna gloria, per amore del quale con giubilo di cuore grido dicendo in verso le sue dilettissime Serve e Spose:

"Ciascuna amante ch' ama il Signore venga alla danza cantando d' amore; venga danzando tutta infiammata, sol bramando Colui che l' ha creata e dal pericoloso stato mondano l' ha disseparata ponendola nel nobilissimo claustro della santa Religione, acciocchè in esso purgata da ogni macula di peccato, e vestendosi lo adornamento delle sante, e nobili virtudi, riformando la bellezza dell' anima, e riducendola al primo stato dell' innocenza acciocchè essa dignamente possa entrare dopo questa peregrinazione nel glorioso talamo del suo castissimo e verginale Sposo Cristo Gesù."[1]

Which passage—far more poetical in conception than the hymn quoted by most of her biographers and given in full in an Appendix—may be broken into lines thus:—

>Ciascuna amante ch' ama il Signore
>Venga alla danza cantando d' amore;
>Venga danzando, tutta infiammata
>Sol bramando Colui che l' ha creata,
>E dal stato mondano l' ha disseparata, etc.

[1] In the name of the Eternal Father, and of His only begotten Son Jesus Christ, the splendour of the paternal glory, for love of whom I cry with joyful heart to his dearly beloved handmaidens and brides, saying: Let every lover who loves the Lord come to the dance singing with love; let her come dancing wholly inflamed, desiring Him alone who created her and separated her from the world's perilous state, putting her into the worshipful cloister of holy Religion, so that in it, purged from every spot of sin, and clothed with noble virtues and the adornment of the saints, renewing the beauty of the soul, and reducing it to its primal state of innocence, so that this pilgrimage ended, she may worthily enter into glorious union with her chaste and virginal spouse, Christ Jesus.

Caterina's life at Court ended in May, 1427. On the twenty-seventh of that month Margherita took back to the Malatesta the lands Parisina had brought as dowry to the Marchese d'Este. She went, poor maiden of fifteen, to an unwilling bridegroom some eighteen months her senior,—the eldest natural son of Pandolfo, Lord of Rimini, Fano, Cesena, and Fossombrone, legitimated and put in the line of succession by Martin V, a pontiff who was particularly obliging in such matters. Galeotto Roberto had no desire for the greatness thrust upon him or for the bride chosen for him. He was sorrowful because he had great possessions; he longed to leave all and follow Christ— in a way of his own choosing. He spent his days in prayer and meditation, fasted, wore a hair-shirt, slept on a table, and refused to live with his young wife till commanded to do so by his confessor. In vain the Pope censured his neglect of the duties of a ruler, and invited him to take up arms on behalf of the Holy See. Galeotto Roberto would not be troubled by politics or war. Like our own Edward the Confessor, he was a good monk spoiled by the force of ancestry and circumstance, and a bad ruler by reason of the preponderance of his religious instincts. Monkish historians represent Margherita as trying his patience by interfering with his devotions and displaying a worldly and ambitious temper; but they never accuse her, neglected young wife as she was, of levity or indiscretion. She may well have been irritated by her husband's neglect of his responsibilities, and, inheriting the Este capacity for affairs, may have taken on herself many of the burdens laid down by the "Beato Roberto."

That the lot of the Lady of Rimini would have been made sweeter by the presence of her well-loved companion we cannot doubt; but Caterina refused to accompany the bride to her new home. She had already chosen what she believed to be the better part. The death of Giovanni dei Vigri a few months previously had severed the strongest tie which bound her to the world; and after Margherita's wedding she left the Court for the family house, on the site of which the chapel dedicated to S. Caterina dei Vigri now stands. There she dwelt with her mother for some months—probably till the widow's year of mourning had expired and Benvenuta contracted her second marriage with a citizen of Ferrara.

It was assuredly not antipathy to a stepfather, or need of a home, which drove Caterina to the shelter of a convent. Friends sought her as companion to their daughters, suitors renewed their offers, relatives were anxious to arrange a marriage. But Caterina had made her choice. One would gladly have had from her own pen an account of the motives which determined it. Failing such direct information, we fall back on a reported speech given us by her friend: " When I left the world,"—thus she spake to Illuminata,—" my sole object was to do the will of God and to love Him with a perfect love; and day and night I had no other desire nor thought save only to be able to love and to know God, and all my strength and study was directed to this end; and I was willing to be despised of all the world, if only I might love God."

That this is a positive and high aim no one will dispute; whether it can be attained only or most perfectly by renunciation of the world is of course another question, the answer to which depends (*a*) on the condition of the world at a given period; (*b*) on the temperament and position of the given individual; (*c*) on the relation of the one to the other.

"Madame," said a distinguished English traveller to a distinguished Abbess, " you are here not from the love of virtue but from the fear of vice."

Caterina, by her own showing, does not deserve the censure implied in this criticism. Yet even the negative aim indicated by the somewhat impertinent Englishman may in certain conditions of society be commendable, nay, perhaps heroic. Charles Kingsley, defending the hermits of the Thebaid, urged that where reformation is impossible, self-expatriation ceases to be cowardice; and that the Roman civilization of the fourth century being irredeemably corrupt, men and women wishful to escape its taint were compelled to fly from infection. Civilized society in the fifteenth century was undoubtedly healthier than in the fourth; nevertheless the environment of Caterina's youth sufficiently indicates the low standards prevailing in the most cultured and enlightened circles of the day. The little girl was placed by tender and pious parents in a household of bastards —affectionately acknowledged by a prince who died the father of three hundred illegitimate children—and in surroundings where it was obvious she would have every opportunity of gathering material for her future generalization, that the crying vices of her time were "ambition, avarice, and that most abominable sin which is contrary to the virginal and chaste beauty of Christ."

Over such surroundings, moreover, a woman had

small influence unless she happened to be of exalted rank or the inmate of a convent. In the one case her example and her commands were of weight in her own circle, while through her husband she might contribute to the welfare of the nation; in the other, her position was a protest against the sins of society, while, if she were of distinguished learning or sanctity, her advice might be sought and taken by the great ones of the earth. Between the cloister and the domestic hearth she must needs choose. There was no place in Caterina's world for the unprotected, independent spinster; and if the cloister were cold, the hearth may well have seemed to her to be lit by a very fitful flame. Conjugal fidelity was rare; conjugal happiness for the weaker partner at least was still rarer; and Caterina was the petted only child of tender parents, a girl with keen susceptibilities, a loving heart, and attenuated passions. It is possible that as an honoured and beloved matron she would have shone in the society of Ferrara, a woman whose price is above rubies; it is far more probable that as a neglected wife she would have covered her wounded pride in a mantle of moody piety. It is possible that sons and daughters would have called her blessed and extended her circle of righteous influence; yet no children after the flesh could have needed her more or have been better loved than the novices she mothered with rare and wise tenderness. It is possible that in looking well to the ways of her house she might have found scope for her rich gifts of mind and heart; but in no capacity could her tact and administrative talents have been more fully exercised than as abbess of a large community.

Again, Caterina was a fragile, delicately organized, tenderly nurtured young woman in a world of robust passions, strong vitality, and scant sympathy with suffering, where the weakly did not cumber the earth and only the fittest survived. Fasts and vigils were probably less exhausting to nerves and digestion than the uncomfortable travelling, unwholesome banquets, and protracted revelry indulged in by the great ladies of her day; while in the matter of discomfort—or what we consider such—there was little difference between the palace and the convent. The winter chill of the cells in the convent of Corpus Domini must have been less icy than that of the great sala in the unwarmed Castello. The nun's pallet was probably cleaner and more comfortable than the silken-covered but ill-stuffed, ill-kept beds[1] of the reigning family. In spite of her self-imposed austerities, Caterina probably lived longer in the convent than she would have done had she continued in the Este Court.

It was from this same Court that a generation later the grandson of Niccolò III's physician fled to the Dominican convent at Bologna. Caterina, artistic, sensitive, fervid, taking herself and the world very seriously, capable of intense emotion, and of burning philanthropy, bears not a little resemblance in character to the great Florentine preacher of righteousness and judgment. She was, moreover, afflicted by the constant, wearing, bodily weakness which deprives its unfortunate possessor of the *joie de vivre*. She had not physically a particle of the buoyant vitality which enabled women

[1] For information as to the beds of the Court of Ferrara see a pamphlet by H. Galandi, published Modena, 1889.

of the type of Isabella d'Este to seize the beauty of their surroundings and be blind to the brutality. Can we doubt that in the great red palace-castle, which seems to symbolize the Este rule alike in its most splendid and its grimmest features, this little pale-faced, sober maid-of-honour was overwhelmed, like Girolamo Savonarola, by the thought of the inequality of society, by "the misery of the world and the iniquities of men?"

CHAPTER III

CATERINA'S NOVICIATE

> Donna più su, mi disse, alla cui norma
> Nel vostro mondo giù si veste e vela
> Perchè in fino al morir si vegghi e dorma
> Con quello Sposo ch' ogni voto accetta
> Che caritate a suo piacer conforma.
> DANTE, *Paradiso*, iii. 98.

THE building in Ferrara which for twenty-four years was Caterina dei Vigri's home was not, when she first entered it, an enclosed nunnery. The house was the property and private residence of a certain pious widow, Bernardina Sedazzi. Her niece, Lucia Mascheroni, lived with her, and little by little aunt and niece gathered round them a society of devout women, who adopted the habit and the rule of the *Pinzochere*, or third order of Augustinians.

Aunt and niece often discussed the possibility of converting their anomalous household into a regular convent under the Augustinian rule; but Bernardina's funds were thought to be inadequate, there were various difficulties to overcome, and she at length died without carrying the project into effect. She bequeathed both her real and her personal property to Lucia, directing that it should be devoted to the purpose so dear to both their hearts.

Lucia at once took steps to carry out her aunt's wish, but she found that the majority of her household was desirous that the new convent should be placed under a stricter rule. The ladies had been accustomed to frequent the Franciscan church (S. Spirito), and to look to the Frati for guidance and spiritual direction. What more natural than that the new foundation should be placed under the rule of the blessed Saint Clare?

Lucia was carried away by these representations; and the zealots of the community—among whom was Caterina—appeared to have gained their end, when resistance suddenly arose from an unexpected quarter. A certain Sister Ailisia, a self-seeking and ambitious woman, protested that Lucia Mascheroni was not free to do what she liked with her inheritance. Bernardina had intended to found an Augustinian house: Lucia, by placing the new convent under another rule, forfeited her right to the property, which consequently passed to those members of the community who were ready to obey the terms of their benefactor's bequest.

Ailisia's obstruction was not restricted to remonstrance, nor even to the creation of dissension and bad feeling in the once harmonious community. Lucia, obliged to enlarge the house, was proposing to purchase a contiguous property. Ailisia, who had influential relatives, contrived to tamper with the owner and to stop the sale. She then brought her case before the civil tribunal of Ferrara, and judgment was given in her favour, the defendant being unheard. Lucia Mascheroni, with all the zealots, was ejected from her old home, and Sister Ailisia reigned in her stead. But the litigation and the bitterness of feeling awakened and revealed, caused so great a scandal in Ferrara that many parents called for their daughters and compelled them to return to their own homes.

But if Ailisia had influence with the judge, Lucia was able to get hold of the Archbishop. A certain Madonna Verde, of the great family of the Pii da Carpi, was active in her behalf. The case was transferred to the Ecclesiastical Court.

Lucia's defence was founded on the perfect harmony of mind and intuition which had always existed between herself and the deceased. They wore the Augustinian habit, and in their plans for the future had never thought of any but the Augustinian rule. Had the desirability of a stricter life been suggested to Bernardina Sedazzi, she would undoubtedly have concurred with the idea.

The Vicar of the Archbishop found that the spirit was more important than the letter. He reversed, doubtless with great satisfaction, the decision of the civil court; and a papal bull was speedily obtained, sanctioning the foundation of the new convent and the adoption of the Franciscan rule.

To adapt the old house to its new character as an enclosed nunnery was to make it for a while uninhabitable. Alterations and enlargements necessitated a general exodus.

The necessity filled Caterina with terror. She refused to go to her mother's house, and "with great sorrow" besought those who came to remove her that they would take her to a place where "she should not be obliged to see nor to speak with any one." She was, in fact, lodged in a convent in the city; but at the earliest possible moment she returned to the old house, living in great discomfort and forwarding the building operations with her own hands. It was at this time that she sustained a painful and lasting injury to the spine, being crushed against a wall by a heavy cart filled with lime.

She was now assailed by an unexpected temptation which she describes as follows in *The Seven Weapons*[1] :—

"After some days as it pleased the Divine Providence she returned to that Place with five others of those sisters who were there from the first: and the rebuilding of the Monastery went on well. But some time elapsed before it was possible to be locked in and cloistered, so that people came to visit the place and entered therein. Whereupon the Enemy attacked her, and instigated certain persons of great state according to the world who in secret besought her to consent to go and stay in their house as companion to one of their daughters left alone; (d' una lor figliuola dismissa) saying that were it necessary to obtain the licence of the Pope or of any other person, she need not doubt but that all and more than she desired for the welfare of soul or body should be duly looked to. To which promises she consented not, but she stood firm and constant in the aforesaid place, in perfect faith that she should yet be cloistered (si serreria in clausura) under the rule of Saint Clare, and so it came to pass."

[1] She always writes of herself in *The Seven Weapons* in the third person.

Now who were these "great persons" who so ardently desired Caterina's company, who were so confident of obtaining the Pope's approbation of her return to the world, and whose appeal came to her as a real and insidious temptation?

A careful observation of the wording of Caterina's narrative and a comparison of dates seem to furnish an answer to the enigma. We find that Caterina was professed and cloistered under the rule of Saint Clare in the year 1432; that early in the same year Galeotto Roberto Malatesta had given up his futile attempts at government and had retired into a monastery; and that in the preceding year the Marchese Niccolò had married for a third time. Margherita, *dismissa*, dismissed, abandoned by her husband, at once returned to her father's house, where the presence of a new stepmother, Ricciarda da Saluzzo, accounts for Caterina's plural forms—" in casa *loro*," " d' una *lor* figliuola," " alcune persone."

A proposal that she should take up her abode with strangers, however great their "state according to the world," would have had no attraction for a woman of Caterina's temperament, while her warm affections and helpful instincts, starved and repressed in her present life, would have yearned towards her lonely friend, and inclined her heart to the appeal of her father's sovereign and benefactor. Margherita's peculiar and unexpected position might well have been interpreted as a real "call"; and since Caterina must have anticipated that her gentle pious mistress, a widow in fact, yet not free to wed again, would lead a life of great retirement—as indeed proved the case—she might have argued with perfect sincerity that in resuming her former duties she might, like Constance, mother of the Emperor Frederick, retain "the veil of the heart."

Whether this hypothesis concerning the identity of Caterina's friends be correct or not, it is certain that in the eyes of her contemporaries her return to the world would have been justified by the late upheaval in the community and the fact that she was not yet "obbligata a religione." It is also certain that her refusal to do so was an act not of cowardice, but of splendid courage.

The autobiographical passages scattered through *The Seven Arms* show that the period of her irregular noviciate was one of acute misery. Parental indulgence and a strong will, physical unfitness, and the lack of tenderness and wisdom on the part of her superiors, combined to make the initial steps in the religious life peculiarly painful and difficult to her; so that in after years she declared that were she bidden to choose between immediate decapitation and a return to the "mortal sadness" of those first five years she would unhesitatingly accept the former alternative. Words such as these reveal the strength of the temptation involved in the invitation of her mysterious friends, and give us the measure of her valour in rejecting it. To accept it would have been to make the "great refusal," to proclaim despair in the Father's power and love, to confess herself beaten, to lay down once for all the "seven arms."

Another passage in her book gives us by implication further information as to her state of mind at this period. We see the reason of her agitation at the enforced exodus of the nuns, of her refusal to return to her mother's house, of her request to be kept secluded, of her furious longing to be shut in by bolts and bars and bound by the vows of a professed religious. The shadow of past struggles with her own affections, of old frantic desiring to go free, lies across her exhortation to her novices.

" No sooner are they within the monastery than they repent of that which they desired with so much ardour, and were it not for very shame they would turn back, that is, go forth. Which thing happens chiefly to those destined to bear great fruit in the way of God ; for not only does it seem to them that they have not found God as they hoped, but they fear that they are deprived of Him and of all favour and devotion ; for before their entrance they desired with great fervour for God's love to abandon relatives and friends ; and now the enemy tempts them to contrary feelings, giving them such tender memories of the same that waking and sleeping they can think of nothing else . . . and devotion becoming utterly insipid to them they fall into great sadness, saying : Truly I was better before I came here, and better I served God, and with more devotion than I do now : and thus the specious enemy tempts them to turn back. But the bride of Christ must in no wise consent to such deception : with hasty and resolute spirit she must constrain her free will, and say to herself even if my Lord permit me to be tempted always, even to the end of my life, I will not yield : and having made this resolution she will fall to prayer with all possible fervour, saying with heart and mouth : My dearest Lord Jesus Christ, by that infinite and unspeakable love which bound thee to the post of scourging, and made thee bear for my sake the cruel and bitter smiting of thy foes, give me, I beseech thee, strength that through thy grace I may have victory over my enemies, and may endure with patience this and every other conflict which thou mayest assign me."

To confess defeat may be courage and prudence on the part of those who are capable of taking up a new and more defensible position. But Caterina recognized no rampart against sin save the religious life, and to evacuate it was to yield herself a captive to the Enemy of Souls. Compromise was to her a loss of knightly honour and therefore of self-respect. She brought to the spiritual combat the temper and standards of chivalry, and bore herself always as *preu chevalier*, without fear and without reproach. It is easy to say her ideals were false: it is difficult to see how she could have deliberately deviated from them without degradation of character.

So, practising first what she preached long afterwards, she stood to her post, and that even when tempted to leave it by another and far more insidious suggestion. This conflict also is described in *The Seven Arms*:—

"In the beginning of her conversion, when she had lived some years in the present Place, she began to taste the sweet savour of divine love in prayer, and for that reason was seized with a great desire to go forth into a desert and solitary place; and considering that she could well do this, because this Place was not yet made into a convent (il Luogo non era obbligato a religione), the desire grew strongly on her."

Did Caterina, we wonder, know how one of her heroes, S. Bernardino of Siena, was once seized by, and yielded to, a similar desire, and how and why the experiment failed? The incident is related by himself with such inimitable humour that with an apology for digression it must be given here.

"One day I was seized with a desire to live as an angel, not as a man." Can we not see the twinkle in the Frate's eyes as he scans his audience after pronouncing these words? "Well, God bless you, listen and see what happened. The idea came to me to live on herbs and water, and I made up my mind to betake myself to the wood. Then I began to ask myself: And what wilt thou do in a wood? what wilt thou eat? Then I answered: 'What did the holy hermits do? I shall eat grass when I am hungry, and when I am thirsty I shall drink water.' ... Then I went seeking a place wherein to establish myself, and I thought I would go as far as Massa.[1] And as I passed through the valley of Boccheggiano, first at this hill and then at that I said: 'I shall do well here. No, there I shall do better still.' At last, not to enter into details, I returned to Siena, and decided to begin to try there the life I wished to lead. And I went down outside the gate of Fallonica and began to gather a salad of grass and sow-thistles; and I had no salt nor bread nor oil. I began, just for once, to wash and scrape it; but next time I meant to scrape it only, and when I was more accustomed to such fare, I should give that up too. And in the name of Christ I began with a bit of sow-thistle. I put it in my mouth and began to chew, chew, chew, chew. But unable to swallow it, I said: 'Well, I will drink a draught of water.' But the water wouldn't go down either and

[1] The village near Siena where Fra Bernardino was born.

the thistles remained in my mouth. I tried several draughts of water, but still I couldn't swallow that bit of thistle.

"Do you guess what I am going to tell you? I wish to say that with a mouthful of thistle I vanquished that temptation."

Caterina vanquished hers by other means. Had she ever considered the subject of a hermit's diet her woman's culinary instincts would probably have preserved her from the Frate's errors; but this aspect of the recluse's life does not seem to have occupied her thoughts. She took herself and the world very seriously, and that she could greatly admire a character so unlike her own as that of Bernardino is a proof not of her power to appreciate his humour, but of the sensible Christian charity which made her, when Abbess, constantly remind her children that the individuality of each sister was to be respected; that there was [1] no one mould of holiness, that *quot homines tot sancti.*

But let us return to her narrative concerning her decision against a hermit's life.

"Somewhat fearful and distrustful of herself, she sought to know the divine pleasure; wherefore she began to make great and almost continual prayer, beseeching the Divine Majesty day and night to show her how she ought to act.

[1] She used to instance the difference between S. Arsenius and "the great Anthony," the former always lachrymose, the latter invariably gay and cheerful. "If these two men," she argued, "had such diverse views and sentiments, why should I be scandalized when I see my neighbours taking another path than that which appears best to me?" (Illuminata Bembo and Father Grassetti.)

"And having for many days made prayer with great anxiety and diligence, it came to pass one morning when she was praying in the Church of the present Place about the hour of terce, that it pleased God to hear her. The Divine Mercy wholly revealed to her what she had asked. And among other things it was told that person that she should remain and dwell in the state and place to which God had called her. Therefore, in obedience to the divine revelation, she resolved to remain in the present Place, understanding clearly that this was the will of God."

Why she felt it to be the will of God that she should continue to live in a community is manifested in an exhortatory passage based on this experience. She is addressing her novices :—

"As soon as the Devil sees that the Religious person begins to taste the sweetness of the divine love in prayer he at once inspires her with a desire to go forth into a desert and solitary place, saying : ' Look now, thou wilt have more opportunity of tasting the sweetness of God and thou wilt be able to stay day and night in prayer as much as thou wouldst.' But be wary, my beloved sisters, and consider that this counsel and desire accords not with the true and most excellent counsel of Christ, who invites us not to follow after mental sweetness and comfort and the pleasing of our own will, but to take up the dear cross, saying, *abneget semetipsum.*"

Caterina's resolution not to quit "the present Place," either for the world or for the desert, is the more remarkable because the recent discussions in the community, and Sister Ailisia's conduct, must have destroyed many of her girlish illusions, and opened her eyes to the worst possibilities of convent life. Her narrative and the exhortation which springs out of it reveal her grit and independence, and the peculiar mingling of mysticism and shrewdness in her character. Life in a religious community, she argues, is a continual crucifixion of self, a continual renunciation of personal affections and desires; therefore it is a more real following of Christ and the precepts of Saint Francis[1] than is the peaceful egotism of the anchorite or hermit. Self-deception, sentimental egotism, weak self-pleasing are impossible and abhorrent to her candid, combative nature. She does not prate of her emotions and desires, nor, as we shall see later, of her visions. She does not seek advice from all her friends, nor does she ask her spiritual superiors to save her from the burden of decision. She believes implicitly in the power of the Holy Spirit to enlighten her judgment, and she patiently awaits the Divine revelation.

The same temper appears in her account of the reasons which induced her to modify some of her original practices. She had "given herself to the service of God with a good conscience," " studying to take for herself every virtue that she had seen or heard of in others, and this not for envy, but to please God in whom she had placed all her love." And then the first flush of girlish enthusiasm had faded, and the inevitable reaction had taken place. The longed-for leisure for religious exercises seemed a disappointing benefit. Meditation, which had been so sweet when the time for

[1] "Il padre nostro S. Francesco," she says, "diceva che piuttosto voleva un Frate che fosse passato per via di tentazione che di dolcezze, e consolazioni, cioè di mentali sentimenti."

it was snatched from worldly occupations, lost its savour. Fervour in prayer was in inverse proportion to freedom from interruption. Worst of all, attendance at the Mass, once a precious privilege, became a tedious obligation.

This "spiritual dryness" was undoubtedly in large measure due to the physical unfitness of a girl in her teens for convent life. The substitution of asceticism, confinement, and monotony for the sunlight, freedom, and ample nourishment needful for the perfection of budding womanhood was a defiance of Nature's laws which brought its own punishment. Caterina became depressed, hysterical, nervous, and irritable. The slightest reproof made her miserable. "Virtues which she used to practise with industry and fervour now seemed impossible." Her weakness was so great that she could not pray or even hear the office without great difficulty and effort. Sometimes she felt "as though she could hardly bear herself" (appena poteva supportare se medesima); and, when alone, she wept so incessantly that in after years it seemed to her that her eyesight had been preserved by a miracle. She believed at this time that for a while she was given over to the power of the Evil One, who was permitted to try her by every sort of ambush and assault. But hand in hand with the vivid imagination which continually materialized the spiritual combat went the shrewdness and independence of judgment which afterwards made Caterina da Bologna a great abbess. Thus—a proof surely of common sense rare in a medieval nun—we find her perceiving to some extent her physical wrong-doing, and this not in old-age retrospect, but during the midst of the "sturm und drang" of her unnatural girlhood. Understanding, she tells us, that her difficulties were partially the result of intemperance in religious exercises, she began "to take more rest, and did not continue to watch during the night; for so much was she used to prayer that she used to get up in her sleep and stand upright crosswise, that is with her arms extended; and I doubt not but that the Enemy induced her to do this, in order that through too much prayer he might make her go mad."

With this experience in her mind, Caterina warned her novices against this subtle device of their "invisible enemies," who, "finding that they cannot succeed in dragging the Religious person from well-doing, attempt to spur her forward with indiscreet practices beyond the common rule. Therefore, rejecting the weapon of discretion, in a little while she becomes weak, or falls seriously ill; and thus she is constrained to give up the pursuit of prayer and of all other virtues. Wherefore being no longer able to exercise herself spiritually, she becomes chill, and, so to speak, unbearable to herself; and God is deprived of worship and her companions of a good example."

The same good sense is manifest in Caterina's dream or vision of the appearance and counsel of Saint Thomas of Canterbury. We do not know the reason of her peculiar devotion to the English Archbishop, or perceive his special fitness for the rôle of teacher in the principles of hygiene; but it is certain that she followed his advice to the benefit of her spiritual and bodily health; and in her breviary she appended the following note to his office :—

"Oratio pro Sancte Thoma meo gloriosissimo Martyre

tam benignissimo qui manus suas sanctissimas ostendit mihi et osculatus sum illas dulciter in corde et corpore meo. Ad laudem Dei scripsi et narravi hoc cum omni veritate."

The occurrence was on this wise: Caterina had for a long while been much tormented by drowsiness—an effort of nature, had she but known it, to heal her tired brain and strained nerves. She struggled helplessly against it, till one evening she actually fell asleep as she knelt beside the table in her cell. Presently she became conscious of a figure in full pontificals, whom, with a dreamer's intuition, she instantly recognized to be her "glorious martyr." He made a sign to her that she should watch and imitate him. Whereupon he put himself in an attitude of prayer, then lay down and seemed to sleep, then rose again and resumed his devotions. After that he drew near to her, holding out his hand. Caterina thought that she opened her eyes and awoke from sleep, but that the figure of the Archbishop, instead of disappearing like the shadow of a dream, continued to stand solidly before her with outstretched hand. Caterina leaned towards him and eagerly kissed his hand, and then the vision faded before her eyes.

"From henceforth," says one of her biographers, the Jesuit Father Giacomo Grassetti, "she used always to remain in prayer for some time after mattins, and then retire to rest, observing with all reverence the teaching of the Holy Bishop."

This salutary apparition belongs to a somewhat later stage of Caterina's life as a religious. The three visions of her unhappy noviciate were regarded by her as the work of lying spirits, who, under the forms of Christ and His Blessed Mother, laid insidious snares for her soul. Her theory of their machinations is ingenious and complicated. "The Devil," she warns her novices, "sometimes puts good and holy thoughts into the mind to deceive it by the semblance of virtue, and then tempts strongly to the vice which is contrary to the same virtue. And this the Enemy does that he may drag the person into the abyss of despair." Wherefore she begs her novices that if they be visited by apparitions, they should "try the spirits" before holding communication with them; and by way of example she quotes, curiously enough, the attitude of Mary towards the Herald of the Incarnation: "Prendete l' arma della Santa Scrittura, la quale manifesta il mode che la Madre di Cristo quando le apparve l' angelo Gabriello, tenne dicendo verso di lui: *Qualis est ista salutatio?*"

Weak and sleepless, and, as she herself perceived, perilously near to insanity, it seemed to Caterina that the Virgin Mother appeared and reproached her for lukewarmness, saying that if she renounced an evil love she should be given a pure love. Pondering distractedly over this enigmatical saying, it seemed to her that an "evil love" could in her case mean nothing but love of self, manifested in self-will and self-indulgence. A growing girl, with the craving for rest and nourishment consequent on growth, she began to find in her own instincts and desires a confirmation of her fears, while weariness and nervous irritability caused her to perform her duties ill, and made her companions accuse her of negligence and sloth.

"The Enemy put into her heart that she was sensual," she says; and the phrase again reveals her common sense struggling with conventual temptations of a kind unknown to men and women, married or single, leading healthy and virtuous lives in the world; "and this he suggested not alone to her, but also to persons with whom she was associated, so that she endured much inconvenience and reproach; and this was all the comfort and support offered to her in her many woes. And her suffering continually increasing, her mind nearly gave way; for within and without were battles."

The severest battle was with her own self-will, and this difficulty in the matter of submission to her superiors perplexed and distressed her greatly. For her keen intelligence perceived that obedience was the foundation of virtue and order in a community, the root whence sprang that spirit of entire resignation to the will of God, that *nichilitade*, which she viewed as the perfect flower of monastic virtue.

But while her intellect recognized the beauty and importance of obedience, she could not refrain from "mentally grumbling at and criticizing almost everything said or done by her superior." She invariably confessed these rebellious feelings to the Mother, and "at least she received strength not to give way to them entirely, though violently drawn to do so." But the continual fret and conflict wore out her nerves and exhausted her spiritual forces.

Her vision of the Crucified, or rather as she afterwards believed, of the diabolic semblance of Christ, was the outcome of this conflict; and the extraordinary dream-dialogue she records is interesting as a revelation of the struggle continually proceeding in her mind. Entering the church one morning to pray, she thought the figure of Our Lord, with arms extended as upon the cross, confronted her, and addressed her as follows :—

"'Thief, why hast thou robbed me? Give me that which thou hast taken from me.' Then she, with great reverence and fear, made answer, saying: 'My Lord, what is this thou sayest? for I have nothing of my own, and am poor and as naught in thy sight, and am in this world subject to others, so that I have nothing.' And he made answer, saying : ' I would have thee know thou art not so poor as thou sayest, and that thou hast something of thine own; for I made thee in my likeness and similitude, giving thee memory, intellect, and will, and the vow of obedience which thou madest, thou madest it to me, and now thou takest it away from me; therefore, I say unto thee thou art a thief.' And she, understanding that he said this on account of the disloyal thoughts which she had in her heart against her Superior, made answer, saying: 'Lord, what shall I do, seeing I possess not my own heart, nor can prevent the thoughts which enter it.' And he replied, saying : ' Do as I tell thee : take thy will, thy memory, thy intellect, and see that thou use them only according to the will of the Superior.' But she said, 'How can I do this, for I cannot withhold my intellect from discerning, nor my memory from remembering.' He answered : 'Put thy will into her will, and make belief that hers is thine, and determine not to exercise the memory and intellect in any contrary way.' But she only said she could not do it, for she did not possess her own heart."

These visions of Christ and his Mother not only did not help Caterina to practise obedience, but increased her disappointment at failure, so that " many times she would have despaired altogether had she not known that despair is the greatest of all sins." On the other hand they inspired her with presumption and conceit. She longed to speak of the favours vouchsafed to her to those who regarded her with suspicion and contempt, and with great difficulty she bridled her tongue. Reticence in respect to all her spiritual experiences was the outcome of victory over the temptation to boastfulness, and this, as she herself perceived, was not an unmixed good. " Let the subject manifest her temptations to her who bears rule," Caterina wrote long after to her novices; "for the hidden wound cannot be dressed nor cured. And the more a thing seems good and safe, the more let her reveal it, that under the semblance of good she may not be deceived, as was the sister abovementioned, to whom the Enemy appeared in the shape of Christ and his Mother." " By their fruits shalt thou know them " was the touchstone which Caterina gradually learned to apply to all supernatural appearances. Those which left her calm and humble she accounted as the work of God. Those which produced presumption and despair she attributed to demoniacal machinations.

Two anecdotes are related by Caterina's friend, Suor Illuminata, which go far to remove surprise at the girl's excessive reserve as well as at her difficulty in the matter of submission. On one occasion, we are told, she was bidden by her Superiors to jump into a large fire: she immediately sprang forward to obey, but found herself forcibly withheld. Another day she was actually commanded to leave the house, and return naked to her mother's dwelling. She at once meekly began to divest herself of her garments, whereupon she was informed that the command was merely given to prove her obedience.

These extravagant demands on her allegiance were possibly abnormal features in the life of the community, final tests of vocation imposed previous to Caterina's reception of the habit of Saint Clare. They mark none the less an arbitrary temper and a lack of discretion on the part of her Superiors which must have made themselves felt in the general government of the house. The only child of admiring parents, who never crossed her will even, in respect to her final settlement in life, a young lady of decided character, accustomed to lead and to rule, it was a foregone conclusion that Caterina dei Vigri would not find it easy to practise the virtue she loved in theory; while the fact that she was intellectually the superior of her Superiors, and that, in spite of her youth, she surpassed them in knowledge of the world, naturally increased the difficulty of absolute submission. Lucia Mascheroni was a holy and amiable person, and Caterina was much attached to "our first mother, who, according to the divine will, received me in this Place, and who was the first who showed me with pure love and maternal affection the way to serve God." She seems, however, to have been deficient in the gifts necessary for the government of a large community. She had not herself been through the mill of conventual training; her household had collected gradually and was very loosely organized. Her conduct in respect of her aunt's legacy, together with Ailisia's rebellion, indicate vacillation of purpose and lack of dignity and strength. It is noteworthy too that she did not become Superior of her own foundation, nor did she doff the Augustinian habit. After a while, indeed, she resumed the life of pious but independent retirement to which she was accustomed, though she certainly had no quarrel with her successor, and at her death left the whole of her property to the convent.

From various passages in *The Seven Weapons* we gain the impression that Caterina herself recognized that under wise guidance the misery of her irregular noviciate might have been averted. Her exhortations to her novices are interrupted by passionate appeals to those who shall be Abbesses in this place " that they diligently watch over the flocks committed to their care." They must not wait " till the poor lamb is actually in the wolf's jaws," but with true magnanimity of temper they must constantly bear in mind the weakness of the human soul and body. Aid given before it is asked for is sweet to the sufferer and pleasing to God, for " the thing asked for is half paid for." To those who are tempted to be disloyal and disobedient they should show not less but greater kindness, knowing that " the Enemy ever pricks the servant of Christ against the very virtue which he perceives she loves." Then again addressing her novices, she cheers them with the assurance that the submission of those who obey with difficulty, doing violence to their own opinion, their own will, their own intelligence and judgment, is not less but more precious and beneficial than the obedience of those who find the virtue easy. But, she adds, let the Superior be careful not to impose on her subjects " a burden greater than they can bear, so that good intention, which God always requires from the soul, may always exceed the work accomplished."

CHAPTER IV

CATERINA THE PROFESSED "CLARISSA"

*That inward eye
Which is the bliss of solitude.*—WORDSWORTH

PROFESSED at twenty, Caterina was still very young when she became Mistress of the Novices. It is noteworthy that her own trials and perplexities faded away when confronted with new interests, occupations, and responsibilities. Her thoughts were no longer concentrated on her own spiritual life, but heart and soul, time, and wealth of tenderness were lavished without stint on "those newly entered on the field of spiritual battle."

Lucia's successor, the Abbess Taddea, was the sister of the convent's friend and benefactress, Dama Verde de' Pii. She came from Mantua, and brought a colony of nuns with her. She was a clever organizer, and the convent under her rule rapidly increased in numbers and prestige. But she was a hard woman of tyrannical temper, careless and unobservant of the physical well-being of her flock. Neither Caterina nor Illuminata allude to her with affection, and the latter tells us that the exclamation, "Oh that you were our Mother!" was not infrequently addressed to the Mistress of the Novices by some young nun who smarted from the Abbess's unsympathetic correction.

Such expressions were sternly repressed by Caterina, but were more than justified by her sisterly tenderness. She became, in truth, *serva servarum*, nor would she ever allow her novices to address her by any title marking superiority. It was for their sakes, "fearing the Divine reproof should I conceal what might help others," that she composed, when she was about[1] five-and-twenty, the first draft of *The Seven Weapons*.

The book was written with the utmost secrecy; for to the shyness of the young author Caterina joined the humility of the saint, and she was fearful of posing as a teacher and displaying her superior education. But secrecy in a convent of Poor Clares was not easy to maintain. The long dormitory was divided into cubicles only by hangings of matting, and "according to the rule of the Blessed Francis the sisters had all things in common," no member of the community possessing even a box or desk where private possessions could be stored. A woman's ingenuity, however, is not easily baffled. Caterina's cubicle contained a large chair with leather-covered seat. Caterina unsewed the leather, laid her papers beneath it, and then tacked the cover down again. She repeated the process whenever she was moved, and found time, to write; and the book grew apace and was larger unfinished than that which she subsequently completed. But, alas! one day when she entered her cell, Caterina found the covering of the chair unsewn. She looked for the MS.; it was there, but in a different position from that in which she had left it. It had clearly been read.

[1] In her preface she says: "Al tempo della nostra Reverendissima Madre Abbadessa Suor Taddea Sorella che fu di Messer Marco de Pii, circa gli anni del nostro Signore Messer Gesù Cristo MCCCCXXXVIII."

Whether a superior had played the spy or a sister had been overcome by curiosity, whether Caterina identified the culprit or feared, even silently, to formulate suspicion, are matters unrevealed by her biographers. But she was certainly filled with immense indignation, and acted with passionate promptness. In the division of manual labour, the oven of the convent was at this time her province. The oven happened to be hot. She took her precious papers and threw them in, and in bitterness of heart she stood and watched their slow consumption.

Another and more cheerful incident is related in connexion with Caterina's duties as chief baker. On one occasion, when she had just put a batch of bread into the oven, the sisters were hurriedly collected to listen to a spiritual discourse from an ecclesiastic visiting the convent. The sermon lasted five hours! At intervals the bakeress thought with anxiety of her bread, and the moment she was released she flew to the oven door. To the wonder of all, the bread, instead of being burnt to a cinder, was unhurt, and when eaten by the hungry nuns was pronounced to have a particularly agreeable flavour. The circumstance was reported beyond the convent walls, and next day many persons made application for a fragment of the loaves, which they named, with Italian felicity of epithet, "the bread of obedience."

Another pretty story with a similar moral is told in connexion with her term of office as portress. Her duties were fatiguing and occasioned perpetual calls from prayer and meditation; but Caterina fulfilled them with alacrity, and like S. Francesca di Romana submitted with joyfulness to interruption and petty trials of patience.

One day an aged man in pilgrim's dress knocked at the convent gate. The portress opened and gave not only alms, but kindly looks and words. His visit was repeated, and Caterina questioned him concerning his travels. He told her of the scenes of the Saviour's life and death, and assuredly no Desdemona ever listened to an amorous traveller's tales with greater eagerness than this cloistered nun listened to the aged pilgrim's stories of the Holy Land.

One day he brought her a little bowl made of a substance she had never seen before. He told her he had brought it from the East, and that out of it the Virgin Mother used to give her Holy Child to drink, and he prayed the Sister-portress that she would keep it safe for him till he should come again to claim it. Doubtless the pilgrim "told the tale as 'twas told to him"; doubtless too he meant the bowl to be a gift, desiring to make some return for kindness and hesitating to presume. Caterina received both bowl and words with grateful and entire credulity; and as the weeks slipped by a supposition stole into her mind which strengthened with the flight of time. The pilgrim came no more, and the nun believed that the object of her charity had been no ordinary man, "but possibly S. Joseph himself." " It is not known," says Grassetti naively, "what foundation she had for this belief, for she never spoke of it, but probably she had some special revelation." To-day in the convent of Corpus Domini in Ferrara, coated without with silver for its preservation, but within gleaming russet and satiny like a polished chestnut,[1] the "Scodella di S. Giuseppe" is still offered to the sight and the kiss of devout visitors.

Preaching what she conspicuously practised, Caterina never failed to exalt the gospel of work. She would sharply reprimand any novice who was heard complaining that appointed manual labours encroached on time which might be profitably spent on religious exercises, declaring that she herself had more joy in mental prayer while she sat spinning or otherwise working with the rest of the community than when she knelt alone in choir or cell. But while reproving indolence she was always ready to spare the weakly by taking on herself their burdens. Thus when she was baker, the heat of the oven tried her health and eyesight, but it was long before she could be induced to ask for a change of office. Some one must do the work, she argued, and "my sisters cannot stand such hard work as I can; they are young";—"forgetting," says Illuminata, "that she herself was young."

With similar unselfishness she strove to mitigate the severity of the rule to weakly and delicately nurtured novices. Illuminata relates with naive admiration the innocent subterfuges to which she resorted for this purpose. She would ask at head-quarters for a couple of eggs as supplement to the day's meagre rations, and would carry them to her place at the long refectory table. Watching her opportunity, she would slip the

---

[1] In substance the "Scodella" resembles closely a set of cups exhibited in the Querini Stampaglia Palace, Venice. No one appears to have identified the wood of which these cups are made.

eggs into a capacious pocket which she wore beneath her gown, at the same time drawing from it some empty egg-shells which she left ostentatiously on the table. Later in the day the eggs found their way into the hands and mouth of some half-starved novice. Sometimes too Caterina would ask for meat, ostensibly for herself, really for convalescents in the infirmary, "that they might have no cause for complaint." Such acts earned for her a reputation for greediness, and at every visitation she was accused of self-indulgence and reproved and punished accordingly. But she proved an incorrigible offender.

She had a true woman's love and capacity for nursing and for "looking after" people, and kept a little medicine chest from which she dispensed medicines to any ailing sister. How much one wishes that Illuminata had given us a detailed inventory of its contents! Caterina had numerous patients, for the course of two centuries had produced such deterioration in the hardihood of Italian women that the rule of the founders, after a fair trial, was felt to be insupportable. The daily fast and the lack of stockings were found particularly hard to tolerate, and sister after sister fell seriously ill. A petition was addressed to Eugenius IV, and in February, 1446, the Poor Clares of Ferrara received the Papal permission to mitigate the severity of their rule.

But if Caterina held that to labour is to pray, she declared still more emphatically that to pray is to labour, and that this labour is the chief duty and privilege of the religious. Constant intercession afforded a vent for her spirit of love and service, and fed its pure flame; it kept her sympathies from shrinking and preserved the suppleness of her mind. Her horizon was never bounded by the convent walls; the ties of blood and friendship were not forgotten; and in spite of her strict seclusion she became through the power of prayer a citizen of the world. By means of this power, and by reason of the spiritual faculties developed in its exercise, she gained that clearness of insight, that certainty of intuition, that triumphant faith, which the vulgar are always apt to represent as gifts akin to magic. Thus, in the anecdotes told of her intercessions, she often appears in the disguise of a wonder-worker or soothsayer; but the true proportions of the yearning tender figure cannot be obscured, while the wide range of her sympathies is strikingly illustrated.

We begin, as is most natural, with two anecdotes telling of her prayer for blood-relations.

Her mother, Benvenuta, as we have already seen, had married again. Of this marriage there were two children,—a son who in early manhood fell into vicious courses, and a daughter who when still a mere child entered the convent of Corpus Domini. This little sister and spiritual daughter was very dear to Caterina's heart. She was remarkable for her gentle piety and religious observance; and "having in a short time fulfilled a long time," she was the first to die in that community, passing hence only five years after the foundation of the new house, in the spring-time of 1437. With a sore heart and with deep fervour Caterina knelt by the death-bed and prayed for the departed soul; and behold, as she prayed, there came to her the full and perfect assurance that little Suor Antonia was already received into the bliss of Paradise.

Fifteen years later we find her in deep distress concerning the welfare of her ne'er-do-well stepbrother. Now she had a very special admiration for that great Franciscan, S. Bernardino of Siena, whose devotion to the name of Jesus particularly appealed to her, and when in May, 1451, the Frate was canonized, she took a keen interest in the event, pictured it to herself, and prayed earnestly that the honour done to God's servant might redound to the glory of the Church. Prayer passed into ecstacy, in which time and space were vanquished. The cell in Ferrara was left behind, the ardent spirit had arrived in Rome. Caterina always believed that in some mysterious manner she actually assisted at the ceremony of canonization.

Then there awoke in her a sentiment similar to that which Browning puts into the mouth of the innocent heroine of *The Ring and the Book*. There was now a new-made Saint in heaven, who was surely less weary and occupied than his older much-prayed-to brethren. She would address herself to S. Bernardino. Undoubtedly he would join his worthy intercessions with her unworthy ones, that the conversion of her wretched stepbrother might be obtained. We do not know when or how her wishes were fulfilled; but the story ends happily with the contrition and amendment of the evil-doer.

From kinsfolk we pass to benefactors and friends. Caterina was deeply grateful for the steady support given to the convent by the good Bishop of Ferrara, Giovanni da Tosignano, who before his appointment to the see had belonged to the Order of the Gesuati. On the 24th July, 1446, she was kneeling in the chapel about the hour of terce, when she suddenly rose to her feet, called one of the Sisters, and exclaimed that she saw the soul of the Bishop ascending up to heaven in the form of a radiant star. The nuns noted the time, and when a little later news of the Bishop's[1] decease reached the convent, it was found that his death-hour corresponded exactly with that of Caterina's vision. Another anecdote of friendship is pleasing only as illustrating the continued affection between Caterina and her old companions. The "Principessa Margherita" had been for some years a widow, Galeotto Roberto dying soon after his longed-for retirement from the world. But a youthful widow had as little place in the scheme of fifteenth-century society as an unmarried maiden, and the girls of noble family were valued only as pawns in the game of matrimonial alliance. Duke Niccolò happened to have an opportunity of placing to advantage the young woman so unexpectedly returned upon his hands, and did not think it needful to apprise her of his schemes till the envoys of the destined bridegroom arrived at Court to take home the bride. She was a dutiful daughter, *bien élevée* after the standard of the day, and endowed to boot with the Este political instinct and aptitude for diplomacy. Her brief married life had been very troublous, and she had no desire to make a second essay in matrimony. Yet she wished to oblige her father and perceived the seriousness of breaking off negotiations at so late a stage. In great agitation she hastened to the convent and poured the tale of her father's schemes and her own repugnance to

[1] The "Diario Ferrarese" (*Muratori*, Vol. XXIV) informs us that the good Bishop made the poor of Ferrara his heirs, and that the hospital of Saint Anna had its origin in this bequest.

them into Caterina's sympathetic ears. The nun promised to pray for Divine help and guidance, and Margherita returned comforted. That night, while Caterina kept vigil in the convent chapel, the " Principessa" slept peacefully in her bed, forgetful of her perplexities and of the morrow's journey. And behold, in a dream her husband, the Beato Roberto, appeared to her, in his Franciscan habit, and once again they plighted their troth; and he told her that she, who had once been his wife after the flesh, was now and for evermore his bride after the spirit; that he asked no other dowry than her free consent, and that he would in no wise suffer her to be pursued by another. As the Beato Roberto had never shown anything but contempt for his bride in life, his post-mortem airs of proprietorship recall the traditional attitude of the dog in the manger. But Margherita received comfort from them, and knew in her dream that she was saved from the detested second marriage, and that this was Caterina's work.

She awoke to receive the news of the death of the elected bridegroom, the " Personaggio grande" whose name is the chroniclers' secret; and untouched by horror or uneasiness at this terrible mode of deliverance, she exhibited such "incredible satisfaction" that Duke Niccolò was moved to question her concerning her real feelings; and understanding them, he promised to let her abide in widowhood and to molest her no further with a talk of suitors.

By far the most striking and pathetic of these tales of intercession is one which recalls the relations of a more famous Caterina with the political prisoner of Siena.

A wicked man of Ferrara, according to the cruel criminal code of the day, had been condemned to be burnt alive. We do not know his name, his life, or his offence, how Caterina heard of his sentence, or whether he had any claim on her interest beyond the hideousness of his sentence and his own impenitence.

During the day preceding his execution, Caterina prayed incessantly for his conversion, and when evening fell she went to the Abbess and asked leave to spend the night in the church. The request was granted, and before the Blessed Sacrament Caterina continued her labour of intercession. The mattin-bell sounded. Caterina rose from her knees and slipped into the choir; but when the office ended, instead of retiring to the dormitory, she resumed her post before the altar. The new day dawned, and still she remained upon her knees; and, "Lord," she cried, "I will never rise from this place till Thou givest me this soul. It is thine, bought with a great price, even thy precious blood. Lord, deny not my unworthy prayers."

Then it seemed to her that a voice came forth from the altar: "I can deny thee no longer, I will give thee this soul."

Caterina was still upon her knees, no longer wrestling in prayer, but rapt in adoring expectancy, when there came a knock at the convent gate. The criminal had sent a messenger in hot haste to ask the prayers of Suor Caterina, and to beg that she would send him a confessor.

The Dominican Tertiary, Caterina Benincasa, could

accompany her penitent to the scaffold; Caterina dei Vigri, the true-hearted daughter of Saint Francis and Saint Clare, physically tied and bound by the "clausura," could only write a letter to the man for whom she had interceded with all the strength of her unshackled will. In the great crises ot our lives the most eloquent of compositions is a poor substitute for the sound of a sweet voice, the sight of a sympathetic tear, the grasp of firm yet gentle hands. Yet even the letter of a true woman, especially if she happens to possess the pen of a ready writer and the calligraphy of an artist, may convey to a lonely man something of the strength and sweetness of her personality. Caterina's convert took courage when he read that letter, and went to his death like a hero. With the meek dignity of the real penitent he accepted as his due the vituperations of the crowd, asking those who railed on him to pardon his offences, and take warning by his life and fate. When bound to the stake, following Caterina's counsel, he called continually on the name of Jesus, and in the strength of that Holy Name patiently endured his torments.

But Caterina's range of sympathy, and therefore of intercession, was not determined by the city walls. She had the faculty, which so many women lack, of really caring about persons and events with whom she had no personal concern. Hence the following anecdote.

On the Vigil of the Assumption, in the year 1443, some very serious news reached the convent of Corpus Domini. The civil war prevailing in Bologna was the opportunity of Filippo Maria Visconti, Duke of Milan. He had a party within the walls. Luigi dal Verme, a valiant mercenary, was besieging it from without. It seemed as though Bologna would once again exchange the easy yoke of the Papacy for the heavy rule of the Milanese.

Caterina was deeply troubled at the news. The cruel outrages which would necessarily follow the taking of the city by a band of greedy mercenaries were present to her vivid imagination. With a sick heart she sought relief in fervent prayer. And as she prayed there came to her a conviction that the danger was passing, that Dal Verme would be defeated, and Annibale Bentivoglio would be his victor. A few days later all Ferrara learned that such had been the case.[1]

Seven years later, when Abbess in Bologna, Caterina foretold the downfall and expulsion of the family whose success in 1445 had caused her such keen joy, and whose ruin actually took place after her own decease.

Some two years after the Milanese defeat, we hear of another political vision. The siege of Constantinople was known to all Italy, and filled the Ferrarese nun with the greatest excitement and consternation. Once more we find her keeping fast and vigil, and making "particular prayer to God" that He would overrule for His people's good this episode of cruel strife. But as she prayed there came to her not this time relief, but the certainty that her supplications were useless, that the Turk was already in possession, that the Christian Empire in the East had fallen. She spoke unhesitatingly of her convictions, and they were only too soon corroborated.

[1] The decisive battle was fought on 14 August, 1445.

But we have not yet taken the extreme measure of Caterina's intercessory energy. Her eschatological ideas may have been crude, but her faith and sympathy were highly matured, and it had never been suggested to this benighted nun that the efficacy of prayer ceases at the grave-side. "The Office of the Dead," says Illuminata Bembo, "was much more prolix in former days than it is now, so that many of the sisters found it very fatiguing to the brain." But on Caterina, even when she was ill and weary, the thought of aiding the souls in Purgatory acted as a tonic. "All my strength comes back," she would say, "so glad I am to be able to give them refreshment."

It is the intensity of this spirit of service and its limited outlet in the life of an enclosed community which gave rise, on the *emotional* side, to Caterina's astounding, and as it seems to us almost blasphemous, petition that she might serve as a scapegoat for the Divine vengeance. The *intellectual* elements in this desire are her strict sense of justice, and her feudal idea of the Atonement.

The idea of substitution—of man for man, of one kind of service for another—was inherent in the feudal system, and even where, as in Italy, that system was but little developed, gave a peculiar tinge to the current conception of the sacrifice of Christ. Christ, as Caterina put it, "left his high Court and Barony and became *a landless man*—a pilgrim, a stranger, a beggar," in order that He might make compensation for the debt of reasonable service due from defaulting man to the Almighty Suzerain. Side by side with this conception of the Atonement went the thought of filling up that which is behind of the sufferings of Christ; and the two ideas, blended in the mystic's mind by a glow of love towards God and towards His creatures, produced a ferment breeding fantastic forms of self-oblation, such as we meet with in the following passage from the *Sette Arme*:—

"Many times have I prayed with tears and of deliberate intent that God would deign to grant me this special grace, that if my damnation could add to the honour of his Majesty He would be pleased to concede me this:—that in the bottom of the infernal abyss (if bottom it can be said to have) He would of his severest justice, form a yet more horrible and indescribable depth, where I as the greatest and most grievous sinner might be placed,—to expiate the guilt of all other sinners who were or are or shall be. And for this with hearty and deliberate will I continually offer myself, believing that the Head will receive more joy from a number of his members than from a single and rotten member. For clearly in the kingdom of our God, his praises would be greatly multiplied if to the great company of the Blessed (Collegio dei Beati) were joined the entire multitude of sinners; and the curse of a single soul would be less dishonouring to thee, my God, than that of a great multitude: albeit I am certain that to thy majesty, most high and incomprehensible God, no dishonour could be done. But if, O Lord, I, unworthy that I am, may not have this favour that through my damnation be multiplied an act of infinite praise and thanksgiving, since the honour of the height of thy Godhead cannot be increased; at least most pitying Lord, grant me this, that by my damnation all sinners may be saved. . . . For this ceaselessly and submissively I offer myself to the Divine Justice, praying that on me may be avenged the guilt of all other sinners, so that their salvations may not be refused for justice sake." [1]

Caterina's conceptions of the working of Divine justice led her astray more than once. She relates— and the episode throws a strong side-light on her mental processes — that during the distressful period of her religious life, she was conscious one morning after mattins of a slight return of interest in her devotions. She had not experienced such a sentiment for many months, and, encouraged by it, she remained on her knees in the choir, when "in her heart was held a disputation, whereby it was shown that since God had enabled man and woman, through giving them the gift of freewill, to choose good or evil, He was obliged, *in justice*, to reward them if they did good. And that the Apostle Paul for this reason said that a crown [2] of justice was laid up for him, because he had used his freewill in doing good, rejecting the evil which he was at liberty to do."

[1] Did Caterina remember the petition of Moses?—"Oh, this people have sinned a great sin, and have made them gods of gold. Yet now, if thou wilt forgive their sin—; and if not, blot me, I pray thee, out of thy book which thou hast written. And the Lord said unto Moses, Whosoever hath sinned against me, him will I blot out of my book."— Exod. xxxi. 32, 33.

Cp. too St. Paul: "For I could wish that myself were accursed from Christ for my brethren, my kinsmen according to the flesh: who are Israelites."—Romans ix. 3.

[2] Caterina's "diceva essergli riposta la corona della giustizia" is of course a version of the Vulgate, "In reliquo reposita est mihi corona justitiae" of 2 Timothy iv. 8. The "crown of righteousness" of the English version is to her a "just crown," a due reward.

CATERINA THE PROFESSED "CLARISSA" 83

The idea took great hold on the poor depressed little nun, and the consolation it inspired made her believe that it came from God. But the following night she worked it out to its logical conclusion, and was horrified to discover whither it had led her. While saying mattins she was overcome with a deadly weariness of mind and body, and it then occurred to her that on account of the fatigue of the office, as well as the other hardships which she bore willingly, she ought to receive as the meed of justice (per debito di giustizia) a higher place than Christ, who knew no sin nor had any taint of vice, while she, who was at liberty to sin and was subject to sin, had nevertheless left the path of vice and sin to exercise herself in virtue.

But she had hardly reached this conclusion before she recoiled in terror from it. An abyss seemed to open in front of her, and she perceived that the thought and the consolation of the preceding night were of the devil's sending (era missione diabolica). And forthwith she recognized that the debt was all upon the other side. For from God had come the gift of goodwill which had inclined her to a right choice. "And albeit we are at liberty to do good, yet are we none the less obliged as a just debt to do it; and do it we cannot without the divine grace." Then seizing the "Second Weapon" of *Propria Diffidenza* she resolved to remember the words of Christ: "Sine me nihil potestis facere."

Thus Caterina dei Vigri in the fifteenth century reached the conclusion formulated by the English reformers of 1571 in the Tenth Article: "Wherefore we have no power to do good works pleasant and acceptable to God without the grace of God by Christ preventing us, that we may have a good will, and working with us when we have that good will."

It is noteworthy that Caterina's speculations on freewill never extend to the subject of predestination. She is unwavering in her belief that all men "start fair," and that the Father willeth not the death of a sinner. The hideous thought of reprobation, of "striving turned to sin," never darkened the gloom of her time of trial. Intellectual difficulties there were, especially doubts concerning the doctrines of the Trinity, the Incarnation, and the Eucharist. The wind of free inquiry, raised by Abelard, and laid by the Council of Sens, was beginning to stir again, and the woman bred in the Court of Ferrara clearly felt its influence even within the cloister walls. Not that Caterina could ever have been a sceptic in the modern sense, or an unbeliever after the pagan type of the later renaissance. Her doubts were invariably viewed as diabolical temptations; they were limited by a strong bias; they were feared less because she knew not whither they might lead her, than because they occasioned a loss of fervour and devotion. There is a touching passage in *The Seven Weapons* describing the agony of this loss.

This "infernal penury," she declares, surpasses in bitterness all the sorrows which women in the world experience from the death of those they love. For God and Paradise lie beyond the loss of present things; but the religious person who has given God all her love, and has "left for Him not only friends and relatives and all created things but *even her own self*, must needs be filled with bitter grief if she be deprived of the sense of His love," for by reason of his infinity there is nothing above and beyond God in which she can take delight.

The nightmare of melancholy and doubt passed in due time, leaving the waker, however, with the conviction that it had been a necessary discipline for the "pilgrim soul." There came a day when communicating without faith or devotion, God "visited her mind," and she saw "in a flash how and in what way it was possible that in the Host consecrated by the priest there should be the whole divinity and humanity of our Lord." And seeing this, she perceived also that "the person who communicates with difficulty, bearing spiritual strife with patience," "does not the less receive the grace of the Sacrament," and that it is well that a soul should learn not to value the sense of joy in worship above the Giver of that gift.

It is characteristic of Caterina's combative and sturdy temperament that this conviction was not the result of tranquil retrospect from the vantage ground of higher things and advancing years, but formed part of that sudden illumination of intellect and spirit which marked an epoch in her life. At the moment when the mysteries of the Catholic religion seemed to grow luminous, when the woman's finite powers of apprehension stretched out towards infinity, when her intellect expanded to receive the doctrines of the Trinity, the Incarnation, and the Real Presence, and her whole being was filled with consolation;—at that supreme moment she perceived the value of spiritual conflict and discomfort, and positively rejoiced in her past painful experience.

If this rejoicing were characteristic of the individual,

the speedy reinforcement of intellectual apprehension by sensuous perception was still more characteristic of her age and country. To the blissful moment in the church of Corpus Domini, when "all her doubts passed away as though they had never been," succeeded a morning when, "having received the Sacred Host in her mouth, she felt and tasted the sweetness of the most pure flesh of the immaculate Lamb Christ Jesus, and that taste was of so sweet a savour as she cannot describe or by any simile make understood. But truly she was able to say : Cor meum et caro mea exultaverunt in Deum vivum."

Such a sensible manifestation of the substance beneath the accidents has, of course, many a medieval parallel from the Lateran Council of 1059 onwards. It is hardly too much to say that a woman of Caterina's training and environment must have expected some material confirmation of these truths so recently, so vividly, so miraculously apprehended by the intellect. What is remarkable in her case is that the material manifestation is secondary and subsequent to the intellectual illumination. It is not the latter, but the former revelation on which she lays stress, and which makes a crisis in her spiritual life. Her mysticism is, as we have seen again and again, leavened by practical common sense, so that it never lays the will to sleep, and limited by intellectual activity. The typical mystic's "testimony of the individual soul" to the statements of the creeds, which suspends intellectual processes and makes intellectual action useless, is not sufficient to Caterina, and when the Lord 'visits her mind' he speaks to her intellectually." (Iddio visitò la mente

CATERINA THE PROFESSED "CLARISSA" 87

sua, e parlando intelletualmente con lei, diedele aperto conoscimento, etc.)

The days of forced and apathetic communions were over, and Caterina's trouble was now her inability to receive the Blessed Sacrament as often as her heart desired. But this spiritual growing-pain passed in its turn as her soul increased in stature. One day as she assisted at Mass, hungry and repining, she was conscious to the full of the sweetness and reality of spiritual communion. (In quell' ora sentì veramente l' anima sua comunicarsi dalla bontà della divina provvidenza.)

Yet the days when she received the Sacrament were the *festas* of her monotonous existence. She was apt to manifest her love of Holy Poverty by wearing the oldest, and we fear we must add, the dirtiest clothes of the community. But on the morning when she communicated she donned a clean and fair habit and dressed herself carefully as one summoned into the presence of a king, thus by outward act expressing the reverence and alacrity of soul which breaks forth in passage after passage of *The Seven Weapons.*

"Let no gentle spirit be so vile," she cries to her spiritual daughters, "as not to take Him who wills to come to you, seeing that with bounteous courtesy He feeds you generously with His Godhead. Hasten, O sinners, delay no more, for He is made your food that ye may take Him." She warns her novices not to be led by the Evil One under pretext of humility to abstain from communicating; and she exhorts them to listen to the Epistle and Gospel "with great and fervent love, as to new letters addressed to you by your Celestial Spouse."

The return of fervour in Communion diffused a glow through all other ceremonies and devotions. When she was saying her office with radiant face and eyes uplifted to the crucifix, Caterina was unmindful of all that passed around her, so that if afterwards in chapter a question arose about anything which had happened at such times, Suor Caterina had seen nothing, knew nothing. "It is not possible," she would say, "to dwell with the angels and occupy one's self in praise and yet have the heart on earth."

Only the extremity of weakness and pain made her renounce attendance in the choir. From an early age to the close of her life, she suffered from a painful and little understood malady,[1] and sometimes when the mattin-bell sounded "it seemed impossible," says Suor Illuminata, "that she could descend the stairs." But taking a mouthful of food and summoning her resolution, she generally managed to creep to the chapel, and once there, "though faint she managed to remain." Once, however, being particularly weak, she begged the mother to dispense her from attendance at Mattins. Leave was given, and the Abbess added that it was unnecessary to apply daily for dispensation, but that as long as the fever lasted she might remain in her cell. The attack proved unusually prolonged; but there came a day when Caterina, though still weak and ill, dragged herself wearily from her cell to attend a chapter. The Abbess, as we have already seen, was a hard and arbitrary woman. Perhaps she had forgotten the scope of her permission: perhaps she thought that if Caterina were sufficiently recovered to attend the chapter she

[1] Hæmorrhoids.

ought to be able to be present at the offices in chapel: perhaps she eagerly embraced an opportunity of humbling a sister whose popularity she grudged. At all events, in presence of the whole chapter, "and this I heard with my own ears," says Illuminata, she addressed her as follows:—

"Sister Caterina, it pleases me not that you should be exempt from the Office because a few days since I gave you leave of absence. I wish you to attend Mattins, and when you cannot, to make excuse, as do the others."

Caterina was now one of the senior members of the community, her conscientiousness was approved, her devotion and also her sickness were known to all. She merely bowed her head, and said, "Mia colpa"; but afterwards many of the nuns gathered round her, asking her indignantly why she did not protest against unjust reproof;—"Well, you are a Christian! Why did you not say you had fever and were ill?" But Caterina answered with gentle dignity—

"My sisters, do you not see that the Holy Spirit spoke to me by the mouth of the mother? I understand that it is His will I should go to the Office: and I shall go believing that the strength of obedience will aid me, and the sweetness of the Divine Office. And I should esteem it a most solemn grace were I permitted to die within the choir singing for the love of obedience and of Christ."

In spite of the supreme moment of illumination and the light which it cast over her entire subsequent spiritual life, Caterina was subject from time to time to the grey days and the spells of apathy which are the peculiar trial of fervent temperaments and delicate organizations, and which, in her case, were usually succeeded by reaction into ecstasy. One of these spells of coldness occurred towards the close of the year 1445. Her well-springs of delight seemed dried up or changed to sources of bitterness, and she wept perpetually from weariness and disappointment.

The Eve of the Nativity had come, and she had no Christmas joy in her heart. From a sense of duty she asked leave of the Abbess to spend the night in church, when, upon her knees, she repeated the Hail Mary, in token of reverence for the Mother of the Lord. By degrees her coldness passed; her normal mood of worship returned,—a mood bordering on the line where its objects become visible or audible to the worshipper. A more than usually severe fast, a prolonged vigil, the eerie stillness of a night watch, and the line is passed.

"About the fourth hour of the night"—thus runs Caterina's own account of the "marvellous grace vouchsafed to her"—"there appeared suddenly before her the glorious Virgin, and in her arms her dearest Son, swaddled after the fashion of newly born children. And drawing near to that Sister, courteously and with great benignity she laid Him in her arms, who perceiving by divine grace that the Babe was Very Son of the Eternal Father, embraced him closely (se lo strinse fra le bracci), laying her face on that of the dear Christ Child (dolcissimo bambino Cristo Gesú) with so much sweetness and delight that her whole being seemed dissolved as wax before a fire. And the sweetness of the odour exhaled by the pure flesh

MADONNA "DEL POMO"
CHAPEL OF THE SANTA, CHURCH OF CORPUS DOMINI, BOLOGNA

of the blessed Jesus no tongue can describe nor mind conceive. O heart insensate, hardest of all created things, which did not crumble away, or melt as snow before the sun, seeing, tasting, embracing the splendour of the paternal glory! For this vision was no dream, nor imagination, neither did it come through mental excitement, but openly and manifestly without any phantasy. But yet it is true that as she bent her face above that of the Babe the vision suddenly faded, and she remained so joyful that it seemed to her as though her heart and all her members would rejoice for ever; and the bitter sorrow which had so long afflicted her by reason of the absence of this same Jesus Christ left her so completely that for a long time melancholy could find no entrance to her heart."

Later writers speak of the odour which lingered in the church and clung to the person of the Saint, awakening the curiosity of the nuns and of the celebrating priest at the Mass on Christmas morning. They tell us too of the celestial joy and beauty of Caterina's aspect; how the sunken eyes were lit and the sallow cheeks flushed by that love which is "a very flame of the Lord"; how the lips which had kissed the Holy Child distilled a strange fragrance; how the skin on jaw and chin which had touched the pure flesh of the Infant Christ had lost its olive tint and become white as milk. Caterina's own narrative has, however, no such sequences. Simple and practical as ever, her only aim is to draw out of her experience a heavenly moral.

"The inexperienced soul thinks itself deprived of divine love when it finds that it no longer enjoys the mental sweetness to which it is accustomed and is deprived *of the presence of the Humanity of Christ*[1] (è sottratta la presenza della Umanità di Cristo). Nevertheless, at this time God in occult mystery is united to that soul in triumphant love. The proof whereof is found in grief's very presence, for the more the love the greater the grief. So the soul which laments because it feels not love, in fact possesses love and grief together: inasmuch as one does not grieve for that one does not love. But mean souls cannot understand this argument, because they love the gift more than the giver. . . . Therefore, dearest Sisters, be wise, and know how to bear with patience the departure of the divine love: and at such times brace yourselves to persistent prayer, and to other holy virtues and good works, till such time as it shall please the Divine Mercy to double the flame of pure and chaste love within your hearts. For God having proved the soul by leaving it widowed for a season, when He sees it constant and faithful in spite of indigence, will be impelled to console it and to give Himself to it again, yea more abundantly and inseparably."

This episode in the life of Caterina dei Vigri, and the language in which she describes it, has its parallels in the lives of other saints and its counterparts in secular poetry and romance. We must remember that there are fashions in sanctity as in other things, recurring cycles of taste in subtle and intimate correspondence with the varying needs and tempers of mankind. We must remember also that the trances and visions, the

---

[1] The italics are mine. The curious phrase seems to mean deprived of the sensible presence of Christ, just as the departure of a beloved person deprives us of the comfort of material contact with him.

miracles and ecstasies of the medieval saint are not isolated phenomena, but translations into the sphere and language of religion of the ideal intensity of love manifested and described by Italian poets of the " spiritual school" from Guido Guinicelli onwards.

A revelling in emotion, a cultivation of sensibility and of the faculty of personification, acuteness of physical sensation, and a tendency to reiterate certain picturesque phrases and experiences, these are the characteristics of the poetry and the religion of the epoch. The groans and tears of the recluse are echoed by the lover. The lamentations of the saint over "spiritual dryness" are couched in the same terms as the poet's complaints of the coldness of his mistress; and a sensible return to favour, human or divine, is accompanied by overpowering emotion. The religious kneels in cell or choir, unconscious of all save the Divine Presence, and seeing with the spiritual eye forms invisible to natural sight; and the youthful Dante in the vicinity of his Beloved is seized with trembling palpitation and faintness and can do naught but look upon "that most gracious being," all his senses being overpowered by the great lordship that love obtained. On the one hand we see the poets idealizing and etherealizing human love till it becomes supersensuous, philosophic, far removed from the commonplace realities of daily life; on the other hand we find the mystics describing the relations of the soul to God in terms of earthly passion. We perceive, moreover, that this terminology helps to create and literally represents the feeling which it designates. When, for example, Caterina speaks of her chastity as that of the affianced bride, of the loss of a sense of devotion as widowhood, of her future bliss as marriage with the Heavenly Bridegroom, it is obvious that she is not using merely conventual figures of speech borrowed from the Apocalypse or the Song of Solomon, but is conveying to the reader with perfect accuracy the peculiar *quality* of her sentiments. The dreams of the *Vita Nuova* are as vivid and as pictorial as Caterina's highly coloured visions of the Last Judgment or the Court of Heaven; while the effect of music, earthly or heavenly, is described in much the same terms by earthly and heavenly lovers. Saint Francis and Caterina feel their souls drawn forth from their bodies by the linkèd sweetness of an angelic chant, and declare that death would have followed the prolongation of that auditory joy; and poet after poet is similarly affected by the singing of some fair and gentle dame.[1]

And just as the phases of feeling pictured in the *Vita Nuova* have innumerable replicas of varying merit and degree in the lesser poets of the "New Style," so it may be doubted whether Caterina would have had her Christmas vision, if Saint Francis and Saint Anthony of Padua[2] had not likewise held in their arms the Holy

[1] As an example I select at random some lines from an unknown writer of the fourteenth century :—

> Ed ella pur cantava.
> Onde l' anima mia, che ciò sentía
> E che vedía—in amor lo cor languire,
> Per gran paura pallida stridia,
> E se ne gía—lasciandomi finire.
> Io gridava merzé, per non morire,
> Piangendo forte.   Ed ella pur cantava.

[2] Another Franciscan, Fra Salimbene of Parma, well known as a chronicler, had a very similar vision.

Child. She was doubtless familiar with the story of these experiences; they formed for her the high-water mark of divine favour. In spite of her humility, she must have felt that what had been might be again.

Even had we not been expressly told that such was the case, it would have been a foregone conclusion that Caterina, like Saint Francis, desired greatly to apprehend the bitterness of the Passion of the Lord Jesus. And once again we note that this desire sprang from a conviction shared by earthly lovers and expressed with equal fervour in the religious and secular literature of the time. Love is a " Lord of Terrible Aspect,"[1] to whom due tribute must be paid. Love is a " Flame of the Lord," scorching those who approach it. The story of Cino da Pistoia and the hot coals may be made ridiculous; it may also be received as a parable.

The sufferings of Love are not merely willingly borne; they are actually desired. And the thought of pain as the concomitant of intense bliss finds its culminating expression in the phenomenon of the stigmata. When we read the impassioned words in which Caterina describes her "Fourth Weapon," *Memoria Passionis,* and recollect that the Poverello's marvellous experience seems to have been more than once repeated, it is almost surprising to find that her intense desire to apprehend the suffering of Christ should be satisfied through the intellect and not through the flesh.

As a revelation of the mystery of the Eucharist came to her primarily through the mind, and only secondarily through the senses, so it seemed to her that

[1] *Vita Nuova.*

Christ spoke to her intellectually (parlava intelletualmente) concerning his sufferings for the salvation of the world; and it is very noteworthy that in a résumé of this *parlamento* the physical pain of the crucifixion is passed over in few words, while stress is laid on the long agony of anticipation arising from foreknowledge, and especially from foreknowledge of man's ingratitude and the grief of the Virgin Mother. This is a remarkable conception at an epoch when the physical sufferings of Christ, of the martyrs, of the souls in Purgatory or in Hell, are set forth in literature and in art in the most brutal, crude, and realistic manner.

The conditions of a life of which the one great work is intercession, and the sole reward celestial sweetness, must needs be complete release from secular interruptions, luxuries, and cares. Poverty and seclusion were essential to Caterina's ideals; and accordingly we find her striving with all her might for the introduction of the strict *clausura* and the maintenance of Franciscan destitution.

When she was professed, she gave an ample donation as her "dowry" to the house; the rest of the large fortune inherited from her father she bestowed on the poor. The proposal made when she was mistress of the novices, by a party in the convent, that the community should no longer be dependent on the daily alms, but should acquire landed property, filled her with indignation and dismay. She arose in chapter, and spoke her mind with a passionate and convincing eloquence which turned the scale in favour of Holy Poverty. No résumé of her discourse can convey its flavour, and it therefore seems well to give a but slightly abridged translation.

"Dearest Sisters, I marvel much how it is possible that among cloistered persons like those here present who profess to follow the standard of our seraphic father, Saint Francis, there should be souls so blind that they fail to recognize that this is most manifestly a temptation of the Devil, who is a spirit of infidelity, and of inexcusable distrust of God. I should like those who are so prudent, according to the world, and who hold that our present mode of life cannot long continue, to tell me where they have learned such doctrine, and on what reasons it is founded. Who will cause such a thing to happen? Will our Lord God, who has brought us together in this place, be unable or unmindful, or—as though he were sick of the trouble of governing us (fastidito dalla lunga molestia del governarci)—indisposed to continue to provide for our needs? Has He not many times praised and commended Poverty? Did He not say: 'Blessed are the poor'? And to another: 'Go sell what thou hast and give to the poor; and when thou art become poor, come and follow me, and I will make thee to have treasure in Heaven'? Did He not say: 'Whosoever for my love shall leave father, mother, possessions, and everything else, shall receive a hundredfold in this world, and in the next the possession of the Kingdom of Heaven'? If He commanded His disciples not to be careful for what they should eat or what they should drink, and to take no thought to procure clothes to cover the nakedness of their bodies, but to leave all care to the heavenly Father, who knew that they had need of these things, to strive only to acquire virtue, and to aspire to the Kingdom of Heaven ; who will be so impertinent as to dare to argue that He who faithfully promises, and who cannot lie, will fail to observe His own word ? For my own part, I do not know with what face a person can dare to call himself a Christian—Christ having said : ' Seek first the Kingdom of God and His righteousness ' and these other things shall be given you in addition,—who is not ashamed to say that a congregation of persons who have deliberately left the world and dedicated themselves to God's service cannot for long maintain themselves lacking provision for livelihood. Will that God who provides for the birds of the air, and who clothes and adorns the flowers of the field, be so improvident as to allow a household, formed for the honour of His Divine Majesty, to be injured for lack of sustenance ? . . .

" How many monasteries of men and of women, of our own Order and of others, have long persevered in this kind of life, and still do persevere ? What they can do why cannot we do likewise with the help of the divine grace ? It seems to you that if this monastery had some estates (poderi) and possessions of its own, whence every year it might draw abundant rents, we should ensure the livelihood of ourselves and our distant successors. What foolishness is this to place more confidence in a few acres of ground (campi di terra) than in God's promises. And tell me : if this land should fail to produce its usual fruit, or if through war, famine, or tempest you should fail to receive the rent which you expect (which would be no new nor extraordinary thing in this world), what would you then be obliged to do? You could do naught but appeal to the Divine Mercy that the hearts of the citizens might be moved to provide you with necessary sustenance. Now what hinders you from doing always what you could do in case of need? . . .

"Poverty spurs us to devotion, for it compels us always to have recourse to God that He may provide for us. Poverty removes from us occasions for disputes and dissensions such as are continually provoked by 'Mine and Thine,' those cruel enemies of fraternal charity. Poverty creates detachment from the world and from the things of this life; for nobody is greatly tempted to love that which he does not possess, but in truth it is very difficult to have no affection for the goods in which one is engulfed. Poverty multiplies our merits in this world and acquires for us inheritance in the Kingdom of Heaven.

"Thus you may clearly perceive by what spirit those are guided who under pretext of providence and prudence go about disturbing the Sisters and filling the minds of the most simple with vain humours."

Caterina's eloquence prevailed. The convent of Corpus Domini acquired no landed property.

She got her way, too, with reference to the strict *clausura*, not this time by a single battle, but by steady gentle resistance and patient watching of opportunity.

Though Lucia's community had deliberately chosen the "strict observance," and though the first Abbess,

Mother Taddea, was in many respects a rigid disciplinarian, there remained considerable freedom of intercourse between the inmates of the convent and their relatives in the city. "The citizens of Ferrara," says Grassetti, "would in no wise permit the house to be thoroughly locked up, because they wished to be able to go in and out at pleasure, and to visit their daughters," and they urged that "in all cases of distress and difficulty they found comfort in this intercourse." It is not suggested that any scandals arose out of this liberty, but to Caterina it seemed, as we moderns would say, *the wrong thing*. Herself a tender daughter, a good sister, a faithful friend, she believed that the nun's real use to her family and to society was in inverse proportion to her intercourse with them. By opening a door to gossip and tittle-tattle, the spiritual tone of the community was lowered, and time and energy were frittered away which should have been devoted to prayer.

But till Mother Taddea died, after a reign of twenty years, Caterina's flame of reform consumed its own smoke. The vacant throne was her opportunity. She turned to Lucia Mascheroni, still a power in the affairs of the convent, and besought her to use her influence with the controlling Fathers and induce them to import an Abbess from a strict community. The facile Lucia assented; but when she found that the Fathers had other views she assented with equal ease to these also. They had determined to choose the new Abbess from the senior members of the community, and of these none appeared more suitable than Suor Caterina herself.

Caterina was summoned before the Committee of Election, and the why and wherefore of the summons were unfolded. For a few moments she remained stupefied and speechless: then she burst into tears. Falling on her knees she besought the electors to spare her, to assign her any subordinate office, however toilsome, in the house, but not to lay on her the heavy burden of rule. The committee, probably embarrassed by her emotion, and perhaps convinced by it that she was indeed not suited to the task, listened to her entreaties and considered her counter-proposals. In April, 1452, a bull was obtained from Pope Nicholas V, authorizing the transportation of an abbess and several sisters from the convent of Poor Clares in Mantua, to the end that the discipline and observance of the convent of Corpus Domini, in Ferrara, should be rendered more strict.

Doubtless the task of the new Mother was not an easy one. We are told of some slight resistance from without; we can conjecture some slight discontent within. But the infusion of new blood, enforced by the influence of Caterina and her friends, told in the end. The old easy coming and going of kinsfolk ceased. Henceforth the professed nun was seen only at stated hours behind the parlour grate.

The four years (1452–6) which passed between the establishment of this new regime and Caterina's departure from Ferrara, were probably the happiest of her life. The struggles of youth lay behind her; the responsibility of her last years was still unforeseen. Her ideal of conventual order was fulfilled, and she was at length in thorough sympathy with her Superior,

Instead of humbling her in chapter, after the manner of tyrannical Mother Taddea, Mother Lenore continually asked the opinion and deferred to the advice of the gentle nun, whom, in the July of 1456, she enthusiastically described to the Bolognese envoys as "a second St. Clare."

CHAPTER V

THE NEW COLONY

Spirit nearing yon dark portal at the limit of thy human state,
Fear not thou the hidden purpose of that Power which alone is great,
Nor the myriad world, His shadow, nor the silent Opener of the gate.
                                                                TENNYSON.

THE convent of Corpus Domini in Ferrara had become fashionable. Ladies of high rank from distant parts were clamouring for admission and waiting disconsolately for vacancies; till at length it occurred to certain leading citizens of Bologna and Cremona that the "venerabile monastero" might be induced to colonize, and that plantations of Poor Clares might be established in their midst.

The moving spirit in Bologna was a certain Battista Mezavacca, who had two daughters in the convent at Ferrara, and whose son was Provincial of the Observant Friars. The Third Order took up the matter, and resolved to furnish the colony with a home, and on the twentieth of July, 1453, the prospective foundation was formally endowed with a house, church, cloister, campanile, and bell. But the Legate Cardinal Bessarion was a shrewd man, and foresaw the popularity of the house. He declared that the premises bestowed by the Third Order were far too limited, and induced the Girolamites of Fiesole to part with the church, cloister, and possessions of S. Cristoforo delle Muratelle which belonged to them. The parochial cure was then transferred to one of the neighbouring churches, while the nuns' procurator purchased an adjacent house, court, stable, and well. In October, 1455, the Pope gave his formal approval to the scheme; and in November, according to the Bolognese historian Ghirardacci, the Commune began the building operations necessary for the housing of a community, and the welding of two detached properties into an enclosed quadrangle.

Nothing now was left but to select and bring home the "suore"; and during the winter and spring months of 1455–56, the dovecot in Ferrara was fluttered by the exciting knowledge that some among them would soon go forth to return no more. There seems to have been a consensus of opinion that Caterina should be one of the colonists, but the prospect of leaving the house which had been her home for so many years was excessively alarming and distasteful to her. Nevertheless, resigned in all things to the Divine Will, she prayed earnestly for a clear revelation of God's purposes concerning her, and resolved to keep the Lenten fast with special devotion and austerity.

But the result of an exclusive diet of "pancotto"—bread soaked in water and beaten to a pulp—seasoned with mental agitation, was a complete failure of physical strength. Caterina was compelled to keep her bed, and the nuns began to doubt whether she would ever leave it. Bodily weakness, however, did but increase the activity of her mind. She meditated constantly and with fresh fervour on the mystery of the Passion of her Saviour, and prayed without ceasing for a direct manifestation of His Holy Will.

But when an answer to her prayers came she did not at first recognize it as such. She dreamed a dream in which she saw two stately seats adorned as for some great persons. "For whom are these prepared?" she asked. And the reply was made that they were for two Sisters, and that the more honourable was for Suor Caterina da Bologna.

She woke with a clear remembrance but no understanding of the vision,—a fact which the good folk of Ferrara, when they claimed her for their own, dwelt on with justifiable satisfaction. Caterina was a common baptismal name; the "cognome" of Vigri was Ferrarese; Caterina da Bologna was as yet non-existent.

The colonizing nuns were more fortunate than most of the brides of the period, whose splendid nuptials were usually arranged for mid-winter, and whose journeys were therefore fraught with extreme hardship and peril. It was on a burning summer's day, July 20th, 1456, that a little company of grave gentlemen and religious presented themselves before the doors of the convent of Corpus Domini in Ferrara and demanded speech with the Reverend Mother. There was the Vicar-General of the Strict Observants with the Minister of the Province of Bologna, who came of the great Fantuzzi house. There was Battista Mezavacca, Doctor of Law, who had been so active in founding the new convent and who was doubtless eager to see his two cloistered daughters; and there were besides many representatives of honourable Bolognese families, whose names, says Father Grassetti, " are lost by reason of his defect who recorded these things with small accuracy."

The veiled Abbess, Mother Leonardo of the great family of the Ordelafi of Forli, duly received the company, who presented the bull of Pope Callixtus III., and prayed her to give them a ruler for their new foundation. She answered, as has already been related, that she would give them a second Saint Clare, a true disciple of the Blessed Saint Francis. The ambassadors withdrew and a chapter was convened. In that chapter Caterina dei Vigri was unanimously chosen as leader of the colonising nuns and Abbess of the Bolognese house.

The decision of the chapter was reported to the expectant Provincial: he inquired as to the family and past history of the abbess-elect, and hearing with great satisfaction that she was born in the city to which she was about to migrate, he ordered that she should henceforth formally describe herself as Caterina da Bologna.

Caterina's vision was now clear to her, but her sorrow at leaving Ferrara was doubled. Reluctance and protestations of unworthiness form the approved attitude of the religious appointed to high office; but in Caterina's case they were certainly genuine and spontaneous. She had always shown herself conspicuously devoid of ambition and of that restless desire for authority so strong in many able women; and she was at this period in such feeble health that many of her friends doubted whether she could even bear the comparatively slight fatigue of the journey to Bologna. It was made as easy and comfortable as possible. The start was arranged to take place at midnight in order that the nuns might be sheltered from the heat of the July sun and from the gaze of curious folk, and a litter was prepared in which the invalid could be carried the few yards down the lane to the main road where the coach of the "Principessa Margherita"[1] was to be in waiting. Caterina was hardly conscious of these preparations for her comfort, or of the moment when she crossed the threshold of the house she had entered in her long-past youth. She was completely overcome with the emotions of the leave-taking; and when her friends lifted the senseless form into the coach, they congratulated themselves on being provided with a consecrated candle.

But the cool night air, the ministrations of her beloved friend Margherita, the unaccustomed novelty of the situation, worked what seemed to her companions a miracle. Colour came back to the ghastly face, strength to the powerless limbs, and when the lumbering vehicle came to difficult places in the deeply-rutted fifteenth-century road, Caterina descended with the rest and walked gaily forwards. Whereat the hearts of her escort were filled with comfort, for they felt that she was evidently called and chosen for the work of God in Bologna.

Before long the jolting coach-road was exchanged for the smooth and easy water-way, which formed the most expeditious route from Ferrara to Bologna, in spite of the "interruptions of the sluices, inventions to raise

---

[1] Margherita must have been visiting her relatives in Ferrara or have come expressly to bid her friend farewell, for since 1449 she had been living at the Court of Sigismondo Pandolfo, her brother-in-law. She died in Rimini in 1475.

the water for the use of mills and to fill the artificial canalls," which were bitterly complained of by the English traveller, Evelyn, when, two centuries later, he made the journey in inverse direction. Caterina, journeying in high summer, was not, like Evelyn, "so pestered with these flying glowworms called *lucciole*, that one who had never heard of them would think the country full of sparks of fire." Nevertheless, used to long vigils and stirred by strange emotions, she did not sleep. She indited some necessary letters and conversed a little with her escort; but for the most part, with her cloak wrapped closely round her [1] and raised above her black veil, she sat silent. Who can tell the thoughts and emotions of those hours of darkness and dawn? How suddenly the current of her life had been diverted into a new and untried channel! With what celerity she had been hurried from the place which had been her home for nearly thirty years! How speedily the Bolognese envoys had executed their long-prepared measure! And now she must look forwards rather than backwards. Moment by moment the stream and fate were bearing her away from the old estate of subjection towards the new estate of authority. Yet in the act they gave her a breathing space, a time when she might possess her soul and rally her physical and spiritual forces. She had leisure to steep her spirit in the elixir of the summer night, whose scents and sounds came to her laden with forgotten memories, stirring sensations

[1] Father Grassetti says: "Then Caterina from humility placed the cloak over the black veil, and was at once imitated by all the company; and from thence began the custom of the Mothers of the Corpus Christi of Bologna to wear the cloak over the black veil, which custom they have not in Ferrara, where the black veil covers the cloak on the shoulders."

which were new and old, while the great open spaces of the plains spoke strongly to one who had long been imprisoned within narrow walls.

Dawn found the woman who had left Ferrara trembling, weeping, scarcely conscious, strong, calm, and alert, ready to bear with meekness and dignity the burdens and the honours laid upon her.

They were considerable. The moment the election of the Chapter was announced the envoys had dispatched a messenger to the Senate, informing the citizens of Bologna that they had obtained for Abbess " that Suor Caterina who had held in her arms the Infant Jesus." The story of the nun's Christmas vision was widely known, and the good folk of Bologna were inclined to be " in all things too superstitious." They required no further testimonials, and determined to give the person thus distinguished a welcome after their own hearts, being, both then and always, " a people most courteous, liberal, and magnificently generous in such external demonstrations of compliment."

The days were very evil. Sante Bentivoglio was sufficiently powerful to hang his foes, but not powerful enough to have undisputed sway. Family feuds were embittered and complicated by enmity between the aristocracy and people, and, as Grassetti naively remarks, the authority of the Holy See was not " an adequate remedy for these dissensions, nor that of the legates, who had not at that time absolute dominion." But for the moment anarchy and dissension ceased, and enemies united to give a welcome to the holy women who were coming to them in the name of the Lord.

Thus it came to pass that when Caterina and her

companions reached Corticella, where the navigable channel ended, they found awaiting them upon the bank, lit by the glow of sunrise, a company of Bolognese matrons with their attendant knights, who had ridden forth three miles to meet them. The nuns were greeted with as much respect as though they had been princesses, and with Margherita d'Este—who was determined not to leave her friend till she saw her safely housed—were conducted to chariots, in which they proceeded towards the city. But before they reached it, they were met by another train of welcomers—the Legate, the wise Greek, Cardinal Bessarion, with the Bishop of Bologna, Cardinal Calandrino, brother of Pope Niccolò V, accompanied by the sixteen senators and the chief clergy and officers of the city, and followed by a jubilant crowd in festal temper and array, were waiting without the Porta Galliera. By this procession the nuns were conducted to the temporary abode prepared for them by the charity of certain members of the Third Order of S. Francis. Italian workmen in the fifteenth century were not unlike their descendants in the twentieth; and the new house, contrary to all hopes and expectations, was not ready for its inmates. Caterina and her companions were therefore lodged in the dwelling which had originally been offered for their use—the little hostel and church of Saint Anthony of Padua in the Via d' Aziglio.

For the remainder of the day they were left in peace; but before taking food or rest they proceeded to the church, and there gave thanks to the Giver of all good for the kindly welcome accorded to them, beseeching a blessing on their benefactors and on their new home.

They were not allowed at once to resume their habitual routine. The two Cardinals decreed that for three days the Abbess should "receive," in order that all the principal persons of the city should have the opportunity of making acquaintance with the Sisters. This was an eminently prudent measure, as Father Grassetti points out; for the community was dependent on the charity of the faithful, who being "incredibly edified by these ladies' rare modesty and truly religious mode of life," went away with quickened generosity and loosened purse-strings. The Abbess's gracious bearing and gentle dignity, her courtesy, her capacity, her ready and persuasive speech, were extolled by all. In spite of long years of retirement, silence, and self-effacement, her inherited instincts, her early training, her old habits, asserted themselves. During her three days' reception, Caterina dei Vigri showed herself endowed with all the social gifts which distinguished the great ladies of the renaissance.

The Abbess prudently decreed that no novices should be admitted during the intense heat of the Bolognese summer, and for five weeks the little company tranquilly endured the August sun, and enjoyed a halcyon period of undisturbed intercourse and freedom from responsibility. For they were all tried persons and old friends, sure of themselves and each other, broken in to conventual life, knowing their duties and earnest in fulfilling them.

First and foremost among them was the noble Venetian lady, Illuminata Bembo, whose *Specchio d' Illuminatione* is the "Urquelle" of every life of the

"Santa." She had been with Caterina in Lucia Mascheroni's semi-religious community, and when others doubted her vocation, believing that a fine lady used to Venetian luxury, gaiety, and culture would soon weary of so hard, narrow, and restricted a life, Caterina had always strengthened her resolution and prognosticated her perseverance. In 1433 the two friends took the Franciscan habit, and their loving companionship was close and unbroken till ·the day Caterina died, and Illuminata discovered, with that pang of sweet remorse which so often rends the true friend and lover, that after all she had never appreciated the lost blessing: "Alas, a thousand times alas!" is her exceeding bitter cry, "that such was my blindness, I did not know the greatness and sublimity of this most excellent soul."

The next two senior nuns were Suor Giovanna of the Lambertini of Bologna, and Suor Anna Morandi, a widow, of Ravenna, both of whom had entered the convent in Ferrara a few months after its foundation.

Then there were Doctor Battista Mezavacca's two daughters,—Paola, a tall, fine woman whom Caterina had chosen to be mistress of the future novices, and Gabriella, who entered religion eight years later, and in a manner which, *pace* Father Grassetti, seems to us somewhat reprehensible. Mezavacca, a pious, learned, wealthy, and much-respected Bolognese citizen, had a large family of sons and daughters, who, as soon as they grew to manhood and womanhood, one after another renounced the cares and perils and pleasures of the world and embraced a monastic life. Gabriella, the youngest, at length found herself alone. She was her father's pet and housekeeper, and would surely be the prop and stay of his old age and the mother of his heirs. He did not guess that her young gaze was already turning from the glare and colour of the world towards the peaceful greyness of the cloister, and pious man as he was, the girl felt intuitively that he would not let her go without a struggle. She had not the moral courage to endure it, and determined to escape it and to effect her purpose by a ruse. Feigning a great desire to see her sister Paola, she set out for Ferrara arrayed in her best clothes, and accompanied by a gay party of friends and relatives. When they reached the convent she asked them to leave her for a while as she wished to talk alone with her sister. The natural request was readily granted. But when the party called at the convent doors a few hours later, Gabriella came to the grating in the habit of a "Clarissa," and bade her companions go back to her father and tell him she should return no more. Mezavacca nearly died of grief at the intelligence; but wonderful and pleasing to relate, he bore no malice against his daughter in particular, or the religious orders in general. He was foremost in promoting the foundation of the new convent in Bologna, his zeal being perhaps inspired by the hope of bringing his children back to their own city.

Another pair of Bolognese sisters were Suor Bernardina and Suor Anastasia Calcina. The former was married, but had agreed to separate from her husband that both might "enter religion." Suore Eugenia and Pacifica Barbieri, kinswomen, were also Bolognese, as was Suor Pellegrina dei Leonori. Suore Samaritana, Modesta, and Innocenzia were Ferrarese; while a certain lachrymose Suor Andrea was from Cremona. Then there were two lay Sisters and one Terzina, or member of the Third Order—even Bernardina, Caterina's mother, who, a widow for the second time, had latterly devoted herself to serving the house in Ferrara, and now gladly accompanied her daughter to their native city.

On the 21st September this little band of colonists received its first new recruits. Six young ladies of Bologna were admitted as novices.

The Abbess was now eager to move into permanent quarters before the approach of winter. She constantly besought the procurators of the monastery to hasten forward the work, and fervently prayed to God that He would dispose the hearts of the citizens towards the convent and its inmates. And her importunity prevailed and her prayers were answered. Funds came in steadily; building went on apace; and at length one November night the nuns were transferred from the Hostel of Saint Anthony to the Abbey of Saint Christopher, which was henceforward known as the Convent of Corpus Domini.

In her first Chapter Caterina sounded the predominant notes of her rule. In it she proposed five measures, which had been matured with much consideration and earnest prayer, and which were unanimously accepted by her devoted company. First, it was ordained that the ancient custom of having all things in common should be faithfully observed; and further that the community should hold no property other than their dwelling-place, and should subsist wholly on the daily alms of the citizens.

Secondly, the *clausura* was to be observed with the same strictness as at Ferrara. Not only might no nun go out, but no outsider might come in, albeit guests were at that time tolerated in many other well-ordered and reputable convents. Furthermore, to discourage intercourse between the nuns and curious visitors, it was decreed that the gratings in the parlour should be covered with thin black linen, Caterina rightly believing that the worldly ladies whose conversation was most likely to be perilous and unsettling to her flock, would not long care to converse with persons who could neither see nor be seen.

While in her first law Caterina maintained the Franciscan principles of poverty, in her third she imitated the Franciscan practice of gratitude. The Senate had exempted the convent from *dazio*, so that gifts from the surrounding country reached it duty free. It had also made *ogni anno in perpetuo* a liberal grant of salt; while the citizens in general had liberally contributed towards the fund for building and maintenance. Caterina, therefore, mindful of the example of S. Francis, who had annually presented a basket of fish to the Benedictines to whom he owed the church of Santa Maria degli Angeli, ordained that the convent should every year present a corporal to the cathedral of Bologna in token of perpetual gratitude for the hospitality of the city.

The fourth regulation related to costume. "As a public sign of modesty and humility," as well as to avoid "abuses and opportunities of vanity such as exist in certain convents by reason of the elegance and coquettishness of veils and collars," it was ordained, that in the choir, when called to parley at the gate, and when receiving the Bishop or other prelates, the nuns of the monastery of Corpus Domini should always wear the cloak above the black veil, after the fashion set by Caterina herself during the journey from Ferrara.

The fifth and last regulation passed in Caterina's first Chapter declared that there should never be prisons in the convent, because she "trusted that by God's mercy no faults should be committed in that holy house deserving so rigorous a punishment."

The first few months after the move were busy and difficult ones for the Abbess. To "get into a new house" was not indeed to a fifteenth-century family, still less to a company of religious, quite the serious undertaking that it is to a modern householder. But Bologna, then as now, was notorious for its winter snow, and a half-finished building, then as now, was cold and uncomfortable; while if the nuns' wants were few their means of supplying them were fewer, dependent as they were on the alms of the faithful with whom they had little direct communication. Hardships were cheerfully endured, for Caterina inspired all her "daughters" with her own pluck and *esprit de corps*, but the health of the community suffered. The infirmary was soon full, and the Abbess, though untiring in her efforts, found it difficult to provide for the necessities of the sick. But the presence of certain physicians is as remedial as their prescriptions, and Caterina's personality and skill and devotion as a nurse largely atoned for her lack of material resources. The first thing in the morning and the last thing at night she visited her sick. She was, besides, always present during the doctor's visits, after which she would retire a while to the church, there "to take counsel with her heavenly spouse," from whence she would return serene and reassuring to the infirmary. And to some, Grassetti quaintly says, " she spoke words of so great consolation that they were perfectly conformed to God's will," and to others she applied the prescribed remedies with a success quite unlooked for by the physicians themselves, so that before long she sent them whole and rejoicing to the church to give thanks for recovery to God. To the power of the Great Physician, flowing through the channel of the medical science of the day, Caterina constantly and unwaveringly attributed these cures. But in vain ; for on the one hand her assertion was a halftruth, and the sick rightly perceived that their recovery was due to their nurse rather than to their doctor, and on the other the ignorant always more readily believe in occult and magical power than in the truly supernatural effects of faith, sympathy, and self-forgetful love. Little by little an atmosphere of enthusiasm and credulity was created. Miracles were expected of the strong and tender woman who lived spiritually and intellectually on a higher plane than the majority of her companions. Miracles were expected—and therefore miracles happened.

Three are specially recorded, and are worth narrating as examples of the Abbess's dealings with her "beloved daughters," and of the way in which they were interpreted and misinterpreted.

First in order of time comes the healing of Lucia Codagnelli, one of the first six novices admitted in

Bologna. To her, in the distribution of offices, was assigned the care of the garden. She was apparently absent-minded or unskilful, for one day, when engaged in digging, she sent the spade or hoe with such force into her own foot as nearly to sever it from the ankle. Her screams of pain and terror speedily drew her companions to the spot, where she lay upon the ground bleeding copiously. They were fifteenth-century nuns, and had not attended ambulance classes. They were, moreover, Italian women, emotional, sensitive to suffering, and easily thrown off their balance. "Not knowing what to do," says Grassetti, "they betook themselves to weeping, the common remedy of women and children."

Then Caterina appeared, self-possessed, self-reliant; and the storm of hysterical emotion at once subsided. She had, as we have already seen, the instincts of a nurse. From her girlhood she had delighted to serve the sick, schooling herself against disgust and nausea, and ardently performing all distasteful offices. The sight of blood did not therefore alarm or distress her now. She knelt by the sufferer, and addressed her with gentle, reassuring playfulness: "Sister Lucia, wilt thou make me a present of this foot?"

Then, making the sign of the cross over the wounded limb, she took the poor leg in her left hand, and with her right drew the half-severed foot into place. The limb *instantly* became whole as before. Whereupon Caterina said, smiling—

"I entrust this foot to you, Sister Lucia, on condition that, as it belongs to me, you will for the future use it well, taking care that you do it no harm whatever."

Lucia wept again, and promised to do as she was bid; the nuns were " incredibly edified," and soon all the city knew that a very notable miracle had been worked by the holy Abbess of the new convent.

It is noteworthy that there is no mention of this " miracle " in the " Mirror " of Illuminata Bembo. Yet the story is so natural and circumstantial it seems reasonable to suppose that the accident and the cure actually took place. To bring them into line with one of the famous miracles of Saint Anthony of Padua—whose life was, of course, familiar to all members and friends of the Franciscan Order—it was only necessary to be blind to such unsightly details as bandages and unguents, and to compress into a single moment a process which, it is likely enough, was remarkably short, the nun being a spare liver, a worker in the open air, and an implicit believer in Caterina's skill.

The second miraculous story is of a novice " much worried by the Devil in various disguises, so that she was reduced to despair by reason of most vehement temptations, occasioned by the rebellion of the flesh against the decrees of the spirit." Prayer and mortification seemed to avail nothing; nay, the more she used these weapons the more increased the diabolical attacks.

At length the tortured and despairing woman went to the Mother Abbess and made a clean breast of her pitiful condition. And the Abbess "*smiled a little.*" She was neither shocked nor horrified; but with a cheerful face said quietly—

" Will you do at once what I tell you ? "

"I will do anything I can and at once," cried the unhappy novice. Then said the Abbess—

"Go, take up the book you see there, and on the first page at which you open you will find the remedy for your distress."

The nun obeyed, and instantly was comforted and reassured; nor from that time onwards was she troubled by the old temptations.

By a very slight twist the narrators of this incident endow the Abbess with something of a magician's power and convert the written page into a kind of spell. Yet the story is in reality simple and matter-of-fact, disappointing in that it omits the name of the book, and interesting only as illustrative of Caterina's tact, discrimination, and common sense. The girl had strung herself up to a high pitch of emotion; so Caterina spoke little. She was taking herself too seriously; so Caterina treated her with bracing cheerfulness. After the manner of young persons, she thought that her difficulties were unprecedented and unique; so Caterina pointed her to a passage which had aided other earnest souls, a passage so often read that the book opened of itself at the marked or well-worn page.

The last of these miraculous histories is a detailed narrative of the first death which took place in the convent.

Sister Samaritana Superbi was a Ferrarese, and was one of the fifteen nuns whom Caterina brought from Ferrara. She was noted for her fervent devotion to the rule and unwavering spirit of submission, and towards the close of her life was able to declare with all humility that she had never consciously sinned in respect to obedience. Soon after her arrival in Bologna her health began to decline, and three years later her case was pronounced hopeless. Finally symptoms of an extraordinary and convulsive nature made their appearance, to the extreme terror of her companions, to whom the drawn face, rolling eyes, groans and twitches seemed indubitable proof of diabolical possession. They stood helplessly round her bed, "more dead than alive, and with copious tears made supplication that God would succour their companion in such a perilous conflict."

The Abbess exhibited as much credulity but vastly more saving faith than her spiritual daughters. She was not more scientific than they were, but she was much more energetic. She "needed to be waited on herself rather than to have to wait on others," for she was more than usually suffering "by reason of her chronic maladies": but self-forgetting as usual she insisted on nursing the unfortunate nun, and for forty-eight hours never left her side.

Towards the end of the second day there was a lull in the storm. The nuns besought their beloved Mother to take some repose. Caterina yielded to their entreaties, but declared that the alleviation was only temporary and that she must be called the moment the bad symptoms returned. The summons was not long delayed. The Sister who was sacristan, presumably thinking that the necessity for such aid was over, extinguished one of the two consecrated tapers which had been placed by the bed, replacing it for purposes of light by an ordinary candle. At that moment the other consecrated taper went out—" was blown out by the Fiend"; whereupon the torments of the sufferer began afresh and with increased violence.

The Abbess had not yet lain down, and she came without delay, grieving greatly not only for Samaritana's sufferings, but on account of the trial of faith and perseverance they occasioned to the novices, who were much distressed that one who had led a holy life should thus on her death-bed be abandoned to the power of the Evil One. Approaching the bedside, she solemnly defied that power, and declared her disbelief in the Adversary's ability to disturb the souls of so many of God's children, and her confidence in the salvation of one who had been the faithful bride of Christ. Turning to the nuns, she bade them be calm and constant in prayer. Then she sprinkled the dying woman with holy water, held her hands, soothed her with words and caresses. Next, kneeling beside her, she repeated over and over again the name of Jesus. Finally, standing up, she said: "Now depart, thou Evil Spirit, thou hast no more power in this place or in the soul of this creature."

And the sufferer lay still: the distorted face became composed, regained its old semblance, nay, seemed to grow younger, "like the face of a girl of fifteen years"; the eyes became clear and calm; the lips parted in a smile; and though speechless, the sufferer clearly expressed her love and gratitude to the mother who bent over her.

"My daughter, you would fain tell me something of your victory?"

The sufferer plainly heard, but she could not answer.

"Rest, rest, my daughter. I understand well what thou wouldst say: but now on thy obedience I bid thee speedily depart in company with thy dear Guardian Angel unto life eternal."

The dying woman lifted her eyes to the speaker's face, and then turned them for a moment on the nuns who stood around her. Then with a smile she bowed her head and gently drew her last breath.

To Caterina, who had assisted so untiringly during the long hours of travail, the soul's delivery and new birth took visible shape. In ecstatic vision she beheld the spirit of the departed Sister borne upwards by angelic hosts. The intensity of her heart's joy acted on her body like some invigorating cordial. She experienced a sudden cessation of her physical trouble, an instantaneous removal of the burden of weakness and weariness which had so long oppressed her. She cast away the stick with which she had hobbled to the sick room and broke into song and verse; the nuns caught the infection, and the extraordinary scene ends almost like some revivalist meeting in a chorus of jubilant, spontaneous, ecstatic singing.

This first death in the convent formed the closing scene of Caterina's first term of office. For in three days the Provincial Beato Fra Marco Fantuzzi, beholding in the houses of Poor Clares within his jurisdiction not a few abuses and disadvantages springing from perpetuity of office, laid before the Pope a proposal that the position of abbess or superior should henceforward be held only for a fixed term of years. The scheme received the papal approbation; the office of abbess was made triennial, and the measure was extended to houses belonging to other orders.

Such a decree was naturally obnoxious to many reigning abbesses ; but to Caterina, wholly devoid as she was of the spirit of domination, the near prospect of laying down the reins of government was genuinely welcome. Only she desired to finish within her term of office a piece of work which her successors might be less eager and able to carry out, namely, the beginning of an orderly " Archivio." To this self-imposed task she devoted all the energies of her closing reign, collecting and cataloguing all privileges, grants, and letters, papal, episcopal, and communal, connected with the founding of the convent in Bologna, and with her own hand making copies of those belonging to the mother house in Ferrara.

Sister Anna Morandi of Ravenna was Caterina's successor, but her office was of short duration. Shortly after her election the poor lady was attacked by a malady of the eyes, and before a year had passed she was almost totally blind.

A new election was imperative, and the Provincial visited the convent for the purpose of conducting it. Conversing privately with the nuns, he was told separately by them all that they did not mean to vote for Sister Caterina because her disposition was so mild, lenient, and compassionate that they feared that the discipline of the convent would be relaxed by her rule.

Great therefore was the visitor's astonishment, as he drew the voting-papers from the nuns, to find that all save one bore the name of Caterina. Surprised and irritated he exclaimed—

" What extraordinary ladies you are ! You tell me

privately you do not wish Sister Caterina to be your Abbess, and then you all vote for her. Which is one to believe, your written or your spoken word?"

There was silence, till the one sister who had not voted for Caterina rose in her place and said—

"Father, I am she who did not vote for Sister Caterina. I persuaded myself I ought not to do so for the reasons of which I told you. But now I see that it is God's will that she should be our Prelate, and I repent and revoke my vote, giving it, like all the rest, to Sister Caterina. And for my part I pray you, Father, to confirm this our unanimous election."

Then the Provincial, convinced that this thing was the work of the Holy Spirit, formally approved the re-election of the first Abbess.

The pressing need and great work of her second term of office was the enlargement of the building. It was a deep grief to her to reject a would-be recruit, not only because such a refusal seemed discourteous and unkind, but because it appeared to involve subtraction from the forces engaged in active conflict against sin, the world, and the devil.

At last it happened that some rejected applicants were children of wealthy and indulgent parents, who, when they realized that their daughters could not be received because every cell in the house was already occupied, came forward with liberal alms for the enlargement of the fabric. Then the Abbess said her Nunc Dimittis. She felt that her strength was failing, and that her earthly course was nearly run, but she had lived to see the answer to her most earnest prayers, and the fulfilment of her pure ambitions.

CHAPTER VI

THE DEATH OF THE RIGHTEOUS

Praised be Thou, O Lord, by our sister, the Death of the body,
Whom no living creature may avoid.
S. FRANCIS OF ASSISI'S *Hymn of the Sun*.

CATERINA'S work in this world was nearly done. The chronic maladies became more acute, pulmonary symptoms appeared, and there was a general failure of strength and vitality.

Her devoted nurse was a young Bolognese, who had entered the convent at the age of ten, and had been professed at twelve. This little Sister, Maddalena Rosa, loved the Mother with the intense, romantic affection which a young girl often conceives for an older woman, and during the last months of Caterina's life she seldom left her side. She slept in her room, helped the "Infirmiere" to prepare her food and medicine, and ministered to her according to the physician's orders. One day it happened that while bathing the invalid's feet she was moved by an access of mingled love, compassion, and apprehension to stoop and kiss them. Caterina made a hasty movement of withdrawal, and chid the child for foolishness. But the little Sister's spirit rose. "You may chide me now, Mother," she cried, "but the time will come when many will do as I have

SANTA CATERINA'S LITTLE VIOL.
PRESERVED IN HER CHAPEL IN THE CHURCH OF CORPUS DOMINI, BOLOGNA

THE DEATH OF THE RIGHTEOUS

done." What she precisely meant by this vindication of her own affection she did not know. But she was wont to declare that the sweet odour proceeding from the Santa's feet and filling the little cell impelled her to this act of reverent love, and in after years her words were remembered and were held to be the prophecy of a child pure of heart.

A full year before the end came there was a sharp premonitory illness and a rehearsal of the final death-bed scene. The Abbess was removed from her cell to a bed in the infirmary. The last sacraments were administered; the nuns stood weeping quietly round one who seemed already to have drifted far beyond their reach.

But after some hours the tide of life turned. Consciousness came back; the eyes opened; the lips quivered into smiles. A few more days, and Caterina was clearly convalescent.

Then it seemed to the nuns that she showed a convalescent's caprice, for she asked constantly and urgently for a little viol, and finally charged the Sisters on their obedience to bring her one.

Where the astonished nuns sought, from whom they obtained, the instrument is not recorded. But after some days a "violetta" was placed in the invalid's hands, to her infinite solace and content. She lay propped up in bed, now playing on her little viol, now reposing with upturned radiant face and far-off gaze, lost to her immediate surroundings, and seemingly absorbed in happy memories. The nuns, finding themselves unheeded and their interrogations unanswered, decided that, in spite of apparent improvement, Caterina's death was near; and at length one of them exclaimed with a touch of bitterness: "Ah! Mother dear, you go away to enjoy music and song in heaven, but we remain below in sorrow and tears."

The words seemed to bring the Abbess back to her children. She told the tearful nun to have no fear. Her hour had indeed come, but her departure was delayed by the prayers of one of their number: the Lord had granted that she should tarry awhile.

Then, little by little, she told them of the vision which had filled the hours when she lay between life and death. Her spirit seemed transported to a fair meadow, "more beautiful than can be told or thought"; and in the midst of it was set a throne resplendent as the sun, and on the throne the Heavenly King. The supporters on either side the throne were the martyrs Laurence and Vincent, and all around them stood the court, even an infinite number of saints and angels. But before the throne was a clear space, and in that space there stood a single angel, holding a little viol, to which he sang. And the song was so exceeding sweet that it seemed to Caterina as though the soul must leave her body for pure joy. But though it never ceased, and the vision lasted long, she could hear no other words but these: *Et gloria ejus in te videbitur.*

Then the Lord Himself stretched forth His arm and took her by the hand, and said: "Listen, O daughter, to this refrain and understand, for it is of thee it speaks." But Caterina seemed dazed and stupefied with joy; yet as she knelt confounded and speechless before the throne, she understood that her hour of deliverance was not yet come, but that prayer was dragging her back to earth.

THE DEATH OF THE RIGHTEOUS

No one can read Caterina's description of this vision of the Court of Heaven without being struck by its pictorial quality. The central throne with its two balls (pomi), on which stand as supporters the two deacon martyrs; the grouping on either side of saints and angels; the background of green and flowery meadow; the open space in front occupied by the single figure on which all interest concentrates;—this is a conventional, carefully balanced composition of a kind familiar to all students of the pictures and miniatures of the *Trecento* and early *Quattrocentro*.[1]

The vision itself furnished a subject to the painter Guido Morina, whose picture hangs in the Sala del Tiarini in the Gallery of Bologna. The two saints represented as supporters of the heavenly throne are wrongly named alike by Mrs. Jameson and the official catalogue, the former calling them S. Stephen and St. Laurence, the latter S. Sebastian and St. Laurence.

The waking remembrance and repetition of a dream-melody recalls a story told of another musical saint, the English Dunstan. One night in sleep he seemed to be present at the espousals of his mother with the Saviour of the world. The angelic choir sang, but he, the dutiful and loving son, was dumb. Then one of the angels, pitying his ignorance, vouchsafed to teach him the song. Next morning, assembling his monks round him, he taught them the music he had learned in the vision of the previous night.

[1] Mrs. Jameson tells us that the deacon martyrs SS. Vincent and Laurence were frequently associated in sacred art, the Spanish legend even making them brothers; but the present writer has not been able to discover any picture thus introducing them which might have been seen by Caterina.

To the nuns who had never heard their Abbess play, her proficiency on the viol seemed miraculous, and following their naïve suggestions, later biographers declared that Caterina had no previous musical knowledge. But the close friend and cultured lady, Suor Illuminata, makes no such assertion. She doubtless understood that the dying woman's mind was wandering back to her girlhood in Ferrara, when Parisina accompanied the singing of her stepson Ugo, when Borso, of an age with Caterina, and his senior Leonello, played on various instruments, and when the little Margherita and her companion were doubtless expected to contribute to the chamber music of the Court.

The Abbess did not long enjoy the selfish delights of convalescence. After a few days the little viol was laid aside, never to be touched again, and Caterina rose from her bed, and to the wonder and anxiety of her nuns, followed her customary routine. She did what she had always done, but with new grace and inspiration. She seemed consumed with zeal, on fire with love; so that in very truth the words of the singing angel were fulfilled, and God's glory was manifested in the daily life of this Saint. It is obvious from the sequence of revelation in Caterina's narrative that she herself accepted the refrain as an injunction to greater holiness during the months unexpectedly added to her allotted span. But after her death and the artificial *réclame* created by her fond but foolish disciples, the words were converted into a prediction of her technical sanctity and its bases.

Long ago Caterina had numbered among her Seven Weapons "Memoria mortis propriæ," but throughout

THE DEATH OF THE RIGHTEOUS

that winter of 1463 she seemed to look forward with chastened impatience to the approach of "Sister Death," whose coming might not be hastened, and the hour of whose arrival was announced. The winter was peculiarly severe, and the Sisters trembled when they saw their Abbess kneel absorbed in prayer for hours in the cold church. At length they offered a remonstrance, whereupon Caterina smiled and bid them have no fear, for "l' ora mia non è venuta." Another time a report was circulated that Caterina was to be transferred as Abbess to another convent; but this fear also she dispelled with great decision, saying that at Ferrara the Lord had revealed to her she should finish her earthly course at Bologna, and that the end was at hand.

On the 25th of February a Chapter was held, and after the dispatch of the usual business the Abbess, as was her custom, addressed her daughters. Her subject was the power of prayer; she spoke with unusual fluency and fervour; her heart seemed full to overflowing; and the little *ragionamento* expanded into a discourse three hours in length. At its close the Abbess begged her daughters to pardon her long speech, giving as her excuse the certainty that this was the last Chapter she would ever hold: "My end has come, and gladly I go hence. I leave you the peace of Christ. Love one another. I shall ever plead before God for you."

The nuns were astonished at these words, and did not take them greatly to heart. Caterina had been ill so frequently, and had frightened them so constantly, and just now she seemed better and stronger than usual.

If they had any apprehensions these were allayed by the bearing of their Mother on the following Sunday. She looked particularly well and seemed unusually bright and cheerful. All day she talked more than was her wont, and in the evening supped gaily with her daughters in the refectory. But in the domitory she spoke briefly to Sister Illuminata concerning the future of the house, bidding her have confidence in the Divine aid and protection, and adding: " Blessed be the Lord who at last has granted me the longed-for end, the longed-for rest."

Then she went to her bed, and did not rise from it again. Next day the old symptoms had returned, accompanied by fever. She suffered greatly, but again, as in her former sickness, found relief in music, singing with great fervour and delight her own canzone,

"Anima benedetta
Dall' alto Creatore,"[1]

to an accompaniment played by one of the Sisters.

Early in the morning of Wednesday, the 9th of March, she asked for the "Vicaria," the sister who acted as *governante* or housekeeper. Suor Giovanna Lambertini duly came to her bedside, and was there directed by the Abbess to put away and carefully preserve the clothes and other effects of a certain recently arrived novice. " Be ready," said the Abbess, " when asked for these things to deliver them at once;

---

[1] Carducci includes this hymn in his anthology, "Primavera e Fiori della Lirica Italiana," but labels it "Ignoto, Secolo XIV." It is however attributed to Caterina by most of her biographers, and we are told that the nuns circulated numerous copies in her lifetime, but always, by her express desire, without giving the name of the author. See Appendix A.

and meanwhile let all pray fervently for this novice, whose need is great." A few weeks later Caterina's judgment and knowledge of character was illustrated by the withdrawal of the novice in question from the religious life.

Later in the day the Abbess sent for the Confessor, and bade her daughters prepare an altar in the room, and place at the foot of her bed a crucifix, candles, and holy water. The command surprised and shocked the nuns, for, though the serious symptoms continued, neither they nor the physician regarded the Mother's condition as critical. But when they had obeyed her, and had prepared for her reception of the last sacraments, she signed to them to gather round her and began to take leave of them.

She commended to them the novices, "both those who are with you now and those who will come in the future." She bade them respect and obey the "Vicaria," Sister Giovanna Lambertini, "who has always been a good and faithful daughter to me; and one better qualified for her work I could not have desired." And she earnestly besought their care and protection for her aged mother, Benvenuta dei Mamolini, who, by special permission of the Pope, was now residing within the convent, though only a "Terzina," she having, a year after her arrival in Bologna, become exceedingly infirm and totally blind.

After these bequests came two solemn warnings: Let no one within or without the house seek or scheme for the removal or the transference of any member of the community, or for the reception of nuns from other convents; and let none give cause for a diminution of the fair fame of the house; and if any thus transgress "I will demand vengeance upon them before the tribunal of the Eternal Judge."

In this trumpet-note of passionate denunciation we have a last glimpse of what may be called the warlike side of Caterina's nature. But it speedily died away into a strain of yearning, maternal tenderness for the spiritual children she was leaving orphaned. Once again, adopting the words of her Lord, she left them the precious legacy of peace; once again she repeated the Johannine injunction to mutual love. And then she comforted them and bade them dry their tears, saying that those who wept for her were not her daughters.

Presently she turned to the portress and commanded her to go instantly to the door; but the portress, stupefied with grief and believing that the Confessor could not possibly arrive so soon, did not stir. Caterina repeated the command, asserting that he whom she expected was even now knocking at the gate. And so, indeed, he was; and the speed with which he had received and obeyed the message of the Abbess seemed to the excited nuns nothing less than miraculous.

Another miracle was created out of the Confessor's confusion, and the Abbess's composure and knowledge of the office. Having made her confession with a strong voice and perfect clearness of mind, Caterina prepared with great devotion to receive the viaticum. But the priest lost his place, failed to "find the words proper to this occasion," and stood helplessly turning and returning the leaves. Whereupon the Abbess said gently: "Father, look in the middle of the book, and you will find what you want." The Confessor followed her direction and proceeded with the office.

Extreme Unction was then administered, and Caterina afterwards placed in the Confessor's hands the book she had long ago composed, but the existence of which she had carefully concealed. Then she turned to the Sisters and said humbly: " I ask pardon of you all for any grief or offence I may have given you. Pray God for me."

She looked up at them with a bright and peaceful face, then her eyelids closed, and with the name of her Saviour thrice repeated on her lips—" Gesù, Gesù, Gesù "—Caterina dei Vigri " breathed forth her happy soul in a little gentle sigh."

CHAPTER VII

CATERINA'S POST-MORTEM HISTORY

> Put a chalk-egg beneath the clucking hen,
> She'll lay a real one, laudably deceived,
> Daily for weeks to come. I've told my lie
> And seen truth follow, marvels none of mine;
> All was not cheating, sir, I'm positive.
> BROWNING, *Sludge the Medium.*

ONE would gladly take leave of the Abbess Caterina lying as though in peaceful sleep upon her narrow bed, her face less corpse-like than it had often been in the days of her suffering life, and wearing the wonderful look of renewed youth and placid childlike innocence which is often the gentle gift of " Sister Death." One would gladly take leave of her thus; but the strange blackened figure in the church of Corpus Domini is so insistent, and the Santa's post-mortem history bulks so large in hagiography, that we must needs consider the events which led to her canonization.

Briefly they are as follows:—

The grave of the deceased Abbess was naturally visited frequently by the sorrowing nuns. Some of them declared that it exhaled fragrance; others discovered that after kneeling on the spot they were cured of various small maladies. After eighteen days the body was exhumed and was found unchanged, beautiful, and positively fragrant. By permission of the Cardinal-Bishop, it was exposed in the chapel, and was visited by numbers of pious Bolognese. By degrees the fame of the Santa spread beyond her city. Pilgrims from all parts of Italy visited the lifelike corpse, and bestowed rich gifts[1] upon it. The first "Life" published in 1503 devotes a lengthy section "to the numerous miracles which God has worked by means of this blessed one." The first printed copy of *The Seven Weapons*, published less than fifty years after its author's death,[2] shows that her cult was thoroughly established. Fourteen years later it was formally authorized by Clement VII, and a special office was appointed for her *festa*. In 1592 the title of Beata was conferred on her. In May, 1707, her canonization was decreed, though the act was not executed till 1713.

We will now examine some of these facts in detail, and will glance at the evidence for them supplied by various persons in the *processo* which preceded the canonization. Let us first, however, prepare our judicial faculties by recalling the passion for relics which characterized the age to which Caterina belonged. The keen competition for them between city and city, monastery and monastery, is a phenomenon with which the modern student of history may not sympathize, but with which he must needs reckon. Fraud and force were exercised in their acquisition, and the end was held to justify the means. Having acquired a

[1] Notably the diadem presented by Isabella, wife of Ferdinand of Aragon, King of Naples, and the splendid robe given by S. Carlo Borromeo. [2] i.e. in 1510.

commercial value, they became subjects of speculation. It was worth while to secure the body not only of an actual but of a prospective saint. Thus the companions of S. Francis persuaded him on his last journey back to Umbria to take the longer route by Gubbio and Nocera, for they feared that the inhabitants of Perugia would attempt by force of arms to seize the person of their dying master.

Now we know that Caterina's reputation for sanctity was established prior to her death. She was welcomed at Bologna as that "Suor Caterina who had held in her arms the Holy Child." Her intercessions were held to have special efficacy. The gifts of healing and of prophecy were attributed to her. The nuns loved her and were proud of her, and naturally desired to spread and to perpetuate her fame. Thus we have an atmosphere in which pious fraud could be executed with little forcing of conscience, and in which it would be received without severe examination.

Furthermore we must note : (*a*) That in the *processo* preceding her canonization the advocates for her sanctity are concerned to prove that embalming did not take place, *not that it could not have taken place*. The argument which would have rendered all others superfluous, i.e. that the art of embalming was wholly unknown or unpractised at that time, or that it was utterly beyond the skill of any of the nuns or of the convent physician, is never advanced. (*b*) That the nuns had time and opportunity for the embalming of the body either before or after its committal to the convent graveyard.

A scene of extraordinary hysterical emotion ensued

CATERINA'S POST-MORTEM HISTORY 139

when the nuns realized that their Abbess had really left them. Sabadini degli Arienti,[1] who wrote the life of the Saint for the benefit of Ginevra Sforza, wife of his patron Sante Bentivoglio, tells us that "the whole convent resounded with sorrowful crying, sighs and sobs." Some of the nuns fell to the ground swooning or cataleptic, and were carried to their cells. "And now this one, now that embraced her sister for sorrow, saying, 'Alas! whom have we now to comfort us? We have lost all! Merciful God, have pity on us.'"

Then the Confessor ordered that the room should be cleared, and that only three or four of the community who retained their senses should be left with the corpse to prepare it for burial. He himself retired to read the MS. which the dying woman had delivered to him, and to confess some of the afflicted and hysterical nuns who appeared to be in a moribund condition. To their aid also the physicians were summoned. Thus a doctor was certainly within the convent during the hours which intervened between the Abbess's death and the removal of the body to the church.

The number of these intervening hours we unfortunately do not know. Assuming that Caterina died between 10 and 11 a.m.[2] on Wednesday, March 9th, the "ufficio funebre" could not have taken place before the morning of Thursday, but we should expect the

---

[1] For his patroness he wrote the biographies of thirty-three women. This collection—Ginevra de le Clare Donne—was republished by Corrado Ricci in 1888. Sabadini was a writer of no distinction, but is a valuable authority, inasmuch as most of the Lives are those of women of the fifteenth century, who were almost his contemporaries.

[2] We are told that she died "sulle ore quindici," and we assume that the reckoning is from the Ave Maria of the preceding evening.

body to have been taken to the church on Wednesday evening. The hagiographers, however, do not tell us that this was done; on the contrary, we might infer from their accounts of the funeral that it followed almost immediately on the transport of the body to the church. They tell us that when the holy Abbess was brought before the altar of the Blessed Sacrament her dead face beamed with joy; but they somewhat destroy the effectiveness of this information by adding that "the afflicted ladies" took no heed of so startling a phenomenon, being "wholly occupied with bitterness and anguished weeping." "And thus," says Sabadini, "with tearful obsequies they bore her to the grave."

Having satisfied ourselves that there was time between Caterina's death and burial for a thorough or for a partial embalmment, let us proceed to note the conduct of the sisters appointed as gravediggers.

"Sorrowing for pity that the face which in life had been to them the mirror of comfort and holiness and which in death appeared the same should be pressed down by earth," the four nuns placed over it a cloth, and above the cloth arranged a board propped on stones, so that the body should not actually come into contact with the soil.

Now follow hints of a mysterious light hovering above the grave by night, and of sweet odours rising from it by day. The light may indicate that the work of embalming was not complete before interment or that preservative or odoriferous substances were being added from time to time; or it may merely have been one feature in a scheme for awakening a belief in the sanctity of the already embalmed Abbess and a demand for her exhumation. Certain it is that the belief grew apace, and that the demand was made with increasing insistency; till at length the Father Confessor yielded so far as to consent that the body should be placed in a coffin, with, however, the proviso that the exhumation should be abandoned if any noxious odour arose from the grave, and that if carried out it should be followed by the immediate reinterment of the coffin. And this, says the earliest Life, he said because the Padri Osservanti "were not well assured of her sanctity, *albeit the grave exhaled the strongest odours.*" The same Life tells us that the sisters had made a coffin *secretly;* which looks as though they did not even wait for a permission which they were determined to extract.

A dramatic account is given of the nocturnal disinterment. The evening was ushered in by thunder, rain, and tempest, and the four sisters waited long beneath the portico adjoining the cemetery, unable to begin their work, and convinced that the hindrance was of the Devil's machination. At length Sister Illuminata Bembo left the sheltering colonnade, advanced into the open, and conjured the tempest and the darkness with the holy cross, praying God to give her a sign whether or no it were His will that the body should be removed. And behold! the sky above the graveyard cleared. "The calm vault of heaven glittering with stars," says Sabadini, "became visible," and beams of light seemed to descend upon the grave.

The Confessor's apprehensions were not justified; the body was uncorrupted; only the board, by reason of the weight of earth above it, had slipped and injured the face, especially the nose. The nuns placed the body in the coffin, cleaned the face, and straightened the nose; whereupon, says Sabadini, there issued from it "living blood."

And now according to the Confessor's instructions the coffin should have been closed and returned to earth. But these four nuns were, strangely enough, unanimously "overpowered by a sudden impulse, which they held to be a divine prompting." Lifting the coffin "with one accord," they bore it through the colonnade to the church, and set it down before the altar of the Blessed Sacrament. Whereupon, they declared, the former miracle was repeated, and the dead Abbess visibly saluted the Body of the Lord. There she lay in the open coffin, her face fresh and fair, her flesh supple, her skin exuding a sweet liquid, which was collected and preserved by the careful nuns. And these things were noised abroad throughout the city, and all the pious citizens by licence of the Legate flocked to visit the blessed corpse. And the Legate himself desired as a relic the cloth wrapped about the face of the holy Abbess, soaked with the mysterious odoriferous "sweat."

The Bishop then ordered the body to be placed in a sort of altar-tomb with two keys, one of which was consigned to the Mother of the convent, the other to its Father Confessor. But this arrangement did not satisfy the sisters. A few days later, on Holy Saturday, they were again overcome by a desire to look upon the Mother's face; the tomb was unlocked, and the silken tunic in which the body had been clothed was found to be soaked with fragrant moisture. Some perturbation was occasioned by the ashen hue and sunken eyes of the corpse, but on Easter morning the disquieting symptoms had disappeared, the eyes were half open and the colour was fresh and rosy, tokens, it was felt, of continued connexion between body and soul, and *therefore*—though the logic of the inference seems obscure—of the latter's beatitude. "And this new marvel," says Caterina's biographer, "was made public, and by a fresh concourse of pious folk was attested and approved."

But, alas! before many months had passed, the nuns were forced to acknowledge that the face was blackening. The woeful change was attributed to the damp of the hastily made sarcophagus, and the dead Abbess was accordingly placed on a litter and borne upstairs to her own dry and airy cell.

But however convenient this habitation may have been for the living, it was found to be unsuitable for the dead. When pilgrims requested an interview, the Santa was placed on a litter and conveyed downstairs into the choir, from which through the "window for Communion" (finestrina della Comunione) she was exhibited to the devout. But the continual ascent and descent of the stairs was somewhat perilous to the precious corpse and made large demands on its guardians' time and strength, while the bulky litter took up much needed space in the nuns' choir. It was felt after some years that a change must be made, and one of the guardians of the body noticing its continued flexibility suggested that it should be placed in a sitting posture in a chair-like tabernacle, which could be kept in a niche in the choir, and be run forward on castors to the window when required.

The plan was accepted, and the tabernacle was made, but Caterina appeared averse to the arrangement. The body was found to be too rigid to assume a sitting posture, and the nuns were at their wits' end when the Abbess Illuminata Bembo [1] commanded her sometime Superior and friend to let herself be placed on the prepared seat. The appeal to "holy obedience" prevailed. As though of her own will and movement Caterina sank upon the seat, and "vi si accomodò con grandissima grazia."

But this arrangement also was cumbersome and inconvenient, and at length the Santa herself suggested a better one. Appearing in a dream to one of her guardians, Suor Leonora Poggi, she indicated as her choice the abode she has ever since occupied, a *camerino* lying between the sacristy of the nuns' choir and the eastern wall, a little to the side of the high altar of the handsome external church of Corpus Domini. Suor Leonora awoke, and behold it was a dream which faded before the dawn of a new day. But next night the dream was repeated, with reproaches, and the nun awoke full of misgivings and indecision. Fearing a diabolic temptation to presumption, she still hesitated to speak, till a third appearance of the Saint, and renewed commands and reproaches, sent her at break of day in great agitation to the Abbess.

Now Mother Illuminata knew naught of the existence of this little room, which belonged to the quarters of the lay sisters and was outside the strictly cloistered portion of the building. But when sought

[1] The Abbess Illuminata does not herself record the fact.

for, all was found to be as the dream-Caterina had revealed, even to the pieces of wood and spare hangings which formed the *camerino's* contents. A window was opened as she had directed, to afford a view of the high altar, and facing it the Santa was placed on the chair she had occupied as Abbess. There she has ever since sat enthroned, only the chair, less incorruptible than its occupant, was in 1584 observed to be rotten and unsafe, and was replaced by a new and more gorgeous seat, carved and gilded according to the taste of the age.

In 1681 a folio volume was published in Rome containing an account of the examination of witnesses, and the facts agreed upon by the Sacra Congregatio de Ritu in reference to Caterina's post-mortem history.

The fragrance, incorruptibility, and unsupported sitting-posture of the body form the chief heads of inquiry. All the witnesses agreed that in their day there had been no issuing of "living blood" from any part of the body, though some of the older nuns mentioned the tradition of their convent that nosebleeding took place one hundred and thirty years after the "Santa's" death. All again admitted that the hair and nails were not actually growing; but Alfonso Arnoaldo, Canon of S. Petronio, drew attention to the fact that the hair was long, and that this was unusual in a nun, while the convent physician affirmed that he had heard growth had ceased only twelve years previously. He loyally attributed the olive tint of the skin to constant exposure to candlelight, and defended himself against further cross-questioning by declaring that his sight was bad and he could not really see. All the witnesses agreed that the skin was discoloured,[1] that the sitting posture was maintained without artificial support, and that beneath the insteps, and on the thighs and chest, the body was soft and flexible, some even auld warm, to the touch. The nuns alone declared that the face changed in expression, sometimes looking pained and severe, at other times sweet and joyful.

The most interesting and accurate evidence is that of certain noble Bolognese matrons, and of a doctor, one Carlo Riario, who was called as an expert. For his part, said this witness, he could not call the body either corrupt or incorrupt, because flesh proper there was none, though the skin—" cute, cuticula e membrana carnosa "—is perfect and entire. When asked whether he considered this state of preservation natural or supernatural, he answered cautiously that he inclined to the belief that it was supernatural—" più tosto lo credero Divino "—and this chiefly because of the continued attachment of hair to the cuticle, " for hair is nourished by the moisture of the body, whereas this body is dried up."

The noble matrons were empowered to examine the body with the object of discovering any traces of corruption on the one hand or embalming on the other. They admit the existence of little creases or fissures, but declare their belief that these are only skin-deep, and attributable merely to " ritiramento della pelle,"

[1] Father Grassetti attributes this *negrezza* to the dampness of the place where the body was kept during the first months after its disinterment.

a shrinking of the skin. They also notice the existence of a little piece of cloth under the *left* arm, which was removed at their request, and was not found to conceal any defect.

One of the nuns appointed as custodian of the Santa admits the existence of a superficial fissure in the *right* arm protected by a piece of linen. A second custodian speaks of little pieces of linen attached by *gomma* to *both* arms, with the object, she declares, of protecting the body from the weight of heavy garments.

As to the odour emanating from the venerated body, it is noteworthy that the short-sighted convent physician declared that " for his sins he had never smelt it "; that the " discreet matrons " said that they did not notice it during their examination of the body, whereas on previous visits to the chapel the air seemed filled with fragrance; and lastly that the nuns of Ferrara, determined not to be altogether eclipsed by their Bolognese sisters, maintained that on certain anniversaries a delicious fragrance pervaded those portions of their building which had been specially frequented by Sister Caterina.

This record of the carefully threshed out reasons for Caterina's canonization is curiously disagreeable reading. The *processo* has the repulsiveness, without the justification, of a coroner's inquest, its ultimate end being not the safety of the living but the glorification of a woman whom many generations of her fellow-citizens had already hailed as blessed. The true odour of sanctity exhaled by *The Seven Weapons* seems tainted by the discussion of the nature of the perfume observed in the chapel. Comments on growing hair and nails and blackened and fissured skin seem unwarrantable liberties taken with a defenceless gentlewoman; and, remembering Illuminata's ridiculous commendation of Caterina's prudishness, we feel a heat of vicarious modesty at the really perfectly decorous proceedings of the Bolognese matrons. The various depositions seem heavy with suggestion of fraud mingling with gruesome but not unparalleled natural phenomena, and the worst features of medieval superstition meet those of modern notetaking realism in the descriptions of the appearance and condition of the corpse, descriptions from which any hint of the sweet personality which once animated it is rigorously excluded.

As for the post-mortem miracles of the "Santa," which in their turn are duly examined and discussed, they are of a kind familiar to all readers of hagiographical literature. Two were cited in the Deed of Canonization—the cure of a stiff hand useless for nine months, and of a violent fever with delirium and coma. Both patients were nuns; both were despaired of by their physicians.

But the greatest miracle of all went unmentioned and won no kudos for its worker. It was this: Caterina being dead ruled the convent of Corpus Domini for the space of an entire year. Her daughters could not bring themselves to make a fresh election, for the spirit of the beloved Abbess seemed as close to them as was her earthly tabernacle. When at length the Vicar-General visited the community he found that order, discipline, charity, and content were perfectly maintained under the ghostly rule of a fair memory. None of the nuns would consent to reign in Caterina's stead, and her successor had at length to be imported from the mother-house in Ferrara.

CHAPTER VIII

CATERINA THE ARTIST

> If at whiles
> My heart sinks, as monotonous I paint
> These endless cloisters and eternal aisles
> With the same series, Virgin, Babe and Saint
>
> .   .   .   .   .   .
>
> At least no merchant traffics in my heart;
> The sanctuary's gloom at least shall ward
> Vain tongues from where my pictures stand apart.
>
> .   .   .   .   .   .
>
> So die my pictures! surely, gently die.
> BROWNING, *Pictor Ignotus*.

> Their works drop groundward, but themselves, I know,
> Reach many a time a heaven that's shut to me,
> Enter and take their place there sure enough,
> Though they come back and cannot tell the world.
> BROWNING, *Andrea del Sarto*.

A CHAPTER dealing with the artistic activity of Caterina dei Vigri is of necessity bald and brief. Her biographers were concerned to spread the fame of the "Santa," not of the artist. Her painting in their eyes as in her own was merely a superfluous expression of religious fervour, of far less importance than many other manifestations of the same grace. Consequently they tantalize us by indicating considerable artistic industry without supplying any details as to its results. Thus Illuminata Bembo, who develops with such satisfactory fullness the character of her friend and the nature of their intercourse, dismisses her paintings in a single sentence: "E volontiere dipingea il Verbo Divino piccolino infasciato, e per molti luoghi del Monastero di Ferrara, e pei libri lo faceva cosi piccolino." (She delighted in painting the Divine Word as a swaddled child, and for many places in the monastery at Ferrara and for the books she did Him thus.)

The earliest "Life," that of 1503, does not even repeat these details, but merely gives us the unillustrated information that "her hands were singularly skilful in the writing of fair books and in illumination in various colours."

These meagre statements at least indicate what is borne out by the few existing specimens of her work, namely, that Caterina, whether she painted moderately large pictures or decorated breviaries, was essentially a miniaturist. We have seen that in thought and feeling she belonged to an age anterior to her own, and this backwardness of temper is expressed by the primitive character of her art. It is very difficult to realize that Gentile Bellini was only eight years her junior; or even that the Dominican, whose gentle mysticism and lack of science were akin to her own, was decorating the walls of S. Marco in Florence at the very time when she was adorning "many places in the convent of Ferrara." Far easier is it to recollect that Duccio was another of her contemporaries; for curiously enough the Bambino in the best authenticated of Caterina's paintings, the really beautiful "Madonna of the Apple," somewhat resembles in facial shape and expression the Infants of the Sienese painter, whose work it seems unlikely she ever saw.

The "Madonna of the Apple" hangs in the chapel of the Santa in the church of Corpus Domini in Bologna. It is unsigned, but has been attributed to the first Abbess by the constant and unbroken tradition of the convent. It is a large miniature on canvas, with carefully stippled colour and the application of burnished gold. The flesh tints are clear, fresh, and beautiful; the expression of the Holy Child is intelligent and engaging; and the crimson tones of the Virgin's robe are wonderfully rich and harmonious. The picture is named from the ripe fruit which she holds in her left hand.

Another Madonna and Child traditionally attributed to Caterina hangs in the convent refectory. It was shown to the writer by the courtesy of two of the Sisters, the Madre Camerlinga and Suor Marianna. Too large to be passed through the aperture in the parlour wall, it could be seen only through the double "grille." But even this imperfect view revealed its likeness and its inferiority to the "Madonna of the Apple." The likeness was most marked in respect to the attitude and expression of the Bambino, and the effect of inferiority in execution was heightened by the misplaced piety of past generations, which had adorned the Mother with earrings and the Child with necklaces of pearl and coral.

Another specimen of work attributed to the Santa was more closely inspected. It was a sheet of vellum about seven inches by eight inches, on which was drawn a half-length figure of the Redeemer and two small

MINIATURE ON VELLUM
CONVENT OF CORPUS DOMINI, BOLOGNA

scenes representing the Annunciation. The Christ is executed in pale transparent tints with golden aureole and collar, against an opaque dull blue background faintly lined with gold. The right hand points to the wounded side, visible through the semi-transparent robe. The left hand grasps an open book, on the pages of which we have a specimen of Caterina's fine calligraphy. On one is written:—

> In me omnis gratia
> in me omnis vie (?) et veritatis.

On the other :—

> In me omnis spes
> Vite (?) et virtutis.

The two little round miniatures above the half-length figure of the Redentore are somewhat superior in execution, and it has been conjectured that they are by another hand, possibly that of her master. To the writer the superiority only seems such as would result from an additional degree of experience and courage. The larger miniature may have been painted when the artist—an amateur it must be remembered—was out of practice, the two smaller when she had "her hand in." Probably, too, she had already attempted an Annunciation. However that may be, her treatment of the subject is distinctly interesting. In one of the little pictures the Virgin sits, in the other the Announcing Angel kneels; and in both the background is a green meadow filled with pre-Raphaelite flowers and shaded by golden trees.

In connexion with this outdoor setting of an event depicted by most of the painters of the time as taking place in the house, or at least in an open cloister or *loggia*, it is interesting to remember that in Caterina's vision of the Heavenly Court the scene is "a great meadow of such beauty as human speech cannot describe." That vision, as we have already said, is the dream of a medieval painter. Another, of an earlier date (1431), is described by Caterina in *The Seven Weapons* as a painter might describe his conception of a picture. The subject is the Last Judgment. God " in human form and aspect, clothed in crimson, with face turned towards the west, stands in the highest clouds of heaven." " A little lower down, to the side but not far away," the Virgin Mother, robed and mantled in pure white, stands in an attitude of admiring expectation. " Some distance below" the twelve apostles sit on flaming thrones. Much lower again a great multitude of men and women stand with faces upturned to God. Caterina herself had a place among those on God's right hand.

Here, wonderful to relate, the picture ends. We should have expected such a description of the torments of the lost and the joys of the saved as arouses our interest and repugnance on the walls of the Spanish chapel, or the painting of Fra Angelico in the Belle Arti, in Florence. But with singular restraint and dramatic feeling Caterina seizes the one moment of supreme expectation and omits subsequent details. Whether this composition was ever transferred from mind to canvas we do not know. Perhaps Caterina was conscious that her technical skill was inadequate to the task; perhaps she tried, and tried in vain, to realize her fine conception.

ST. URSULA AND HER MAIDENS
PINACOTECA, BOLOGNA

The two best-known pictures ascribed to Caterina dei Vigri are unfortunately far less pleasing and less well authenticated than the works already described. The "St. Ursula" in the Bolognese Gallery (No. 202) is a lady of enormous stature with flat, fair, expressionless face of a Dutch type. She is, however, most gorgeously and harmoniously attired in a rose-madder, white-cinctured, gold-embroidered gown, under a green-lined mantle of cloth of gold. Her virgins, the tallest of whom hardly reaches to her ankles, shelter themselves in the folds of this splendid cloak, and tremblingly support the scaffolding poles from which float the emblematic red and white pennons.

The "St. Ursula" of the Accademia of Venice (No. 54, Sala III) is in features, dress, and colouring not unlike the giantess of Bologna, but she has only four attendants, does not tower above them, and carries her own red and white banner. Red, tawny, and brown tones prevail through the picture. The pose of the second lady on the right is graceful and unexpected, reminding us slightly of Perugino, and she has a very curious scarlet horn projecting from her curly hair. In the foreground kneels a nun in a white habit with a black wimple.

The signature, "CATTERINA VIGRI F BOLOGNA. 1456," is almost certainly a later addition.

The white habit of the kneeling figure has inclined some Italian experts to believe that the picture was painted, not by Caterina, but by a Dominican nun. The well-known name of the Santa of Bologna would undoubtedly be affixed by later generations to a picture traditionally attributed to a forgotten fifteenth-century religious. But is it quite certain that the kneeling figure in the foreground is a Dominican? The nun does not indeed wear the grey or brown serge of a Poor Clare; but a white habit was worn not only by Dominicans but also by some communities emanating from the Augustinian Order.[1] The distinguishing mark of a Dominican is of course the knotted cord; but the position of the arms of this small kneeling figure prevents us from seeing whether this is present. The straight fall of the white folds suggests, however, the absence of any cincture.

Now if we assume that this figure may be Augustinian, various interesting possibilities present themselves. If the date 1456 be altogether imaginary, we may see in the nun an early *auto-ritrattro* of the painter, or a portrait of her friend Suor Illuminata; and in either case the picture may have been a gift to the latter's family, the great Venetian house of Bembo. If on the other hand we accept the date as correct even though its inscription be not contemporaneous, we may imagine that Caterina, warned by a vision of her approaching departure to Bologna, determined to take with her as a precious souvenir a portrait of "our first Mother," Lucia Mascheroni. We know that Lucia never abandoned the habit and rule she had first adopted, while her early work among the young ladies of Ferrara might certainly entitle her to the special protection of St. Ursula. Such a picture, carried by Caterina to Bologna, would have no interest for any members of the new community with the exception of Illuminata, who had also been one of Lucia's maidens, and on Caterina's

[1] St. Bridget of Sweden, however, wore a black tunic, white wimple, and white veil with red band. St. Rosalia of Palermo wore a black tunic *fastened by a leather belt*, a black veil, and white wimple.

death it may have passed to her friend and successor, and from her again, by gift or bequest, to a Venetian relative[1] or friend, who would prize it for the sake of some old memory or association.

Venice possesses yet another painting ascribed, and with great probability, to the Santa. It is stowed away in a room above the church of S. Giovanni in Bragora. The picture is in four compartments: each contains two female martyrs in richly coloured and embroidered robes, drawn on a gold background.[2]

The question naturally asked in respect to every artist—who was his or her teacher?—is not answered by any of Caterina's biographers. The tradition—founded perhaps on a general resemblance in style—that she was the pupil of Lippo di Dalmasio, is disproved by a comparison of dates. Probably at the Court of Ferrara she had lessons from some deservedly unremembered artist, and was for the rest self-taught. It is perhaps an insignificant, but certainly it is an interesting, coincidence that in Ferrara to-day nothing can be found resembling the work of Caterina dei Vigri save only some fragments in the gallery taken from a demolished church dedicated to her patron Saint. Is it, then, a too fanciful conjecture that Margherita d'Este's young companion, fired by a special devotion for her name-saint, drew her chief artistic inspiration from the pictured walls of the church of S. Catherine of Alexandria?

[1] The donors to the gallery were the Molins, a very ancient Venetian family.

[2] One can distinguish S. Margaret, S. Catherine, S. Barbara, and perhaps S. Lucy. The faces are pleasing though expressionless. I owe the discovery of this picture to a clue kindly given me by Dr. Fogolari of the Venetian Accademia. It is not mentioned by the biographers.

AUTHORITIES

Suor Illuminata Bembo. *Specchio d' Illuminatione sulla Vita di Caterina da Bologna.*

(Completed in 1469. The MS. is in the Archivio of the convent of Corpus Domini. There is a printed copy in the Library of the University of Bologna. The writer has not been able to discover any other copy.)

Sabadini degli Arienti. Biography 4 in *Gynevra de le Clare Donne.* Edited by Corrado Ricci. *Curiosità Letteraria.*

Sabadini's Life of Caterina was published separately in 1502 by Zuan Antonio, of Bologna: it was entitled *Vita della Beata Catherina Bolognese de lordini de la diva Clara del Corpo de Christo.* It was republished with thirty-one other biographies in the volume called *Gynevra de le Clare Donne.* It reappeared again with a few variations and additions and divisions into chapters in 1536. The additions are accounts of the numerous miracles "which God has worked by this blessed one," with poems and prayers composed by her or about her.

Sabadini's Life and the archives of the convent are the *Urquelle* from which Cristoforo Mansueti and Giacomo Grassetti compiled the acts for her canonization.

P. Grassetti. *Vita di S. Caterina da Bologna* (Bologna, 1724) treats the subject exhaustively, and contains "The Seven Weapons" and Caterina's discourse on poverty.

The Seven Weapons was published for the first time in 1510 by Hieronymo Platone de Benedictis, citadino da Bologna. It was republished with the Life of 1536, and has since repeatedly reappeared.

AUTHORITIES

Numerous small biographies of S. Caterina and sermons and orations in her honour have been examined. None of them add anything to the information obtained from the above-mentioned sources, save that a Ferrarese, Bruffaldi, writing in the eighteenth century, gives the pedigree of the Vigri family.

For her post-mortem history and the evidence of her sanctity:—

" Congregatione Sacrorum Rituum coram Sanctissimo Card. Parpine Bononień. Canonizationis B. Catharinae a Bononia Monialis Professae Ordinis S. Clarae."

Roma. *Ex Typographia Reverendae Camerae Apostolicae* (1680).

For an estimate of her work as a painter:—

MALVASIA. *Felsina Pittrice*, Vol. I.
TIRABOSCHI. *Storia Lett. Ital.*, Vol. VI.
LANZI. *Storia d' Arte*, Vol. V.
MARCO MINGHETTI. *Le Donne Italiane nelle Belle Arte* (1877).

MS. SOURCES. Dossier, in Archivio Arcivescovile, Bologna, labelled "Memorie della Lite et Pretensione de Ferrarese che la nostra B. Cat. da Bologna si dovesse chiamare da Ferrara."

APPENDIX A

CATERINA'S HYMN

Anima benedetta
Dall' alto Creatore,
Risguarda il tuo Signore,
Che confitto t' aspetta.

Risguarda i piè forati
Confitti da un chiavello,
Stan così tormentati
Pe' colpi del martello:
Pensa ch' egli era bello
Sopra ogni creatura,
E la sua carne pura
Era più che perfetta.

        Anima benedetta, etc.

Risguarda quella piaga,
Ch' egli ha dal manco lato,
Vedi che' l sangue paga
Per tutto il tuo peccato,
Mira il Cuor trapassato
Dalla lancia crudele,
Che per ciascun fedele
Il passò la saetta.

        Anima benedetta, etc.

APPENDIX A

Risguarda quelle mani
Sante, che ti plasmaro,
Vedi come que' cani
Giudei lo conficcaro:
Ora con pianto amaro
Piangi il Signor, che in Croce
Soffrì pena sì atroce,
Perche tu fussi lieta.

   Anima benedetta, etc.

Mira il capo sacrato,
Ch' era sì di lettoso
Vedil tutto forato
Di spine, e sanguinoso;
Anima, egli è il tuo Sposo;
Dunque perche non piagni,
Sicchè piagnendo bagni
Ogni tua colpa in fretta.

   Anima benedetta, etc.

Another of Caterina's compositions is of immense length and small literary merit. It is a proof that she was conversant with the Latin tongue, and had no notion of making Latin verses.

"Desirous of meditating daily," says Father Grassetti, "on the Life and Passion of her Redeemer," she composed a Rosary, which she divided into three parts, each part having five subdivisions. There are in all five thousand six hundred and ten lines, each ending in the syllable "is." Eight of them will probably more than satisfy the reader's curiosity.

 O Bone Jesu, nunc libenter te laudarem in terris,
 Et meum post obitum tunc te libentissimè in Cœlis,

Cum infinitas laudes à nobis dignè promerearis.
Creasti etenim hunc orbem, nunc gubernas, conservasque hunc gratis,
Et quidem in necessitatibus quibuscumque nostris
Tam animæ, quam corporis, nec unquam nos derelinquis,
Sed, quod incomparabile est, tu etiam pro omnibus nobis
Delesti originale peccatum primi parentis.

The most interesting part of this Rosary is its title, which runs as follows :—

Jesus, Maria, Franciscus, Clara.

Rosarium antiquum, et devotum Beatissime Matris Dei, Virginum Virginis Mariæ humillimæ, purissimæ, ac dignissimæ, non minus historicum, quam contemplativum, ut penitus exclusa sint, et intelligantur, si quæ apocrapha aliquibus fortasse viderentur, a me Catharina Moniali, ac serva vilissima, indigna et inutile hic in Conventu Sanctissimi Corporis Christi Ferrariæ ad Dei Filii et Matris gloriam et honorem, ob singularissimam gratiam infrascriptam ibidem nostra in Ecclesia genuflexè à me obtentam, inspiratè conscriptum.

The reference is to Caterina's Christmas vision. The *inspirate conscriptum* is worth noting.

APPENDIX B

Decreto della Canonizazione della Beata Catarina emanato à 17 Maggio 1707

CUM in Congregatione generali coram Sanctissimo habita die 31 Maii anni 1701 discussum fuisset dubium, An, et de quibus Miraculis constaret post indultam Beatae Catharinae de Bononia Venerationem : Cumque S.S.D.N. exquisitis Consultorum, et Eminentissimorum, et Reverendissimorum D.D. Sac. Rituum Congregationi Praepositorum Cardinalium suffragiis, die 5 Mensis Decembris anni 1703 ex octo Miraculis à Postulatoribus allatis, et in discussionem adductis duo approbaverit : nempè.

Sextum instantaneae Sanationis Sororis Justinae de Calcinis Monialis Monasterii S.S. Corporis Christi, à luxatione manus à novem mensibus inflexibiles, et a Medecis derilectae.

Et octauum subitae sanationis Sororis Mariae Gertrudis de Ghirardellis Monialis ejusdem Monasterii S.S. Corporis Christi à gravissima infirmitate febris cum delirio et lethargo ad dies ferè sexaginta protracta, et a Medecis deplorata Tandem die 18 Novembris 1704 denuo accitis consultoribus, et praehabita per Eminentissimum et Reverendissimum D. Card. de Carpinea ad prescriptum Decretorum plena, ac distincta relatione omnium in causa gestorum. Sac. Congregatio unanimi consensu censuit posse annuente Sanctissimo juxtà Ritum S.R.E. et Sacrorum Canonum dispositionem ad solemnem ejusdem Beatae Canonizationem quandocumque deveniri.

Proindequè SS.D.N.PP Clemens XI ut Christi Ecclesia Agni Sponsa nouo decore induta in Cœlestis Regis oculis gratiam inveniat et tamquam Civitas in Monte posita majoribus in dies irradiata fulgoribus semitas justorum dirigat, atque iis, qui in tenebris ambulant lumen veritatis, et viam salutis clarius ostendat, saepius ad Deum fusis, et indictis precibus, et pluries Secretario et Pro. Promotore Fidei auditis, prasens Canonizationis Decretum expederi et publicari mandavit.

Dic 17 Maii Anni 1707
G. Card. Carpineus

Loco + sigilli.   B. Inghirami Sac. Rit. Cong. Sec.

PROPERZIA DE' ROSSI

THE SCULPTOR

(1500?–1530)

PROPERZIA DE' ROSSI

> Fero splendor di due begli occhi accrebbe
> Già marmi a marmi; e stupor nuovo e strano
> Ruvidi marmi delicata mano
> Fea dianzi vivi, ahi ! morte invidia n' ebbe.
> *Properzia's Epitaph written by Vincenzo Bonacorso Pitti.*

> Le donne son venuti in eccellenza
> Di ciascun' arte ov' hanno posto cura.
> ARIOSTO, *Orlando Furioso*, Canto xx.

A LOVELY highly gifted woman, who is persecuted by professional jealousy, is unsuccessful in love, and dies at the height of her fame in the hey-day of her beauty—have we not here all the elements for melodrama and romance? And in truth the story of Properzia de' Rossi, so vague in outline, so brilliant in colour, has been the subject of a successful tragedy, and of much bombastic fiction masquerading in the guise of history.

To avow that Vasari is the sole original source for the majority of our facts is equivalent, it will be said by superior persons, to proclaiming that Properzia's story is a myth. But in defence alike of Vasari and the present sketch it must be urged that the worthy painter came to Bologna when Properzia lay a-dying, and that he heard first-hand the laments and reminiscences of her fellow-citizens; and secondly, that modern investigation has reversed the doubts thrown on some of his statements concerning her, and amply justified his disputed assertions.

Thus in the *Lives of the Painters*, Properzia was described as the daughter of a Bolognese citizen. Alldosa, however, in his *Istruzione della Cose notabile di Bologna*, confidently declared that she was the daughter of Giovanni Martino Rossi da Modena. He was followed by several subsequent writers, till at length an early nineteenth-century biographer,[1] chiefly on the ground that she is generally styled *Madonna* Properzia, suggested that Rossi was her married, not her maiden, name. But that industrious delver among civic MSS., Gualandi, has discovered documents of the years 1514, 1516, and 1518, in which mention is made of "Domina Propertia, filia q. Iieronymi de Rubeis Bononiae civis," and he believes this Girolamo to have been the son of a notary, who in 1480 was living in Strada Maggiore (now Via Mazzini), and in 1489 in Strada San Donato (Via Zamboni). Thus we may once more hold with Vasari that Properzia was a Bolognese.

The date of her birth is given us neither by Vasari nor by any one else : that of her death is fixed unmistakably by a great public event. She died on the day of Charles V's coronation by Clement VII, i.e. February the twenty-fourth, 1530. From the amount of work she had accomplished and the fact that her admirers represented her as cut off in the fullness of her beauty, we may conclude that she was not less than twenty-

[1] Carolina Bonafede, *Cenni Biografici e Ritratti d' Insigni Donne Bolognese*.

eight or much over thirty when she died, and that her birth consequently took place when the fifteenth century was very old or the sixteenth very young.

Beyond the name of her drawing master, we know nothing of her education save its results. Vasari says that she was highly accomplished in every way and especially distinguished for her musical gifts—" singing and playing on instruments better than any woman of her day in the city of Bologna."

Now this was very high praise, for Bologna was "in her day" the most musical city in Italy. In the middle of the fifteenth century it actually possessed a chair of music, occupied by a Spaniard, one Bartolomeo Pareia, and though for some unknown cause his lectures and his office had but a brief existence, its institution is significant and probably was not unfruitful.

The pedantic Achillini in his poem the "Viridario," printed in 1530, declares that the city is full of musicians who can improvise on any given theme; that there is a sprinkling of more scientific composers and one noted authority on counterpoint; that there are five organists of extraordinary skill, players on the lute and on the lyre, and one gentle youth who has rare skill upon the pipe. No great wedding could be celebrated without the accompaniment of a complete orchestra.[1] A drum and fife band performed daily in the long balcony of the palace of the Podestà; and a certain Ludovico Felicini had charming chamber concerts in his house attended

[1] In the Diario of Jacopo Rainieri we have a list of instruments in general use: "Liuti, violle, dolsemelle, ciavasembali, manacorde, organi, violunni, pifari, cornitti."

by all the great people of the city. May we not fancy that the gifted Properzia de' Rossi was sometimes heard on these occasions?

We do not know who were her music masters, but we do know that her instructor in drawing was that Marc Antonio Raimondi who was Francia's pupil and Raphael's friend, who engraved many of the latter's pictures "in such a manner that all Rome was thrown into amazement," and who figures as one of the bearers in the "Expulsion of Heliodorus from the Temple." It was natural that he should set his pupil to copy some of Raphael's works, and Vasari, who himself possessed some of these copies, tells us that they were extremely well done.

It would seem that at first Properzia, like many another gifted young person, was uncertain which of Art's paths to pursue, what mode of self-expression to make her own. She had that keen, full, rounded sense of beauty which makes the perfect dilettante and is apt to make the imperfect professional. Such a sense was the special dower of the women of the renaissance. They played, they sang, they danced, they dabbled in the classics, they wrote letters and made verses, and were altogether charming companions, excellent critics, graceful amateurs. Such was Properzia, and might have been no more when, through a mere accident, a feminine caprice, the true direction of her genius was discovered. The discovery once made, the step from the grade of gifted amateur to that of hard-working professional was definitely taken.

It happened on this wise. Properzia took to carving the kernels of fruits—apricot and peach and cherry

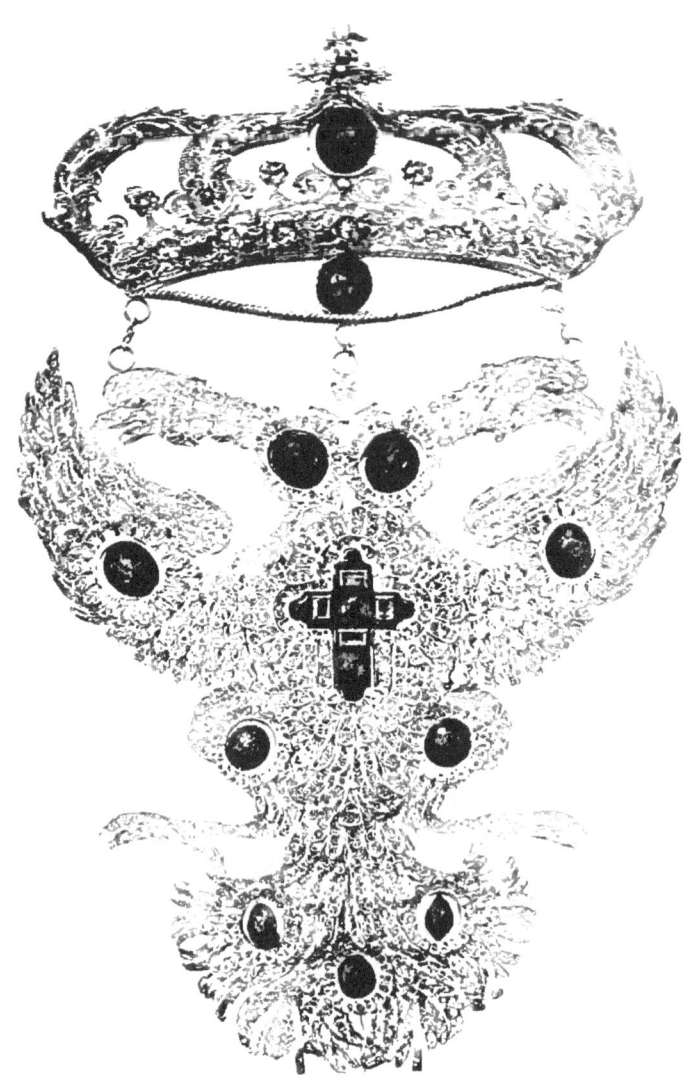

MINUTE CARVINGS ON ELEVEN PEACH STONES
MUSEO CIVICO, BOLOGNA

stones. At length she produced a crucifixion—the central figure, the onlookers, mourners, and executioners being grouped in a pleasing composition, and each separate figure treated with accuracy and spirit—all upon a single peach stone. The subtlety and delicacy of the work is described by Vasari as miraculous. In the collection of gems in the Uffizi Gallery in Florence is a pendant, in the midst of which is set a cherry stone carved with about sixty minute heads. It is generally attributed to Properzia. An entire series of similar carvings in the Museo Civico in Bologna is certainly by her hand. It was presented to the city by Conte Marsigli, heir of the Grassi family, the original owners. Eleven peach stones are set in a device of filigree silver. This is suspended so that both sides of the stones can be seen. Unfortunately the device cannot be removed from its place and examined by a window, and the room is badly lighted; so that the minute carvings can be better studied in some engravings published and described in 1829. (*Descrizione di alcuni minutissimi intagli di mano di Properzia de' Rossi*, by Bianconi and Canuti.) On one side of the stones are eleven apostles, each with his name and a clause of the Apostles' Creed; on the other side are virgin saints, each with a motto alluding to her special virtue or attribute.

We do not know when Properzia exchanged her delicate knives and needles for mallet and chisel, or by what transitional stages she passed from her "feminine accomplishments" to professional labour hitherto monopolized by the sterner sex. But this is certain: the second decade of the sixteenth century finds her equipped for competition with the first sculptors of the day, and with a budding, but not yet assured, reputation.

She must have carved something more than fruit stones before, in the year 1524, the Vice-Legate invited her to decorate the canopy of the high altar in the church he had just restored outside the gate of S. Stefano. Properzia joyfully undertook the commission, and a more beautiful specimen of the best period of renaissance carving can hardly be conceived than the lovely intertwining of flambeaux and birds' heads, of fruit and foliage and sphinxes, which wreathes the altar arch in the church of S. Maria del Baraccano.

About this time (whether a little before or a little after her work in the church without the walls is uncertain) there came to Properzia, as to all other young sculptors in Bologna, a unique opportunity for making money and a name.

In the last decade of the fourteenth century the Bolognese, fired by the architectural achievements of Florence, determined to build a church which should exceed in size and splendour the lately completed Santa Maria del Fiore, which boasted itself the largest of Italian churches.

In February, 1390, the Council of Six Hundred ordered Antonio Vincenzio to prepare a design. In June the work of construction and destruction had begun. The two arms of the immense Latin cross were to abut on spacious piazzas, so there was a wholesale and most sanitary clearing of unsavoury alleys and crowded tenements, together with the demolition of eight churches and some of the hundred towers [1] with which

---

[1] See Gozzadini in *I Torri Gentilizie di Bologna*. The two famous leaning towers, Asinelli and Garisenda, remain as specimens.

the fourteenth-century city bristled. The work of construction was necessarily less rapid, and little by little its pace slackened, till in 1659 it came altogether to a standstill, and has never since been resumed. S. Petronio, as we know it, represents but one-half of Vincenzio's original design, and ends abruptly with an apse where the arms of the Latin cross should have begun.

Even this half is imperfect in decoration. The western façade, which was to have been its peculiar glory, which Jacopo della Quercia came from Arles to begin, and from which the youthful Michael Angelo drew inspiration, remains unfinished, in spite of the fifty designs for its completion which repose in the museum of the church. At the beginning of the sixteenth century there was, however, a flicker-up of zeal. It was pronounced to be a civic disgrace that while the central western portal was glorious with Jacopo di Quercia's work, the lateral doors should remain bare, ugly, and insignificant. The administrators of the fabric prepared to act with vigour. They invited the sculptors of the city to compete for work and to send in specimens of their skill.

This is the chance of a lifetime for Properzia. She quietly places herself among the ranks of male professional artists, and enters on the path hitherto untrodden by women's feet, and rarely since her day successfully pursued by them. Her test-work was a likeness of Count Guido Pepoli—perhaps the bust preserved in the first room of the *Museo della Fabbrica*, but more probably a basso-relievo discovered in the middle of the last century in a villa of the Pepoli.

It has been argued that Properzia's carving in the church of the Baraccano must have been executed after this event, for, had it been anterior, no test-work would have been required of her. But, in truth, no such positive inference can be drawn from the requirements of the administrators. Red-tape existed even in the sixteenth century, and the carving in the Baracano—a conventional design of intertwining fruit, flowers, foliage, and birds—gave no guarantee that Properzia was capable of dealing with the human form.

Vasari tells us that the bust not only satisfied the administrators but "delighted the whole city"—a little touch revealing that solidarity of civic life and intelligent general interest in artistic and architectural matters which was so marked a feature of the Italian city-state and is so conspicuously absent in the modern town.

We do not know what portion of the work upon the great west front of S. Petronio was assigned to Properzia de' Rossi, nor do the registers of the Fabbrica greatly help us. They contain, however, the following entries:—

"June 1, 1525. To Madonna Properzia de' Rossi, lire 11 for a Sibyl in marble executed by her.

"September 8, 1525. To Madonna Properzia de' Rossi for an Angel executed by her, 10 lire and 19 soldi.

"August 4, 1526. To Properzia, 40 lire and 3 soldi for the remaining two Sibyls, an Angel, and two pictures."[1]

[1] The writer was unable to inspect the MSS. of the registers. The entries quoted above come from Davia's accurate and detailed study, "Sculture delle Porte di San Petronio."

JOSEPH AND THE WIFE OF POTIPHAR
MUSEUM OF S. PETRONIO, BOLOGNA

We do not know what has become of the sibyls. The angels are doubtless those in the chapel of Tribolo's Assumption, the eleventh off the nave to the right from the west entrance. They are graceful figures, but are rather thin for their height, and do not quite correspond with the great reputation of the sculptress. Vasari, however, tells us that Properzia was not responsible for their proportions, but worked from Tribolo's models.

The pictures were probably the bas-reliefs in the museum of S. Petronio. They represent the visit of the Queen of Sheba to Solomon, and Joseph and Potiphar's wife. In the first the king sits on his throne, his guards and great men around him. A figure kneels at his feet, offering a garment of needlework. The Queen and her maidens stand respectfully aloof. In the second Joseph turns from the temptress, who, seated at the end of a canopied couch, lays a detaining hand upon his flying cloak. The picture expresses natural, vigorous movement and action, but withal without violence or contortion. The gestures are graceful, the harmony of line unbroken. We perceive that Properzia has been studying classical models.

Glancing backwards with the mind's eye to Caterina dei Vigri's "Madonna of the Apple," we measure the pace at which Art has travelled. Between the work of our first two women artists of Bologna lie, to use the famous formula of Michelet, "the discovery of the world and the discovery of man." Yet, paradoxical though it seem, the primitive Italian Madonnas and their Byzantine forerunners had something of the essential spirit of antiquity which the classical imitations of the sixteenth and seventeenth century did not possess. For Greek pagan sculpture at its best, and Greek Christian painting even at its worst, strove to express the abstract and the permanent as opposed to all that was merely personal and momentary. Then came the struggle of medieval introspectiveness and lively religious faith against the bonds of Byzantine conventionalism. The actors in Sacred Story were conceived and portrayed as men of like clothes and passions with the artist,—though perhaps of rather different anatomy ; till, in due time, the social organism was reinvigorated by the strong wind of Humanism setting from Constantinople. Men bared their heads to the breeze, and drew the intoxicating draughts into their lungs. Pallid monastic fears were dispersed, the cobwebs of scholasticism were blown away. " The shapes of things, their colours, lights and shades" became a source of unforbidden joy, and it was freely recognized that

> If you get sense of beauty and naught else
> You get about the best thing God invents.

But the intellectual awakening of the renaissance was penetrated by the inwardness and introspection of the days preceding it ; and thus was generated an abnormal development of individuality which was really fatal to a re-creation of the spirit or art of antiquity. Man, by the laws of nature, is " heir of all the ages," and cannot, however much he may wish it, cut off the entail. To the race, as to the individual, rare moments may be given in middle life when the world is viewed anew with the fresh and fearless vision of a child. But to both youth comes but once, nor have any been permitted to retrace Time's stream towards its source. Self-consciousness is the burden of sane maturity, and the men and women of the renaissance steeped themselves in pagan culture only to quicken the self-consciousness which was commensurate with their immense vitality. As they understood the richness of their heritage the desire to enjoy it to the utmost grew apace. Their passion for self-realization was a flame consuming all the barriers of morality. Their egotism was insatiable and unabashed. The moment and the actual meant so much, that the abstract and eternal were ignored. The repose, simplicity, and objectiveness of the "older world" and its art were as remote from them as from the modern American of fashion.

Let us now glance again at Properzia's bas-relief, and note how in all respects it is characteristic of the art and spirit of her time.

Secular art does not yet go abroad naked and unashamed: therefore she takes for her nominal subject a Bible story. Biblical archæology is still in the womb of time: therefore, as was expected of her, she provides classical costumes and *mise en scène*. And with this sacred pretext, and this Greek disguise, she tells a modern love story, nay, if Vasari's gossip is to be believed, her own, giving us in the woman an *auto-ritratto*, and in the man a portrait of her lover.

One of her biographers—Carolina Bonafede—indignantly repudiates this *on dit* as unimaginably inconsistent with womanly reticence and proper pride. To the present writer it seems perfectly consistent with all that we know of Properzia and the society of her day. "It is not too much to say"—this is the late Mr.

Addington Symond's summing-up against that society —"it is not too much to say that neither public nor private morality, in our sense of the word, existed." And if there be any fact more patent to the student of this period than the one thus emphatically stated, it is that what we mean by reticence was an utterly unknown quality. The only sensations it was held becoming—especially in the male sex—to conceal were physical fear and pain. For the rest the suppression of emotion was a proof of callousness or guile—an opinion still in some measure prevalent among Latin peoples. Men gazed on all the facts of human life with a frank childish curiosity, blinking none of them, holding none of them common or unclean ; and freedom of speech was the natural correlative of this fearless vision. See how Vasari records what he hears of his heroine's amour. He writes of it as his contemporaries spoke of it, not as a scandal to be told in whispers, but as an ordinary, if pitiful, incident to be discussed at the family dinner-table with brutal simplicity. He greatly pities the fair and gifted lady who was "successful in all things but love," and he does not strike the faintest note of blame, contempt, incredulity, or extenuation.

One half of Vasari's report of the fact of the amour has been corroborated, if not actually confirmed, by the documentary researches of Gualandi. A certain Francesco da Milano, described as a velvet merchant, brings an action against Properzia for damage done to his garden which adjoins her own. He describes her as the "mistress of Anton Galeazzo di Napoleone Malvasia." Anton Galeazzo denies the charge, and incidentally declares that he lives at a distance from Properzia. The plea was dismissed from the criminal to the civil court. On April 12, 1521, Anton Galeazzo di Napoleone Malvasia and Properzia dei Rossi are again summoned: the action is again suspended; and then we hear no more of it, the parties concerned probably coming to an amicable understanding.

The information afforded by this case is tantalizingly vague and insufficient; but at least these three facts emerge from it:—First: Properzia's address, which we learn from no other source, and which shows us that the " distance" at which Anton Galeazzo resided from her was about three minutes' walk.[1]

Secondly: The existence of some kind of connexion between them, and his joint responsibility for damage done to adjacent property.

Thirdly: The popular belief as to the nature of that connexion. It is possible, of course, that this belief was a crude misrepresentation of a flirtation which was a pastime for the man and the " whole existence" of the woman; or of one of those platonic friendships which, in the case of young and handsome persons of artistic and ardent temperament, usually end in the misery of one or the other. It is possible also that the damages done to Francesco da Milano's garden were the outcome of a gay party at Properzia's house, when Anton Galeazzo was the ringleader in some of the intolerable and in-

---

[1] The velvet merchant, and consequently Properzia also, lived in the Via S. Lorenzo, a narrow turning out of the Via delle Casse, which leaves the Via Ugo Bassi opposite the Hotel Brun. At the end of the Via delle Casse we reach the bank of the Canal of the Reno. Here, between the Via delle Casse and the Via delle Lame, was the Malvasia house.

credible horseplay which was so frequently the recreation of the fashionable society of the day. Such suppositions are perfectly compatible with Vasari's story as to the bas-relief and Properzia's broken heart. But the velvet merchant's accusation remains—an accusation not made in an anonymous or private letter, but written by a notary's pen as the formal description of a person sued for damages. Anton Galeazzo's denial of connexion with Properzia is subtly worded. It is not retrospective, and may mean anything or nothing.

Three years after the close of this incident Anton Galeazzo took his bachelor's degree (1524). Two years later again Properzia was paid for her "pictures." Some time, then, between 1524 and 1526 their relations were severed, doubtless by the natural development of the career of a well-educated young man of good family. Of Anton Galeazzo di Napoleone Malvasia we know nothing more, save that he married in September, 1538, when Properzia had been eight years in her grave.

Another action brought against Properzia corroborates another of Vasari's statements. He says that she was persecuted by the mean and jealous painter, Amico Aspertini, who maligned her to the administrators of S. Petronio, and caused the price of her work to fall; and that on this account she gave up sculpture and took to engraving on copper, which she did to great perfection. Now in January, 1525, an action was brought against Properzia and a painter named Domenico Francia by another painter, Vincenzo Miola. The two had come to his house, he complained, and had abused and attacked him, Properzia scratching his face. *One of the witnesses against the accused was Amico Aspertini.*

After this show of weapons and flourish of trumpets the plaintiff doubtless accepted some small compensation for the injuries to his visage and his sensibilities. There is at least no further record of proceedings. But what a pleasing side-light is thrown on the manners and customs of sixteenth-century Bohemia! And how familiar is the scene which it illumines! The angry voices and excited gestures, the torrent of select insults, the clenched fists, the feline fury of the woman; the threat "to make a process"; the initial steps towards the realization of that·threat, shortly succeeded by conviction that money will be saved by mutual capitulation; then the dismounting of both parties from their high horses, followed by prolonged bargaining, the balance being held by some wily *avvocato;* lastly, the handshaking, smiles, bows, and *complimenti, servo suo* and *riverisco* and *di nuovo* of polite leave-taking—most dwellers in Italy have witnessed repetitions of this little bit of low comedy.

But one would fain know what was the subject of this quarrel between Properzia and Miola, whether the latter was Master Amico's tool and accomplice, and whether Domenico Francia was the disinterested champion of so fair and persecuted a fellow-artist. One is tempted to hope that the ugly and malicious Amico came in for a share of Properzia's summary revenge, since from all accounts the words of Shakespeare's Beatrice might have been applied to him: " Scratching could not make it worse an' 'twere such a face as yours."

This ill-conditioned fellow had doubtless no grudge against Properzia beyond the fact that she was an artist of rare talent. To suppose that he disapproved of female competition and was indignant that a woman should have a share in the work going forward on the west front of S. Petronio is to endow the sixteenth century with one of the most curious and ugly features of recent times. For "the notion of rivalry between the sexes" is, as Bishop Creighton has pointed out,[1] as foreign to the Italian Renaissance as that of "rivalry between classes in the State. All were at liberty to do their best." Only here and there a dog in the manger like Master Amico snarled sullenly at superiority of any kind,—"never," says Vasari, "speaking well of any one, however distinguished by excellence and ability, or however well endowed whether by virtue or the gift of fortune." This lack of magnanimity accompanied by various eccentricities made him an object of general ridicule and dislike. He was an industrious and facile worker, had travelled much and made an immense number of copies and models. These, however, he always destroyed in order that no other artist might benefit by them. As an assistance to rapid execution he was wont to gird himself with a leather belt hung round with little paint pots and bottles. Then he would sit down, his great spectacles on his nose, and begin to paint with both hands at once, chatting all the while like a parrot—"a figure," says Vasari, "to make stones laugh." One is not surprised to learn that in advanced age he became quite insane.

Properzia was doubtless in no mood to humour or propitiate this incipient madman. Stings and pricks ignored in days of happiness are felt acutely when the heart is sore. A profession may often be an excellent

[1] "A Learned Lady," in *Historical Essays and Reviews*.

substitute for a husband, and may become an idol on whose shrine all the affections of a life are laid. In nine cases out of ten, moreover, the "labour we delight in" does "physic pain"; but in the tenth case there may be no reserve of physical energy necessary for reorientation. Sorrow and disappointment may beget, and in turn be nourished by, bodily disease; and that useful remedy, change of air and scene, so readily prescribed and taken in our own day, was not available to a woman of Properzia's class and time. One move, however, she at length made, exchanging the house and garden in the Via S. Lorenzo for a dwelling in a very central situation. The beginning of the year 1530 found her lying sick in the Spedale della Morte.

This admirable institution owed its name of ill-omen to the origin of the society from whose work it sprang. The Confraternity of Death represented the efforts of certain devout persons to meet for the love of God some obvious needs of their fellow-men. In days when street frays and nocturnal assassinations, conspiracies and their discovery, were common occurrences, these persons dedicated a portion of their wealth and time to attendance on condemned criminals,[1] the nursing of the injured, and the burial of the dead. The work steadily expanded, changing its character with the varying requirements of successive generations; till by the sixteenth century the nursing of the sick had become the *raison d'être* of the society, their hospital a school of medicine, and their premises a large block of buildings lying between the Via Clavatura and the Archiginnasio,

---

[1] See Appendix to this part of the work.

with an entrance on the great Piazza.[1] The members of the Confraternity no longer gave personal service in the wards. A Rector, a Prior, and Administrators appointed a Warden who was responsible for the internal administration. There was an established hierarchy of male and female nurses, a chaplain, visiting physicians, house surgeons, students, and an apothecary —in fact, in embryo, all the paraphernalia of the modern hospital system.

But neither here, nor in any other hospital until very recent times, were there rooms for paying patients possessing relatives and means, who could well be nursed at home if sickness were not such an inconvenient interruption of the household's money-getting, pleasure-seeking routine. Properzia's presence in the Ospedale della Morte indicates one of two things—poverty or absolute friendlessness.

As she lay in the women's ward sick unto death, the sound of many voices and of many feet must have reached her from the Great Piazza near at hand.[2] All her old associates were active and bustling. Master Amico was erecting an immense triumphal arch in the Piazza. Other artists were decorating a temporary wooden bridge which should unite the Sala degli Anziani and the great west door of S. Petronio; and

---

[1] The Farmacia and the Portico della Morte still mark the site of the old Spedale, which was the city hospital till the year 1801. Then a new building rose on the banks of the Reno, and its revenues were mingled with those of the Confraternity, whose oratory in the Via Clavatura is now the office of the administration of the hospital and also its "Archivio."

[2] We have the most detailed information as to the occurrences and ceremonial of these days from Giovio and from the Bolognese Cardinal, Ugo Buoncompagni, afterwards Pope Gregory XIII.

THE MEETING OF THE EMPEROR CHARLES V WITH
POPE CLEMENT VII IN BOLOGNA, 1529

DETAIL OF A PICTURE BY MARCO VECELLIO IN THE HALL OF THE
COUNCIL OF TEN, DUCAL PALACE, VENICE

the administrators of the building were arranging and adorning the vast church against the day when Charles V should receive at the hands of the Pontiff, whom three years earlier he had humbled to the dust, the crown and sceptre which twenty-six years later he voluntarily laid down.

For days the narrow, roughly-paved, arcaded streets must have echoed to the roll of lumbering coaches and the tramp of horses' feet as the imperial troops marched into the city, and the representatives of foreign powers and the rulers of Italian States arrived to honour or propitiate the spiritual and temporal potentates who had been in Bologna since the previous October.

Did Properzia realize the meaning of these sounds, and ask her nurses and physicians for news of what was passing in the world without? Or did the tumult merely strike upon her fevered brain with a vague sense of unintelligible suffering? Was the sleep which comes with the dawn after a restless night disturbed at daybreak on the Feast of S. Matthias (24 February) by the clang of bells from every church tower in Bologna? Or was her hold on life so far relaxed that all the voices of this world seemed blurred and dulled as echoes from a distant shore?

Vasari, though he was a unit in the crowd which employment, or hope of it, brought to Bologna at this time, tells us few out of the many things we would fain know concerning the last days of this unhappy, highly gifted woman. But this he does relate :—

The business of the great day was over. For the first time a king of the Romans had been crowned with the imperial diadem outside the walls of Rome; for the last

186 THE WOMEN ARTISTS OF BOLOGNA

time in history the medieval Empire had received the papal benediction. Clement VII must have retired to his apartments well pleased with the result of negotiations which had secured the supremacy of Spain and the Papacy in Italy, and made its smaller states his vassals. But true, though base-born,[1] Medici that he was, he did not dwell on matters of statecraft, but prepared to recreate himself with thoughts of art. He had heard much, he said (perhaps from Marc Antonio in Rome), of one Properzia di Rossi, a sculptress. He would like to have converse with her. Could she be summoned and presented to him?

Inquiries were made, but the reply was unfavourable. It was most unfortunate, but His Holiness was just too late. Another Potentate, mightier than Pope or Emperor, had forestalled him. Properzia had died[2] that morning in the Ospedale della Morte.

---

[1] Clement VII was the illegitimate son of Lorenzo's brother Giuliano, assassinated by the Pazzi.

[2] There is some uncertainty as to her place of burial. Vasari says that by her own request she was buried in the Spedale della Morte. By this he must mean one of the hospital cemeteries, or the Confraternity church of S. Maria della Vita in the Via Clavatura. He tells us that her fellow-citizens, who had never been slow to recognize her merit, mourned her greatly.

AUTHORITIES

The main authority for the life of Properzia de' Rossi is

Vasari. Vol. V (Firenze, 1878).

All other sketches and notices in the biographies of artists or hand-books of art are repetitions of Vasari's facts.

Fresh discoveries from contemporary legal documents have, however, been made and published by

Gualandi, *Memorie intorno a Properzia de' Rossi*, Osservatore Bolognese, Numeri 33, 34, 35 (1851), and *Memorie delle Belle Arti*, Serie V; and something has been drawn from the rolls of the Fabbrica by

Davia, *Sculture delle Porte di S. Petronio*.

Nothing really new is contributed by

Saffi, *Discorso intorno a Properzia de' Rossi* (1832); or by

Carolina Bonafede, *Cenni Biografici e Ritratti d' Insigni Donne Bolognese* (1845).

For engravings of her work, see

Cicognara, *Storia della Scultura*, I, II.

Bianconi and Canuti, *Descrizione di alcuni minutissimi intagli di mano di Properzia de' Rosse* (1829).

APPENDIX

THE "COMFORTING" OF CRIMINALS

On the day of execution the members of the Confraternity of Death accompanied the criminal to the west door of S. Petronio, where he heard mass. Then the procession walked round the Piazza and proceeded eastwards, in the direction of the modern railway station, to the market-place (now Piazza dell' otto Agosto), where they had built a little church "dedicated to the decapitation of S. John Baptist." In this church the condemned man heard mass for the second time. He was then conducted to the Monte del Mercato (now Montagnola), the place of execution. When he laid his head upon the block, the member of the Confraternity whose office was that of "Confortatore" held before his eyes a little picture (*tavoletta*) which might bring some images of hope before the mind of him who was about to be sent so rudely from this world; and the "Comforter" was instructed not to withdraw the *tavoletta* till the blow fell, "so that he who must die need not perceive its withdrawal." If the criminal were hanged, not beheaded, the "Comforter" was bidden to mount the steps of the gallows and hold the *tavoletta* before his eyes till the moment he was pushed off, and then to cry to him to think upon Christ's passion and call upon the Mother of Sorrows. The night after the execution some of the brethren came and removed the corpse for burial. This pity and consideration for condemned criminals shines brightly in a world of barbarous punishments and furious retaliations.

In 1351 the Confortatori were given by the Pope the privilege of releasing on the day of San Rocco one prisoner under sentence of death.

The statutes and regulations of the hospital, which became in later times the chief work of the Confraternity, are very interesting reading. Some of these regulations, notably those dealing with visiting hours and food introduced by patients' relatives, have a curiously modern sound; but the spirit of religious tenderness and of minute care for economy, which is noticeable in all of them, cannot be said to have many modern parallels. The life, conduct, outgoings and incomings of the medical students, who were not taken under the age of fourteen, were regulated with great exactness, as were their relations to physicians and patients. One curious rule declares that the gratuities given to their instructors were the perquisite of the first surgeon, who was however obliged on the Feasts of Christmas and Easter to make a gift of eatables to the second surgeon. The students, if Bolognese, were allowed only a fortnight's holiday in the year, if *forestiere*, one month.

The hospital was pre-eminently for accident and emergency cases: the administration was forbidden to refuse any accident case, and to keep two or three beds always vacant and ready. Infectious and incurable diseases were refused, and it is noteworthy that phthisis was placed in the former category.— *Regole e Capitoli da osservari da i ministri e serventi dell' Ospitale di Santa Maria della Morte.* Bologna. Per Gaspara de Franceschi.

PORTRAIT OF LAVINIA FONTANA, PAINTED BY HERSELF
UFFIZI GALLERY, FLORENCE

CHAPTER I

LAVINIA FONTANA

> This is her picture as she was:
> It seems a thing to wonder on,
> As though mine image in the glass
> Should tarry when myself am gone.
> I gaze until she seems to stir,—
>
> .   .   .   .
> .   .   .   .
>
> And yet the earth is over her.
> D. G. ROSSETTI, *The Portrait.*

IN the first of the four rooms in the Uffizi Gallery which are devoted to the portraits of artists painted by themselves, there hangs, "skyed," and in a bad light, the picture of a figure in rich severe dress, with a round white ruff, and dark smooth hair melting into a dark background, whose sex can hardly be determined without reference to the catalogue. And if a bright light or Brogi's excellent photograph enables us to examine this picture more minutely, we shall see that not the accessories alone, but also the countenance has a curiously hermaphrodite character. The upper half of the face—the straight, rather thick nose, the strongly marked eyebrows, the high cheek-bones—is distinctly man-like. The lower half—the large flexible mouth, the plump chin, the rounded jaw—is altogether feminine. Eyes and mouth both smile; but the smiles have different meanings. The eyes are shrewd, intelligent, humorous, critical. The mouth droops with a gentle compliancy.

Yet in spite of its complexity, the face is reassuring. It at least does not suggest any baffling gulf between the artist and her work. It harmonizes with the little that we know of Lavinia Fontana's life, and with all that her painting reveals of her personality. It is the face of a woman one could do business with, capable of looking after her own interests, but incapable of heartless dealing. It is the face of a woman who smiles at, but also with, the world; who is never blind to the failings of her friends, but who regards them with kindly tolerance. It is the face of a woman with a refined, but not a sensitive, nature; who cherishes few ideals in respect to either art or life, but in both has a keen eye for values. It is the face of a woman who has reached "the middle of the pathway of our life," who is well content with her journey, and who has travelled the easier for being unweighted with the impedimenta of good looks. Lavinia Fontana, if not positively plain, had none of Properzia's classical beauty nor Elisabetta Sirani's pretty grace. She was neither capable of inspiring nor of feeling a great passion; but she attracted many suitors and married a good husband. She alone of the four artists whose lives are here recorded experienced all the phases of a normal woman's life, and enjoyed an existence of commonplace happiness.

The happiness was, of course, not unclouded. Her middle life must have been shadowed by the financial difficulties of her father's old age; and we know that her husband was stupid, that her only son was positively wanting, and that her elder daughter became blind through an accident in childhood. But her male relatives, if foolish, were fond; and against maternal anxieties she could set the advantage of a cheerful temper, the inalienable possession of a happy youth, and the boon of professional occupation.

All three gifts she owed to her father, Prospero, a genial good-hearted man, and a singularly successful, though really mediocre, painter. His master was Innocenzo da Imola, whose virtues he caught and retained, but whose defects he exaggerated. Leaving him while still a mere youth, Prospero proceeded to Rome with an introduction to Michael Angelo, who received him kindly and presented him to the Pope. From this time onward he continuously enjoyed papal favour, and from Julius III he received a pension of three hundred scudi a year.[1]

When barely forty, he returned to his native city, married, and settled down to a life of ease and comfort. He was an intelligent man, with great social talents. He had travelled with observation, had acquired a smattering of classical learning and antiquarian knowledge, and possessed a showy acquaintance with what Oretti terms " the fables of sacred and profane history." He was moreover an excellent cicerone, knowing *au fond* the story and the treasures of his native

---

[1] Oretti, *Pittori*, t. II, Gozzadini MS. (122), says that Prospero was "provisionato" and made Pittore Palatino by this Pope. There is mention too of another pension of five scudi a month for the maintenance of his family.

city. Best of all he had the faculty—which he transmitted to his daughter—of making many friends and few enemies, and of enjoying prosperity without exciting envy. Such a faculty implies not only personal charm —though that too must be present—but also a nice blending of qualities and a rare balance of character and manner. Consciousness of merit must be shown without arrogance, generosity without patronage. A tact-producing sensitiveness to the opinion and susceptibilities of others must co-exist with a skin too thick to feel gnat-stings, and a nervous system too healthy to quiver under imaginary wrongs.

Little by little the Fontana dwelling became the rendezvous not only of artists, but also of men of letters and dilettanti of all kinds ; and of this circle the master of the house was not only the centre, but also " the oracle and judge," so that, according to Malvasia," " it was held sacrilegious to disobey his counsels or dissent or appeal from them." His repeated election as *Massero* or Steward of the Artists' Guild was but the outward and visible sign of the position tacitly accorded to him.

Now it happened that when Prospero had been settled for some nine or ten years in Bologna, the progress of the great public works brought together within its walls a rare company of foreign architects [1] and artists, with a crowd of lesser craftsmen of skill and talent.

Bologna was rich with the prosperity of fifty peaceful years of stable government. The papal rule, which

---

[1] By which I mean "forestieri" from other Italian cities.

began in 1506 and lasted till the French Revolution, suited her well. It preserved her from internecine strife and Milanese rapacity; while allegiance to a distant power was always more congenial to her temper than submission to a native despot. Even a republic must have a visible and ornamental head, and she was always well content to receive and do honour to a Legate who "reigned but did not govern." In the year 1560, the man who filled this office was the Pope's sister's son, the young and saintly Carlo Borromeo; and in Bologna, as elsewhere, his energies were chiefly directed to two objects—the reformation of ecclesiastical abuses and the amelioration of the condition of the poor. A year of terrible dearth was occasioning great distress among the people;—but the city treasury was full. San Carlo accordingly determined to provide bread for the starving by carrying into effect his uncle's cherished scheme of providing the scattered "Scuole" of Bologna with a single worthy habitation. Thus, in the year 1561, the first and nobler [1] home of the University of Bologna was begun as a relief-work.

It was finished in a single year, and must have furnished a livelihood to a multitude of unemployed. It was faced by the fine colonnade which is to-day the Bond Street of Bologna—the Pavaglione; while the following year (1563) a block of old houses on the north side of S. Petronio was demolished to form the open space, now named after the ugly statue of Galvani in its midst, but originally known as the Piazza

[1] In 1803 the University was united to the Istituto delle Scienze and transferred to the Palazzo Poggi in the Via Zamboni. The beautiful Archiginnasio is now occupied by the Communal Library.

dell' Accademia. Borromeo's architect was Francesco Terribilia, who had just completed the adjoining Portico della Morte.

On the other side of this portico another work was proceeding. The northern side of the Piazza Maggiore (now the inevitable Vittorio Emanuele) was assuming its present dignified aspect under the direction of Jacopo Barozzi da Vignola. With a minimum of destruction, and much skilful uniting and reconstructing of existing houses—traces of which appear in the unequal windows—Vignola created an imposing block of buildings faced with the fine Portico dei Banchi.[1]

Again, on the opposite side of the great piazza a third work was in progress, so that all the centre of the city, between the years 1560 and 1563, must have rung with the sound of axes and hammers. The Piazza del Nettuno, with its great fountain, which seems to the modern Bolognese almost as characteristic a feature of their city as the two towers, was now coming into being. An island of mean houses was demolished, and the work of construction was then entrusted to a Sicilian artist, Tomaso Laureti. The Sicilian divided the lower part of the fountain among three young sculptors, and entrusted its canalization[2] to an architect named Grisante; but for an artist worthy to execute the colossus which was to surmount it, he journeyed across the Apennines to Florence to bring back with him that John of Douay

---

[1] This portico meeting the Portico della Morte, which again joins the Pavaglione, forms an unbroken colonnade from the Via Farina to the Via Orefici.

[2] Water was brought from a spring found to the south-west of the city. Now the water is from the aqueduct of the Setta.

who ever after the completion of his *chef d'œuvre* was known as Giam Bologna.[1]

The progress of great public works such as these must have occasioned a perfect ferment of expectation and discussion among the art-loving inhabitants of an Italian sixteenth-century city. The reunions in the house of Prospero Fontana must have been unusually animated and interesting; and his little daughter Lavinia, watching the strangers passing up her father's stairs and sipping wine round his table, listening to the criticism of little groups and to the general chorus of mutual admiration, hearing each difficulty surmounted described as a famous victory, and completion celebrated as an event of world-wide importance, must have become acquainted early with the charms and failings, the naïve egotism, the ever-youthful enthusiasm of the artistic temperament, and have accumulated between her ninth and eleventh years a series of indelible and educative impressions.

Her father's hospitality was becoming more and more lavish, and doubtless many a needy artist preyed on his good-nature. " Visse alla grande e trattosi bene "—he lived like a lord and did himself well—is Oretti's comprehensive description of Prospero's housekeeping. He enjoyed entertaining his friends handsomely, and he liked now and then to give away a picture and make a present of a portrait. Such acts of lavishness and display were but the natural expressions of a careless

[1] Two arches of the partially-finished portico of the Pavaglione were walled up to form Giam Bologna's workshop. There, aided by a skilful modeller and caster named Zanobi Portigiani, he worked at the great Neptune with his attendant sirens, water-babies, and dolphins.

generosity of temperament, which in art revealed itself in copiousness of invention, slovenliness of treatment, an almost Venetian opulence of colour, and extraordinary rapidity of execution. It is said that he painted *in eighteen days* that chapel in the Palazzo Pubblico where Charles V had received the iron crown of Lombardy prior to his coronation; and this, and similar *tours de force*, won for him a cheap popularity which continually spurred him to greater speed of production. His facility, a proof of indolence rather than of activity, grew like an insidious malady consuming his power of taking pains, and thus exposing him in advanced life to the attacks of the laborious eclectic school.

Already in his studio Prospero was hatching the serpents who would later sting him to death. His pupils[1] were at one time numerous, and many of them afterwards became famous—in spite, as they averred, rather than through the aid of their master. And indeed a man of Prospero's temperament is necessarily an indifferent teacher. The possessor of great natural quickness and acquired facility is apt to be intolerant of a beginner's maladroitness; and he whose stock of patience does not suffice for the perfecting of his own work has little to spare for the blundering efforts of a conscientious learner.

Such a learner was Lodovico Carracci; and one day his master intimated to him that he had mistaken his vocation, and that Nature had not intended him to be a painter. Carracci, whose mind and hand worked slowly, and whose capacity for painstaking labour was as great

---

[1] Among them were Lodovico and Agostino Carracci, Calvart, "Il Fiamingo," and Tiarini.

as that of his master was small, went away sorrowful, but not despairing. He betook himself to Venice to see Titian, and copied with untiring diligence the work of the Venetian school. Subsequent visits to Parma and to Florence completed his artistic education. He returned to Bologna the complete eclectic, and at once took a position which mortified and amazed his sometime teacher. Prospero perhaps saw no reason to reverse his original judgment, but he recognized that the despised disciple had become, *à force de travail*, an accomplished master, and that he who in derision of his slowness used to be called the Ox (Il Bue) had managed to leave behind all his swifter contemporaries.

Soon odious comparisons were instituted between Prospero Fontana and his successful pupil. Seeds of sedition were sown among his students, which, after a period of fermenting discontent, ripened to revolt. Prospero's studio was emptied, and the new school of Carracci was proclaimed the Only Way.

To one of Prospero's pupils both rebellion and a change of masters was denied. Lavinia Fontana—as, later, Elisabetta Sirani—had the advantages and disadvantages of being a painter's daughter. On the whole the advantages preponderated. But for the relationship it is improbable that Lavinia would have received any art education at all. The maidens of her day were, as a rule, intended and trained for only one profession—that of matrimony; and the *convenances*, and social and economic conditions of the time conspired to prevent them from dabbling in any other. The guild spirit and regulations, with which the arts and crafts were hedged, excluded even the most earnest amateur, and the non-existence of the artist's colourman prevented the emergence of the people who "paint a little." When a boy first entered a studio he had to learn how to prepare canvases, grind and compound colours, and mix varnishes. Every school of painting had its cherished recipes,[1] and the painter's technical knowledge, like that of every other craft, was transmitted to the apprentice for a consideration, and to the son as an heirloom.

Thus Lavinia Fontana had reason to be grateful for the state of life to which she was called—a state which enabled her to exercise an art or "mystery," and incidentally gave her a liberal education. For it was necessary for her equipment as a painter that Prospero should impart to her some of his knowledge of "the fables of sacred and profane history," while her duty as his daughter entailed that association with educated men which is the best possible stimulus and complement to book-learning. To enjoy the conversation of her father's friends, to help in the material preparations for their entertainment, and to have in the background, correcting dissipation of energy and tendencies to frivolity, the steady, daily routine of studio work—this surely is a training of intelligence and character equal to any devised by educational theorists and carried out in modern schools and colleges.

Lavinia probably resembled her father too much to excite the irritation which pupils of the tortoise type

---

[1] We all know the story of how Baccio Bandinelli went to Andrea del Sarto ostensibly to have his portrait taken, really to discover his secrets, and how the faultless painter found means to reveal nothing but the intentions of the sitter.

roused in him. She managed to assimilate the good and reject the evil of his teaching. She avoided the failings which sprang from his impatient haste; she reproduced his sombre sumptuousness of colour, and she added to it a power of seizing and conveying individual expression which was never his.

No record of work accomplished, like the catalogue kept by Elisabetta Sirani, helps us to assign Lavinia's paintings to their proper dates, and to trace the development of her talent. We know only that it was her faculty of "catching a likeness" and for making her portraits both truthful and pleasing, which first won her a reputation. The days had gone by when the harmless desire "to have one's picture taken" had to be concealed beneath the cloak of religious fervour, and men and women wishing to transmit their features to posterity had to stand aside as supporters to a central Madonna, or to kneel in humble adoration before the Divine Child. Oretti tells us that the smart ladies of Bologna found Lavinia's colouring so pretty, and her representation of their finery so satisfactory, that "they all wanted her to paint them, and made a pet of her." They began, too, to give her large prices. Baglioni asserts that before long she could command as much as Vandyke.

In 1572 an event occurred which altered the current of her life while facilitating her successes. Pius V died, and was succeeded on the papal throne by that Cardinal who had so graphically described the coronation of the Emperor Charles—the Bolognese, Ugo Buoncompagni. His pedigree, on both sides, was interesting and unexceptional. His mother was of the Mareschalchi; his father's ancestors were famous in the annals of the University.[1] Following the family traditions he studied law, took his doctor's degree, and acquired a reputation as a teacher. Three cardinals to be—Carlo Borromeo, Alexander Farnese, and Cristoforo Maduzzi—were among his pupils.

By lawyers Gregory XIII will always be honoured for his collection of legal treatises, *Dei Trattati Magni*.

Englishmen know him as the inspirer of fresh sedition and favourer of the Armada.

French protestants execrate his memory for his rejoicings at the Massacre of St. Bartholomew.

Italians generally respect him as the untiring promoter of education, the founder of many schools and colleges, notably the Jesuit colleges in Rome, Vienna, and Gratz, and the school for Greeks in Venice.

The Japanese perhaps remember him as the kindly host of the first Japanese[2] ambassadors ever sent to Europe.

All Europe—save the great tract of Russia—is grateful to him for his reformed Calendar.

But to the Bolognese this man of many parts and aspects was and is first and foremost a Bolognese. Every pope might be expected to leave in his birthplace some memorial of himself and his pontificate, and to bestow preferment when possible on its inhabitants. But when his own city was also one of his temporal possessions, his love for it could find yet more substan-

---

[1] A Buoncompagni was a very famous teacher of rhetoric in the first half of the thirteenth century.

[2] They took three years to come from their own country to Rome.

tial expression. The day after his election, Gregory XIII addressed a letter to the Senate assuring the people of Bologna of his special favour and protection. And these promises he fulfilled. He converted the bishopric into the see of a metropolitan, originated some beneficial changes in the government, liberally dispensed those cheap ecclesiastical alms—indulgences, and in spite of his immense need and expenditure of money always dealt leniently with Bologna in matters of taxation. The great bronze statue [1] placed in his lifetime above the portal of the Palazzo Pubblico is the enduring token of the gratitude of the Bolognese to their fellow-citizen, Ugo Buoncompagni.

Gregory XIII had none of the innate love of art, the real *flair* of the Medici popes; but he could appreciate merit when it was pointed out to him, and was particularly disposed to see it in a Bolognese. Prospero Fontana, moreover, had enjoyed the favour of three of his predecessors, and papal protection seemed almost to be his daughter's natural heritage.

We now hear of journeys made by Lavinia for the exercise of her profession to the country houses of the Buoncompagni and their friends, of the approaches to Sora and Vignola being lined with men-at-arms, of speeches and receptions, and other extraordinary marks of honour shown to the gifted and charming young woman, who was too modest and level-headed to be spoiled then, or afterwards, by the favour of the great.

[1] The statue was designed by Menganti and cast by Anchise Censori in 1580. In 1797 it was saved from destruction by a curious subterfuge. The triple crown was removed and a mitre was substituted for it, the statue being rechristened by the name of Bologna's patron, S. Petronio.

And then, as the climax of this growing reputation, came the papal invitation, amounting to a command, to go to Rome.

Lavinia had already sent thither a specimen of her powers,—a picture ordered by Cardinal Ascoli for S. Sabina on the Aventine. A little later she was commissioned to paint a picture for S. Paolo fuori le Mura on the "Stoning of S. Stephen." The subject and the size of the picture were chosen for her, and on this account it was something of a failure. She was not accustomed to draw figures larger than life-size, and was incapable of representing vigorous action and muscular play and development. The study of anatomy and hard drawing from the nude had been neglected. Here it was that Prospero's training had been fatally deficient.

But as a portrait painter her fame deservedly increased. Her doors were besieged by fair ladies and fine gentlemen, and the number of her commissions was always in excess of the time at her disposal. In Rome, too, as formerly in Bologna, her sitters were not only delighted with her work but fascinated by her personality. All doors were open to her; she was received with marked favour in every society. More than this, she had numerous offers of marriage from men whose station in life was far more exalted than her own.

But Lavinia Fontana was not to be diverted from the narrow way of Art. She foresaw clearly that marriage with a man of wealth and birth would mean the termination of her professional career; that she would inevitably become absorbed in his pursuits and his advancement; that the claims of his position would grow ever more insistent and those of her work would take a secondary place; that little by little her social slavery would be complete. She had found another scheme of life and she adhered to it. The most desirable matches—"i più belli partiti"—were refused, and the young painter would say with a laugh she "would never take a husband unless he were willing to leave her the mistress of her first-beloved Art." Probably she already knew well that such a husband was ready to offer himself whenever she chose to whistle for him.

Her union with the son of a wealthy grain-merchant of Imola exactly answered her requirements. It was not the outcome of youthful passion, still less was it the ideal "marriage of true minds." But it gave her the protection indispensable for her good name, and left her free to follow her true calling. The young man, while content to take a secondary place in her life and affections, seems to have regarded her with a kind of dog-like fidelity; while on her side there was perhaps that maternal interest and pity, which with many women is Love's proxy rather than his kinsman.

The intimacy between the Fontana and De Zappis families began in a manner predictive of Lavinia's future attitude. Her father-in-law to be was one of Prospero's numerous acquaintances, and was probably accustomed to enjoy the artist's boundless hospitality when his business brought him in from Imola. One day he had a favour to ask Lavinia. A little difficulty had arisen concerning the export of grain. A petition to head-quarters, a word of explanation would set things right. Every one said that the Legate refused Lavinia nothing. Would she befriend him?

The popular young woman did as she was asked. The grain-merchant was satisfied and grateful; and Lavinia began to feel interested in the family she had placed under an obligation. A stupid young son fancied he had a taste for art, and craved permission to enter Prospero's studio. He was found to be lacking, not only in genius, but also in ordinary capacity. But Lavinia probably perceived at this time both his incipient admiration and the solid moral qualities underlying the dull exterior. He had learnt, at least, to talk the painter's jargon, to understand the technicalities of art, to realize its difficulties, to value its triumphs. Lavinia by and by found in the younger Zappis a very appreciative and useful helpmeet; and now and then she allowed him to put in a background or help her with a bit of draping—though she never permitted him to touch the more important portions of her pictures.

Three children, two daughters and a son, were born of this curious but peaceful union. None of them perpetuated the gifts of their mother and maternal grandfather, while the son unfortunately inherited in a cumulative degree the simplicity of his father.[1] Gregory XIII gave him a nominal position in his household and attached to it a pension sufficient to relieve his mother from all anxiety for the material future of her "idiot boy." He passed his time chiefly in the corridors and ante-rooms of the Papal Court, where he was treated with kindly tolerance as a harmless buffoon.

Though Lavinia's married home was in Rome, it is

[1] "Confessavasi aver tratto egli quella simplicità dalla parte del Padre," says Malvasia.

THE GOZZADINI FAMILY
GOZZADINI PALACE, VIA SANTO STEFANO, BOLOGNA

clear from the dates of two of her best pictures, the Gozzadini family group (1584) and the Madonna with portrait of the donor, of S. Giacomo Maggiore (1589), that she paid at least two visits to her native city. Probably her father's declining strength and financial difficulties called for her presence. For Prospero, after the fashion of Bohemia, had, in the days of his prosperity, more than lived up to his income. In spite of constant employment and papal pensions he had saved nothing against the inevitable day when the hand loses its cunning and those which look out of the windows are darkened. He had once been "the fashion," but the public taste had changed. The Eclectics held the field.

A letter has been preserved by Malvasia which pathetically illustrates the reversed positions of the Carracci and their sometime master. It is written by one Pompeo Vizzani in Bologna to Monsignore Ratta in Rome, who wished to present a picture to a church in the former city :—

"As to the picture, I have spoken to the Carracci and got others to speak to them, and they were willing to undertake it; but when it came to speaking about the price, their decision did not please me; for they said they wanted *two hundred scudi*, which seems to me a very big price, since till now they have always done their pictures for sixty or seventy; but now they begin to trade upon their name. I have heard though that it is their way to take much less than they ask at first, and that they are apt to have their work on hand a long time before finishing it.

"I have talked to M. Prospero, who said a great deal

P

about wishing to serve you. He would not be explicit about price "—(how characteristic is this passage of Italians in general, of Prospero in particular)—" but he said that to other people he should ask one hundred scudi, but from you he would be content with whatever you chose to give, and that he would get it finished by the end of April, and would do it with his own hand ; there was no question of Madonna Lavinia."

The letter is dated December, 1593. Lavinia was certainly in Bologna at that time, working on the Gozzadini portraits, hence Vizzani's assertion that Prospero, not his daughter, could paint the picture required by Monsignore Ratta. The remark possibly indicates that, portraiture apart, the work of the father was still preferred by his contemporaries. Prospero, when he so eagerly bid for this commission, was eighty-two. He hungered not for bread alone, but for the incense of admiration which had once filled his atmosphere. To the end he could not realize that the old order had changed, and that he must give place to a younger generation.

He lived to be eighty-five, passing hence in the year 1597. His life and that of his daughter together fill exactly a century (1512–1612).

Neither the death of her father nor that of her munificent patron, Gregory XIII, which took place in 1585, materially affected the even tenor of Lavinia's prosperous life, about which little is recorded, precisely because it was of the happy, tranquil type which has no history. We know, however, that during her long residence in the Eternal City, which was her *pays d'adoption*, she must have seen extraordinary changes alike in its outward aspect and in its social conditions.

" I am in Rome after an absence of ten years," wrote Don Angelo Grillo at this period, "and I hardly recognize it, so new does everything seem,—monuments, streets, piazzas, fountains, aqueducts, obelisks, and other marvels, all the work of Sixtus V."

The best remembered of these public works was the completion in twenty-two months of the dome of St. Peter's, and the erection in the great square in front of it of the obelisk which had once stood in Caligula's circus. The latter achievement was accomplished by a young architect named Domenico Fontana, a fellow-countryman and probably a relation of Lavinia. But the really stupendous marvel, and one which intimately affected the life and comfort of every man and woman in the city, was the breaking up of the alliance between the nobles and the *bravi*, and the expulsion of the latter from the papal states.

The story that Felix Peretti entered the conclave a bent, infirm man on crutches, and that immediately after his election he stood straight and erect, and informed his terrified electors that he meant to be implicitly obeyed, is one of those fictions which are truer than accurate statements of fact. The Pope, whom our English Queen Elizabeth, in admiration of a spirit as determined as her own, declared to be the only man in Europe worthy to be her husband, lost no time in showing that he meant to be master in his own city. A few hours after his election, an infringement of the law against carrying arms was punished with immediate death. Soon the wits of Rome had reason to compose a dialogue between the statues of S. Peter and S. Paul on the bridge of S. Angelo,[1] in which the former is made to explain that he is preparing to leave Rome, fearing to be punished for the cutting off of Malchus' ear. Within a year of his election, life and property were tolerably secure in Rome.

After the death of Sixtus V, Lavinia saw the brief reigns of eight popes. One of these, Innocent IX, was a Bolognese, though as his pontificate lasted but two months, he can hardly have had time to benefit his countrywoman. But in fact Lavinia no longer stood in need of patronage. Popes might come and popes might go; the eclectics might create a new mode in art; young Guido Reni might visit Rome; and still the current of the portrait painter's prosperity flowed evenly along. Her talent was at once too limited, and too unique and individual to be disturbed by the emergence of new ideals and methods. Her fame never grew less, and a few years before her death a medal was actually coined in her honour.

[1] The usual place of execution. There, in Lavinia's lifetime, the Cenci family were executed (1599). Readers of Browning's *Ring and the Book* will remember how the Pope changes the place of execution in order to make the punishment of Pompilia's murderers more public and impressive.

"The substituting, too, the People's Square
For the out-o'-the way old quarter by the Bridge."

This *cause célèbre* took place just a century after that of the Cenci.

CHAPTER II

LAVINIA FONTANA'S WORKS

THE best known, and perhaps the most characteristic, of Lavinia Fontana's larger paintings is the picture—No. 75 Sala C—in the Accademia of her native city.

It represents a noble lady with her four attendants kneeling at the feet of a tall friar, to whom they present for benediction a naked, smiling babe. The babe is the friar's godson, afterwards known to history as Francis I, King of France. The noble lady in whose arms, or rather in whose *hands*, he lies, is his mother, Louise de Savoie, Duchesse d'Angoulême. The friar is the Calabrian, Francesco di Paola,[1] founder of that reformed order of Franciscans known as Minimes—the least.

The miserable superstitious Louis XI, lying sick unto death at Plessis-le-Tours, heard of the miracles of healing wrought by the holy friar in far-off Southern Italy, and straightway sent for him, promising him great advantages for his order. But Francesco di Paola, like his namesake and exemplar, the " poverello " of Assisi, wanted nothing, and believing that his visit to France would not advance the spiritual welfare of the King, declined the invitation. His refusal added fuel to the

[1] Paola is a village on the road between Reggio and Naples.

fire of Louis' sick desire, and he besought Pope Sixtus IV to command Francesco to repair to Tours. The Pope obeyed the King, and the friar obeyed the Pope. When Francesco reached Plessis, Louis grovelled at his feet, beseeching him in a passion of hope and fear to obtain from heaven a prolongation of his days. The friar replied that life and death were in the hands of the Creator, and that perfect submission to His will was the duty of the creature. Little by little Francesco's words and personality calmed the wretched king; he succeeded in imbuing him with some of his own faith and courage; he soothed his dying moments, and administered the last sacraments.

Louis' successors, Charles VIII and Louis XII, would seldom permit Francesco to leave France; and by degrees the order took root there, and the name of *Bons-hommes*, originally given to the Minimi by derisive courtiers, was adopted and cherished by the French people. He exercised a great and salutary influence over Louise de Savoie, the wife of Charles of Orleans, and when in 1507 the friar died, lamented by all the court and household, she prepared with her own hands the winding-sheet for his burial. In 1519 he was canonized by Leo X; and when Lavinia was twelve years old, a burst of righteous indignation at the outrage of the Huguenots, who rifled his tomb and burned his remains, caused a great recrudescence in the new Saint's popularity.

Lavinia has represented him as a tall gaunt man, whose height is increased by the wearing of high clogs. He stands, holding in his left hand a pole as long as an alpenstock, with his right hand raised to bless his

THE INFANT FRANCIS I OF FRANCE PRESENTED BY HIS MOTHER
LOUISE DE SAVOIE FOR THE BLESSING OF S. FRANCESCO DI PAOLA
PINACOTECA, BOLOGNA. SALA DEL TIARINI

infant godson. The babe is being held by his mother in an uncomfortable and seemingly precarious position, but instead of weeping, wriggling, and slipping backwards, as we might have expected, he seems to stiffen his little spine into a sitting posture, while gazing with heavenly serenity into the friar's face.

His mother and three of her ladies are upon their knees: the fourth attendant stands behind them, her hands uplifted with a gesture of pious admiration. The Duchess wears a sleeveless tunic like an ephod, the hem of which is encrusted with jewelled embroidery. The four ladies are in the ordinary French costume of the period—tight-fitting, square-cut bodices, ruffs, puffed sleeves, and close-fitting little caps. Their faces, attitudes, and gestures are worthy of Lavinia's reputation as a portrait painter; and their adornments are painted with the peculiar skill which won her the patronage of all possessors of costly jewels. Each pearl and gem has its value, yet they are not painted in the niggling, microscopic manner of the miniaturist. The whole is never sacrificed to the parts; broad effects and masses are preserved in spite of elaboration of detail.

The pillow and cloth held by the lady immediately behind Louise de Savoie are very characteristic of Lavinia's manner of treating the minutiæ of feminine costume. Look carefully into the picture; place a photographic reproduction of it under a microscope. You will see that the insertion in the pillow-cover and the edging of the cloth are of the fine *reticella* embroidery which is the peculiar needle-craft of Bologna and the neighbourhood, recently revived under the name of *Æmilia Ars*. All this is clearly revealed by close examination; but this detail of ornamentation does not obtrude itself, and we might long be familiar with the picture without even noticing the pillow or its lace.

Behind the kneeling figures is a flight of stone steps down which come dancing two bare-legged damsels, affectedly holding up their skirts, apparently for the benefit of a group of men-at-arms who stand a little farther back in the hall, but not so far but that they seem to be relatively too small.

Above, badly shown in the photograph, is a musician's gallery, in which one can dimly discern some figures blowing long trumpets.

The background of the picture is rather confused and purposeless, but the composition as a whole is entirely pleasing, and the colouring, warm, rich, splendid yet sombre, is characteristic of both Lavinia and her father. The brown robe of the Franciscan tones with the dull red tiles of the hall, and these again with the red under-dress and golden tunic of the Duchess, whose costume supplies the strongest colour of the picture.

There are three other pictures by Lavinia Fontana in the Bologna Gallery. All are portraits. One, a man's head (Camera G, 523), is hardly larger than a cabinet photograph. The gentleman wears the black dress, the round white ruff, and little pointed beard which constituted the regular uniform of all her male sitters.

The second portrait (Corridor N. 2, 686) is of an unknown lady in a black velvet gown cut open at the throat to reveal a fine white chemisette embroidered with seed pearls and finished by the inevitable round white ruff. The face is three-quarters, the eyes full. The dark hair is drawn back from the intellectual brow. The lady is not of an Italian type; we might almost fancy her a modern Englishwoman masquerading in sixteenth-century costume. In the same room is another portrait, a little picture of a young girl.

The pictures of a painter whose contemporary fame exceeded her posthumous reputation, and whose *forte* was portraiture, must necessarily be sought for chiefly in the collections of private persons, or with dealers who have bought from these collections; and a steady search in Roman and Bolognese lumber-rooms and palazzi would doubtless bring to light many forgotten specimens of Lavinia's work. The subsequent division or disposal of collections, the extinction of families, and the transference of property have destroyed the practical value of Oretti's long list of the houses where in his day her pictures might be found, and it is interesting only as a proof of her industry and popularity.

There is, however, one picture which still hangs in the place where Oretti saw it, and for which it was painted —the large Gozzadini family group reproduced on the opposite page. A photograph, however, necessarily conveys a very unworthy idea of this picture. It emphasizes the limitations imposed on Lavinia by her subject and her sitters, and does not indicate how she triumphed over them. It presents us with a photographic group, two plain, self-conscious women and three commonplace men, who seem to have posed before a camera—five people who have put on their best clothes and are very anxious that these should "come out well." But it does not show the character and beauty of these garments, and the amazing quality and workmanship of the ornaments so lavishly displayed; still less does it convey the witchery of rich harmonious colour by means of which Lavinia converted what might have been a portrait group interesting only to the Gozzadini family into a really fine and exceedingly decorative work of art.

As an illustration of the dress and goldsmith's work of the period the picture has extraordinary and unique interest; and every student of the history of costume should take a little trouble to obtain access to the Gozzadini Palace, No. 58, Via San Stefano. Failing to do this, he should examine the coloured reproduction in Litta's *Famiglia Celebre Italiana*. Litta, bowing no doubt to the limitations of colour printing, omits Lavinia's charming background. The figures stand out against white paper, and a dignified picture appears as a banal fashion plate. As such, however, its value is considerable, particularly if it be studied together with a short paper describing it, published by the last direct representative of the great Gozzadini house, the learned Count Giovanni Gozzadini. (*Atti e Memorie della Reale Deputazione di Storia Patria per le Romagne*, Serie III. Vol. I.) In this paper extracts are given from a family book of accounts and memoranda which contains careful record of the purchase of some of the jewels depicted by Lavinia.

The order for the picture came from one of the two ladies who appear in it—she who caresses the little dog, a spaniel of the type we call after their fancier "King Charles." Both ladies were natural daughters, subsequently legitimated, of the elderly gentleman in the centre of the group, the Senator Ulisse Gozzadini, and both were married to brothers belonging to another branch of the same family, so that the name of Gozzadini is common to the entire group.

The picture is signed : " Lavinia Fontana De Zappis, fecit M.DLXXXIIII." But Ulisse Gozzadini died in 1561 (when the painter was only nine years old), and Ginevra—the plump lady on whose arm Ulisse lays an affectionate hand—in 1581. But in 1538 the Senator's portrait had been taken by Samachini, and Lavinia may well have worked from this. Ginevra she must have remembered, and may have sketched or painted previously. No imaginary portraits would have satisfied Madonna Laodamia, who wished to have a memorial of all her dear ones ; and the plump figure, described by Count Gozzadini as "tozza, rincignata, assai brutta " (ill-shaped, enceinte, and very ugly), is painted with almost brutal truthfulness to life.

Ginevra is arrayed in white brocade with an over-dress of marvellous black lace, and a girdle of wrought gold, jewels, and enamels. Behind her stands her husband, Annibale Gozzadini, as " peaky," cadaverous, and anxious as his wife is podgy and self-satisfied. He was forty-five when his portrait was taken.[1]

The central figure, Paterfamilias Ulysses, is seated behind the little table which separates his daughters. He is a grave dignified man with an intelligent anxious face, hardly looking the fifty-six years which he had when he died, and which Lavinia, working from the portrait taken when he was only thirty-three, doubtless

[1] He holds an open letter in his left band. The writer has not been able to discover whether this has any special significance.

found it difficult to realize. He wears the senatorial *zimarra* and round black cap. Both he and his two sons-in-law have little beards and moustaches clipped in the French mode.

Camillo, who stands behind his wife Laodamia, is a stouter, darker, more genial person than his brother, whose junior he was by six years, albeit he married the elder of the two sisters.

Laodamia is perhaps the most pleasing and certainly the most gorgeously arrayed of the five figures. Her face is that of an intelligent, cheery, but unimaginative and rather prim woman of thirty, though possibly the " prunes and prisms " expression is due to the self-consciousness of the amateur model. She wears a crimson robe and an over-dress of black lace. On her bosom gleam the double row of those oriental pearls, to the number of fifty-five, which Camillo Gozzadini notes, in the previously mentioned account-book, as purchased for " Madonna Lavinia mia sposa " for the sum of two hundred and fifty-six ducats. On the thumb of the right hand, laid on the lap-dog's head for the purpose of exhibiting its adornments, is one of the two diamond and ruby rings which cost her husband eighty ducats, the other gleams on the forefinger of the left hand ; while two of the four " pendenti da orecchii " of pearls and crystals, priced at eighteen ducats, hang from her ears, the other two perhaps appearing in those of Madonna Ginevra.

All five figures wear round pleated ruffs of fine cambric edged with lace.

The table separating the ladies and serving for the display of their hands is covered with a dull green cloth. The background, a warm brown in tone, is a room in the palace, with a vista through an open door of a second room, where a latticed window forms the vanishing point, and gives a sense of air and light.

Oretti speaks of "many pictures" in the Gozzadini Palace. The writer has only been able to discover one other. This is the head and shoulders portrait of an elderly lady with a fat, pleasant countenance. As is the case with all Lavinia's portraits, it is at the face that the beholder first gazes, and only when this has been examined does he look at the elaborate details of the dress. The dress in this case is black, but—again a characteristic of Lavinia—the *texture* is hardly indicated; we cannot tell whether the pleasant old dame is habited in cloth, silk, or velvet. She wears a peaked "Marie Stuart" cap, and a curious necklace, composed of pearls and black lozenged-shaped stones.

Portraiture, as we have already seen, was not obliged in Lavinia Fontana's day to go abroad masked with religious fervour. When a man wanted to have his picture taken it was unnecessary to simulate a longing to make a votive offering. But it was of course possible to entertain both desires, and it was convenient and economical to satisfy them simultaneously, and for a single price. Moreover, when a handsome gift was given to a church, it was surely well to acquaint posterity with the name and features of the donor.

So thought a certain Bolognese citizen, by name Scipio Calcina, who at the close of the sixteenth century restored the chapel in S. Giacomo Maggiore erected by a member of his family one hundred and seventy years previously. He determined further to supply the Calcina Chapel with an altar-piece, and to put his portrait into it, instead of merely recording his generosity on a mural tablet as his ancestor had done.

So Lavinia Fontana was commissioned to paint a Madonna and Child with attendant saints, and a very fine picture she produced, rich and mellow in colour as the work of the Venetian school. Her Virgin is a fair and noble figure, in a red robe and dark green cloak, seated on a throne canopied with dark green curtains. The Babe—although the face is very sweet and the pose graceful—is far less satisfactory; the poor modelling of the limbs reveals the great defect in Lavinia's training: the lack of careful drawing from the nude.

On either side of the throne are SS. Cosmo and Damian in red robes and ermine tippets—life-like studies of Bolognese doctors. Just below the dais of the throne kneels a woman in a rich gold-coloured robe ornamented with gems. She is looking up into the face of the Virgin, whose arm embraces her with a familiar gesture of protection. The lack of dignity in her attitude, so different from the restrained adoring reverence of earlier Saint Catherines, makes us at first overlook her emblems—the coronet and a curious scimitar lying beside her on the ground—and take her for another suppliant member of the Calcina family. With the right hand, from which she has evidently dropped the scimitar, she points backwards, with a gesture of introduction, to a man in a white ruff with a little pointed beard, the donor Scipio, who kneels with his body curiously bent backwards from the knees.

In the church of S. Maria della Pietà is a large canvas which differs somewhat in character from any of Lavinia's other pictures. The subject—the Multiplication of the Loaves and Fishes—brought her face to face with a difficulty which her usual choice of subjects seldom presented—the difficulty of delineating a large and confused crowd, while concentrating the interest of the picture in a small group of foreground figures. This difficulty is on the whole very successfully met. Lavinia depicts not the feeding of the multitude, but the moment when the power of the compassionate Master is put forth on their behalf. Jesus is seated in the foreground with his right hand uplifted to bless the little bare-legged lad who, brought forward by Philip, presents his dish of fishes. To the left, one of the disciples is holding a flat loaf, while in front of him another, seated on the ground, holds a stilus and a tablet, perhaps for the purpose of calculating the number of persons to be fed, more probably to record the miracle he was about to witness.

The vermilion robe of this figure and the dull pink and deep blue and green draperies of the Master are the strongest masses of colour in the picture, which is otherwise low in tone. But in spite of the grey rocks, the grey cliffs, the distant glimpse of a grey lake, and the grey sky overhead, the atmosphere of the picture is warm. We know that it is a hot evening, not a sunless afternoon.

In S. Maria del Baraccano—the church which contains Properzia de Rossi's carved "arco"—there is a Holy Family by Lavinia. The Virgin sits beside a table in a natural but ungraceful posture, sideways, yet with body and head turned full. On the table is a curious wicker cradle—a long basket lined with dull yellow cushions. The Mother is taking her Child out of this cradle. He stretches out his arms to the little Saint John Baptist, a lovely laughing child standing by the table. S. Joseph from the background watches the three, his head propped on his hands. There is nothing in this domestic group to inspire devotion; but the colouring is charming. The Virgin's robe is red; so is the drapery of the Baptist; a red book lies on the table. The whole picture is flushed with red gold tones, harmonious and mellow as the tinting of ripe fruit.

Those who would see any specimens of Lavinia Fontana's drawings—and in the rougher sketches of an artist we always find the most intimate note, the surest indication, of his quality—can do so by making due application to Ispettore Ferri, of the Uffizi Gallery in Florence. Ten of her sketches are in his keeping. They are :—

No. 4327—A St. Ursula and her virgins in pen and ink. The saint stands, crowned; the virgins, all in late sixteenth-century costume, kneel around. The sketch is squared for reproduction on a larger scale, but the writer has been unable to discover whether Lavinia ever used it for this purpose.

No. 4326—A large sketch in red chalk, representing the Presentation in the Temple. The Virgin and her attendants are in classical draperies. The high priest is an undignified figure, but the composition as a whole is pleasing.

No. 12,189—A very slight sketch of a young girl's head.

No. 12,190—A child's full face.

No. 12,191—The portrait of a little boy, with face turned to the right.

No. 12,193—The head of a man slightly turned to the left. He has a moustache, and wears a small cap.

No. 12,194—A large and interesting study in black pencil and water-colour of two half-length figures—a woman whose face is seen in left-side profile, a man turning to the left and looking down.

No. 12,195—The head of a man turned to the left but looking straight. His face has a pained, anxious expression. He wears the usual ruffs and pointed beard.

No. 2196—A man's head, full face.

AUTHORITIES

ORETTI. *Pittori*, Tomo II. Gozzadini MS. 122 (the only MS. source).

MALVASIA. *Felsina Pittrice*, Vol. I.

GIOVANNI GOZZADINI. "Atti e Memorie della Reale Deputazione di Storia Patria per le Romagne" (on the Gozzadini portrait).

ABECEDARIO PITTORICO. Merely a recapitulation.

ZANOTTI. *Vite dei Pittori*, I.

BLANC ET DELABORDE. *Histoire des Peintres*.

MARCO MINGHETTI. *Le Donne Italiane*.

ELISABETTA SIRANI

THE DISCIPLE OF GUIDO RENI

(1638–1665)

PORTRAIT OF ELISABETTA SIRANI, PAINTED BY HERSELF
PINACOTECA, BOLOGNA

CHAPTER I

A SEVENTEENTH-CENTURY FUNERAL

> Giusta sembra la doglia, e ben conosco
> Quanto sia grave altrui
> Perder sul fior degli anni amata prole.
> FULVIO TESTI, *Si consola la Marchesa Vittoria*
> *Lurcari Calcagnina per la morte di sua figlia.*

HALF-WAY up the stately nave of the Dominican church in Bologna are two chapels larger and more imposing than the rest. That on the south side contains the beautiful sarcophagus enclosing the bones of the founder of the order. That on the north side, bedecked with artificial flowers, and frequented all day long by kneeling worshippers, is the Cappella del Rosario.

Entering this chapel we notice on the left-hand wall a slab bearing the following inscription :—

HIC JACENT
GUIDO . RENIUS . ET . ELISABETHA . SIRANA
VIXIT . GUIDO . LXVII . OBIIT . XV . K .
SEPT . A . MDCXLII
VIXIT ELISABETHA . A . XXVI . OBIIT . V . K .
SEPT . A . MDCLXV

The vault marked by this tablet was the property of Signor Saulo Guidotti, a distinguished gentleman of

Bologna, a lover of painting and a friend of painters. He had held the infant Elisabetta in his arms at the baptismal font, and when "Death lay on her like an untimely frost," he offered her a last hospitality—a place in his own tomb. Thither, twenty-three years earlier, Guido Reni had preceded her; and, to the fancy of her contemporaries, there was something peculiarly fitting in this post-mortem union of the two painters; for though Elisabetta was a mere babe when Guido Reni died, she called him Master and was both the ablest and the most faithful of his disciples.

In this vault in the chapel of the Rosary, on the evening of 28 August, 1665, the girl-artist was laid to rest—quietly, as she had lived. But Elisabetta Sirani had never been without honour in her own country and among her own kindred, and her fellow-citizens were determined to give public expression to their admiration and their grief. And thus it came to pass that, on the fourteenth day of November following, the Dominican church was crowded and adorned as for a princely funeral. The walls were hung, the pillars swathed with sable cloth, gold-fringed. There were gilded wreaths, swaying lamps, and shields displaying a variety of mottoes, emblems, and devices—among them one which excited marked and peculiar attention, the picture of a fruitful tree with an axe laid to the trunk, surmounted by the words: "*Invida Manus.*"

The crowd which filled the church doubtless resembled a modern Bolognese congregation assembled for some high festival or solemn ceremonial. That is to say, it was at once devout and irreverent; skilful in making the best of both worlds; greeting acquaintances and singing responses with equal heartiness; circulating freely and persistently from one point of interest to another, but withal without noise or unseemly push or jostling. We are told that it was not only *numerissima* (most numerous), but also *fioritissima* (most distinguished), including many nobles and *virtuosi;* and this implies a brave show of satins, velvets, and laces, the gleam of jewels, and the glint and clank of swords. These fine gentlemen—many of them good musicians, more of them indifferent poets, most of them dilettanti—listened with rapture to "the exquisite music" of Signor Maurizio Cazzati, which accompanied the function, praised the invention of the artist Matteo Borbone, who was responsible for the scheme of decoration, and gave admiring ears to the lengthy funeral oration pronounced by Signor Giorgio Luigi Picinardi, Prior of the Lawyers in the University of Bologna. And meanwhile the vulgar herd pressed towards the picture of the tree stricken by the hand of envy; and we can imagine with what expressive pantomime, what shrugging of the shoulders, show of extended palms, and shaking of clenched fists the Bolognese proletariat communicated and expressed their suspicions and their execrations.

But the point towards which all currents in the crowd ultimately tended was the catafalque rising in the middle of the nave, intended to represent the Temple of Fame. It was an extraordinary structure of imitation marble; octangular, with cupola-shaped roof supported by eight columns of sham porphyry. Seven sides of the base were decorated with angelic figures, mottoes, and emblematic pictures. On the eighth side a flight of steps, guarded by siren-shaped candelabra —an admired allusion to the name of the deceased— led to the platform or tribune; and there, in the glare of lighted torches, was placed the life-sized, lifelike figure of the dead artist, seated before her easel, in the act of painting.

The portentous erection, with its gilding and its sham marble, its fantastic emblems, intricate conceits, allegorical devices, and touch of startling realism, seems the very symbol and embodiment of *barocco* taste and feeling.

The funeral oration was its counterpart in rhetoric. Nay, in comparison with the bombastic grandiloquence of Picinardi (who had profited only too well by the teaching of the famous Achillini), the architecture of the catafalque was of Gothic simplicity. The lawyer's stream of eloquence almost bears us off our feet. His periods are long lanes with only too many turnings. We must needs take a classical dictionary as a road-map if we would not lose ourselves in his wood (scarce visible for the trees) of allegory and trope. Yet this oration, "extant and writ in very choice Italian," under the title " Il Pennello Lagrimato " (" The Lamented Paintbrush "), is not unprofitable reading. Here and there among its gaudy flowers of rhetoric we may gather sprigs of rosemary, fragrant reminiscences of the painter's life, obtainable from no other quarter. Here, too, we find a tribute to her spotless innocence, a virtue rare among the ladies of her century and city. Here, again, we have a list of her foreign patrons, and of the distinguished persons who went to see her paint.

But chiefly is the oration worthy of our note because

we are informed that Picinardi moved his audience to tears. Such emotion argues not only art and artifice on the part of the orator, but also a close bond of sympathy between himself and his audience. We ask ourselves what were "the cords of a man" by which this bombastic, self-satisfied lawyer drew his hearers; and the "Pennello Lagrimato" supplies an answer to the question. In it we recognize the twofold cord of artistic perception and civic patriotism.

This public mourning for a girl of humble, middle-class family is the seventeenth-century counterpart in black of the many-tinted scene in thirteenth-century Florence when the Borgo Allegro installed the Rucellai Madonna in the church of Santa Maria Novella; or of that yet gayer procession of the whole population of Mantua in the summer of 1495, when Mantegna's "Our Lady of Victory"[1] was borne from the painter's house to the chapel erected for its reception. It was the expression of a love and respect for art which was not confined to certain strata of society, but was diffused through all classes, and sprang from the deepest founts of popular feeling.

This popular, instinctive, artistic perception is unknown in modern Europe. It was seen in perfection only in the Italian city-state, where it was trained and intensified by a sense of civic solidarity. Elisabetta Sirani was, to the Bolognese, not merely a talented

[1] The chapel and its altar-piece commemorated the success of the Duke of Milan and his ally, Francesco Gonzaga, over the French. It is one of "life's little ironies" that the Madonna della Vittoria is now one of the most valued possessions of the Louvre.

artist—*she was their own painter.* She had been born in their midst. They had seen her womanhood and her genius bud and blossom. She filled them with the pride of ownership. She became one of the sights of their city. They took their strangers to see her paint. They greeted her pictures with sonnets. When she lay in mortal agony they discussed her every symptom. When she died they wept and demanded vengeance on her suspected murderers.

" She is mourned by all," wrote the Gonfalonier of Justice to Cardinal Leopoldo de Medici; " the ladies especially, whose portraits she flattered, cannot hold their peace about it. Indeed, it is a great misfortune to lose such a great artist in so strange a manner."

And this letter was preceded by one from Count Annibale Ranuzzi (for whom Elisabetta's last finished picture was executed), who wrote on August 30 :—

" The day before yesterday, about 21 o'clock,[1] Signora Elisabetta Sirani died in twenty-four hours, of pain in the stomach and bowels, to the extreme grief of the whole city ; for day by day her power increased, so that the greatest expectations were entertained concerning her."

Nowadays we give and we receive less in the way of neighbourly sympathy. The modern painter, trained in London or Paris, lost in a crowd of art students, working and rising to fame far from his native place, never receives the homage which the Bolognese accorded to their Carracci, to Guido Reni, Domenichino, Guercino, and the Sirani, father and daughter. Nor can the

[1] That is, according to our reckoning, between five and six o'clock in the evening.

modern art critic, with his cosmopolitan standards of comparison, see with the eyes, at once keenly discerning and blinded with local prejudice, of the medieval Italian citizen. Our impressions are weakened by the speed of their succession. Our sympathies and affections are diffused and diluted: frequent posts, facilities of travel, the telegraph, the daily newspaper, have made us citizens of the world. It is very difficult for us to comprehend the power of appreciation, the lack of perspective, the intensity of emotion created by restricted space and immense leisure: it is well-nigh impossible for us to realize the excitement caused by events of minor importance within those city walls which shut out the *forestiere* and shut in the seething strength of class and civic sentiment.

It would never have occurred to Picinardi's hearers to criticize his oration on the ground that it was less a eulogy of the artist than a panegyric on her birthplace. Yet, in fact, an assertion that she took her first steps towards fame by coming into the world *fra i Penati di Felsina*, forms the starting-point for a sketch of Felsinean history from the earliest times and an excuse for a perorating rhapsody of civic patriotism: " City which for the clemency of its air, for the benignity of its climate, the vastness of its circumference, the fertility of its fields, the amenity of its hills, the magnificence of its edifices, the wonder of its spectacles, the number of its inhabitants, the charm of its paintings, the nimbleness of its spirits, the doctrine of its professors, the venerable order of its masters, the concourse of foreign students, the splendour of its nobility, the gallantry and generosity of its gentlemen, the beauty and gaiety of its ladies, is with reason esteemed the centre of mirth, the garden of delight, the dwelling of Flora, the throne of Spring, the treasure of Pomona, the abode of Diana, the inn of Fortune, the museum of Apollo, the school of painters, the camp of Mars, the asylum of the Graces, the nest of Love, the Venus of cities; city

> That hath 'mong other towns the place I trow
> That hath the cyprus 'mong viburnums low."

We do not speak thus of London, Paris or Berlin; and Picinardi's attitude towards the dead artist reminds us irresistibly of the commendation bestowed in Gilbert and Sullivan's most popular operetta on the man who "resisted all temptations to belong to other nations." But the Bolognese who gathered round the rostrum greedily inhaled the incense of the lawyer's eloquence. They thrilled with pride at the reminder that the painter whose death they commemorated had been a native of "no mean city." Picinardi spoke not merely *to*, but *for* them; "and the energy of his words," says one who was himself among that congregation, "drew from our eyes tears, from our hearts sighs"; so that the temple "but lately filled with sweet harmonies and sonorous chanting, echoed to the sound of sobs and groans."

CHAPTER 11

ELISABETTA AT HOME

I saw her upon nearer view,
A spirit, yet a woman too !
Her household motions light and free
And steps of virgin liberty ;
A countenance in which did meet
Sweet records, promises as sweet ;
A creature not too bright or good
For human nature's daily food ;
For transient sorrows, simple wiles,
Praise, blame, love, kisses, tears, and smiles.

And now I see with eye serene
The very pulse of the machine ;
A being breathing thoughtful breath,
A traveller betwixt life and death ;
The reason firm, the temperate will,
Endurance, foresight, strength and skill ;
A perfect woman, nobly planned
To warn, to comfort, and command.

THE Via Urbana is a quiet turning out of one of the main thoroughfares of Bologna—the street of late rechristened Via d' Azeglio, for centuries known as Via S. Mamolo. On the right-hand side, above a house-door marked by the number 7, we find a tablet bearing this inscription :—

NEL GIORNO VIII, GENNAIO MDCXXXVIII
QUI NACQUE
ELISABETTA SIRANI
EMULATRICE DEL SOMMO GUIDO RENI.[1]

The house has been enlarged and internally reconstructed, and is now let in separate apartments; in the seventeenth century it was a two-storied, modest, private dwelling. It was Elisabetta's only home—the scene, not only as the tablet states, of her entrance into this world, but also of her exit from it, and of all the astounding activity of her brief existence.

Of her childhood we know nothing save the solitary fact recorded with mingled satisfaction and remorse by Count Carlo Cesare Malvasia,[2] Canon of the cathedral church of San Pietro. This distinguished Bolognese art critic and patron, whose *Felsina Pittrice*, in spite of prejudice, inaccuracies, and omissions, remains a standard work on the history of Bolognese painting, was a frequent visitor in the Sirani household, where the pretty little Elisabetta, twenty years his junior, was his especial friend. He tells us that, noting the child's artistic bent, he with difficulty persuaded her father, a painter of some note, to number her among his pupils. When her talent developed, he encouraged her efforts. When his prognostications of success were fulfilled, he everywhere sounded her praises. But when she died,

---

[1] Here was born on January 8, 1638, Elisabetta Sirani, emulator of the most excellent Guido Reni. Born in January, 1638, dying in August, 1665, Elisabetta lived twenty-seven years and seven months. The "Vixit A. xxvi" on the tablet in the church of S. Dominic is, in fact, an error.

[2] Son of Conte Galeazzo Malvasia. B. 1616. D. 1693.

the victim as he believed of professional jealousy, he was filled with morbid regret at having "dedicated her to art"; nay, he "almost wished" he "had never known her or aided her."

Elisabetta's father, Giovanni Andrea, had been Guido Reni's favourite pupil. His pictures, touched up by his master, were often mistaken for Guido's own; and on the other hand, when Guido died Gianandrea successfully completed several of his unfinished pictures. He became, in a sense, Guido's successor as a teacher, and was one of the first masters and directors of the Life school held in the house of Count Ettore Ghislieri. Elisabetta could hardly have found a better instructor, and Gianandrea must soon have taken pleasure in the progress and the industry of his new pupil. The theory that his original reluctance to teach her proceeded from a suspicion that her fame would eclipse his own accords ill with the paternal pride in her success which he subsequently exhibited. It probably sprang from a man's conception of "a woman's true sphere" and a masculine contempt for female art. Elisabetta's astonishing success and unalterable filial devotion appear to have effected his conversion, for both his younger daughters, Barbara and Anne, became professional artists. Their teaching, however, fell chiefly to their sister, for Gianandrea early in life became a martyr to rheumatic gout, which crippled his hands and prevented him for weeks together from holding a pencil.

It is evident that Elisabetta's education included the outlines of Bible history, the stories of Greece and Rome, a smattering of heathen mythology, and a slight acquaintance with the legends of the saints. Such attainments were *de rigueur* in polite society, and were an indispensable equipment for an artist.

Incidentally, moreover, we learn that Elisabetta received regular instruction in music and was an apt pupil. Picinardi alludes to her harp-playing; and a poem of one of her admirers informs us that she sang; while in her " List of pictures made by me, Elisabetta Sirani," are three entries of paintings executed as gifts "for my music master." Her sister Barbara subsequently married a professional musician; and we may fairly conclude that the Sirani household were to some extent infected by the " musical and theatrical frenzy," as Signor Corrado Ricci calls it, prevalent in seventeenth-century Bologna. Young and old, laymen and clerics, flocked to the opera. There was street music and chamber music; music in the churches, oratorios and operettas in seminaries and convents. Towards the close of this century the civil and religious authorities, finding these musical tendencies subversive of public decency and conventual discipline, made strenuous but futile efforts to destroy them. It was decreed that marriage with a dancing-girl or singer should be held a disqualification for public office. The Archbishop prohibited instrumental or concerted music in churches. The Pope forbade the heads of households to " admit any music-master or professional musician, whether lay, secular, or regular," to instruct their women folk, seeing that "music is most detrimental to the modesty fitting to the sex, distracting them from their proper activity and occupation."

Little as we know of Elisabetta's youth we confidently affirm that it did not justify the papal apprehensions. Neither her modesty nor her industry were impaired by her love of harp and song. The sonnets of her admirers, the disjointed statements of Picinardi, the naïve entries in her own catalogue, and the biographical sketch of Malvasia, together give us a perfectly distinct and singular pleasing impression of her character.

She has a warm heart and a lively temper, and is what Jane Austen and her contemporaries would have called a *quiz*, habitually amusing her family and friends with her caricatures. But her manners are gracious and winning, and she is always a courteous listener. She is sincerely pious; and, " su l' imbrunire del giorno," when the fading light compels her to leave her easel, it is her custom to retire for private prayer and meditation. She is assiduous in tending her ailing father —a sufferer from gout, and not always an amiable patient. She holds his wishes as commands, save when he urges her to spend time and money on her own adornment. She believes in plain living and high thinking. Her art is a pearl of great price; she is luxurious in colour, opulent in invention, and can afford to eat simply and dress plainly; "quella," says Picinardi, "che ritendo la maestà nelle opere non la ricercava nelle gonne, nè su le mense." She looks out upon the world with the candid gaze and dignified composure exhibited by her portrait in the Pinacoteca of Bologna. Her activity is immense. She rises early, and disdains none of the occupations which Clement XI considered so much more "proper to the sex" than the study of music. She cheerfully performs the most menial tasks. She has her own *atelier*, too, with quite a large number of girl students. Oretti gives us the names of some of them. There were her own two sisters, both of whom became more than tolerable artists. There was Veronica Fontana, later known throughout Italy as a first-rate wood-engraver: the engravings in Malvasia's *Felsina Pittrice* were by her. Then there was Caterina Pepoli and Maria Elena Panzacchi, of whom we know nothing save that they came of good old Bolognese families; Camilla Lanteri and Lucretia Forni, who painted several large and tolerable sacred pictures; and Veronica Franchi, whose predilection was for mythological subjects. Lastly, there was Ginevra Cantofoli, sometimes, but groundlessly, represented as Elisabetta's enemy and rival, who had much more talent than any of her companions. Her portrait, painted by herself, hangs in the Bolognese room in the Brera Gallery; and there is a good picture by her in that Calcina Chapel in the church of S. Giacomo Maggiore for which Lavinia Fontana painted her large Madonna.

Thus between teaching, and executing a steadily increasing number of commissions, Elisabetta becomes at an early age the principal bread-winner of the family. All her earnings go to her father; only the presents, the jewels and trinkets she receives over and above the stipulated prices of her pictures, are retained for her own use. She rejoices in work and in success, and is unspoilt by flattery. "All the gentlemen and great persons who visit Bologna" go to see her paint; and she has so much self-assurance, and so little self-consciousness, that their presence is no embarrassment to her. Her sweetness is not insipid. Her strength is free from self-assertion. She is comely and devoid of vanity, eminently attractive, and entirely virtuous. Even the ugly publicity of a poisoning case fails to sully the whiteness of her fame.

It is a fair picture, and seems all the fairer because it hangs in a seventeenth-century Italian portrait gallery. Around it are likenesses of frail beauties and professed libertines; of women whose passions and extravagance were equally boundless; of men who had made a fine art of vice, who were epicures and *conoscenti* in debauchery; of ecclesiastics who lived in pagan self-indulgence and cared not at all for the feeding of their flocks; of "sheep" who never dreamed of "looking up," and were hungry for no spiritual food.

It is surely a tribute to the healthy and enduring influence of English Puritanism that the immorality of the Restoration Court never filtered down to the lower strata of English society; whereas in Italy the corruption confined in the sixteenth century to courts and palazzi had in the seventeenth infected the whole body politic. There was, moreover, something peculiarly repulsive in the vice of the seventeenth century; it had neither barbaric grandeur nor medieval *naïveté*, neither renaissance splendour nor rationalistic consistency—it was merely *barocco*. The crimes of the period are bizarre; the tissue of adulterous intimacy is of ugly and whimsical design.

In such an environment Elisabetta Sirani passed a pure and industrious life, finding in the retirement of her sick father's home, and in unceasing labour, the shelter which in an earlier age she would have sought, perhaps, like Caterina Vigri, in a cloister. Her life was one of conventual monotony and calm; the arrival of an order, the completion of a picture, the visit of some distinguished person who came to see her paint, the feasts of the Church and the public spectacles and processions connected with them, are its only milestones. Now the country without a history may be happy but is seldom progressive, and the individual without one obtains tranquillity at the price of complete self-development. Elisabetta's pictures reflect the beauty and the limitations of her life. They display no feminine weakness, sentimentality, or indecision; indeed, the girl's sure touch and bold invention were the features which most impressed her contemporaries; they are never pretentious *tours de force;* they are never without dignity. But they have no *élan;* they do not set the beholder thinking, wondering. All is on the canvas before him, "all is placid and perfect." Elisabetta's execution was more than equal to her conception.

It is perhaps futile, but it is certainly interesting, to speculate on the effect which change of scene or of emotions would have produced on this woman-artist's work. Picinardi tells us that she longed to travel; and to estimate the fervour of her desire and the pain of its non-realization, we must remember that her training and her principles were those of the Bolognese Eclectic school. The sonnet[1] is well known in which

---

[1] Chi farsi un buon pittor cerca, e desia,
Il disegno di Roma abbia alla mano
La mossa coll' ombrar Veneziano
E il degno colorir di Lombardia.

Annibale Carracci formulated his artistic creed: He who would be a good painter must go to Rome for his drawing, to Venice for his chiaroscuro, to Lombardy for his colouring: he must unite Michael Angelo's grand manner with Correggio's sweetness, and imitate Titian's truth to nature and Raphael's balanced composition. To a modern mind Annibale's prescription contravenes the essence of great and sincere art; and is calculated to produce an effect similar to that arrived at by Portia's English lover who "bought his doublet in Italy, his round hose in France, his bonnet in Germany, and his behaviour everywhere."

But the sonnet represents the creed which Elisabetta professed; and *it is a counsel of impossible perfection to an untravelled painter*.

We cannot doubt that even a brief sojourn in Rome, in France, or in Venice would have enlarged her horizon and enriched her imagination. It is more difficult to prognosticate the effects of marriage and maternity. It is possible that a subtler beauty, an intenser feeling would have stolen into the faces of her sweet Madonnas had she herself known a mother's joys and sorrows; but it is at least as possible that excessive or defective

> Di Michael Angiol la terribil via,
> Il vero natural di Tiziano,
> Del Corregio lo stil puro e sovrano,
> E di un Rafael la giusta simmetria.
>
> Del Tibaldi il decoro, e il fondamento
> Del dotto Primatticio l'inventare,
> E un po' di grazia del Parmigianino.
> Ma senza tante studii, e tanto stento
> Si ponga l'opre solo ad imitare
> Che qui lasciocci il nostro Nicolino.

matrimonial happiness would have quenched her genius and suspended her artistic activity.

> Had I been two, another and myself,
> Our head would have o'erlooked the world,

is the cry which Browning puts into the mouth of the "Faultless Painter," while showing how his art was crippled and debased by the influence of an unworthy spouse.

That this gifted and attractive woman should have died unwedded at the age of twenty-seven—an age regarded as young indeed for death, but hopelessly late for marriage—is a fact which perplexed her fellow-citizens, and has been discussed by her biographers. There were two contemporary explanations of the artist's celibacy. Some held, Malvasia tells us, that Gianandrea prevented his daughter from marrying; while others believed that for art's sake she elected to live single, and that indeed her only true affinity was the master she joined in the grave.[1] The mere existence of the latter theory is a proof of the unique impression which Elisabetta's strong and pure personality produced on the mind of her contemporaries. For we must remember that happy and respected spinsterhood of the modern Anglo-American type is still somewhat of a puzzle to Latin nations and was unknown in earlier epochs. A right-minded Italian parent in the seventeenth century married his daughters young to preserve

---

[1] Innupta
Quia nulli digne nubenda
Parem sibi thalamum reservavit in tumulo
Guidoni Rheno conjuncta.

their reputations and provide for their protection ; and when a life of chastity was deliberately embraced, it was accompanied by retirement from this world, and inspired by the hope of corresponding compensations in the next.

That Elisabetta, with her refined temper and artistic sensibility, was hard to please, that like Lavinia Fontana she may have vowed to marry no one who would not leave her " mistress of her art," we may readily believe : that, as Count Berò's sonnet declared, she was "a lady who knew not love"[1] is probably too large an assumption. Her latest and most conscientious biographer, Signor Manaresi, has constructed a pretty if vague romance out of certain entries in her catalogue. In the year 1661, when she was twenty-three, she painted Love for the first time ; and her Cupid, with his bow and arrows bound together beneath his feet, pointed to his quiver which was full of gold pistoles. In 1665 the Duchess of Brunswick visited Elisabetta's studio, and in her presence the artist painted a cupid in the act of wounding himself with an arrow, while contemplating his own reflection in a glass. " Intendami chi può che m' intend' io ec.," are the words added to the entry of this picture. It is an ambiguous phrase, and the concluding "ec." may indicate that it is merely a quotation. It is noteworthy, however, that contrary to her usual habit, Elisabetta does not name the purchaser or ultimate possessor of this cupid ; and it does not appear that the Duchess of Brunswick ordered it. Signor Manaresi believes that both pictures alluded to personal experience and are charged with specific messages, and that we may

[1] " Fu donna in terra e non conobbi amore."

possibly infer from them that a deficient dowry was an obstacle in love's true course. But if this fancy comes near the truth, it after all merely reinforces the well-founded and popular opinion that paternal selfishness was the cause of Elisabetta's celibacy. There is a passage in Malvasia's *Felsina Pittrice* which illuminates the situation. He tells us that Elisabetta's catalogue does not represent her total output of work;[1] among other things it excludes sundry "small heads and little figures" executed on the sly (de soppiato) without her father's knowledge, in order that with the proceeds she might oblige her mother in some domestic difficulty. The father chained to his couch and irritable from gout: the mother unable to make both ends meet and afraid to ask for money: the grown-up daughter obliged to aid her mother secretly, and unable even to enter her little pictures in her catalogue, because it was subject to the greedy scrutiny of her father, who claimed "for the account and common benefit of the house" the earnings which might have been spent on travel or saved for a dowry;—it is a little sketch of domestic tryanny, and it enables us to understand why Elisabetta's parents were not anxious to arrange a marriage for their daughter.

The interrogatories of the witnesses in the "Processo" throw vivid side-lights on the condition of the Sirani household during the last six months of Elisabetta's life. The state of things is dreary and depressing. Gianandrea is a helpless sufferer: his wife has

[1] Oretti tells us of twenty of these pictures done "senza saputa di suo Padre." (Gozzadini MS., 120).

lately had a paralytic seizure: there are "servant worries"—petty annoyances felt keenly by a busy woman. The necessity for work is greater than ever, while the combination of labour and anxiety is beginning to tell on the artist's health and spirits.

In Lent, 1665, she experienced premonitory symptoms of her fatal disease: the pain in the stomach "went away of itself without the aid of any remedy"; but the buxom, cheerful girl began to lose flesh and colour, and to grow pinched and melancholy, so that every one noticed, and wondered at, the transformation.

Towards the middle of August the pain returned, increasing in intensity after eating. The family physician was at that time attending Barbara Sirani, who lay in bed, sick of a fever, and Elisabetta took this opportunity of seeking medical advice. Dr. Gallerati said her suffering was due "to some slight fluxion or catarrh"; and since "it was no time to take medicine, the sun being in Leo," he prescribed merely "a little acid syrup" to be taken in the morning fasting. The syrup was duly made by Aunt Giacoma, Gianandrea's sister, who presided in the kitchen, and Elisabetta thought it did her good—"at times she felt the pain, but it did not really trouble her"—and upon August the twenty-fourth, Saint Bartholomew's Day, she was well enough to go with her mother to see the brave shows and gay doings in the Piazza del Gigante.

The Festival of the Little Pig, *porchetta* or *porcellina*, annually held on the day of Saint Bartholomew, was the most characteristic of the many festivals which brightened the life of the populace in medieval Bologna. Its origin is obscure. The older historians declare that it commemorated the fall of Faenza, that is to say, the complete victory of the Bolognese Guelfs, and that its name was derived from the fact that Faenza was betrayed by one Tebaldello[1] (whom Dante consequently consigns to the Inferno) because the Lambertazzi, leaders of the Bolognese Ghibellines, had stolen from him "duos pulcherrimos porcos."[2] But modern writers, less ready to accept specious derivations, have discovered traces of the Festival of the Porchetta[3] thirty years before the fall of Faenza.[4] The festa probably commemorates the luckless Enzio's entry as a captive on August 24, 1249; while the peculiar feature of the day's proceedings, the throwing of eatables from the balcony of the Palazzo Pubblico to the crowd in the Piazza below, undoubtedly represents an ancient Roman usage. The appearance and importance of the sucking pig among these articles of largesse—roast fowls, bread, salt meats—was doubtless due to the Bolognese partiality for pork,[5] a taste by no means extinct, as the large manufacture of *salumi* and *mortadella* testifies. Moreover, we find that sucking pig and roast fowls were prizes given both at Ferrara and Modena[6] at the annual horse-races, and this previous to the Bolognese victory at Faenza, and " secundum consuetudinem."

[1] " Tebaldello, Ch' apri Faenza, quando si dormia " (*Inferno*, XXXII, 122).
[2] Benvenuto da Imola, c. *Inferno*, XXXII.
[3] Guidicini, *Cose notabili di Bologna*, Vol. II.
[4] Savioli, *Annali*, III, 232.
[5] John Evelyn, who visited Bologna twenty years before Elisabetta's death, remarks : " This Citty is famous also for sausages."
[6] Muratori, *Antiq. Ital.*, II, 856. Mazzoni-Toselli, *Racconti Storici*, II, 523–6.

The festival, after having been celebrated some five hundred and forty-seven times, was killed by the entrance of the French in 1796. It would, however, have been extinguished naturally and inevitably by the growing habit of the *villeggiatura*. In the seventeenth century wealthy aristocrats repaired in summer to their suburban villas; but the majority of citizens sweltered in the dark and airless alleys of Bologna like rabbits in a warren, enjoying long social evenings on the cool pavements underneath the colonnades, and inhaling, untroubled by sanitary scruples, the miasmas arising from the open sewers in the centre of the streets, where every sort of garbage festered till slowly removed by intermittent flushing. But in this twentieth century the Feast of Saint Bartholomew finds Bologna emptied of all but the poorest and most indispensable of its inhabitants; and a crowd could hardly nowadays be drawn to the Piazza in the August heat even by a spectacle similar to that with which Marchese Ferdinand Cospi delighted his fellow-citizens in the year of grace 1665.

To celebrate his third election as Gonfalonier, and to welcome and impress the new Legate, Cardinal Caraffa, Cospi determined to keep the Feast of the Porchetta with more than usual magnificence. Besides the customary largesse to the crowd, sweetmeats, fans, and gloves were bestowed on the noble ladies who filled the windows and balconies of the Palazzo Pubblico; while in the square below a marvellous pageant was arranged. A pasteboard Vesuvius vomited flames; two lesser mountains were the abode respectively of a knight and of a sorcerer, and battle in mid-air was waged between the two, the knight being mounted on a pasteboard steed, the sorcerer upon a dragon.

As Elisabetta and her mother stood looking at this spectacle (we may presume from some reserved and secure place, for accidents were common in the Saint Bartholomew crowd), Margherita more than once inquired how her daughter felt. And Elisabetta answered that "she was better"; that "if she did not think about the pain she did not feel it."

Perhaps the novelty of the spectacle, the greetings of friends, the gaiety of the scene, were really a nervous stimulus cheating the girl into belief in her own cure; she was at all events cheerful and uncomplaining till, on the twenty-sixth, the pain returned with violence after she had dined. Still she did not give in; and next day, after the mid-day meal, while her mother went to her room to enjoy a customary siesta, and Aunt Giacoma went out to see the fair which accompanied and extended the Feast of the Porchetta, the artist repaired to her studio upstairs and began to work at the picture she was executing "for the Empress," that is, for Eleanore Gonzaga, Ferdinand III's widow.

But "about twenty of the clock," that is, about 4 p.m.,[1] Aunt Giacoma, coming in from the fair, found her niece descending the stairs with great difficulty. She entered the room on the ground-floor where Barbara lay ill in bed, and, sinking on to a stool, gasped, "Sister, I have such horrible pain in the stomach, I feel as though I

[1] The Bolognese reckoned their time from the Ave Maria of the preceding evening; twenty hours after the last Ave Maria, that is from our 8 p.m., would be 4 p.m.

should die." And indeed Barbara thought she would die there and then.

Margherita hurried in, drew her daughter into her own room, and put her into her own bed. She was already but half-conscious and bathed in a cold sweat. Dr. Gallerati was sent for, but was not at home, and so, the case being urgent, Dr. Matessilani was summoned from the near Ospedale della Morte.

In the evening the family physician called, but his remedies were useless, or worse. All night the mother and Aunt Giacoma applied hot cloths to the cold body. Sometimes they brought a lamp to the bedside, and saw with sinking hearts that the patient's face was drawn and death-like, her feet and fingers a dull purple. From time to time the faintness and perspiration returned; there was no sleep, no cessation of pain.

Morning brought the doctor's visit. He bade Margherita send for the parish priest. The dying girl confessed, and received the last sacraments.

As the day wore on she seemed a little easier, a little warmer, and hope revived in the heart of the poor father who lay in bed upstairs listening to the sounds below, waiting anxiously for news and feverishly turning it over in his mind. But towards evening the patient was again seized with faintness, and very quickly and quietly, in the presence of the doctors, Gallerati and Matessilani, she passed "from this to another life."

The bereaved father demanded a post-mortem examination. It took place next day, "the first doctors in Bologna" being present. Some of them—and of these was the family physician, Dr. Gallerati—thought they discerned clear traces of the administration of "corrosive poison," and on the last day of August Giovanni Andrea Sirani addressed a memorial to the Legate and set the machinery of the law in motion.

CHAPTER III

A SEVENTEENTH-CENTURY TRIAL

> So in this book lay absolute truth,
> Fanciless fact, the documents indeed,
> Primary lawyer-pleadings for, against.
> . . . . .
> the trial
> Itself, to all intents, being then as now
> Here in the book and nowise out of it;
> Seeing there properly was no judgment-bar,
> No bringing of accuser and accused,
> And whoso judged both parties, face to face
> Before some court, as we conceive of courts.
> There was a Hall of Justice; that came last;
> For Justice had a chamber by the hall
> Where she took evidence first, summed up the same,
> Then sent accuser and accused alike,
> In person of the advocate of each
> To weigh its worth.
> BROWNING, *The Ring and the Book.*

"THE death is announced of the poor Sirana from poison given, it is believed, by a wretched maid-servant now in the Archbishop's prison."[1] Thus the Marchese Ferdinando Cospi, writing a few days after Elisabetta's death. And from that time to this the *on dit* has been repeated in romance, in guide-books, in

[1] *Archivio della R. Galleria di Firenze*, published by Jacopo Cavallucci Rivista di Firenze, 1858.

histories of art, until it has acquired the consistency and strength of indisputable fact.

Recently, however, a very powerful battering-ram has been brought to bear upon an edifice founded on the quicksands of medical ignorance and built of successive suppositions. With the object of "cutting short once for all the erroneous and unwholesome tradition concerning the cause of the painter's death," Signor Antonio Manaresi has published the entire *Processo di Avvelenamento*, translated into Italian, and abridging the Latin portions. To this publication we shall do well to turn, not only, or even chiefly, because it affords material for a right judgment on a specific question, but because the nature of the accusation and the conduct of the trial are intensely characteristic of the country and the period.

The seventeenth century is the golden age in the history of secret poisoning. Throughout the sixteenth century the mania gathered force; in the seventeenth it spread to France and touched the shores of England. In Rome there existed a secret society of women poisoners to which some of the wealthiest and best-born Roman ladies belonged; while in Paris it was found necessary to institute a special court for the investigation of poisoning cases—La Chambre Ardente. It is hardly an exaggeration to say that the apprehension of poison attended any and every malady the causes of which were not obvious and certain. It has sometimes been stated that in Elisabetta's case suspicion was primarily awakened by certain post-mortem phenomena —the body swelled, the nose thickened, the face was strangely transformed and aged. But in reality these changes in the corpse merely gave a picturesque *vraisemblance* to the rumour of foul play already current in the city. " I heard it said publicly in this city of Bologna "—this is the evidence of Donzelli, one of Gianandrea's pupils—" that the aforesaid Elisabetta had been poisoned, and this I heard before she died, even when she was seized, as I heard say, with great pain in the stomach."

The report probably originated in a dark hint from Dr. Gallerati, who was completely puzzled by his patient's symptoms and the powerlessness of his own prescriptions to relieve them.

Elisabetta's death was rapid, painful, and mysterious; therefore it must have been caused by poison. This is the first tier in the fantastic edifice of supposition. And the second is like unto it: *Poison is generally given in food; therefore the poisoner was probably the maid-of-all-work in the Sirani family.* " I know not who could have given poison to my daughter,"—it is the mother who speaks,—" but truly I have suspected that Lucia Tolomelli our servant must have been the person who gave it, either in soup or in drink, or in some other way, because while serving in the house she did not lack the means of doing this treachery to my daughter." Gianandrea and Margherita discussed the possibility of poison as a cause of death much as a modern parent in like case might consider the possibility of sewer gas. They cast about them for a criminal as a householder to-day seeks for a defective drain-pipe: and as the latter, having localized his suspicions, sends for a sanitary inspector, the former, having formulated his accusation, addressed a memorial to the Legate.

S

Those who are depressed by " the servant problem " of the present day may find comfort in studying the manners and customs of seventeenth-century lackeys and waiting-women. Never were servants more worthless and more numerous. Display rather than necessity regulated their numbers; and the comfort in which they lived relatively to that of the class to which they belonged formed an attraction to the least desirable characters. Wages were low, but the practice of tipping was carried to a preposterous extent. Pert waiting-maids were fee'd by the lovers of their mistress, and successfully copied her intrigues. Greedy lackeys presumed at their own pleasure to dismiss or admit their master's visitors, while they involved him in their inter-household quarrels, imitated his vices, and wasted his substance in riotous living.

Lucia Tolomelli was not, however, a fine lady's waiting-maid. She was merely a maid-of-all-work in a humble establishment, and had much the same characteristics, virtues, and defects as an average modern "general." She came with a good character, and though no " treasure," evidently gave satisfaction, for her mistress was surprised, annoyed, and distressed when, after nearly three years' service, she suddenly " gave notice." Her duties were to sweep and dust, help Aunt Giacoma in the kitchen, and open the door to the visitors who came to see Elisabetta paint. When such guests were expected Lucia was allowed to comb and dress her hair ; otherwise this luxury was forbidden her save on Thursdays and Sundays, and then " she did it over-night so as not to lose time in the morning." She had no " evenings out," nor was she permitted to leave the house save when required to accompany one of her mistresses. She had her meals with the family, and was treated with the kindly familiarity more common in Italian than in English households. She received the magnificent wage of four pauls a month, less than twenty shillings a year, but she doubtless got an occasional *mancia* from Elisabetta's visitors, and, like other servants, she received a little present from the family on the occasion of the annual St. Bartholomew Fair.

But in her third year of service, shortly before the Porchetta Festival, she announced her intention of quitting the Sirani household. Elisabetta told her "to sleep over it." She awoke next morning in the same mind. Gianandrea summoned her to his bedside, and made an appeal to her better feelings. Did she not see that her departure was peculiarly ill-timed, considering that he, his wife, and his daughter Barbara were ill? He would never have believed Lucia could have treated the family so badly as to depart without giving them time to find another servant.

But Lucia was obdurate, and the week's notice, usually required both by master and servant in Bologna in the present day, does not seem to have been obligatory in the seventeenth century. Accordingly the Sirani, anxious in spite of their annoyance to do what was right by an orphan girl, sent for her cousin, one Casarini, a tailor, who had placed her with them, and for her brother-in-law, servant to Signor Gualandi, the Government Secretary.

Now Lucia had fully intended to go to the house of this Pagliardi, her sister's husband, but when Signor

Sirani asked the two men if either of them could receive the girl, they both answered no. Casarini then interviewed his tiresome young cousin in the kitchen, and appealed to her self-interest, pointing out that an orphan should not lightly lose a comfortable place. Lucia was as little moved as she had been by the arguments of the " Padrone."

Then by the advice of Gianandrea, Lucia's relatives determined to place her temporarily in the " Mendicanti," or Poor House; and the poor, then as now, having little love for such institutions, they resorted to a stratagem, telling her they would put her in "a family outside the walls."

Thus "on the day of the vigil of the Madonna" (i.e. on August 14), Lucia, accompanied by her brother-in-law and cousin, left the little house in Via Urbana, and made her way past the two famous leaning towers, and along the street, and out through the gate of S. Donato,[1] to the institution founded by S. Carlo Borromeo, when Legate in Bologna in 1560.

Ten days later, when Elisabetta lay in mortal anguish, " it was said publicly in this city of Bologna " " that the poison was given to Signora Elisabetta by Lucia when servant in the house; because"—such is the evidence of one of Gianandrea's pupils—" the aforesaid Lucia after she had heard the aforesaid Signora complain of pain in the stomach, gave notice and departed without having any reason, albeit, as I have heard said, she was entreated not to leave the aforesaid service; but she was determined to go away, without being able to state any cause for doing so, and albeit it was nigh upon the

[1] Now Zamboni.

time of the fair, when, according to custom, she might expect a present."

Thus described, the fact and date of Lucia's departure become a presumption of her guilt. But was that departure—as the Sirani and their friends represented it to be—(1) quite sudden ; (2) quite groundless ; (3) consequent on Elisabetta's symptoms?

Now (1) Lucia herself asserted, and her statement was confirmed by another witness,[1] that she wished to depart many months previously, and that Elisabetta's kindness and persuasion alone induced her to remain. Moreover (2) it is by no means true that she was " unable to state any cause for her departure." On the contrary, she stated a number of causes which were perhaps intrinsically inadequate, but which to her seemed weighty and cogent. She was "sick of being scolded" she told her cousin Casarini, sick of Margherita's nagging tongue, and of the sense that, try as she might, she never succeeded in giving satisfaction. Most of all she resented the phrase of her Padrona that she " ate the bread of idleness." Silly little servant-girl as she was, she wearied of the dreary routine, the watchful strictness of the invalidish household. She was probably not uncomely,—we are told that she had lovely hair,—and her master declared " she was ready to fall in love with every one she saw." She wanted to "go out sometimes," and to dress her hair " as other girls do." She admitted that she was " well treated," but she was not happy in the

[1] "Io son informata che la detta Lucia, avanti che si partisse di casa delli Signori Sirani, diasse di voler partire, chè lo cominciò a dire di Natale; ed io lo so perchè glie l' ho sentito dire." Interrogatorio di Anna Maria Donnini, 26 giugno, 1666.

Sirani household. She knew, she told the judge, that she should lose her fairing by giving notice previous to the Feast of the Porchetta, but "she couldn't stand it any more."

Again, (3) it is difficult after comparing and collating the evidence of various witnesses to connect Elisabetta's symptoms with Lucia's departure. It is indeed true that Lucia is the only person who mentions the attack of pain during the preceding Lent; but the testimony of aunt and mother as to Elisabetta's pallor and emaciation corroborate their servant's statement. The pain returned, according to Margherita, on "the second or third day after San Lorenzo," i.e. on 12 or 13 August, a day or two before Lucia's departure on the 14th; but Lucia declared that her young mistress was ailing for "a good while," *un pezzo*, before her departure, and Anna Maria Donnini, the charwoman, speaks of "a month."

And while it can hardly be said that Lucia departed "as soon as she heard the Signora Elisabetta complain of pain in the stomach," it is equally clear that the girl spoke what she believed to be the truth when she protested that the Signora was not *ill* when she took leave of her. For neither the father nor the family physician viewed Elisabetta's indisposition seriously. Dr. Gallerati prescribed "a little acid syrup"; and Gianandrea, when he reasoned with the obstinate Lucia, did not number his eldest daughter among "the invalids of the house,"[1] who would be inconvenienced by the absence of a servant.

[1] Gianandrea's words are: "ritrovandosi ammalata mia moglie, Barbara mia figliola ed io."

A SEVENTEENTH-CENTURY TRIAL 263

The Sirani family found an additional proof of Lucia's guilt in the illness of the before-mentioned Anna Maria Donnini, a girl whom they frequently employed as messenger and charwoman. Now Anna Maria was a minx, and hysterical to boot. She was made much of by her employers, and discussed them freely with their servant. She encouraged Lucia's grumbling, listened to her silly but innocent confidences and sympathized with her girlish vanity, and then reported to the Padrone all that the girl "said or did." Gianandrea affirmed that Lucia became aware of this espionage and bore ill-will to Anna Maria. But Lucia assured the examining magistrate that Anna Maria had always been her friend, and that there had never been any unpleasantness between them.

Anna Maria and her mother were both employed in the Sirani house on 14 August, 1665. The mother, Antonia Donnini, went home to dinner; the daughter remained that she might "take a picture to the house of Count Annibale Ranuzzi," doubtless Elisabetta's "Carità" in which Count Ranuzzi's sister was portrayed as "Charity," the children being his little nephews.

Gianandrea said that Anna Maria had better have some food before she started on her errand, so that if she "were kept waiting by the Signor Count she might not suffer"; and the minx accordingly repaired to the kitchen. *Was Lucia alone there?* This was the crucial question of the trial. Lucia asserted the presence of Aunt Giacoma; Anna Maria declared that she found no one in the kitchen but the servant.

It was a fast day—the vigil of the Assumption—and

the family meal was to consist simply of a little fish and *pancotto*, that is, bread soaked in water and then beaten with a spoon to the consistency of thick gruel, when it is flavoured with spices or eaten with salt and olive oil. This common food of the poorer classes in Italy was simmering in an earthenware vessel on the fire when Anna Maria appeared and asked for her meal. Lucia took a ladleful of the as yet unflavoured *pancotto* and put it on a plate. Anna Maria tasted it and said it was insipid. Lucia forthwith added something to the tasteless pap. *What was this flavouring?* Lucia declared that it was merely pepper taken from the kitchen pepper-box which stood on the shelf among the pewter plates. Anna Maria asserted that it was a reddish powder, which Lucia called cinnamon and took from a paper which she drew from her bosom. Pepper or cinnamon, Anna Maria found it gritty, ate only a few spoonfuls, and then went about her business.

Lucia then served the family meal in the chamber on the ground floor, which for coolness Signora Margherita occupied in summer; and as soon as she and her mistresses had eaten she prepared to leave the house.

Anna Maria was not kept waiting by Count Ranuzzi, and she returned at the moment when Lucia's cousin, Casarini, was conversing with Signora Margherita, who had retired to bed for a siesta. Whether the minx went in boldly to report herself, or whether she listened at the door, she somehow learned to what kind of "country house" the unfortunate Lucia was about to be conducted. She wanted to warn her, but opportunity was wanting; for Lucia was by Barbara's bedside taking leave of the sick girl and of the Signora Elisabetta. Anna Maria looked in and was included in the good-byes, Lucia adding: "Anna Maria, se ho fatto delle ciarle ne haveto fate ancor voi: ricordatevi però che siamo tutte due nell' istessa posta." (If I have done any silly tricks you have also: remember we are both in the same boat.) The natural interpretation of the phrase is that Lucia when the moment of departure came was a little regretful and a little jealous. Anna Maria was now indispensable to the employers who had always spoilt her. She had been told to report to them if Lucia had "followers" or stood at the windows; and Lucia, aware of the espionage, wished to remind her late companion that she was after all no better than herself. But the word *ciarle* is ambiguous and may be translated *jugglery*. And the following year, when the Sirani had enlarged the bounds of their suspicions, Barbara remembered Lucia's parting shaft and Anna Maria's immediate burst of weeping; and the little incident is recorded on a loose sheet of paper lying among the MS. pages of the *Processo*, as one of the reasons for suspecting Anna Maria's complicity in Lucia's crime.

The following day the minx complained of giddiness and pain in the stomach, and for fifteen days remained in a more or less ailing state in the Sirani service. We do not know when she told her mother that she believed "Lucia had put something bad in the *pancotto*"; but it is a relief to hear that Antonia Donnini promptly told her daughter that she "was a silly, fanciful girl." Nor do we know on what day Dr. Gallerati, after paying Barbara a visit, was requested to "look at this poor young woman who is continually crying and has become insensible." Dr. Gallerati complied with Margherita's request, and then sternly told the minx to go about her work, informing her mistress that there was "nothing the matter with the girl, who must be in love or have some nonsense in her head."

But when Elisabetta had breathed her last, Anna Maria again became insensible, and the confessor of the deceased hastened to her side. He felt her pulse, and then remarked: "This is a queer attack! She looks as though she were dead, and her pulse has not changed."

In spite of doctor and priest, Gianandrea and his wife never seem to have suspected that Anna Maria was shamming. They regarded her as co-victim with their daughter of Lucia's practices, and they sent her to the Ospedale della Morte, where she was treated by one of the physicians who had attended Elisabetta, Dr. Matessilani. He gave her "ordinary remedies, not antidotes or medicaments against poison," and he added, "if her illness had been poisoning I should have known or at least should have suspected it." He did not unfortunately give his diagnosis of the case, at least he did not do so in his formal interrogatory. It is quite probable, and quite conformable to the usages of the times, that he privately gave the examining magistrate his opinion of Anna Maria's health and of the value of her testimony. To a modern reader of the text of the *Processo*, it seems clear that she was an unhealthy girl, nervous and hysterical or epileptic. "People said she was consumptive," according to Lucia; while Gianandrea owned that she had been poorly before her attack of giddiness and pain, and that on the occasion of the previous Carnival, i.e. at a time of special excitement, "gli casca un poco di goccia," a vague phrase indicating some sort of fit, doubtless of the same character as her subsequent attacks of unconsciousness.

Anna Maria, discharged from the hospital, called at the Sirani house. She found its attitude towards her strangely changed. She was told, indeed, that she need not call again. Shortly afterwards she was arrested. With her examination on June 1st, 1666, a new phase of the trial begins.

But here we must look back to the summer of the preceding year, and review the course of the legal proceedings up to this point.

The poor-house of San Gregorio dei Mendicanti belonged, as a religious foundation, to the jurisdiction of the Archbishop. There Lucia was arrested by the Archbishop's officers in consequence of the report current in Bologna which represented her as the murderer of the popular artist. When, on the last day of August, Gianandrea addressed his memorial to the Legate—that is, to the head of the civil government—the unhappy girl was already lodged in the Archiepiscopal prison, and the fact that she was arrested without the instance of the Public Prosecutor, under pretext that she should not escape from the aforesaid place—i.e. "the Mendicanti"—quickened and enlarged the suspicions of the unhappy father. He saw in it an attempt to shelter the murderess of his daughter from the extreme penalties of the law, for the inmates of "the Mendicanti" enjoyed ecclesiastical immunities.

Cardinal Caraffa transmitted Signor Sirani's memorial to the Auditor of the Torrone, and the *Processo verbale* opened the following day (September 1st, 1665) with the clinical examination of Giovanni Andrea Sirani by the Sub-Auditor of the Torrone.

On September 2nd Anna Maria was visited in the hospital, and her deposition taken; while the Court of the Torrone *ad effectum ut constet de corpore delictu* required a certificate of death from the priest of the parish, and the depositions of three persons who had seen and recognized the body after death.

A locksmith whose shop faced the Sirani dwelling, and who had curiously looked through the window into the ground-floor room where the dead artist lay: a carpenter wont to stretch her canvases, who had measured the body for a coffin: a guardian of the parish of S. Mamolo, who had helped to bear the coffin to the church of S. Domenico—these three persons declared that they had known the deceased and that they recognized the corpse in spite of its strange disfigurement.

On the evening of the following day, the keeper of the prisons in the Torrone presented himself in the office of the examining magistrate, and said that the Archbishop's officer had consigned to his keeping the person of Lucia Tolomelli.

Elisabetta's mother and aunt were next examined; then Gianandrea's three pupils; and, on September the seventh, Domenico Casarini, Lucia's cousin. The two doctors who were foremost in maintaining the theory of "administered poison," Dr. Gallerati and one Fabri who had assisted at the autopsy, were examined on the ninth and tenth of September.

Thus ends the first act of the trial. An interval of several months ensued. Gianandrea chafed and fretted at "the law's delay," and wrote bitterly to Cardinal Leopoldo de' Medici that he "turned from the higher powers of Bologna" to a heavenly tribunal, "where justice is not suffocated; for up to now, under pretext of ecclesiastical immunity, this monstrous deed remains hid."

But in fact the delay seems to have been occasioned by hostility, rather than favour, to the prisoner. Her removal to the Torrone did not imply a renunciation on the part of the Archbishop of his carefully guarded ecclesiastical immunities. Lucia's arrest in the Mendicanti protected her from capital punishment. But when the evidence of the doctors furnished real ground for the belief that a murder had been committed, the girl was first returned to the Archiepiscopal prison and then sent back to the "Mendicanti." At once discharged from this asylum, she betook herself to the dwelling of her sister, the wife of Pagliardi, in Via Maggiore (now Via Mazzini). In this street, on April 11th, 1666, she was again arrested.

This time she was taken straight to that part of the Palazzo Municipale called the Torrone, wherein were the prisons and the rooms of the auditors and notary of the Criminal Court. Here she was placed in the women's prison, constructed early in the century by Pietro Fiorentino.[1] And on the twenty-fourth of April,

[1] "And I arranged the prisons under the Legation of the aforesaid Cardinal. But first I had made the sick-room (infirmaria) and the women's prison; and I raised the Tower and made a big room where the punishment of the strappado is given. And I repaired other prisons which were uninhabitable under the government of Monsignore Dandino, then vice-legate of Cardinal Montalto." (MS. record of Pietro Fiorentino in the University Library, Bologna.)

1666, she appeared for the first time before the examining magistrate.

This is the end of the second act of the trial. After it, proceedings are again suspended. Nine weeks later Act III opens with the appearance of Anna Maria in the character of Second Murderer.

The girl still stuck to her tale of the "reddish powder" taken from a packet drawn from Lucia's bosom; but the tone of her *interrogatorio* is very different from that of her previous deposition in the hospital. There, petted and influenced by the Sirani, she declared that Lucia "wished her ill" and had certainly put "something bad" in the *pancotto*. Now, with the Sirani doors closed against her, Lucia was "a good girl" who had ever been and was still her friend. Nor had she herself suspected that "her sickness came from poison given in the form of the powder, but Signora Margherita had told her it must have been poison, like that which had been given to Signora Elisabetta."

On the same loose sheet among the MS. records of the *Processo* on which Anna Maria's strange seizures are described, there is the following curious note: "As to the matter of the powder given to Anna Maria *it may be that it was really innocuous*, but was christened poison by the aforesaid Anna Maria to cover her crime and throw the guilt back upon Lucia."

But if the reddish powder were innocuous, what indication was there that the Sirani's servant girl ever had poison in her possession? As long as Anna Maria is held to be Elisabetta's fellow-victim, who escaped death only because she consumed but two or three spoonfuls of the poisonous *pancotto*, we have a coherent and fairly plausible case against Lucia. But when she is transformed into an accomplice, and her illness and its cause are subtracted from the sum of the evidence against the accused, it is difficult to see what is left to indicate Lucia's guilt. There remains only the fact of her departure from a house where she had long been discontented.

On August the fourth, Lucia was again examined. Her straightforward answers are repetitions of those given in the previous April. The two girls were then confronted. Each stuck to her previous statement as to the flavouring added to the *pancotto*—which was cinnamon-coloured according to Anna Maria, and was ordinary pepper from the kitchen pepper-box according to Lucia. Lucia was invited, but refused, to question Anna Maria. Thus ended the third act of the trial.

The fourth act opens with the orations of the lawyers for the defence and for the prosecution. Nicola de Lemmi, who appeared *procuratore intercessore et escusatore*, was probably called by the Committee for the Defence of the Poor (Ufficio della Difesa dei Poveri), a body which has, unfortunately, no modern counterpart. He contended that there was no case against the accused, while her previous good character and her orderly and religious habits—she " was accustomed to confess and communicate regularly every year and also upon the great festivals "—formed a presumption of innocence. On the other hand Bianchini, the counsel for the prosecution and the personal friend of the Sirani, vehemently maintained the dangerous juridical doctrine that the graver the crime and the harder to prove, the more allowable it is "to proceed by way of conjecture, presumption, and partial indication." The perforation of the stomach, he maintained, was an indication of administered corrosive poison. Again, the sudden sickening in the midst of robust health (a mistaken assertion this, for Elisabetta had ailed for months), the purple extremities, the changes in the corpse, were the very signs and tests of poison enunciated by Galen. In short, the medical evidence sufficed to prove the fact of the crime; while it was unlikely that anything more definite would be discovered unless the prisoner were tortured.

Torture was not resorted to—an omission which the Sirani and their friends viewed as an evidence of the prisoner's protection by some person in authority. But by the seventeenth century torture was kept within certain prescribed limits. It was illegal when there was no actual proof of crime, and here, in spite of Bianchini's assertion to the contrary, it was held "non constare satis corpore delicti." It was known that two at least of the doctors present at the autopsy held the theory of "generated poison" in contradistinction to that of "administered poison"; and that they had not already been examined, though Dr. Gallerati and Dr. Fabri had appeared as experts for the prosecution more than a year before, sufficiently indicates that there was no miscarriage of justice in favour of the accused, and that if "the trial" were "ill-conducted," it was because, as Malvasia reluctantly admits, "the Auditor always seemed to favour Signor Sirani."

At the eleventh hour these two doctors, Matessilani

A SEVENTEENTH-CENTURY TRIAL 273

and Oretti, were summoned by Monari, "Advocate of the Poor," as experts for the defence. They declared that to the best of their belief Elisabetta Sirani had died a natural death.

Lucia Tolomelli's guilt was non-proven; nevertheless, in deference to the strong popular feeling against her, she was banished from the Legations. "A light sentence if guilty, a heavy and undeserved if innocent" is Malvasia's comment; and he points out that if there were no ground for torture, there could be none for exile. His own attitude appears to be one of suspended judgment as regards Lucia's instrumentality, but of certainty respecting the fact of Elisabetta's death by a mysterious *invida manus*. He declares that his Christianity and his cloth hardly restrain him from cursing the impious being who had deprived the world of so great an artist; while he alludes to some one who, when the proud parents used to display the gifts presented to their daughter by illustrious sitters, looked on with such greedy eyes and such obviously reluctant praises that the observant Canon warned his friend Sirani that this person was consumed with envy. Lucia was asked by the examining magistrate if she knew one Lorenzo Zanichelli. Anna Maria was asked if she had ever talked with a red-haired painter. Both girls answered in the negative. Perhaps this red-haired artist was the person Malvasia mentally accused; perhaps Gianandrea also had him in his mind when he declared: "I suspect that the aforesaid Lucia has administered poison at the instance of another, because we are not at enmity with any one, therefore I hold that the aforesaid, my daughter, has been poisoned on account of

T

her talent, that is, that some one has caused her to be poisoned out of envy."

Besides alluding obscurely to his own theory of the Envious Hand, Malvasia mentions two other current explanations of Elisabetta's fate. Some said that it was compassed " by a high and powerful hand " whose proffered attentions the artist had rejected. This supposition is consonant with the belief that the course of justice was prevented in favour of the accused; and Gianandrea's above-quoted letter to the Cardinal Leopoldo de' Medici would seem to indicate that he forsook his original theory of professional jealousy in favour of this more romantic explanation. Others, again, spoke of a certain "cavalier grande" mortally offended because the artist had drawn him in caricature.

But Malvasia dismisses with scorn both these popular suppositions; those who hold them are "much deceived." Certainly they presuppose that an honest if silly girl could easily be induced to murder a beloved mistress. Her affection for Elisabetta is mentioned, or is taken for granted, by every witness in the trial; none of them ever suppose that the girl was actuated by enmity or spite. Malvasia even makes the curious conjecture that she was induced to administer the poison by the assurance that it was a love potion, something "which had power to make the signora, whom she loved only too well, love her in return." There is nothing in the *Processo* which lends colour to this fancy, nor does it diminish the difficulty which attends any theory which makes Lucia the instrument of another's malice, i.e. how and when she held com-

CARICATURE OF THE OLD MAN RIALI
FROM A TRACING OF THE COPY PRESERVED WITH THE MS. OF THE PROCESSO
IN THE ARCHIVIO DI STATO, BOLOGNA

munication with any one belonging to the outside world. She was closely questioned as to the company she kept; and the single fact elicited was that she once talked with a whitesmith called in to mend a kitchen pot, a man who had made love to her when she lived with her mother. But Margherita promptly sent her son and one of her daughters to the cellar to act as chaperons; and for the rest the girl was kept in convent-like seclusion.

In spite of its inherent improbability, and of Malvasia's scorn, the story of the caricature was probably seriously considered in court, and has been revived in modern times. In the year 1844 Signor Michel Angelo Gualandi found a curious pen-and-ink drawing in the possession of a certain Bolognese artist in Florence. The drawing represented a hideous old man in flopping hat and long cloak, and appended to it was this description: "Portrait from life of one of the family of Riali, original by the famous Elisabetta Sirani, on account of which she was poisoned by the same Riali, and a celebrated painter perished in her prime."

Signore Gualandi had this drawing engraved, and the copy now lying with the MS. of the *Processo* is doubtless, as Signore Manaresi conjectured, one of these impressions, placed there by Gualandi when he made his transcript of the MS. Unfortunately, Signore Manaresi carried his conjecture a step further, and declared that the engraving had no seventeenth-century original. When the painter, Liverati, died the caricature was not found among his effects—"suddenly as rare things will it vanished." Signore Manaresi argued from this disappearance that the too credulous Gualandi had been the victim of a practical joke on the part of his artist friend.

But the hoax theory had an obvious weakness: it involved the further supposition that Liverati was an accomplished paleographer; for although the inscription on the caricature does not correspond precisely with any one handwriting in the records of the *Processo*, it is thoroughly seventeenth century in character. Happily before this paper was concluded, the existence of the original caricature was no longer a question of inference and hypothesis. Among the drawings kept, and recently put in order by Signore Ferri, Ispettore of the Uffizi Gallery in Florence, the writer discovered Elisabetta's grotesque sketch of the hideous old man Riali. It came to the gallery in 1866 as part of the magnificent collection of Professor Emilio Santarelli, to whom it had doubtless been sold or given by the Bolognese painter.

There is a curious appendix to this seventeenth-century poisoning case. Perhaps, after the first distress and panic were outlived, the unhappy father began to feel less certain of Lucia Tolomelli's guilt. Perhaps Anna Maria confessed to exaggeration or misstatement. Perhaps some positive indication of the little servant's innocence came unexpectedly to light. At all events on January 3rd, 1668, Giovanni Andrea Sirani subscribed, for himself and his family, to a very singular document. He declared that freely, and for the love of God, he made peace with Madonna Lucia Tolomelli, cancelling all suits against her, and consenting to the erasure of her name from the registers of the third bench of the Torrone.

In the following February Lucia's sentence of banishment was revoked, and two years later Gianandrea passed to his long home.

CHAPTER IV

ELISABETTA'S PHYSICIANS

> Thy pardon for this long and tedious case
> Which now that I review it, needs must seem
> Unduly dwelt on, prolixly set forth !
> BROWNING, *Epistle of Karshish*.

THE trial of Lucia Tolomelli for the supposed murder of her mistress throws a lurid light on the medical knowledge and practice of the seventeenth century—a century at the beginning of which Bacon, in his marvellous review of human learning, had declared that "Medicine is a science which hath been more professed than laboured, and yet more laboured than advanced ; the labour having been rather in a circle than in progression."[1]

We note first the medieval mingling of astrology and medicine in Dr. Gallerati's reply to Elisabetta's first complaints of pain. He prohibited purgatives—not because his diagnosis of "a slight catarrh" was contradictory to their use, but because "the sun was in Leo" and therefore "it was no time to take medicine."

The remedy he actually prescribed was "a little simple acid syrup," to be taken in tablespoonful doses the first thing in the morning. This *Sciroppa Acetosa*

[1] *Advancement of Learning*, book II, X. 3.

was made by Aunt Giacoma, doubtless according to a recognized recipe similar to that given by Lemery in his *Farmacopea Universale*, which is as follows :—

"In a glazed earthenware pipkin put two parts powdered sugar and one part white wine vinegar. Put it over the fire till the sugar liquefies. Skim and pour off.

"It is good as a cooling beverage in burning fevers, alleviates thirst, arrests spitting of blood and other hæmorrhage, and resists poison."

About the middle of August Elisabetta was troubled with an eruption with small pustules which appeared on the neck under the chin and at the angle of the jaws. She did not consult the family physician for this annoying complaint, but successfully employed some ointment which Aunt Giacoma "kept in the house." It was one of those convent preparations which were the medieval equivalents of the modern patent medicine. Aunt Giacoma said she was wont to procure it from the Sisters of S. Peter Martyr.

If Elisabetta Sirani were indeed the victim of foul play, she was given from first to last every chance in the way of antidotes. We have seen that the Simple Acid Syrup was said to "resist poison"—an assertion probably based on the observed efficacy of acids in counteracting alkaline poisons; and when her mortal agony began, and the arrival of the physician was delayed, Elisabetta's terrified relations gave her "a little Triaca," an electuary which enjoyed for centuries a great reputation as a "counter-poison," besides being a specific for a vast number of infirmities not arising from poison.

This Triaca, Theriaque or Venice Treacle, was, according to Bacon, one of the very few remedies in respect of which physicians were content "to tie themselves severely and religiously to receipts": and for this licence he blames them, declaring that they "frustrate the fruit of tradition and experience in adding and taking out and changing *quid pro quo* in their receipts, commanding so over the medicine as the medicine cannot command over the disease."[1] It is singular that treacle should have been thus signally exempted from medical caprice, seeing that the prescription of Andromach, the physician of Nero, contained over sixty ingredients, some of which were compounds. Nevertheless, it was not till the middle of the seventeenth century that any one of them was "taken out or changed," and then a certain M. d'Aquin, of Paris, first physician to the King, ventured to issue a "reformed recipe," and to place the same in the Royal Gallican Pharmacopea.

But if the physicians respected the venerable prescription, the apothecaries were less scrupulous. There was an immense quantity of cheap counterfeit treacle in the market. Venice had at first a practical monopoly of the manufacture of triaca; later a good deal was made at Montpellier. But as Sieur Pierre Pomet, the Paris druggist, tells us, there were sold at fairs whole barrelfuls of so-called *Theriaque de Montpellier*, which was merely common honey mingled with mouldy roots; while more fastidious customers were tempted by pretty *faïence* pots, on which were painted two vipers crowned with fleurs-de-lis, with the inscription *Theria-*

[1] *Advancement of Learning*, book II, x. 8.

que fine de Venise, "quoiqu'elle soit faite à Orleans ou à Paris."

In a lengthy treatise on the making of treacle published in 1570 by a physician of repute in Naples, we find an ingenious justification of the portentous number of ingredients used in Andromach's prescription. There are, says the writer Bartolomeo Maranta, many different kinds of poison and much diversity in the nature and complexion of men. A simple remedy aids one person and is useless to another; it is an antidote against one sort of poison and does not withstand a second; it helps a single infirmity, but cannot include virtue equal to a great number of maladies. Therefore the first maker of Triaca was moved to make a great collection of simples to compose an electuary which should be a singular antidote against all kinds of poison, "for all natures and complexions," and should further be helpful to all other kinds of infirmities.

Headache, dimness of sight, mental disturbances; female complaints; diseases of the liver, stomach, and spleen; congestions, asthma, shortness of breath, blood-spitting; ague, gout, and rheumatic fluxions;—these are some of the complaints for which Triaca, taken in varying doses, at various times, undiluted, or mixed with water, wine, or acid syrup, is said to be a notable and sovereign remedy. Children alone must abstain from this universal panacea; for once, it is naïvely stated, *Galen saw a child die the night after he had taken treacle*, which is too powerful a compound for the infantile digestion. There is one other limitation to its use: it is too heating to be taken in the height of summer—an injunction disregarded by Elisabetta's relatives. For the rest, "if any man is not helped by its means, the failure must be attributed solely to its bad composition, resulting either from ignorance or the negligence of physicians and apothecaries."

When Dr. Matessilani from the Ospedale della Morte reached the patient's bedside, he ordered an injection of sweet oil, and friction about the heart with an unguent. In the evening Dr. Gallerati, who probably at once suspected poison, ordered an emetic. The nature of the embrocation and emetic is not stated; but Gianandrea is careful to declare that all the medicaments ordered by the doctors were procured at the pharmacy of San Petronio or of San Paolo, and that the injection was given by a nurse from the Ospedale della Morte. These facts were important as legal evidence, tending to eliminate the possibility that poison was administered subsequent to the departure of Lucia Tolomelli. The clyster, especially in France, was sometimes a vehicle for the introduction of poison; but to deal with well-known druggists, who were employed by physicians of repute, and whose shops were situated in the best and most public quarters of the city, was something of a guarantee that the medicaments used had not been tampered with; whereas many an obscure and starving Italian apothecary was ready, like him whom Romeo found in Mantua, to brave the penalties of the law and sell his fatal knowledge and his drugs for bread.

When Dr. Gallerati arrived on Friday morning and found his patient no better, he prescribed the preparation called *Elescoff* or *Episcopi*, a purgative electuary containing scammony and cream and salt of tartar. It was duly given in a little broth.

But the patient's condition became hourly more alarming. The confessor was sent for; and the doctor, as a last resource, administered some *Oil of the Grand Duke* and a little *Bezoar*. Beyond the fact that it was an esteemed antidote the writer has discovered nothing concerning the first-named remedy; but Bezoar was a medicine of great repute. It was a concretion found in the stomach and intestines of ruminating animals, and the supply being inadequate to the demand, a chemical imitation was sometimes employed. It is told of Charles IX of France that he resolved to test the alleged virtues of Bezoar on the vile body of a cook who was believed to have stolen two silver spoons. The thief was given a dose of corrosive sublimate followed by a dose of Bezoar. The antidote was ineffectual, and the wretched man died in agony seven hours later.

Elisabetta likewise died in spite of Bezoar, plus treacle, Elescoff, and Oil of the Grand Duke;[1] and the unhappy father, counselled by Dr. Gallerati, demanded a post-mortem examination.

The body was opened by Master Ludovico, Surgeon of the Ospedale della Morte. Of the seven physicians present, Dr. Fabri alone, and once only, touched the corpse. Surgery and dispensing were alike beneath the attention of these professors of medicine; nay, acquaintance with such " manual arts " were sometimes held to be disqualifications for a doctor's degree.[2]

[1] One is reminded of the conduct of Benvenuto Cellini's Roman physician, who despaired of his life and left his bedside with the direction: " Apply the five medicines one after another." (*Memoirs*, ch. x, vii.)

[2] *Vide* Niccolo Lemery's Preface: "As if," he says indignantly, "exercises necessary to the perfection of medicine could be unworthy of a physician."

In the present day in a case of suspected poison the autopsy is followed by a chemical examination of the various organs of the body. This analysis largely determines the verdict. If traces of poison are discovered, its quality and approximately its quantity are indisputably established. But this seventeenth-century post-mortem examination left the doctors divided—not indeed as to the facts observed, but as to their interpretation—and augmented public suspicion without furnishing substantial evidence against the suspected person. Five out of the seven bystanders who from a distance noted the perforations of the stomach attributed it to the action of *corrosive poison*. Dr. Gallerati, who had previously administered antidotes at random, did not venture further than this generic statement. The "administered poison" was never named specifically.

Malvasia, however, who doubtless knew the private opinion of the doctors, declares that it was clearly "foul and plebeian, such as caustic, commonly called *fuoco morto*"; which fact seems to him an argument against the theory that the poisoner was a gentleman of importance.

It would seem that arsenic was the poison most affected by aristocratic Italian poisoners. It was almost certainly the weapon of the Borgias. It was also the deadly principle of the colourless, tasteless liquid circulated in Italy, in the latter half of the seventeenth century, in small glass phials, labelled "Aqua Toffana, Acquetta di Napoli," or "Manna di San Niccolo di Bari." For upwards of fifty years the maker of this liquid, La Toffana, carried on a lucrative business of indiscriminate murder. At last, her secret becoming widely known, she took refuge in a convent in Naples. But public fear and indignation overcame the scruples of superstitious piety; the convent was broken into, and the wretched beldame handed over to the civil authorities, by whom, in 1709, she was executed. Her preparation was reputed to cause the victim's death at any determinate period of weeks, months, or even years, and that in a peculiarly insidious way, causing languor, weariness, loathing for food, and a general gradual decay, without any marked symptoms of fever, vomiting, or such violent pain as attacked the unfortunate Elisabetta.

While fully admitting the terrible prevalence of secret poisoning in the seventeenth century, it is certain that many deaths described as murders were due to natural causes and to diseases unrecognized or misunderstood by the physicians of the day. Ptomaine poisoning, for instance, was not known; and many seemingly suspicious deaths after the consumption of eel-pie, or similar pasties, were doubtless due to these mysterious animal poisons. Little, again, was known concerning septic poisons; while blood poisoning, as a result of impure water or insanitary surroundings, was recognized dimly if at all. Yet the majority of town-dwellers habitually drew their water from wells polluted by the infiltration from filthy streets, while advances in public decency were converted into dangers to public health by a lack of knowledge of the elements of sanitary engineering and a blissful ignorance of the perils of ill-placed cesspools and leaking drain-pipes.

Again, when chemistry was still in swaddling clothes, and suspicion could not be confirmed or dispelled by the analyst, the suggestion of poison was an absolutely secure refuge for the ignorant physician. And all seventeenth-century physicians were ignorant, needlessly ignorant, of what Bacon calls "the footsteps of diseases and their devastations of the inward parts." The great lawyer justly arraigns the medical profession for the lack of systematic and recorded observation, for the "discontinuance of medicinal history." While members of his own profession have for centuries been careful to report new cases and decisions for the direction of future judgment, physicians had made no notes of things which "might have been observed by the multitude of anatomies" (i.e. post-mortem examinations), but which "now upon opening of bodies are passed over slightly and in silence."

The opening of the body of Elisabetta Sirani illustrates and justifies this condemnation of the medical profession. Only one of the seven doctors present—i.e. Doctor Fabri, shown by his interrogatory to have been a more careful observer than the rest—took the trouble to introduce one of his fingers into the perforation,[1] and thereby discovered that the circumference was ringed round by hardened tissue. But the doctor did not perceive the significance of his own observations. To-day it is recognized as an indication of *prolonged inflammation*.

The professional evidence for and against the asserted traces of poison, and the probable cause and nature of the artist's sufferings and death, assuming both to have been natural, can be discussed adequately only in the

[1] "Io intromessi il dito auricolare della mano destra e toccai la circonferenza di detto foro osservando come qualche poco incallita."

pages of a medical journal, and were actually discussed in the *Bulletino delle Scienze Mediche di Bologna*, in May, 1898. Suffice it to say here that competent medical authorities have asserted that Elisabetta's symptoms—the pain felt more or less for a long period, its intensity after eating, the patient's changed appearance, pallor, and emaciation, the acute symptoms of 27 August, the difficulty of lying down—and all the post-mortem appearances, notably the position of the perforation in the stomach and the ring of hardened tissue surrounding it, are all consonant with the diagnosis of ulcer in the stomach, causing sudden perforation and consequent peritonitis. On the other hand, experts have declared that a dose of corrosive poison powerful enough to produce perforation could not have taken twelve days (from 15 to 27 August) to accomplish its work; while small doses repeated over a long period would not have produced a lesion at a single point.

It is noteworthy that Dr. Matessilani, one hundred and seventy years before this disease was recognized, expressed a belief that generated poison had caused "an ulcerous inflammation."

CHAPTER V

ELISABETTA'S WORK

> Work of his hand
> He nor commends nor grieves;
> Pleads for itself the fact;
> As unrepenting Nature leaves
> Her every act.

THE statement graven above the portal of the house in the Via Urbana is repeated *ad nauseam* in every guide-book to Bologna and every history of Bolognese Art. Elisabetta Sirani is universally proclaimed the "Emulatrice del Sommo Guido Reni."[1]

In accepting this statement we need to remind ourselves of three facts:—

(1) That in the opinion of her contemporaries and of art critics and art lovers for two successive centuries it was regarded as a very high praise.

---

[1] The English traveller, John Evelyn, echoed this judgment, but, it would seem, in merely a parrot-like fashion. In the midst of his description of Bologna we find this phrase: "This Citie is full of rare pieces especially of Guido, Domenichino, and a Virgin named Isabetta Sirani, now living, who has painted many excellent pieces, and imitates Guido so well that many skilful artists have been deceived." Now when Evelyn visited Bologna in the year 1645, Elisabetta, or Isabetta as she is sometimes called, was only *seven years old*. One cannot avoid the conclusion that the worthy gentleman improved his diary with the accounts of later travellers, without realizing the shortness of Elisabetta's life. He thought she was painting in 1645, and imagined he remembered her work. Probably he confused it with that of her father.

(2) That it is true, but not the whole truth.

(3) That we of the twentieth century, in considering the work of the seventeenth, are almost certain to err on the side of condemnation.

The books which recorded the impressions or guided the steps and opinions of early Victorian or eighteenth-century travellers give us the measure of the change which has taken place in the attitude of the cultured public towards the Eclectic school. What is now reprobated as a baneful form of decadence was once hailed as a second and glorious renaissance. We worship what our grandfathers and great-grandfathers burned; we burn what they adored. We go to Bologna to see Francia. Mrs. Stark's celebrated guide-book did not even mention him. We delight in the lovely colouring of Lippo di Dalmasio. Mr. Eustace and his contemporaries waxed eloquent and sentimental over the great canvases of the Carracci and their followers.

Of all those followers Guido Reni was the most fervidly, fulsomely, and deservedly belauded. No master has ever been overrated to a greater degree or for a longer period than the painter of the *Ecce Homo*. He alone among the Eclectics retains a portion of his sometime popularity. Among painters who, in the felicitous phrase of a French critic, were "peintres beaux-esprits au lieu de peintres inspirés," he was undoubtedly relatively great; but his very superiority was injurious to the welfare of Art, in that it gave rise, to quote again from M. Henri Delaborde, to "the regrettable successes of mediocrity." It is comparatively easy to imitate a painter whose virtues are chiefly technical, and whose sentiment is superficial. And whereas in the Golden Age of painting discipleship meant the assimilation of what was best in the master for the nourishment of original gifts, in the Bronze Age it meant merely the perpetuation of a manner. Guido's manner was copied with extraordinary success by artists of inferior ability; and among these imitators none was more successful, or less inferior, than the young daughter of Giovanni Andrea Sirani.

She was, we have already seen, his pupil only indirectly. But just as in natural relationship, characteristics of mind and body are often seen to skip a generation, so in this artistic kinship Elisabetta resembled the master whom she never knew more nearly than did her father who had been Guido's favourite pupil. She caught with singular exactness the characteristics of his "second manner," his mild dignity, his inept serenity, his plaster-like flesh-tints, his gentle diffused light. But for good and evil, in expression as in range of subjects, she is far more limited. She never rises to Guido's heights nor sinks to his depths. Her sweetness is less cloying, her artificiality less obvious. She has no conception of deep grief or stormy passion, but she indulges in no theatrical horrors. She has no keen sense of beauty; her men and women are pleasing, comely, graceful, not supremely lovely; they are commonplace and plain, not ugly and repulsive. She never could have painted the radiant Aurora of the Rospigliosi Palace in Rome, nor the thorn-crowned Man of Sorrows of the Bolognese Gallery. She never would have painted the vulgar Samson drinking from the jawbone, nor the Slaughter of the Innocents, with its stage terror and its absence of natural grief. Her work is far from being weak, but there is a constant negative quality about it which makes it somewhat unsatisfying. To describe it justly one must employ comparatives rather than superlatives. Before beginning to examine it in detail let us again remind ourselves that we shall be disposed to underrate it. Owing to many different causes, which cannot be discussed here—which in part defy analysis and elude classification,—we are nowadays far more in sympathy with the spirit of the thirteenth and fourteenth centuries than with that of the seventeenth and the eighteenth.

Not the art alone, but the music, literature, architecture, oratory, religion, and social life of the *Seicento* are distasteful and incomprehensible to the men and women, more especially the English men and women, of the twentieth century. The theatrical scenes of the Bolognese masters are antipathetic to a generation to whom the work of the early Florentine and Sienese schools makes peculiar and intimate appeal. We cannot feel the precise thrill, the particular quality of emotion which the tearful Madonnas of Guercino and the suffering Christs of Guido Reni awakened in contemporaries. We are at home in the severe and spacious churches of the friars, and strangers in the decorated *barocco* temples of the Society of Jesus. We are interested in the early history of Minorites and Dominicans, and comparatively indifferent to the schemes and struggles of Ignatius Loyala. We can understand the fervour of the Crusades, not that of the Catholic reaction. S. Francesco and S. Chiara are our friends,

S. Filippo Neri and S. Teresa are hardly acquaintances. We read the *Little Flowers*, but not the once popular *Flaming Heart* or *Life* of St. Theresa. For one modern Englishman who knows the sometime belauded poets, Achillini and Marini, for five who have glanced through Metastasio, there are fifty who study Dante with pious regularity.

In justice to the Eclectics we must admit :—

First, that they were more truly artistic than their creed. The very reason of our distaste for their work is that it embodies and expresses the *Zeitgeist* of an age with which we are out of sympathy. Borrowers and imitators by profession, they thoroughly fused and welded their material in the fire of *barocco* sentiment. *Secondly*, that in giving us the quintessence of the time they give it rectified and refined. The art of the *Seicento* was less degraded than its society or its religion, less bombastic than its rhetoric, less monstrously artificial than its poetry. Guido Reni and Guercino, Domenichino and Tiarini, Giovanni Andrea Sirani and his gifted daughter were influences for good and not for evil. They show us the best and noblest aspect of an age of decadence, an age devoid of true dignity and destitute of great ideals.

The natural starting-point for any study of Elisabetta Sirani's work is the " Baptism of Christ" on the left wall of the first chapel to the left from the entrance door of the church of the Campo Santo in Bologna. It is, as she records with naïve satisfaction in her catalogue, " un quadro grandissimo"; and it was her first important order.

Malvasia gives us a pretty little account of the arrival

of this commission and of the young artist's joy at receiving it. The good Canon, according to his frequent custom, was paying an evening visit to the invalid Giovanni Andrea. There was a knock at the door, a man's step upon the stairs, and one Gozzini was ushered into the upstairs-room where the sick painter lived and taught. He came from the Fathers of the Certosa, for whom some four or five years earlier Giovanni Andrea Sirani had painted a large picture representing the Supper in the house of the Pharisee. They now desired a companion picture for the opposite wall of the chapel; and this time the commission was given not to the father but to the daughter. Elisabetta was still in her teens, and on learning Gozzini's errand she jumped for joy. Withdrawing to a corner of the room with a sheet of white paper, some water-colour, and a camel-hair pencil, she then and there sketched in the whole composition. It was finished before her elders had concluded their evening chat, and was her only study for a large and important work.

Malvasia further tells us that she subsequently presented him with the sketch, and that it was thoroughly typical of her mode of composition. Her invention and execution were extraordinarily quick. She conceived her subject at once and conceived it whole; and, as a rule, after a few rough pencil lines she drew it with water-colour and brush on white paper, putting in light and shade at the same time—" the method," says the admiring Canon, " of the greatest masters," and one to which her father never aspired. Several examples of this method of sketching may be seen in the collection of Elisabetta's drawings in the Galleria degli Uffizi in

Florence, where they are shown on application to the Signore Ispettore. For the sake of Elisabetta's reputation it is unfortunate that this collection is almost unknown to the public. For a painter's finished work never seems to proclaim his true rank, or to bring us quite so close to him as do his first studies and rough sketches. In them his capacity lies, so to speak, uncovered before us; undistracted by colour and ornament we measure his naked strength and weakness. Now Elisabetta's studies are certainly in "the manner of the greatest masters." They possess precisely the qualities in which women's work is most frequently deficient— qualities notably lacking in the drawings of her Bolognese predecessor, Lavinia Fontana. They are easy, dexterous, spirited, unhesitating, self-confident — the work of one thoroughly mistress of herself and of the technical side of her art.

But to return to the young artist's first important picture, the Baptism in the church of the Certosa. It hangs in a bad light and is not easy to see in detail, still less easy to photograph. It is not a beautiful or a pleasing picture; but it is astonishingly powerful and bold—one might almost say audacious, when one remembers that it is the work of a girl under twenty. From clouds of glory in the centre of the sky, emerges the figure of God the Father with right hand uplifted in blessing. On either side are angels,—rather solid feminine shapes with floating draperies. From below the clouds the Dove descends upon the Son of God, who kneels on a rock in the shallow river. The Precursor in red drapery stands with hand uplifted above the Saviour's head—the pose of hand and arm are un-

THE BAPTISM OF CHRIST
THE CERTOSA, BOLOGNA

fortunate.[1] The stream in which the feet of the Christ and the Baptist are half immersed is flat, unwatery, untransparent.

To right and left of the two central figures are groups of spectators, presumably the Baptist's audience. They appear to be much interested in one another, unobservant of the baptism, and ignorant of any celestial manifestations. In the middle distance some one is hanging towels to dry on the branches of a tree, while noticeable in the foreground is the vigorous lifelike figure of a woman in a yellow turban suckling a child. In the opposite corner of the picture, a seated youth, with devout and joyful countenance, looks up into the face of a brawny half-naked old man who stands beside him. The painter seems to indicate that these are newly-baptized persons, who have just come up out of the stream. The youth is putting on his hose—an action exceedingly interesting to the student of costume. One stocking lies on the ground beside him—he is drawing on the other; they are of coarse grey material, are attached by red ties, and are *toeless*.

There is a figure yet more interesting than this handsome youth performing his toilet. Behind him, on the same side of the picture, in close attendance on Our Lord, are two "Santine,"—young girls, chattering together in girlish fashion. One in blue has towels or garments folded over her arm; one in pink, looking upwards, raises a hand emphatically to enforce the words pouring from her lips. Now in this pretty, curly-headed, animated, and very human "little saint," Elisa-

[1] Slightly suggesting the offer of a perch for the Dove who hovers above.

betta, as she herself tells us, gave her own portrait to the Fathers of the Certosa.

It is difficult to perceive much resemblance between this slim fair-haired child and the buxom comely young woman who looks out at us from the little picture in the smallest room of the Bolognese Gallery (9503). This little picture has always been described as an "auto-ritratto," and expert opinion agrees with the tradition. Elisabetta's latest biographer, Signor Manaresi, is, however, inclined to ascribe it to Barbara Sirani, since Barbara is known to have painted her sister's portrait not long before the latter's tragic death ; and he argues, with much plausibility, that the younger sister's technique might well be undistinguishable from that of the elder, under whom, and with whom, she worked.

Whoever was the artist, one feels instinctively that the likeness is a good one. Elisabetta stands, a palette in her left hand, a brush in her right, in the act of painting. She wears a tight-fitting blue velvet bodice, with fine, lace-trimmed, white fawn chemisette. Gems fasten the bodice, and loop a drapery round the arm-holes. There is a string of pearls at her throat. Her hair is drawn back tightly save for a few flat curls upon the forehead and falls in ringlets on each side of her face, after the fashion of seventeenth-century coiffures alike in England and on the Continent.

At Castelguelfo there is yet a third portrait of Elisabetta occupying a middle position in time between the "Santina" of the Certosa and the little picture of the Pinacoteca. Again we see the artist in the act of painting. This picture has long been in the Hercolani

THE CHRIST-CHILD ON THE GLOBE
PINACOTECA, BOLOGNA

collection. Oretti, however, mentions it as being in "Casa Oretti," and says that it is not by her own hand.

There is a tradition, recorded even by the official catalogue, that the head of a nun—a small canvas in the second corridor of the Bologna Pinacoteca—is an "auto-ritratto." If this be the case, it must have been taken during the last months of the painter's life, and would corroborate the testimony of Aunt Giacoma as to her niece's altered looks. It is difficult to trace any resemblance between the mournful nun and the fair, plump, cheerful young woman of the little portrait in Camera G.

This little room in the Pinacoteca contains seven small pictures by Elisabetta Sirani. Most noticeable among them are the *Virgine Addolorata* and the *Bambino Gesù sul Mondo*, which have a certain poetic beauty and suggestiveness possessed by none of her large paintings.

In one of his wonderful Dreams Jean Paul Richter describes the vast ocean of life through which suns and planets float as motes in light. Brain and senses are reeling before the contemplation of the universe when he sees sailing towards him through galaxies of stars a dark globe. And on the globe stands a child. And the child turns on him a look so bright and loving that he wakes for very joy.

Elisabetta's *Bambino Gesù sul Mondo* might serve as an illustration for the Dream of the German transcendentalist. The perfectly infantile features of her Christ-Child are touched with subtle majesty. His little hand is uplifted with authority to bless. The olive-branch in his left hand is the sceptre of the Prince of Peace. He stands on the globe of the world, its pilot through vast misty space, and the clouds behind the infant head are touched with brightness and glow into an aureole. The scheme of colour is delicate and characteristic. A floating scarf of dull pinkish mauve connects the flesh tints with the blue streaks in the sky. This little picture (it is 38 by 27 centimetres) was painted, like her earlier " quadro grandissimo," for the Fathers of the Certosa.

Beside it, even smaller in size, and on copper instead of canvas, hangs the *Virgine Addolorata*. The sorrowing Mother, in under-dress of dull carnation and deep blue draperies, sits holding on her knees the crown of thorns. Her attitude expresses sorrowful contemplation and restrained grief. In the background, to the left of the Virgin Mother, rises the cross. Two angels embrace its arms; a third with clasped hands stands at its foot gazing upwards, as though he mystically beheld its divine burden; a fourth kneels weeping in the foreground beside the instruments of the passion.

Elisabetta was only nineteen when she painted this really beautiful and poetic little picture. To its entry in her catalogue is added the note: " E l' intagliai anco in rame"; and this engraving is mentioned by Adam Bartsch with unstinted admiration. The order for the picture came from a certain Padre Ettore Ghisilieri, of the church of the Madonna di Galliera; and the oratory of the church was its first home. Four of Elisabetta's pictures still hang there; all were ordered by the same priest. One of them, a " Conception," painted in the last year of her life, is a very graceful little picture on copper. Its composition reminds one of her father's treatment of the same subject in the canvas numbered 176, Corridor 2, of the Pinacoteca. The Virgin stands on a white crescent moon which rests upon the head of a greenish serpent with curled tongue and feline expression, who lies coiled on the terrestrial globe. Angels, holding white lilies, hover in the clouds. The stars of heaven have come together to form a faint, crown-like nimbus round the Virgin's head. Her brown hair falls smoothly parted round her sweet oval face : her beautiful hands are crossed submissively upon her breast : she is the willing handmaid of the Lord.

A larger picture, removed like the *Virgine Addolorata* from the Madonna di Galliera to the walls of the Pinacoteca, represents the vision of S. Filippo Neri. The Saint, vested for Mass, kneels near an altar; in front of him stands the Virgin, tendering her child for his adoration. Elisabetta's catalogue describes the picture as an altar-piece, and states that the order came from the Signore Fabri Dottore. This was probably the physician who maintained the theory of "administered poison" in the trial of Lucia Tolomelli, and whose evidence was remarkable for its superior accuracy and observation.

Two other pictures by Elisabetta hang in Corridor 2 close to the S. Filippo Neri.

Number 176 is the *Madonna of the Rosary*. The Virgin's face—very sweet and framed in light brown hair—her attitude, the background of spacious sky, the starry nimbus, recall the little *Concezione* in the church of the Galliera,—with the difference of a total change of expression. The Virgin of the Rosary is the Queen of Heaven, standing, a sceptre in her right hand and the Divine Child on her left arm, to receive the homage of the World.

In his right hand, which rests against his mother's heart, the Infant Christ is holding a crimson rose; in his left he extends a rosary of pearls. There is no aureole round his head, no dignity in the sweet but inexpressive little face. He is a pretty earthly child playing a quiet game with a string of beads. His feet are ugly and coarse. His robe is of the peculiar pinkish purple of pastel consistency which Elisabetta much affected, especially in her later work. The Virgin's draperies are hard and smooth. The picture is low in tone, and would gain in effect were it in a less obtrusive frame.

A little further off is a *Holy Family* (No. 616), which in colouring and conception differs somewhat from Elisabetta's usual and most characteristic work. The Virgin is a handsome contadina; her shapely head is turbaned by a gay striped scarf: her robe is a deep pure red: the sky is a deep blue. Her Child sits in front of her on a cushion placed on a wall: he bends forward to see the Dove held up to him by a curly-headed St. John.

No entry corresponding to this canvas appears in Elisabetta's catalogue; but it is probably indirectly referred to in her mention of "a Blessed Virgin on copper, with the Infant Christ and St. John, who holds a bird in his hands which the former desires and asks for"; for she adds: "*This was copied from a larger picture.*"

Another *Holy Family* (No. 178, Room G) likewise displays a richness, warmth, and purity of colour unusual in her work. It is a pleasing composition. A looped-back curtain, disclosing a loggia, through the arches of which we get a distant glimpse of sky, gives a sense of restfulness and space. S. Joseph reads peacefully in the background. The Bambino sleeps in the Virgin's lap. Her red bodice and deep blue cloak, the white and gold scarf covering her head, a copper pot with red flowers in the loggia behind her, are bright warm bits of colour.

The most important picture by Elisabetta in the Bolognese Gallery is fitly hung in the Sala di Guido, in juxtaposition to the works of the master whose style it so closely approaches. But in none of Guido's pictures in Bologna or elsewhere do we find the pretty, fresh, Greuze-like children in whom Elisabetta delighted. Here the cell of the monk, Anthony of Padua, is filled with lovely human children who have entered in the thin disguise of heavenly visitants. Chubby cherubs, with wings about their little ears, are playing peep-bo over substantial clouds; a little angel, with more developed wings, is saying its prayers with sweet, childish solemnity; and a pretty *ragazza*, with untidy hair, appears on the right of the picture. The Bambino himself, in spite of the little floating cloud on which he sits, is simply an English baby, fair, rosy, dimpled, smiling, almost mischievous. The Saint, young, gentle, and effeminate, is no ascetic dreamer, bowing in rapt devotion before a celestial apparition, but a lover of children, bending tenderly forward to fondle the beautiful little foot of an engaging infant.

The picture, in spite of its graceful composition,

pleasing colour, and technical virtues—note, for example, the finely-painted hands of the Saint—is curiously commonplace and unsatisfactory. In a room we should quickly weary of it. On the walls of a church it would not inspire devotion. For a church it was painted, i.e. for S. Leonardo in the Via S. Vitale, a new building in Elisabetta's day. It would be interesting to know when the cult of S. Anthony of Padua reacquired popularity in Bologna; for Fra Salimbene writing at the end of the thirteenth century tells us that their defeat by the people of Faenza, on the feast of S. Anthony, in the year 1275, rankled so terribly in the memory of the Bolognese, that they would not even have him named within their city—"nolunt ipsum audire in Bononia nominari."[1]

Two other pictures by Elisabetta hang in the Sala di Guido,—a Magdalene and a S. Jerome, both painted in 1660 for one "Signore Giovanni Battista Cremonese, a jeweller." They are both "skied," and in a bad light. S. Jerome is very busy with literary work; he is mending a pen, and using the head of his mild lion as a book-rest. The Magdalene lies on a rough mat, con-

---

[1] Elisabetta's *Vision of S. Anthony* was probably painted in 1662. In that year she painted, according to her catalogue, an almost incredible number of pictures, while none are assigned to the year 1663. Signor Manaresi conjectured that the artist had forgotten to enter the date of the new year, and had run the work of 1662 without a division into that of 1663. He subsequently discovered in the archives of the Leopardi family a confirmation of this supposition; a letter from Giovanni Andrea Sirani, dated *March 9, 1663*, alludes to two pictures—Iolus and Hercules spinning—as just finished and sent off. These two pictures are entered under the heading 1662.

templating a crucifix; one hand rests on a skull, and is very finely drawn.

Works from Elisabetta's facile and industrious brush, purchased by the distinguished strangers who went to see her paint, are scattered throughout Europe; but, seeing that in Italy alone her fame is yet green, that the Bolognese Gallery contains thoroughly typical specimens of her work, and that pictures in private collections are often difficult to trace and sometimes difficult to see, it seems sufficient to indicate here those which are publicly exhibited in her native city.

Furthermore, there are three pictures placed in prominent positions in Roman galleries which are easily seen, and are worth seeing. One, numbered 90, in Room 6 of the Borghese Gallery, is invariably called *Lucretia*. No picture is thus named in Elisabetta's own catalogue; and though, as we have already seen, that catalogue is not exhaustive, it is noteworthy that it does describe a composition which appears to correspond with the so-called Borghese *Lucretia*, to wit: " Una Porzia in atta di ferirsi una coscia quando desiderava saper la congiura che tramava il marito." (A Portia in the act of wounding herself in the thigh when she desired to know of the plot her husband was hatching.) The expression of the nude figure gazing upwards with sentimental tranquillity is certainly more appropriate to a happy woman about to do herself a trifling injury for her own fanciful satisfaction, than to an outraged wife preparing to commit suicide to save her honour and her husband's life.

In the first room in the Pinacoteca of the Capitol, facing the statue of Benedict XIV, is a bold picture, representing a soldier, wearing a helmet with nodding scarlet and white plumes, and a crimson mantle, taking leave of a golden-haired lady in purple and gold, reclining on a throne-like crimson dais, shadowed by purple curtains. Elisabetta has placed a delicate, stemmed glass in the lady's left hand, and called the picture *Circe and Ulysses*. By any other name it would please us better; for the anachronisms of the pseudo-classical painters of the seventeenth century are irritating, though those of earlier and more child-like workers are touching and endearing. This richly coloured *Circe and Ulysses* is in Guido's first, rather than his second, manner.

More pleasing and characteristic is the Amorino, in the room which contains Guercino's enormous and repulsive S. Petronilla. The winged boy sits on a carmine cushion, placed on the stone steps of an Italian garden. Above him is a bush of pink roses in full bloom. He holds a spray of roses in his dimpled left hand, and stretches out the right to gather more. A dull purple curtain falls behind him, looped back in Elisabetta's favourite manner to show a glimpse of distant landscape.

Though singularly successful as an etcher, Elisabetta seems to have cared little for this delightful form of art, and to have abandoned it entirely for painting after her first youth. She was only nineteen when she engraved on copper the *Virgine Addolorata*, of which the painted replica is in the Bolognese Gallery; and only

THE CONVERSION OF ST. EUSTACE

seventeen when she executed the S. Eustachio, pronounced by Adam Bartsch to be one of the finest known specimens of this kind of work.

The attitude of the suddenly converted hunter, who kneels in amazement and devotion before the miraculous stag, is exceedingly fine and expressive, and conveys no hint of immaturity of conception, or of the indecision of a prentice hand. The sylvan surroundings—thicket, rocks, and streams—are suggested with spirit and reality, and without excessive detail, while the background of breeze and space are admirable. There is little in Elisabetta's etching to distinguish S. Eustace from S. Hubert, about whom a similar legend is related. The short tunic and cloak belong as much to medieval times as to the days of Trajan.

The blot on this otherwise super-excellent composition is the horse, whose body is happily concealed by a bush, but whose face peeps over it with a comic expression of pained astonishment. We might almost fancy that the strange animal was merely emblematical, and that the head emerging from the brushwood was that of the brazen bull in which S. Eustace is said to have been enclosed and roasted.

The skill in line-drawing shown in this admirable etching is visible even in the slightest of the studies which are preserved in the Uffizi Gallery. Nothing perhaps so really reveals the capacity of an artist as his sketch-book, and this collection, which may be seen on application to Ispettore Ferri, deserves to be visited by all who are interested in the work of the unfortunate, highly gifted Bolognese artist. We give a list of these

x

monochrome studies, with their numbers in the official catalogue.

1. 1664. The Angel of the Annunciation, holding a lily in the right hand. Swift motion cleverly indicated. Pen and ink; coarse lines.
2. 1665. The Virgin sitting on the ground (described in catalogue simply as "figura muliebre") with the Holy Child leaning against her, his arms upraised so as to shape a cross. An interesting sketch. Pen and ink, on white paper.
3. 1666. Virgin and Child with youthful Baptist. The figures commonplace and rather ugly. Pen and ink, on white paper.
4. 1667. Sylvan scene. Before a rough tent supported by a tree trunk are two women; one holds a ram; a child is on the ground at her feet. Large drawing in pen and ink. On the left margin a fly is carefully drawn.
5. 4192. Kneeling figure with pretty child. Pencil, on greenish paper; high lights in body colour.
6. 4193. Child holding up a curtain. A very slight sketch. Black pencil.
7. 4194. Figure of Comedy. Brush, on white paper, in bistre.
8. 4195. The famous caricature of the old man in the long cloak, supposed to be Elisabetta's poisoner. Pen and ink, on white paper.
9. 4196. Virgin kneeling with Infant Christ. Signed. Brush, on white paper, in bistre.
10. 4197. A cupid sitting by a table, on which are a dish and flagon. Brush, in bistre; a few rough lines in red chalk.

ELISABETTA'S WORK

11. 4198. Holy Family. A large and very slight sketch. Pen and bistre, on brownish paper.
12. 4199. Holy Family. A very small sketch in black pencil, with slight water-colour wash.
13. 4200. Magdalen with skull in her right hand, standing with left hand raised. Outlined with a pen; shading with brush and bistre wash.
14. 4201. Virgin and Child. Pretty and graceful. In red pencil.
15. 4202. Holy Family. The Infant Christ plays with the Baptist: the Virgin kneels, holding her hands over them. Very rough sketch in red pencil.
16. 4203. Magdalen divesting herself of her worldly adornments. A large half-figure. Three cherubs appear in the clouds to the right. To the left a little angel holds a basket of flowers and fruit, and points to the skies. A very characteristic sketch. Pen and black ink, with indigo wash, on white paper.
17. 4204. Half-length figure of an old man wearing spectacles, with a strong, humorous, kindly countenance. Full of vigour and spirit. Probably a portrait. Red pencil.
18. 4205. A caricature: two friars. Red pencil.
19. 4206. A graceful female figure standing. Red pencil.
20. 6299. Youthful head, three-quarter face, turned right. Signed. Coloured pencils, on white paper.
21. 6300. *Shown under glass in the corridor with work of Bolognese school.* Beheading of S. John the Baptist. The executioner is in the act of placing the head in a basin held by a child. A few black pencil lines and water-colour wash, on white paper.

22. 6301. The Scourging of Christ. A very rough and very vigorous sketch of doubtful authenticity. On it is written : "Lascia stare questo disegno per che è buono." Pencil, pen, and brown ink and brown wash, on white paper.
23. 6302. A man lying on a bed near which stand two women. Black pencil and bistre wash, on white paper.
24. 6303. The rape of Deianira. A beautiful spirited drawing in red chalk, on yellowish paper.
25. 6304. Catalogued as "Three studies for half-length figure of a Christ." The first holds a cross, the second a globe, the third a book. Possibly symbolical of the Three Persons of the Trinity. Black pencil and bistre wash, on white paper.

AUTHORITIES

MALVASIA. *Felsina Pittrice.*

MINGHETTI. *Le Donne Italiane nelle Belle Arti.* Firenze, 1877.

PICINARDI. *Il Pennello Lacrimato.* Bologna, 1665.

PICINARDI. *La Poesia Muta.* Bologna, 1666.

Processo per il creduto veneficio di Elisabetta Sirani. 1665–6. MS. Archivio di Stato, Bologna.

ORETTI. *Pittori.* MS. Gozzadini, 122. Archigninasio, Bologna.

VACCOLINI. *Biografia di Elisabetta Sirani.* Roma, 1844.

BIANCHINI. *Prove Legali dell' Avvelenamento della Celebre Pittrice Bolognese Elisabetta Sirani.* Bologna, 1666.

CAROLINA BONAFEDE. *Cenni Biografici e Ritratti di Insigne Donne Bolognese.* Bologna, 1845.

GUALANDI. *Memoria su Elisabetta Sirani.* Indicatore Modenese, anno II, num. 50.

MAZZONI TOSELLI. *Di Elisabetta Sirani, e del Supposto Veneficio.* Bologna, 1833.

ANTONIO MANARESI. *Elisabetta Sirani.* Bologna, 1898.

ANTONIO MANARESI. *Processo di Avvelenamento.* Bologna, 1904.

CORRADO RICCI. *Vita Barocca.* Bologna.

LODOVICO FRATI. *Vita Privata di Bologna*, dal secolo xiii. al xvii. Bologna, 1900.

Rivesta di Firenzo. 1858. Article by JACOPO CAVALLUCCI.

SIEUR PIERRE POMET. *Histoire Générale des Drogues.* Paris, 1699.

Farmacopea Universale. Venice, 1720.

BARTOLOMEA MARANTA. *Treatise on Triaca.* Naples, 1570

APPENDIX I

LETTER FROM DR. GALLERATI TO CONTE ANNIBALE RANUZZI, 4 SEPTEMBER, 1665.

(Archiv. della R. Galleria di Firenze. Cod. ix, Inserto 15.)

"PER servire alla richiesta che mi fa la S. V. Illustrissima con la sua lettera gli participio quello che s'è osservato nell' apertura del cadavero della signora Elisabetta Sirana, che sabbato mattina, 29 del caduto, fu considerato; il quale, prima d'aprirlo, si vide tutto gonfio, con la faccia tanto deformata che più non si conosceva, ed il ventre intumidito come un otre pieno di vento, che al primo taglio sboccò un flato così fetente, che necessitò gli circostanti a ritirarsi per qualche tempo. Dipoi, col taglio in croce fatto luogo per osservar gli visceri, si vide la rete lacerata in pezzi, parte sparsa sopra gli intestini, parte mescolata con un seriosità gialla e torbida, nella quale s' immergevano le budelle, le quali, nella tunica esterna, come anco il peritoneo, erano abrasi et infiammati ; e perchè la ditta seriosità scaturiva con abondanza, fatto diligenza di dove venisse, si ritrovò da un foro fatto da un lato della bocca inferiore dello stomacho, che nella parte di dentro d' intorno aveva l' escara, come se fosse stato fatto da un grano di fuoco morto, ed era di grandezza quanto una piccola palla di schizzetto, senza che d' altra parte la tunica interna del ventricolo fosse offesa in alcuna parti, fuorchè un poco distante dal detto forame, dove si vedevano ave macchiette rosse e minute come punti o morsi di pulci. Nella parte di dentro alle budelle non sè osservata veruna alterazione, ma solo nella parte esterna la ridetta abrasione cagionata da quella seriosità che similmente aveva roso le tuniche di tutti gli altri visceri di questo ventro inferiore.

APPENDIX II

PICTURES BY ELISABETTA SIRANI IN THE PINACOTECA, BOLOGNA

Number in Catalogue.		Room
178.	Holy Family, from Certosa	G
179.	The Infant Christ on the Globe	G
180.	Our Lady of Sorrows, from S. Maria de Galliera	G
280.	Mary Magdalene	G
503.	Portrait of herself	G
554.	Virgin in Prayer, from Zambeccari Gallery	G
561.	The Saviour in the act of blessing, from Zambeccari Gallery	G
		Corridor
379.	Portrait of a nun, a fragment: said to be herself	2
177.	Appearance of the Blessed Virgin and Child to S. Filippo Neri, from S. Maria di Galliera	2
176.	Madonna of the Rosary, from S. Maria Nuovo	2
616.	Madonna and Child with the Dove, from Zambeccari Gallery	2
		Room
565.	S. Jerome in the Desert, from Zambeccari Gallery	A
750.	The Magdalene in the Desert, from Zambeccari Gallery	A
175.	The Vision of S. Anthony of Padua, from the Monastery of S. Leonardo	A

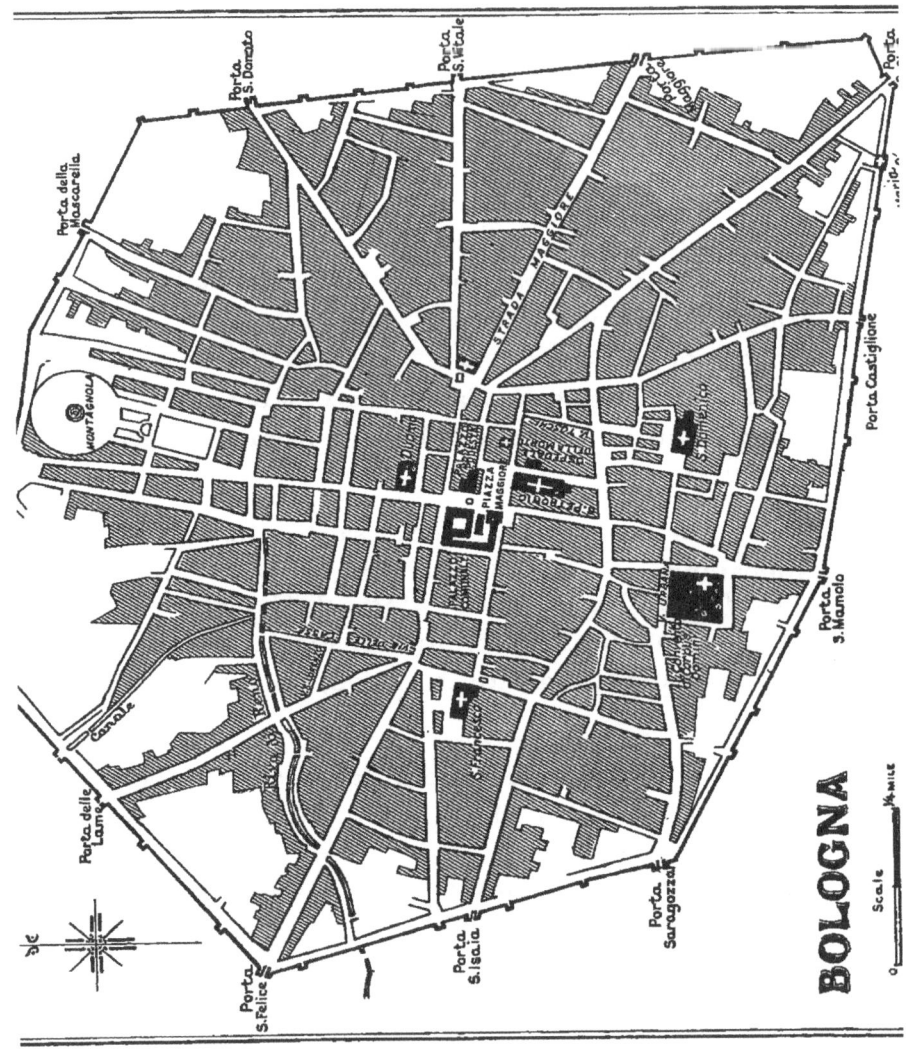

INDEX

Accursius, 1
Achillini, 169, 232, 292
Acquin, d', French physician, 280
Ailisia, Sister, 47, 65
Alfonso Arnoaldo, Canon, witness in Processo for Caterina dei Vigri's canonization, 145
Alidosi, Bolognese historian, 168
Andromach, Nero's physician, 280
Angelico, Fra, 151, 154
Angelo, S., Bridge of, Rome, 212
Angelo, Michael, 173, 245
Anna Morandi, Abbess, 124
Anthony, S., of Padua, 94, 301, 302
Anthony, S., of Padua, Hostel of, in Bologna, 114
Antonia, Sister, the half-sister of Caterina dei Vigri, 73
Archiginnasio, Bologna, 183, 197
Archivio of the convent of Corpus Domini, Bologna, 124
Arsenius, S., difference in temperament between him and S. Anthony, 55 *n*.
Ascoli, Cardinal, 206
Aspertini Amico, painter, 179, 181, 182
Assumption, Vigil of Feast of, 264
Atonement, Feudal idea of, 80
Augustinian rule, 46
Augustinian habit, 156
Austen, Jane, 241

Bacon, Francis, 278, 280, 286
Bandinelli, Baccio, 202
Bartsch, Adam, 305
Bellini, Gentile, 151
Bembo family, 156. *See* Illuminata
Bentivoglio, Annibale, 79
Bentivoglio, Ginevra, 139
Bentivoglio, Sante, 109
Bernardina Sedazzi, 46, 48
Bernardino, S., 36; his humour, 36, 55; attempts to lead a hermit's life, 53, 54; his canonization, 74
Berò, Count, his sonnet, 247
Bessarion, Cardinal Legate, 103, 110
Bezoar, 283
Bianchini, Bolognese lawyer, 271
Bianconi and Canuti, description of carving by Properzia de' Rossi, 171
Bologna, birthplace of Caterina dei Vigri, 13
Bologna :—
  Churches :
  Certosa (Campo Santo), 292, 294, 296, 298
  S. Cristoforo delle Muratelle, 104, 114
  S. Domenico, 229 *sqq*.
  S. Giacomo Maggiore, 209, 242
  S. Leonardo, 302
  S. Maria di Galliera, 298, 299

313

Bologna (*continued*) :—
  Churches (*continued*):
    S. Maria del Baraccano, 172, 174, 223
    S. Maria della Pietà, 223
    S. Maria della Vita, 186
    S. Mammolo, 16, 227
    S. Petronio, 172 *sqq.*
    S. Pietro, 238
  Gates:
    S. Donato, 260
    Galliera, 110
  Piazzas:
    Maggiore (now Vittorio Emanuele), 198
    del Nettuno, o del Gigante, 198, 249
    dell' Accademia (now Galvani), 198
  Palazzi:
    Archiginnasio (now Communal Library), 197
    Pubblico, 200, 205, 250, 251
    Poggi (now the University), 197
  Porticoes:
    Their possible origin, 17
    Dei Banchi, 198
    Della Morte, 184, 198
    Pavaglione, 197
  Streets:
    Clavatura, 183, 184, 186
    delle Casse, 179
    S. Donato (now Zamboni), 168
    Lamme, 179
    S. Lorenzo, 179
    Maggiore (now Mazzini), 168, 184, 269
    Mammolo (now d'Azeglio), 16, 237
    Toschi, 19
    Urbana, 237, 260, 288, 315

Bologna (*continued*) :—
  Giam, sculptor, 199
  Music in Bologna, 169, 240
  Scuole di Bologna, 16, 17, 197
  Senate of Bologna, 115, 205
  Students' life in Bologna, 15-19
Bonafede, Carolina, 168, 177
Borbone, Matteo, 231
Borgias, 284
Borromeo, Carlo, 197, 204, 260
"Bread of Obedience," 69
Brunswick, Duchess of, her visit to the studio of Elisabetta Sirani, 247
Buoncompagni. *See* Gregory XIII

Calandrino, Cardinal, 110
Calcina Chapel, 221, 222, 242
Callixtus III, Pope, 106
Cantofoli, Ginevra, painter, pupil of Elisabetta Sirani, 242
Canonization of S. Caterina, 137, 148
Caraffa, Cardinal Legate, 251, 267
Carducci, 1, 24, 132
Carracci, Lodovico, 200, 201, 209
Carracci, Annibale, 245
Casarini, cousin of the Sirani's maid-servant, 260, 261, 264, 268
Castelguelfo, 296
Caterina, S., of Alexandria. In a picture by Lavinia Fontana, 222
Caterina, S., of Alexandria, church of, at Ferrara, 157
Caterina of Bologna, 3, 1-164, 243
Caterina of Siena, 77
Catholic reaction, 4, 291
Cazzati, Maurizio, 231
Cellini, Benvenuto, 283
Certaldo, Paolo da, 30, 31
Certosa. *See* Bologna
"Chambre Ardente," 256
Charles V, Emperor, 168, 185, 200

INDEX

Cino da Pistoia, 95
Civic Patriotism, 234
Clare, S., Rule of, 49, 50, 65, 72
Clausura, Strict, 49
Clement VII, Pope, 137, 186
"Comforter" (Confortatore), office of, 188
Constantinople, 79, 176
Convent of Corpus Domini (in Bologna), 11, 114
Convent of Corpus Domini (in Ferrara), 49, 73, 99, 101, 105
Correggio, 245
Cospi, Ferdinando, Marchese, 251, 255
Creighton, Bishop, 182
Cupid, Elisabetta Sirani's painting of, 247

Dalmasio, Lippi, 157, 289
Dante, 93, 250, 292
Delaborde, Henri, 289
Domenichino, 237, 288, 292
Donnini, Anna Maria, charwoman to the Sirani, 262-70
Donzelli, 257
Doubts, Santa Caterina's, 84, 85
Duccio, 151
Dunstan, S., 129

Eclectic school, 201, 244, 289
"Elescoff," an electuary, 282
Elisabetta Sirani, 6, 201, 203, 229-308
Elizabeth, Queen of England, 211
Enzio, 250
Este, d', Niccolò, 20, 22, 25 sqq., 50
Este, d', Leonello, son of Niccolò, 27, 35
Este, d', Margherita, "Principessa," daughter of Niccolò, 22, 23 sqq., 50, 75, 107

Este, d', Ugo (Aldobrandini), son of Niccolò, 27
Este, d', Isabella, 27, 35, 45
Este, d', Beatrice, 35
Este, d', Borso, 28, 135
Eugenius IV, Pope, 72
Eustace, English traveller, 289
Evelyn, English traveller, 108, 288

Fabri, Dr., 268, 272, 283, 286, 299
Faenza, 250, 302
Fantuzzi, Beato Fra Marco, 123
Felsina, 234
Ferrara, Court of, 24-45
Ferrara, described by Carducci, 24
Ferrara, described by Shorthouse, 25
Ferrara, disputes with Bologna for possession of Santa Caterina, 13-15
Ferrara horse-races, 250
Fiorentino Pietro, architect, 269
Florence, 172, 201, 233
Fontana. See Lavinia and Prospero
Fontana, Domenico, employed by Sixtus V, 211
Fontana, Veronica, pupil of Elisabetta Sirani, 242
Forni, Lucretia, pupil of Elisabetta Sirani, 242
Francesca, S. di Romana, 70
Francesco, S. d' Assisi, 94, 115
Francesco, S. di Paolo, 213, 214
Franchi, Veronica, pupil of Elisabetta Sirani, 242
Francia, Francesco, 179, 289
Francis I, King of France, 213
Franciscan rule, 48
Free-will, Santa Caterina's conception of, 83, 84

Galen, 272, 281

Gallerati, Dr., 249, 253, 254, 257, 262, 265, 268, 272, 279, 282, 283, 284
Galleries:—
  Bologna, 155, 213, 215, 216, 248, 290, 296, 297, 298, 299, 300, 301, 302, 304
  Florence (Uffizi), 171, 193, 224, 293
  Milan (Brera), 242
  Rome (Borghese), 303
  Rome (Capitol), 304
  Venice, 155
Ghislieri, Ettore, Count, 239
Gigliola da Carrara, wife of Niccolò III, d' Este, 22
Giovio, 184
Gonfalonier of Justice, 234, 251
Gonzaga, Eleonora, Empress, 252
Gozzadini, family, 209, 217, 218, 219
Gozzini, 293
Grassetti, Padre, 15, 60, 106, 108, 109, 161
Grassi, family, 171
Gregory XIII, Pope, 184, 204, 210
Grillo, Don Angelo, 210
Grissante, architect, 198
Gualandi, Michael Angelo, 168, 178, 275
Gualandi, Secretary, 257
Guercino, 234, 291, 292, 304
Guerino, 34
Guido Reni. *See* Reni, Guido
Guidotti, Saulo, senator, 229
Guinicelli, Guido, 93

Hospital (Ospedale della Morte), 183, 184, 186, 189, 253, 266, 282

Illuminata, Sister (Bembo), 14, 18, 64, 67, 71, 119, 132, 141, 144, 148, 156

Ignatius Loyola, 291
Imola, 20
Imola, Innocenzo da, 195
Innocent IX, Pope, 212
Intercessions, S. Caterina's, 73-7, 80, 81

Japanese Ambassadors, 204
Joseph, St., Bowl of, 70, 71
Joseph and wife of Potiphar, bas-relief by Properzia, 175
Julius III, Pope, 195

Kingsley, Charles, on Monks of Thebaid, 42

Lambertazzi, Bolognese family, 250
Lanteri, Camilla, pupil of Elisabetta Sirani, 242
Laurence, St., 129
Laureti, Tommaso, architect, 198
Lavinia Fontana, 5, 6, 193-225, 242, 246
Lemery's *Farmacopea Universale*, 279
Lemmi, Niccolò, 7
Leonarda, Abbess, 102
Leonello. *See* Este
Leonora, Sister (Poggi), 144
Leopardi, family, 302
Life school, 239
Liverati, painter, 275
Lombardy, 245
Louis XI, King of France, 213
Louise de Savoie, Duchesse d'Angoulême, 213
Lucia, Sister (Codagnelli), 117, 118
Lucia, Sister (Mascheroni), 46, 47, 48, 65, 100, 156
Lucia Tolomelli, 257-87, 299
Ludovico, Master, barber of Spedale della Morte, 283

INDEX

Maddalena, Rosa, Sister, 126
Maduzzi, Cristoforo, 204
Malatesta, Sigismundo, 26
Malatesta, Pandolfo, 40
Malatesta, Parisina. *See* Parisina
Malatesta Roberto. *See* Roberto
Malvasia, Anton Galeazzo, 178, 179, 180
Malvasia, Canon, 237, 241, 246, 248, 272, 274, 284, 292, 293
Mamolini, family, 19
Manarese, Antonio, biographer of Elisabetta Sirani, 247, 256, 275, 296
Mantegna, 233
Mantua, 101, 233
Marconi, 1
Marini, 291
Martin V, Pope, 28
Massero, 196
Matessilani, Dr., 252, 266, 272, 282, 286
Medici, Leopoldo, Cardinal, 234, 269, 274
Mendicanti (Poor House), 260, 267, 269
Metastasio, 292
Mezzavacca, Battista, 103, 105
Milano, Francesco da, 179
Minghetti, Marco, 35
Minimes (Reformed Franciscans), 218
Miola, Vincenzo, painter, 179
Miracles, S. Caterina's, 117-23
Modena, horse-race at, 250
Molins, Venetian family, 157
Monari, Advocate of the Poor, 273
Montpellier, 280
Morina, Guido, 129
Museo Civico (Bologna), 171
Museo della Fabbrica (Bologna), 173, 174
Music. *See* Bologna

Neri, S. Filippo, 292, 299
Nicholas V, Pope, 110

Office, Daily, in the choir, 88, 89
Office of the Dead, 80
"Oil of the Grand Duke," 283
Ordelaffi, family of Fortè, 102
Oretti, 195, 199, 203, 217, 221, 242, 273, 297

Padua, 21
Pagliardi, 259, 269
Panzacchi, Maria, pupil of Elisabetta Sirani, 242
Paolo, S., Fuori delle Mura (Rome), 206
Pareia, Bartolomeo, Professor of Music, 169
Parisina, wife of Niccolò III, d' Este, 26, 130
Parma, 20
Pepoli, Caterina, 243
Pepoli, Guido, 173
Pepoli, Romeo, 18
Pharmacy of S. Petronio, 282
Pharmacy of S. Paolo, 282
Pia de Carpi, Madonna Verde dei, 48, 65
Pia de Carpi, Abbess Taddea. *See* Taddea
Picinardi, funeral oration of, 232-41, 244
Pinzochere, 25
Pius V, Pope, 203
Plessis-le-Tours, 213
Poisoning in seventeenth century, 256, 284, 285
Pomet, Pierre, Paris druggist, 280
Porchetta, Festival, 249, 251, 259
Post-mortem examination, 253, 268, 283-6
Poverty, S. Caterina's love of, 96-9

Processo of Caterina's canonization, 145
Processo di avvelenamente (Elisabetta Sirani), 255 *sqq.*
Properzia de' Rossi, 167–86
Prospero Fontana, 195, 196, 199, 200, 201, 206, 209, 210
Public Prosecutor, 267

Quercia, Jacopo della, 173
Queen Elizabeth. *See* Elizabeth

Raimondi, Marc' Antonio, 170, 186
Rainieri, Jacopo, 169
Rangoni, Aldrovandino di, 28
Ranuzzi, Annibale, Count, 234, 263, 264
Raphael, 170, 245
Ratta, Monsignore, 209, 210
Reni, Guido, 7, 212, 229, 230, 234, 238, 239, 288, 290, 292, 301, 304
Reno, Canale di, 179, 184
Riali, 275
Riario, Carlo, Dr., 146
Ricci Corrado, 240
Ricciarda Saluzzo, 50
Richter, Jean-Paul, 297
Roberto Beato, 40, 50, 75
Rome, 185, 195, 206, 208, 209, 212, 218, 290
Rossetti, Dante Gabriel, 193
Rossi, Giovanni Martino, 168
Rossi, Girolamo, 168
Rossi, Properzia. *See* Properzia

Sabadino degli Arienti, 139, 140, 141
Sabina, S., Church of (Rome), 206
Salimbene, Fra, 94, 302
Saluzzo, Ricciarda. *See* Ricciarda
Samaritana, Sister, her death, 120–123

Sarto, Andrea del, 202, 246
Savonarola, 44, 45
Sciroppo Acetoso, 278–9
Sedazzi Bernardina. *See* Bernardina
Servants in the seventeenth century, 258, 259
Sette Arme, S. Caterina's book: its opening, 13, 32; its characteristics, 37, 38; its object and first draft, 68, 69
Sforza, Galeazzo Maria, 26
Sforza, Ginevra. *See* Bentivoglio
Siena, 54
Sirani family, 234, 238, 242, 257, 263
Sirani, Elisabetta. *See* Elisabetta
Sirani, Gian Andrea, 239–63
Sirani, Barbara, 240–65
Sirani, Giacoma, 249, 297
Sirani, Margherita, 252–62
Sixtus V, Pope, 211
Stark, Mrs., 289
Symonds, Addington, 178

Taddea, Abbess, 66, 88, 99, 100
Tebaldello, 250
Teresa, S., 37, 38, 292
Terzina, 113, 114
Teste, Fulvio, 229
Third Order of Franciscans in Bologna, 101
Thomas, St., of Canterbury, 59, 60
Tiarini, 292
Titian, 201, 245
Toffana, La, 284
Torrone, Prison, 268, 269
Torrone, Auditor of, 267, 269, 272
Torrone, Sub-Auditor of, 268
Torture, 272
Tosignano, Giovanni da, Bishop of Ferrara, 74
Tower of the Lions, Ferrara, 28

INDEX 319

Triaca ("Venice Treacle"), 279, 280, 281
Tribolo, 175
Trombetti, 1

Uffizi. *See* Galleries
Uffizio della difesa dei Poveri, 271

Vasari, 169, 170, 171, 177, 178, 182, 185
Veil, manner of wearing, 116
Venice, 201, 245, 280; and *see* Galleries
Verme, Luigi dal, Mercenary, 78
Vesuvius, in pasteboard, 251
Vignola, Barozzi da, 198
Vigri family; pedigree, 14
Vigri Benvenuta (de' Mamolini), 19, 20, 73, 114, 133
Vigri Caterina. *See* Caterina
Vigri Giovanni, 15-24, 41

Vincent, St., 129
Vincenzio, Antonio, architect, 172
Vinidani, Jacopo dei, teacher in Bologna, 17
Violetta of S. Caterina, 127
Viridario, 169
Visconti, Filippo Maria, 78
Visions of S. Caterina, 59-64, 90, 91, 105, 106, 162
Vita Nuova of Dante, 94, 95
Vizzani, Pompeo, 209, 210

Wages of servants in twelfth century, 258, 259
Whitesmith, 275
Women's education, 30
Women, learned, 1, 2, 31

Zanichelli, Lorenzo, 273
Zappis, de, 207, 208

PLYMOUTH
WILLIAM BRENDON AND SON, LTD.
PRINTERS

A CATALOGUE OF BOOKS PUBLISHED BY METHUEN AND COMPANY: LONDON 36 ESSEX STREET W.C.

CONTENTS

	PAGE		PAGE
General Literature,	2-24	Little Library,	32
Ancient Cities,	24	Little Quarto Shakespeare,	33
Antiquary's Books,	25	Miniature Library,	33
Arden Shakespeare,	25	New Historical Series,	34
Beginner's Books,	26	New Library of Medicine,	34
Business Books,	26	New Library of Music,	34
Byzantine Texts,	26	Oxford Biographies,	34
Churchman's Bible,	26	Romantic History,	34
Churchman's Library,	27	School Examination Series,	35
Classical Translations,	27	School Histories,	35
Classics of Art,	27	Simplified French Texts,	35
Commercial Series,	27	Simplified German Texts,	35
Connoisseur's Library,	28	Six Ages of European History,	36
Handbooks of English Church History,	28	Standard Library,	36
		Textbooks of Science,	36
Illustrated Pocket Library of Plain and Coloured Books,	28	Textbooks of Technology,	37
		Handbooks of Theology,	37
Junior Examination Series,	29	Westminster Commentaries,	37
Junior School-Books,	29		
Leaders of Religion,	30		
Library of Devotion,	30	Fiction,	37-45
Little Books on Art,	31	Books for Boys and Girls,	45
Little Galleries,	31	Novels of Alexandre Dumas,	46
Little Guides,	32	Methuen's Sixpenny Books,	46

SEPTEMBER 1909

A CATALOGUE OF

MESSRS. METHUEN'S
PUBLICATIONS

In this Catalogue the order is according to authors. An asterisk denotes that the book is in the press.

Colonial Editions are published of all Messrs. METHUEN's Novels issued at a price above 2s. 6d., and similar editions are published of some works of General Literature. Colonial editions are only for circulation in the British Colonies and India.

All books marked net are not subject to discount, and cannot be bought at less than the published price. Books not marked net are subject to the discount which the bookseller allows.

Messrs. METHUEN's books are kept in stock by all good booksellers. If there is any difficulty in seeing copies, Messrs. Methuen will be very glad to have early information, and specimen copies of any books will be sent on receipt of the published price *plus* postage for net books, and of the published price for ordinary books.

I.P.L. represents Illustrated Pocket Library.

PART I.—GENERAL LITERATURE

Abraham (George D.). THE COMPLETE MOUNTAINEER. With 75 Illustrations. *Second Edition. Demy* 8vo. 15s. net.

Acatos (M. J.). See Junior School Books.

Addleshaw (Percy). SIR PHILIP SIDNEY. With 12 Illustrations. *Demy* 8vo. 10s. 6d. net.

Adeney (W. F.), M.A. See Bennett (W. H.)

Ady (Cecilia M.). A HISTORY OF MILAN UNDER THE SFORZA. With 20 Illustrations and a Map. *Demy* 8vo. 10s. 6d. net.

Aeschylus. See Classical Translations.

Ainsworth (W. Harrison). See I.P.L.

Aldis (Janet). THE QUEEN OF LETTER WRITERS, MARQUISE DE SÉVIGNÉ, DAME DE BOURBILLY, 1626-96. With 18 Illustrations. *Second Edition. Demy* 8vo. 12s. 6d. net.

Alexander (William), D.D., Archbishop of Armagh. THOUGHTS AND COUNSELS OF MANY YEARS. *Demy* 16mo. 2s. 6d.

Aiken (Henry). See I.P.L.

Allen (Charles C.). See Textbooks of Technology.

Allen (L. Jessie). See Little Books on Art.

Allen (J. Romilly), F.S.A. See Antiquary's Books.

Almack (E.), F.S.A. See Little Books on Art.

Amherst (Lady). A SKETCH OF EGYPTIAN HISTORY FROM THE EARLIEST TIMES TO THE PRESENT DAY. With many Illustrations and Maps. *A New and Cheaper Issue Demy* 8vo. 7s. 6d. net.

Anderson (F. M.). THE STORY OF THE BRITISH EMPIRE FOR CHILDREN. With 42 Illustrations. *Cr.* 8vo. 2s.

Anderson (J. G.), B.A., NOUVELLE GRAMMAIRE FRANÇAISE, À L'USAGE DES ÉCOLES ANGLAISES. *Crown* 8vo. 2s.
EXERCICES DE GRAMMAIRE FRANÇAISE. *Cr.* 8vo. 1s. 6d.

Andrewes (Bishop). PRECES PRIVATAE. Translated and edited, with Notes, by F. E. BRIGHTMAN. M.A., of Pusey House, Oxford. *Cr.* 8vo. 6s.
See also Library of Devotion.

'Anglo-Australian.' AFTER-GLOW MEMORIES. *Cr.* 8vo. 6s.

Anon. THE BUDGET, THE LAND AND THE PEOPLE. *Second Edition. Crown* 8vo. 6d. net.
HEALTH, WEALTH, AND WISDOM. *Crown* 8vo. 1s. net.
THE WESTMINSTER PROBLEMS BOOK. Prose and Verse. Compiled from *The Saturday Westminster Gazette* Competitions, 1904-1907. *Cr.* 8vo. 3s. 6d. net.
VENICE AND HER TREASURES. With many Illustrations. *Round corners. Fcap.* 8vo. 5s. net.

Aristotle. THE ETHICS OF. Edited, with an Introduction and Notes by JOHN BURNET, M.A., *Cheaper issue. Demy* 8vo. 10s. 6d. net.

Asman (H. N.), M.A., B.D. See Junior School Books.

Atkins (H. G.). See Oxford Biographies.

Atkinson (C. M.). JEREMY BENTHAM. *Demy* 8vo. 5s. net.

Atkinson (C. T.), M.A., Fellow of Exeter College, Oxford, sometime Demy of Magdalen College. A HISTORY OF GERMANY, from 1713 to 1815. With 35 Maps and Plans *Demy* 8vo. 15s. net.

General Literature 3

Atkinson (T. D.). ENGLISH ARCHITECTURE. With 196 Illustrations. *Fcap. 8vo.* 3s. 6d. net.
A GLOSSARY OF TERMS USED IN ENGLISH ARCHITECTURE. With 265 Illustrations. *Second Edition. Fcap. 8vo.* 3s. 6d. net.

Atteridge (A. H.). NAPOLEON'S BROTHERS. With 24 Illustrations. *Demy 8vo.* 18s. net.

Auden (T.), M.A., F.S.A. See Ancient Cities.

Aurelius (Marcus). WORDS OF THE ANCIENT WISE. Thoughts from Epictetus and Marcus Aurelius. Edited by W. H. D. ROUSE, M.A., Litt. D. *Fcap. 8vo.* 3s. 6d. net.
See also Standard Library.

Austen (Jane). See Standard Library, Little Library and Mitton (G. E.).

Aves (Ernest). CO-OPERATIVE INDUSTRY. *Crown 8vo.* 5s. net.

Bacon (Francis). See Standard Library and Little Library.

Bagot (Richard). THE LAKES OF NORTHERN ITALY. With 37 Illustrations and a Map. *Fcap. 8vo.* 5s. net.

Bailey (J. C.), M.A. See Cowper (W.).

*****Bain (R. Nisbet).** THE LAST KING OF POLAND AND HIS CONTEMPORARIES. With 16 Illustrations. *Demy 8vo.* 10s. 6d. net.

Baker (W. G.), M.A. See Junior Examination Series.

Baker (Julian L.), F.I.C., F.C.S. See Books on Business.

Balfour (Graham). THE LIFE OF ROBERT LOUIS STEVENSON. With a Portrait. *Fourth Edition in one Volume. Cr. 8vo. Buckram,* 6s.

Ballard (A.), B.A., LL.D. See Antiquary's Books.

Bally (S. E.). See Commercial Series.

Barham (R. H.). See Little Library.

Baring (The Hon. Maurice). WITH THE RUSSIANS IN MANCHURIA. *Third Edition. Demy 8vo.* 7s. 6d. net.
A YEAR IN RUSSIA. *Second Edition. Demy 8vo.* 10s. 6d. net.
RUSSIAN ESSAYS AND STORIES. *Second Edition. Cr. 8vo.* 5s. net.
Also published in a Colonial Edition.

Baring-Gould (S.). THE LIFE OF NAPOLEON BONAPARTE. With nearly 200 Illustrations, including a Photogravure Frontispiece. *Second Edition. Wide Royal 8vo.* 10s. 6d. net.
THE TRAGEDY OF THE CÆSARS: A STUDY OF THE CHARACTERS OF THE CÆSARS OF THE JULIAN AND CLAUDIAN HOUSES. With numerous Illustrations from Busts, Gems, Cameos, etc. *Sixth Edition. Royal 8vo.* 10s. 6d. net.
A BOOK OF FAIRY TALES. With numerous Illustrations by A. J. GASKIN. *Second Edition. Cr. 8vo. Buckram.* 6s., also *Medium 8vo.* 6d.
OLD ENGLISH FAIRY TALES. With numerous Illustrations by F. D. BEDFORD. *Third Edition. Cr. 8vo. Buckram.* 6s.
THE VICAR OF MORWENSTOW. Revised Edition. With a Portrait. *Third Edition. Cr. 8vo.* 3s. 6d.
OLD COUNTRY LIFE. With 69 Illustrations. *Fifth Edition. Large Crown 8vo.* 6s.
A GARLAND OF COUNTRY SONG: English Folk Songs with their Traditional Melodies. Collected and arranged by S. BARING-GOULD and H. F. SHEPPARD. *Demy 4to.* 6s.
SONGS OF THE WEST: Folk Songs of Devon and Cornwall. Collected from the Mouths of the People. By S. BARING-GOULD, M.A., and H. FLEETWOOD SHEPPARD, M.A. New and Revised Edition, under the musical editorship of CECIL J. SHARP. *Large Imperial 8vo.* 5s. net.
A BOOK OF NURSERY SONGS AND RHYMES. Edited by S. BARING-GOULD. Illustrated. *Second and Cheaper Edition. Large Cr. 8vo.* 2s. 6d. net.
STRANGE SURVIVALS: SOME CHAPTERS IN THE HISTORY OF MAN. Illustrated. *Third Edition. Cr. 8vo.* 2s. 6d. net.
YORKSHIRE ODDITIES: INCIDENTS AND STRANGE EVENTS. *Fifth Edition. Cr. 8vo.* 2s. 6d. net.
THE BARING-GOULD SELECTION READER. Arranged by G. H. ROSE. Illustrated. *Crown 8vo.* 1s. 6d.
THE BARING-GOULD CONTINUOUS READER. Arranged by G. H. ROSE. Illustrated. *Crown 8vo.* 1s. 6d.
A BOOK OF CORNWALL. With 33 Illustrations. *Second Edition. Cr. 8vo.* 6s.
A BOOK OF DARTMOOR. With 60 Illustrations. *Second Edition. Cr. 8vo.* 6s.
A BOOK OF DEVON. With 35 Illustrations. *Third Edition. Cr. 8vo.* 6s.
A BOOK OF NORTH WALES. With 49 Illustrations. *Cr. 8vo.* 6s.
A BOOK OF SOUTH WALES. With 57 Illustrations. *Cr. 8vo.* 6s.
A BOOK OF BRITTANY. With 69 Illustrations. *Second Edition Cr. 8vo.* 6s.
A BOOK OF THE RHINE: From Cleve to Mainz. With 8 Illustrations in Colour by TREVOR HADDEN, and 48 other Illustrations. *Second Edition. Cr. 8vo.* 6s.
A BOOK OF THE RIVIERA. With 40 Illustrations. *Cr. 8vo.* 6s.
A BOOK OF THE PYRENEES. With 25 Illustrations. *Cr. 8vo.* 6s.
See also Little Guides.

Barker (Aldred F.). See Textbooks of Technology.

Barker (E.), M.A. (Late) Fellow of Merton College, Oxford. THE POLITICAL THOUGHT OF PLATO AND ARISTOTLE. *Demy 8vo.* 10s. 6d. net.

Barnes (W. E.), D.D. See Churchman's Bible.

MESSRS. METHUEN'S CATALOGUE

Barnett (Mrs. P. A.). See Little Library.
Baron (R. R. N.), M.A. FRENCH PROSE COMPOSITION. *Fourth Edition*. *Cr. 8vo.* 2s. 6d. *Key,* 3s. *net.*
See also Junior School Books.
Barron (H. M.), M.A., Wadham College, Oxford. TEXTS FOR SERMONS. With a Preface by Canon SCOTT HOLLAND. *Cr. 8vo.* 3s. 6d.
Bartholomew (J. G.), F.R.S.E See Robertson (C. G.).
Bastable (C. F.), LL.D. THE COMMERCE OF NATIONS. *Fourth. Ed. Cr. 8vo.* 2s. 6d.
Bastian (H. Charlton), M.A., M.D., F.R.S. THE EVOLUTION OF LIFE. With Diagrams and many Photomicrographs. *Demy 8vo.* 7s. 6d. *net.*
Batson (Mrs. Stephen). A CONCISE HANDBOOK OF GARDEN FLOWERS. *Fcap. 8vo.* 3s. 6d.
THE SUMMER GARDEN OF PLEASURE. With 36 Illustrations in Colour by OSMUND PITTMAN. *Wide Demy 8vo.* 15s. *net.*
Bayley (R. Child). THE COMPLETE PHOTOGRAPHER. With over 100 Illustrations. With Note on Direct Colour Process. *Third Edition*. *Demy 8vo.* 10s. 6d. *net.*
Beard (W. S.). EASY EXERCISES IN ALGEBRA FOR BEGINNERS. *Cr. 8vo.* 1s. 6d. With Answers. 1s. 9d.
See also Junior Examination Series and Beginner's Books.
Beckett (Arthur). THE SPIRIT OF THE DOWNS: Impressions and Reminiscences of the Sussex Downs. With 20 Illustrations in Colour by STANLEY INCHBOLD. *Demy 8vo.* 10s. 6d. *net.*
Beckford (Peter). THOUGHTS ON HUNTING. Edited by J. OTHO PAGET, and Illustrated by G. H. JALLAND. *Second Edition.* *Demy 8vo.* 6s.
Beckford (William). See Little Library.
Beeching (H. C.), M.A., Canon of Westminster. See Library of Devotion.
Beerbohm (Max). A BOOK OF CARICATURES. *Imperial 4to.* 21s. *net.*
Begbie (Harold). MASTER WORKERS. Illustrated. *Demy 8vo.* 7s. 6d. *net.*
Behmen (Jacob). DIALOGUES ON THE SUPERSENSUAL LIFE. Edited by BERNARD HOLLAND. *Fcap. 8vo.* 3s. 6d.
Bell (Mrs. Arthur G.). THE SKIRTS OF THE GREAT CITY. With 16 Illustrations in Colour by ARTHUR G. BELL, 17 other Illustrations, and a Map. *Second Edition*. *Cr. 8vo.* 6s.
Belloc (H.) PARIS. With 7 Maps and a Frontispiece in Photogravure. *Second Edition, Revised*. *Cr. 8vo.* 6s.
HILLS AND THE SEA. *Second Edition*. *Crown 8vo.* 6s.
ON NOTHING AND KINDRED SUBJECTS. *Second Edition*. *Fcap. 8vo.* 5s.
*ON EVERYTHING. *Fcap. 8vo.* 5s.
MARIE ANTOINETTE. With 35 Portraits and Illustrations, and 22 Maps. *Demy 8vo.* 15s. *net.*
THE PYRENEES. With 46 Sketches by the Author, and 22 Maps. *Second Edition*. *Demy 8vo.* 7s. 6d. *net.*
Bellot (H. H. L.), M.A. See Jones (L. A. A.).
Bennett (Joseph). FORTY YEARS OF MUSIC, 1865-1905. With 24 Illustrations. *Demy 8vo.* 16s. *net.*
Bennett (W. H.), M.A. A PRIMER OF THE BIBLE. *Fifth Edition*. *Cr. 8vo.* 2s. 6d.
Bennett (W. H.) and **Adeney** (W. F.). A BIBLICAL INTRODUCTION. With a concise Bibliography. *Fifth Edition*. *Cr. 8vo.* 7s. 6d.
Benson (Archbishop) GOD'S BOARD. Communion Addresses. *Second Edition*. *Fcap. 8vo.* 3s. 6d. *net.*
Benson (A. C.), M.A. See Oxford Biographies.
Benson (R. M.). THE WAY OF HOLINESS. An Exposition of Psalm cxix. Analytical and Devotional. *Cr. 8vo.* 5s.
Bernard (E. R.), M.A., Canon of Salisbury THE ENGLISH SUNDAY: ITS ORIGINS AND ITS CLAIMS. *Fcap. 8vo.* 1s. 6d.
Berry (W. Grinton), M.A. FRANCE SINCE WATERLOO. With 16 Illustrations and Maps. *Cr. 8vo.* 6s.
Beruete (A. de). See Classics of Art.
Betham-Edwards (Miss). HOME LIFE IN FRANCE. With 20 Illustrations. *Fifth Edition*. *Crown 8vo.* 6s.
Bethune-Baker (J. F.), M.A. See Handbooks of Theology.
Bindley (T. Herbert), B.D. THE OECUMENICAL DOCUMENTS OF THE FAITH. With Introductions and Notes. *Second Edition*. *Cr. 8vo.* 6s. *net.*
Binns (H. B.). THE LIFE OF WALT WHITMAN. Illustrated. *Demy 8vo.* 10s. 6d. *net.*
Binyon (Mrs. Laurence). NINETEENTH CENTURY PROSE. Selected and arranged by. *Crown 8vo.* 6s.
Binyon (Laurence). THE DEATH OF ADAM AND OTHER POEMS. *Cr. 8vo.* 3s. 6d. *net.*
See also Blake (William).
Birch (Walter de Gray), LL.D., F.S.A. See Connoisseur's Library.
Birnstingl (Ethel). See Little Books on Art.
Blackmantle (Bernard). See I.P.L.
Blair (Robert). See I.P.L.
Blake (William). THE LETTERS OF WILLIAM BLAKE, TOGETHER WITH A LIFE BY FREDERICK TATHAM. Edited from the Original Manuscripts, with an Introduction and Notes, by ARCHIBALD G. B. RUSSELL. With 12 Illustrations. *Demy 8vo.* 7s. 6d. *net.*
ILLUSTRATIONS OF THE BOOK OF JOB. With General Introduction by LAURENCE BINYON. *Quarto.* 21s. *net.*
See also I.P.L., and Little Library.

GENERAL LITERATURE 5

Bloom (J. Harvey), M.A. See Antiquary's Books.
Blouet (Henri). See Beginner's Books.
Boardman (T. H.), M.A. See French (W.).
Bode (Wilhelm), Ph.D. See Classics of Art.
Bodley (J. E. C.) THE CORONATION OF EDWARD VII. *Demy 8vo.* 21s. net. By Command of the King.
Body (George), D.D. THE SOUL'S PILGRIMAGE: Devotional Readings from the Published and Unpublished writings of George Body, D.D. Selected and arranged by J. H. BURN, B.D., F.R.S.E. *Demy 16mo.* 2s. 6d.
Bona (Cardinal). See Library of Devotion.
Bonnor (Mary L.). See Little Books on Art.
Boon (F. C.), B.A. See Commercial Series.
Borrow (George). See Little Library.
Bos (J. Ritzema). AGRICULTURAL ZOOLOGY. Translated by J. R. AINSWORTH DAVIS, M.A. With 155 Illustrations. *Second Edition. Cr. 8vo.* 3s. 6d.
Botting (C. G.), B.A. EASY GREEK EXERCISES. *Cr. 8vo.* 2s. See also Junior Examination Series.
Boulting (W.) TASSO AND HIS TIMES. With 24 Illustrations. *Demy 8vo.* 10s. 6d. net.
Boulton (E. S.), M.A. GEOMETRY ON MODERN LINES. *Cr. 8vo.* 2s.
Boulton (William B.). SIR JOSHUA REYNOLDS, P.R.A. With 49 Illustrations. *Second Edition. Demy 8vo.* 7s. 6d. net.
Bovill (W. B. Forster). HUNGARY AND THE HUNGARIANS. With 16 Illustrations in Colour by WILLIAM PASCOE, 12 other Illustrations and a Map. *Demy 8vo.* 7s. 6d. net.
Bowden (E. M.). THE IMITATION OF BUDDHA: Being Quotations from Buddhist Literature for each Day in the Year. *Fifth Edition. Cr. 16mo.* 2s. 6d.
Bower (E.), B.A. See New Historical Series.
Boyle (W.). CHRISTMAS AT THE ZOO. With Verses by W. BOYLE and 24 Coloured Pictures by H. B. NEILSON. *Super Royal 16mo.* 2s.
Brabant (F. G.), M.A. RAMBLES IN SUSSEX. With 30 Illustrations. *Crown 8vo.* 6s. See also Little Guides.
Bradley (A. G.). ROUND ABOUT WILTSHIRE. With 14 Illustrations, in Colour by T. C. GOTCH, 16 other Illustrations, and a Map. *Second Edition. Cr. 8vo.* 6s.
THE ROMANCE OF NORTHUMBERLAND. With 16 Illustrations in Colour by FRANK SOUTHGATE, R.B.A., and 12 from Photographs. *Second Edition. Demy 8vo.* 7s. 6d. net.
Bradley (John W.). See Little Books on Art.
Braid (James), Open Champion, 1901, 1905 and 1906. ADVANCED GOLF. With 88 Photographs and Diagrams. *Fifth Edition. Demy 8vo.* 10s. 6d. net.

Braid (James) and Others. GREAT GOLFERS IN THE MAKING. Edited by HENRY LEACH. With 24 Illustrations. *Second Edition. Demy 8vo.* 7s. 6d. net.
Brailsford (H. N.). MACEDONIA: ITS RACES AND THEIR FUTURE. With 32 Illustrations and a Map. *Demy 8vo.* 12s. 6d. net.
Brentano (C.). See Simplified German Texts.
Brightman (F. E.), M.A. See Andrewes (Lancelot).
*****Brock (A. Clutton).** SHELLEY: THE MAN AND THE POET. With 12 Illustrations. *Demy 8vo.* 7s. 6d. net.
Brodrick (Mary) and Morton (A. Anderson). A CONCISE DICTIONARY OF EGYPTIAN ARCHÆOLOGY. A Hand-Book for Students and Travellers. With 80 Illustrations and many Cartouches. *Cr. 8vo.* 3s. 6d.
Brooks (E. E.), B.Sc. (Lond.), Leicester Municipal Technical School, and **James (W. H. N.),** A.M.I.E.E., A.R.C.Sc., Municipal School of Technology, Manchester. See Textbooks of Technology.
Brown (S. E.), M.A., B.Sc., Senior Science Master at Uppingham. A PRACTICAL CHEMISTRY NOTE-BOOK FOR MATRICULATION AND ARMY CANDIDATES. Easy Experiments on the Commoner Substances. *Cr. 4to.* 1s. 6d. net.
Brown (J. Wood), M.A. THE BUILDERS OF FLORENCE. With 74 Illustrations by HERBERT RAILTON. *Demy 4to.* 18s. net.
Browne (Sir Thomas). See Standard Library.
Brownell (C. L.). THE HEART OF JAPAN. Illustrated. *Third Edition. Cr. 8vo.* 6s. Also *Medium 8vo.* 6d.
Browning (Robert). See Little Library.
Bryant (Walter W.), B.A., F.R.A.S., F.R. Met. Soc., of the Royal Observatory, Greenwich. A HISTORY OF ASTRONOMY. With 47 Illustrations. *Demy 8vo.* 7s. 6d. net.
Buckland (Francis T.). CURIOSITIES OF NATURAL HISTORY. Illustrated by H. B. NEILSON. *Cr. 8vo.* 3s. 6d.
Buckton (A. M.) THE BURDEN OF ENGELA. *Second Edition. Cr. 8vo.* 3s. 6d. net.
EAGER HEART: A Mystery Play. *Seventh Edition. Cr. 8vo.* 1s. net.
KINGS IN BABYLON: A Drama. *Cr. 8vo.* 1s. net.
SONGS OF JOY. *Cr. 8vo.* 1s. net.
Budge (E. A. Wallis). THE GODS OF THE EGYPTIANS. With over 100 Coloured Plates and many Illustrations. Two Volumes. *Royal 8vo.* £3, 3s. net.
*****Buist Massac (H.).** THE COMPLETE AERONAUT. With many Illustrations. *Demy 8vo.* 12s. 6d. net.
Bull (Paul), Army Chaplain. GOD AND OUR SOLDIERS. *Second Edition. Cr. 8vo.* 6s.

Bulley (Miss). See Dilke (Lady).

Bunyan (John). THE PILGRIM'S PROGRESS. Edited, with an Introduction by C. H. FIRTH, M.A. With 39 Illustrations by R. ANNING BELL. *Crown 8vo.* 6s.
See also Standard Library and Library of Devotion.

Burch (G. J.), M.A., F.R.S. A MANUAL OF ELECTRICAL SCIENCE. Illustrated. *Cr. 8vo.* 3s.

Burgess (Gelett). GOOPS AND HOW TO BE THEM. Illustrated. *Small 4to.* 6s.

Burke (Edmund). See Standard Library.

Burn (A. E.), D.D., Rector of Handsworth and Prebendary of Lichfield. See Handbooks of Theology.

Burn (J. H.), B.D., F.R.S.E. THE CHURCHMAN'S TREASURY OF SONG: Gathered from the Christian poetry of all ages. Edited by. *Fcap. 8vo.* 3s. 6d. net. See also Library of Devotion.

Burnet (John), M.A. See Aristotle.

Burns (Robert), THE POEMS. Edited by ANDREW LANG and W. A. CRAIGIE. With Portrait. *Third Edition. Wide Demy 8vo, gilt top.* 6s.
See also Standard Library.

Burnside (W. F.), M.A. OLD TESTAMENT HISTORY FOR USE IN SCHOOLS. *Third Edition. Cr. 8vo.* 3s. 6d.

Burton (Alfred). See I.P.L.

Bury (J. B.), M.A., Litt. D. See Gibbon (Edward).

Bussell (F. W.), D.D. CHRISTIAN THEOLOGY AND SOCIAL PROGRESS (The Bampton Lectures of 1905). *Demy 8vo.* 10s. 6d. net.

Butler (Joseph), D.D. See Standard Library.

Butlin (F. M.). AMONG THE DANES. With 12 Illustrations in Colour by ELLEN WILKINSON, and 15 from Photographs. *Demy 8vo.* 7s. 6d. net.

Cain (Georges), Curator of the Carnavalet Museum, Paris. WALKS IN PARIS. Translated by A. R. ALLINSON, M.A. With a Frontispiece in Colour by MAXWELL ARMFIELD, and 118 other Illustrations. *Demy 8vo.* 7s. 6d. net.

Caldecott (Alfred), D.D. See Handbooks of Theology.

Calderwood (D. S.), Headmaster of the Normal School, Edinburgh. TEST CARDS IN EUCLID AND ALGEBRA. In three packets of 40, with Answers. 1s. each. Or in three Books, price 2d., 2d., and 3d.

Cameron (Mary Lovett). OLD ETRURIA AND MODERN TUSCANY. With 32 Illustrations. *Crown 8vo.* 6s. net.

Cannan (Edwin), M.A. See Smith (Adam).

Canning (George). See Little Library.

Capey (E. F. H.). See Oxford Biographies.

Carden (Robert W.). THE CITY OF GENOA. With 12 Illustrations in Colour by WILLIAM PARKINSON, and 20 other Illustrations. *Demy 8vo.* 10s. 6d. net.

Careless (John). See I.P.L.

Carlyle (Thomas). THE FRENCH REVOLUTION. Edited by C. R. L. FLETCHER, Fellow of Magdalen College, Oxford. *Three Volumes. Cr. 8vo.* 18s.
THE LETTERS AND SPEECHES OF OLIVER CROMWELL. With an Introduction by C. H. FIRTH, M.A., and Notes and Appendices by Mrs. S. C. LOMAS. *Three Volumes. Demy 8vo.* 18s. net.

Carlyle (R. M. and A. J.), M.A. See Leaders of Religion.

Carmichael (Philip). ALL ABOUT PHILIPPINE. With 8 Illustrations. *Cr. 8vo.* 2s. 6d.

Carpenter (Margaret Boyd). THE CHILD IN ART. With 50 Illustrations. *Second Edition. Large Cr. 8vo.* 6s.

***Carter (George),** M.A. THE STORY OF MILTON'S 'PARADISE LOST.' *Crown 8vo.* 1s. 6d.

Cavanagh (Francis), M.D. (Edin.). See New Library of Medicine.

Celano (Brother Thomas of). THE LIVES OF FRANCIS OF ASSISI. Translated by A. G. FERRERS HOWELL. With a Frontispiece. *Cr. 8vo.* 5s. net.

Chambers (A. M.). A CONSTITUTIONAL HISTORY OF ENGLAND. *Crown 8vo.* 6s.

Chamisso (A. von). See Simplified German Texts.

Chandler (Arthur), Bishop of Bloemfontein. ARA CŒLI: AN ESSAY IN MYSTICAL THEOLOGY. *Third Edition. Crown 8vo.* 3s. 6d. net.

Channer (C. C.) and Roberts (M. E.). LACEMAKING IN THE MIDLANDS, PAST AND PRESENT. With 17 full-page Illustrations. *Cr. 8vo.* 2s. 6d.

Chapman (S. J.). See Books on Business.

Chatterton (Thomas). See Standard Library.

Chesterfield (Lord), THE LETTERS OF THE EARL OF CHESTERFIELD TO HIS SON. Edited, with an Introduction by C. STRACHEY, with Notes by A. CALTHROP. *Two Volumes. Cr. 8vo.* 12s.

Chesterton (G. K.). CHARLES DICKENS. With two Portraits in Photogravure. *Fifth Edition. Cr. 8vo.* 6s.
ALL THINGS CONSIDERED. *Fourth Edition. Fcap. 8vo.* 5s.
TREMENDOUS TRIFLES. *Fcap. 8vo.* 5s.

Childe (Charles P.), B.A., F.R.C.S. See New Library of Medicine.

Cicero. See Classical Translations.

Clapham (J. H.), Professor of Economics in the University of Leeds. THE WOOLLEN AND WORSTED INDUSTRIES. With 21 Illustrations and Diagrams. *Cr. 8vo.* 6s.

Clarke (F. A.), M.A. See Leaders of Religion.

Clausen (George), A.R.A., R.W.S. SIX LECTURES ON PAINTING. With 16

General Literature

Illustrations. *Third Edition. Large Post 8vo. 3s. 6d. net.*
AIMS AND IDEALS IN ART. Eight Lectures delivered to the Students of the Royal Academy of Arts. With 32 Illustrations. *Second Edition. Large Post 8vo. 5s. net.*
Clay (Rotha Mary). See Antiquary's Books.
Cleather (A. L.). See Wagner (R).
Clinch (G.), F.G.S. See Antiquary's Books and Little Guides.
Clough (W. T.) and Dunstan (A. E.). See Junior School Books and Textbooks of Science.
Clouston (T. S.), M.D., C.C.D., F.R.S.E. See New Library of Medicine.
Coast (W. G.), B.A. EXAMINATION PAPERS IN VERGIL. *Cr. 8vo. 2s.*
Cobb (W. F.), M.A. THE BOOK OF PSALMS: with an Introduction and Notes. *Demy 8vo. 10s. 6d. net.*
*Cockshott (Winifred), St. Hilda's Hall, Oxford. THE PILGRIM FATHERS, THEIR CHURCH AND COLONY. With 12 Illustrations. *Demy 8vo. 7s. 6d. net.*
Collingwood (W. G.), M.A. THE LIFE OF JOHN RUSKIN. With Portrait. *Sixth Edition. Cr. 8vo. 2s. 6d. net.*
Collins (W. E.), M.A. See Churchman's Library.
Colvill (Helen H.). ST. TERESA OF SPAIN. With 20 Illustrations. *Demy 8vo. 7s. 6d. net.*
Combe (William). See I.P.L.
Conrad (Joseph). THE MIRROR OF THE SEA: Memories and Impressions. *Third Edition. Cr. 8vo. 6s.*
Cook (A. M.), M.A., and Marchant (E. C.), M.A. PASSAGES FOR UNSEEN TRANSLATION. Selected from Latin and Greek Literature. *Fourth Ed. Cr. 8vo. 3s. 6d.*
LATIN PASSAGES FOR UNSEEN TRANSLATION. *Cr. 8vo. 1s. 6d.*
Cooke-Taylor (R. W.). THE FACTORY SYSTEM. *Cr. 8vo. 2s. 6d.*
Coolidge (W. A. B.), M.A. THE ALPS. With many Illustrations. *Demy 8vo. 7s. 6d. net.*
Cooper (C. S.), F.R.H.S. See Westell (W.P.)
Corkran (Alice). See Little Books on Art.
Cotes (Rosemary). DANTE'S GARDEN. With a Frontispiece. *Second Edition. Fcap. 8vo. 2s. 6d.; leather, 3s. 6d. net.*
BIBLE FLOWERS. With a Frontispiece and Plan. *Fcap. 8vo. 2s. 6d. net.*
Cotton (Charles). See I.P.L. and Little Library.
Coulton (G. G.). CHAUCER AND HIS ENGLAND. With 32 Illustrations. *Second Edition. Demy 8vo. 10s. 6d. net.*
Cowley (Abraham). See Little Library.
Cowper (William). THE POEMS. Edited with an Introduction and Notes by J. C. BAILEY, M.A. Illustrated, including two unpublished designs by WILLIAM BLAKE. *Demy 8vo. 10s. 6d. net.*

Cox (J. Charles). See Ancient Cities, Antiquary's Books, and Little Guides.
Cox (Harold), B.A., M.P. LAND NATIONALIZATION AND LAND TAXATION. *Second Edition revised. Cr. 8vo. 3s. 6d. net.*
Crabbe (George). See Little Library.
Craik (Mrs.). See Little Library.
Crane (C. P.), D.S.O. See Little Guides.
Crane (Walter), R.W.S. AN ARTIST'S REMINISCENCES. With 123 Illustrations by the Author and others from Photographs. *Second Edition. Demy 8vo. 18s. net.*
INDIA IMPRESSIONS. With 84 Illustrations from Sketches by the Author. *Second Edition. Demy 8vo. 7s. 6d. net.*
Crashaw (Richard). See Little Library.
Crispe (T. E.), K.C. REMINISCENCES OF A K.C. With Portraits. *Demy 8vo. 10s. 6d. net.*
Cross (J. A.), M.A. THE FAITH OF THE BIBLE. *Fcap. 8vo. 2s. 6d. net.*
*Crowley (Ralph H.). THE HYGIENE OF SCHOOL LIFE. *Cr. 8vo. 3s. 6d. net.*
Cruikshank (G.). THE LOVING BALLAD OF LORD BATEMAN. With 11 Plates. *Cr. 16mo. 1s. 6d. net.*
Crump (B.). See Wagner (R.).
Cruttwell (C. T.), M.A., Canon of Peterborough. See Handbooks of English Church History.
Cunynghame (H. H.), C.B. See Connoisseur's Library.
Cutts (E. L.), D.D. See Leaders of Religion.
Daniell (G. W.), M.A. See Leaders of Religion.
Dante (Alighieri). LA COMMEDIA DI DANTE. The Italian Text edited by PAGET TOYNBEE, M.A., D.Litt. *Cr. 8vo. 6s.*
THE DIVINE COMEDY. Translated by H. F. CARY. Edited with a Life of Dante and Introductory Notes by PAGET TOYNBEE, M.A., D.Litt. *Demy 8vo. 6d.*
THE PURGATORIO OF DANTE. Translated into Spenserian Prose by C. GORDON WRIGHT. With the Italian text. *Fcap. 8vo. 2s. 6d. net.*
See also Little Library, Toynbee (Paget), and Vernon (Hon. W. Warren).
Darley (George). See Little Library.
D'Arcy (R. F.), M.A. A NEW TRIGONOMETRY FOR BEGINNERS. With numerous diagrams. *Cr. 8vo. 2s. 6d.*
Daudet (Alphonse). See Simplified French Texts.
Davenport (Cyril). See Connoisseur's Library and Little Books on Art.
Davenport (James). THE WASHBOURNE FAMILY. With 15 Illustrations and a Map. *Royal 8vo. 21s. net.*
Davey (Richard.) THE PAGEANT OF LONDON. With 40 Illustrations in Colour by JOHN FULLEYLOVE, R.I. *In Two Volumes. Demy 8vo. 15s. net.*
See also Romantic History.
Davies (Gerald S.). See Classics of Art.

MESSRS. METHUEN'S CATALOGUE

Davies (W. O. P.). See Junior Examination Series.
Davis (H. W. C.), M.A., Fellow and Tutor of Balliol College. ENGLAND UNDER THE NORMANS AND ANGEVINS: 1066-1272. With Maps and Illustrations. *Demy 8vo.* 10s. 6d. *net.*
Dawson (Nelson). See Connoisseur's Library.
Dawson (Mrs. Nelson). See Little Books on Art.
Deane (A. C.). See Little Library.
Deans (Storry R.). THE TRIALS OF FIVE QUEENS: KATHARINE OF ARAGON, ANNE BOLEYN, MARY QUEEN OF SCOTS, MARIE ANTOINETTE and CAROLINE OF BRUNSWICK. With 12 Illustrations. *Demy 8vo.* 10s. 6d. *net.*
Dearmer (Mabel). A CHILD'S LIFE OF CHRIST. With 8 Illustrations in Colour by E. FORTESCUE-BRICKDALE. *Large Cr. 8vo.* 6s.
*****D'Este (Margaret).** IN THE CANARIES WITH A CAMERA. Illustrated. *Cr. 8vo* 7s. 6d. *net.*
Delbos (Leon). THE METRIC SYSTEM. *Cr. 8vo.* 2s.
Demosthenes. AGAINST CONON AND CALLICLES. Edited by F. DARWIN SWIFT, M.A. *Second Edition. Fcap. 8vo.* 2s.
Dickens (Charles). See Little Library, I.P.L., and Chesterton (G. K.).
Dickinson (Emily). POEMS. *Cr. 8vo.* 4s. 6d. *net.*
Dickinson (G. L.), M.A., Fellow of King's College, Cambridge. THE GREEK VIEW OF LIFE. *Sixth Edition. Cr. 8vo.* 2s. 6d.
Dilke (Lady), Bulley (Miss), and Whitley (Miss). WOMEN'S WORK. *Cr. 8vo.* 2s. 6d.
Dillon (Edward), M.A. See Connoisseur's Library, Little Books on Art, and Classics of Art.
Ditchfield (P. H.), M.A., F.S.A. THE STORY OF OUR ENGLISH TOWNS. With an Introduction by AUGUSTUS JESSOPP, D.D. *Second Edition. Cr. 8vo.* 6s.
OLD ENGLISH CUSTOMS: Extant at the Present Time. *Cr. 8vo.* 6s.
ENGLISH VILLAGES. With 100 Illustrations. *Second Edition. Cr. 8vo.* 2s. 6d. *net.*
THE PARISH CLERK. With 31 Illustrations. *Third Edition. Demy 8vo.* 7s. 6d. *net.*
THE OLD-TIME PARSON. With 17 Illustrations. *Second Edition. Demy 8vo.* 7s. 6d. *net.*
Dixon (W. M.), M.A. A PRIMER OF TENNYSON. *Third Edition. Cr. 8vo.* 2s. 6d.
ENGLISH POETRY FROM BLAKE TO BROWNING. *Second Edition. Cr. 8vo.* 2s. 6d.
Dobbs (W. J.), M.A. See Textbooks of Science.
Doney (May). SONGS OF THE REAL. *Cr. 8vo.* 3s. 6d. *net.*

Douglas (Hugh A.). VENICE ON FOOT. With the Itinerary of the Grand Canal. With 75 Illustrations and 11 Maps. *Fcap. 8vo.* 5s. *net.*
Douglas (James). THE MAN IN THE PULPIT. *Cr. 8vo.* 2s. 6d. *net.*
Dowden (J.), D.D., Lord Bishop of Edinburgh. FURTHER STUDIES IN THE PRAYER BOOK. *Cr. 8vo.* 6s.
See also Churchman's Library.
Drage (G.). See Books on Business.
Driver (S. R.), D.D., D.C.L., Regius Professor of Hebrew in the University of Oxford. SERMONS ON SUBJECTS CONNECTED WITH THE OLD TESTAMENT. *Cr. 8vo.* 6s.
See also Westminster Commentaries.
Dry (Wakeling). See Little Guides.
Dryhurst (A. R.). See Little Books on Art.
*****Duff (Nora).** MATILDA OF TUSCANY. With many Illustrations. *Demy 8vo.* 10s. 6d. *net.*
Duguid (Charles). See Books on Business.
Dumas (Alexandre). THE CRIMES OF THE BORGIAS AND OTHERS. With an Introduction by R. S. GARNETT. With 9 Illustrations. *Cr. 8vo.* 6s.
THE CRIMES OF URBAIN GRANDIER AND OTHERS. With 8 Illustrations. *Cr. 8vo.* 6s.
THE CRIMES OF THE MARQUISE DE BRINVILLIERS AND OTHERS. With 8 Illustrations. *Cr. 8vo.* 6s.
THE CRIMES OF ALI PACHA AND OTHERS. With 8 Illustrations. *Cr. 8vo.* 6s.
MY MEMOIRS. Translated by E. M. WALLER. With an Introduction by ANDREW LANG. With Frontispieces in Photogravure. In six Volumes. *Cr. 8vo.* 6s. *each volume.*
VOL. I. 1802-1821. VOL. IV. 1830-1831.
VOL. II. 1822-1825. VOL. V. 1831-1832.
VOL. III. 1826-1830. VOL. VI. 1832-1833.
MY PETS. Newly translated by A. R. ALLINSON, M.A. With 16 Illustrations by V. LECOMTE. *Cr. 8vo.* 6s.
See also Simplified French Texts.
Duncan (David), D.Sc., LL.D. THE LIFE AND LETTERS OF HERBERT SPENCER. With 17 Illustrations. *Demy 8vo.* 15s.
Dunn (J. T.), D.Sc., and **Mundella (V. A.).** GENERAL ELEMENTARY SCIENCE. With 114 Illustrations. *Second Edition. Cr. 8vo.* 3s. 6d.
Dunn-Pattison (R. P.). NAPOLEON'S MARSHALS. With 20 Illustrations. *Demy 8vo. Second Edition.* 12s. 6d. *net.*
Dunstan (A. E.), B.Sc. (Lond.). See Textbooks of Science, and Junior School Books.
Durham (The Earl of). A REPORT ON CANADA. With an Introductory Note. *Demy 8vo.* 4s. 6d. *net.*
Dutt (W. A.). THE NORFOLK BROADS. With coloured Illustrations by FRANK SOUTHGATE, R.B.A. *Second Edition. Cr. 8vo.* 6s.

General Literature

WILD LIFE IN EAST ANGLIA. With 16 Illustrations in colour by FRANK SOUTHGATE, R.B.A. *Second Edition*. *Demy 8vo*. *7s. 6d. net*.
SOME LITERARY ASSOCIATIONS OF EAST ANGLIA. With 16 Illustrations in Colour by W. DEXTER, R.B.A., and 16 other Illustrations. *Demy 8vo*. *10s. 6d. net*. See also Little Guides.

Earle (John), Bishop of Salisbury. MICROCOSMOGRAPHIE, OR A PIECE OF THE WORLD DISCOVERED. *Post 16mo*. *2s. net*.

Edmonds (Major J. E.), R.E.; D.A.Q.-M.G. See Wood (W. Birkbeck).

Edwardes (Tickner). THE LORE OF THE HONEY BEE. With 24 Illustrations. *Cr. 8vo*. *6s*.

Edwards (Clement), M.P. RAILWAY NATIONALIZATION. *Second Edition, Revised*. *Crown 8vo*. *2s. 6d. net*.

Edwards (W. Douglas). See Commercial Series.

Egan (Pierce). See I.P.L.

Egerton (H. E.), M.A. A HISTORY OF BRITISH COLONIAL POLICY. *Second Ed., Revised*. *Demy 8vo*. *7s. 6d. net*.

Ellaby (C. G.). See Little Guides.

Ellerton (F. G.). See Stone (S. J.).

Epictetus. See Aurelius (Marcus).

Erasmus. A Book called in Latin ENCHIRIDION MILITIS CHRISTIANI, and in English the Manual of the Christian Knight. *Fcap. 8vo*. *3s. 6d. net*.

Erckmann-Chatrian. See Simplified French Texts.

Evagrius. See Byzantine Texts.

Ewald (Carl). TWO LEGS, AND OTHER STORIES. Translated from the Danish by ALEXANDER TEIXEIRA DE MATTOS. Illustrated by AUGUSTA GUEST. *Large Cr. 8vo*. *6s*.

Ezekiel. See Westminster Commentaries.

Facon (H. T.), B.A. See Junior Examination Series.

Fairbrother (W. H.), M.A. THE PHILOSOPHY OF T. H. GREEN. *Second Edition*. *Cr. 8vo*. *3s. 6d*.

Fea (Allan). THE FLIGHT OF THE KING. With over 70 Sketches and Photographs by the Author. *New and revised Edition*. *Demy 8vo*. *7s. 6d. net*.
SECRET CHAMBERS AND HIDING-PLACES. With 80 Illustrations. *New and revised Edition*. *Demy 8vo*. *7s. 6d. net*.
JAMES II. AND HIS WIVES. With 40 Illustrations. *Demy 8vo*. *10s. 6d. net*.

Fell (E. F. B.). THE FOUNDATIONS OF LIBERTY. *Cr. 8vo*. *5s. net*.

Ferrier (Susan). See Little Library.

Fidler (T. Claxton), M.Inst. C.E. See Books on Business.

Fielding (Henry). See Standard Library.

Finn (S. W.), M.A. See Junior Examination Series.

Firth (J. B.). See Little Guides.

Firth (C. H.), M.A., Regius Professor of Modern History at Oxford. CROM-

WELL'S ARMY: A History of the English Soldier during the Civil Wars, the Commonwealth, and the Protectprate. *Cr. 8vo*. *6s*.
*****Firth (Edith E.)**. See Beginner's Books and Junior School Books.

FitzGerald (Edward). THE RUBÁIYÁT OF OMAR KHAYYÁM. Printed from the Fifth and last Edition. With a Commentary by Mrs. STEPHEN BATSON, and a Biography of Omar by E. D. ROSS. *Cr. 8vo*. *6s*. See also Miniature Library.

FitzGerald (H. P.). A CONCISE HANDBOOK OF CLIMBERS, TWINERS, AND WALL SHRUBS. Illustrated. *Fcap. 8vo*. *3s. 6d. net*.

Fitzpatrick (S. A. O.). See Ancient Cities.

Flecker (W. H.), M.A., D.C.L., Headmaster of the Dean Close School, Cheltenham. THE STUDENT'S PRAYER BOOK. THE TEXT OF MORNING AND EVENING PRAYER AND LITANY. With an Introduction and Notes. *Cr. 8vo*. *2s. 6d*.

Fletcher (C. R. L.), M.A. See Carlyle (Thomas).

Fletcher (J. S.). A BOOK OF YORKSHIRE. With 16 Illustrations in Colour by WAL PAGET and FRANK SOUTHGATE, R.B.A., 16 other Illustrations and a Map. *Demy 8vo*. *7s. 6d. net*.

Flux (A. W.), M.A., William Dow Professor of Political Economy in M'Gill University, Montreal. ECONOMIC PRINCIPLES. *Demy 8vo*. *7s. 6d. net*.

Foat (F. W. G.), D.Litt., M.A. A LONDON READER FOR YOUNG CITIZENS. With Plans and Illustrations. *Cr. 8vo*. *1s. 6d*.

Ford (H. G.), M.A., Assistant Master at Bristol Grammar School. See Junior School Books.

Forel (A.). THE SENSES OF INSECTS. Translated by MACLEOD YEARSLEY. With 2 Illustrations. *Demy 8vo*. *10s. 6d. net*.

Fortescue (Mrs. G.). See Little Books on Art.

Fouqué (La Motte). SINTRAM AND HIS COMPANIONS. Translated by A. C. FARQUHARSON. With 20 Illustrations by EDMUND J. SULLIVAN, and a Frontispiece in Photogravure from an engraving by ALBRECHT DÜRER. *Demy 8vo*. *7s. 6d. net*. *Half White Vellum*, *10s. 6d. net*.
See also Simplified German Texts.

Fraser (J. F.). ROUND THE WORLD ON A WHEEL. With 100 Illustrations. *Fifth Edition* *Cr. 8vo*. *6s*.

French (W.), M.A. See Textbooks of Science.

Freudenreich (Ed. von). DAIRY BACTERIOLOGY. A Short Manual for Students. Translated by J. R. AINSWORTH DAVIS, M.A. *Second Edition*. *Revised*. *Cr. 8vo*. *2s. 6d*.

Fursdon (F. R. M). FRENCH AND ENGLISH PARALLELS. *Fcap. 8vo*. *3s. 6d. net*.

Fyvie (John). TRAGEDY QUEENS OF THE GEORGIAN ERA. With 16 Illustrations. *Second Ed*. *Demy 8vo*. *12s. 6d. net*.

A 2

MESSRS. METHUEN'S CATALOGUE

Gellaher (D.) and Stead (W. J.). THE COMPLETE RUGBY FOOTBALLER, ON THE NEW ZEALAND SYSTEM. With 35 Illustrations. *Second Ed. Demy 8vo.* 10s. 6d. *net.*

Gallichan (W. M.). See Little Guides.

Galton (Sir Francis), F.R.S.; D.C.L., Oxf.; Hon. Sc.D., Camb.; Hon. Fellow Trinity College, Cambridge. MEMORIES OF MY LIFE. With 8 Illustrations. *Third Edition. Demy 8vo.* 10s. 6d. *net.*

Gambado (Geoffrey, Esq.). See I.P.L.

Garnett (Lucy M. J.). THE TURKISH PEOPLE: THEIR SOCIAL LIFE, RELIGIOUS BELIEFS AND INSTITUTIONS, AND DOMESTIC LIFE. With 21 Illustrations. *Demy 8vo.* 10s. 6d. *net.*

Gaskell (Mrs.). See Little Library, Standard Library and Sixpenny Novels.

Gasquet, the Right Rev. Abbot, O.S.B. See Antiquary's Books.

Gee (Henry), D.D., F.S.A. See Handbooks of English Church History.

George (H. B.), M.A., Fellow of New College, Oxford. BATTLES OF ENGLISH HISTORY. With numerous Plans. *Fourth Edition Revised. Cr. 8vo.* 3s. 6d.
A HISTORICAL GEOGRAPHY OF THE BRITISH EMPIRE. *Fourth Edition. Cr. 8vo.* 3s. 6d.

Gibbins (H. de B.), Litt.D., M.A. INDUSTRY IN ENGLAND: HISTORICAL OUTLINES. With 5 Maps. *Fifth Edition.\ Demy 8vo.* 10s. 6d.
THE INDUSTRIAL HISTORY OF ENGLAND. With Maps and Plans. *Fifteenth Edition, Revised. Cr. 8vo.* 3s.
ENGLISH SOCIAL REFORMERS. *Second Edition. Cr. 8vo.* 2s. 6d.
See also Hadfield (R. A.), and Commercial Series.

Gibbon (Edward). MEMOIRS OF MY LIFE AND WRITINGS. Edited by G. BIRKBECK HILL, LL.D *Cr. 8vo.* 6s.
*THE DECLINE AND FALL OF THE ROMAN EMPIRE. Edited, with Notes, Appendices, and Maps, by J. B. BURY. M.A., Litt.D., Regius Professor of Modern History at Cambridge. Illustrated. *In Seven Volumes. Demy 8vo. Gilt top. Each* 10s. 6d. *net.*

Gibbs (Philip). THE ROMANCE OF GEORGE VILLIERS: FIRST DUKE OF BUCKINGHAM, AND SOME MEN AND WOMEN OF THE STUART COURT. With 20 Illustrations. *Second Edition. Demy 8vo.* 15s. *net.*

Gibson (E. C. S.), D.D., Lord Bishop of Gloucester. See Westminster Commentaries, Handbooks of Theology, and Oxford Biographies.

Gilbert (A. R.). See Little Books on Art.

Gloag (M. R.) and Wyatt (Kate M.). A BOOK OF ENGLISH GARDENS. With 24 Illustrations in Colour. *Demy 8vo.* 10s. 6d. *net.*

Glover (T. R.), M.A., Fellow and Classical Lecturer of St. John's College, Cambridge. THE CONFLICT OF RELIGIONS IN THE EARLY ROMAN EMPIRE. *Third Edition. Demy 8vo.* 7s. 6d. *net.*

Godfrey (Elizabeth). A BOOK OF REMEMBRANCE. Being Lyrical Selections for every day in the Year. Arranged by. *Second Edition. Fcap. 8vo.* 2s. 6d. *net.*
ENGLISH CHILDREN IN THE OLDEN TIME. With 32 Illustrations. *Second Edition. Demy 8vo.* 7s. 6d. *net.*

Godley (A. D.), M.A., Fellow of Magdalen College, Oxford. OXFORD IN THE EIGHTEENTH CENTURY. With 16 Illustrations. *Second Edition. Demy 8vo.* 7s. 6d. *net.*
Also published in a Colonial Edition.
LYRA FRIVOLA. *Fourth Edition. Fcap. 8vo.* 2s. 6d.
VERSES TO ORDER. *Second Edition. Fcap. 8vo.* 2s. 6d.
SECOND STRINGS. *Fcap. 8vo.* 2s. 6d.

Goldsmith (Oliver). See I.P.L. and Standard Library.

Goll (August). CRIMINAL TYPES IN SHAKESPEARE. Authorised Translation from the Danish by Mrs. CHARLES WEEKES. *Cr. 8vo.* 5s. *net.*

Gomme (G. L.). See Antiquary's Books.

Gordon (Lina Duff) (Mrs. Aubrey Waterfield). HOME LIFE IN ITALY: LETTERS FROM THE APENNINES. With 13 Illustrations by AUBREY WATERFIELD and 15 Illustrations from Photographs. *Second Edition. Demy 8vo.* 10s. 6d. *net.*

Gorst (Rt. Hon. Sir John). See New Library of Medicine.

Gostling (Frances M.). THE BRETONS AT HOME. With 12 Illustrations in Colour by GASTON FANTY LESCURE, and 32 from Photographs. *Demy 8vo.* 10s. 6d. *net.*

Goudge (H. L.), M.A., Principal of Wells Theological College. See Westminster Commentaries.

Graham (Harry). A GROUP OF SCOTTISH WOMEN. With 16 Illustrations. *Second Edition. Demy 8vo.* 10s. 6d. *net.*

Graham (P. Anderson). THE RURAL EXODUS. The Problem of the Village and the Town. *Cr. 8vo.* 2s. 6d.

Grahame (Kenneth). THE WIND IN THE WILLOWS. With a Frontispiece by GRAHAM ROBERTSON. *Fourth Edition. Cr. 8vo.* 6s.

Granger (F. S.), M.A., Litt.D. PSYCHOLOGY. *Third Edition. Cr. 8vo.* 2s. 6d.
THE SOUL OF A CHRISTIAN. *Cr. 8vo.* 6s.

Gray (E. M'Queen). GERMAN PASSAGES FOR UNSEEN TRANSLATION. *Cr. 8vo.* 2s. 6d.

Gray (P. L.), B.Sc. THE PRINCIPLES OF MAGNETISM AND ELECTRICITY. With 181 Diagrams. *Cr. 8vo.* 3s. 6d.

Green (G. Buckland), M.A., late Fellow of St. John's College, Oxon. NOTES ON

General Literature

GREEK AND LATIN SYNTAX. Second Ed. revised. Crown 8vo. 3s. 6d.

Green (Mary Anne Everett). ELIZABETH; ELECTRESS PALATINE AND QUEEN OF BOHEMIA. Revised by her Niece S. C. Lomas. With a Prefatory Note by A. W. Ward, Litt. D. Demy 8vo. 10s. 6d. net.

Greenidge (A. H. J.), M.A., D. Litt. A HISTORY OF ROME: From the Tribunate of Tiberius Gracchus to the end of the Jugurthine War, B.C. 133-104. Demy 8vo. 10s. 6d. net.

Gregory (Miss E. C.). See Library of Devotion.

Grubb (H. C.). See Textbooks of Technology.

Gwynn (Stephen), M.P. A HOLIDAY IN CONNEMARA. With 16 Illustrations. Demy 8vo. 10s. 6d. net.

Hadfield (R. A.) and Gibbins (H. de B.). A SHORTER WORKING DAY. Cr. 8vo. 2s. 6d.

*Hall (Cyril). THE YOUNG CARPENTER. With Diagrams, and Illustrations. Cr. 8vo. 5s.

Hall (Hammond). THE YOUNG ENGINEER: OR MODERN ENGINES AND THEIR MODELS. With 85 Illustrations. Second Edition. Cr. 8vo. 5s.

Hall (Mary). A WOMAN'S TREK FROM THE CAPE TO CAIRO. With 64 Illustrations and 2 Maps. Second Edition. Demy 8vo. 16s. net.

Hamel (Frank). FAMOUS FRENCH SALONS. With 20 Illustrations. Third Edition. Demy 8vo. 12s. 6d. net.

Hannay (D.). A SHORT HISTORY OF THE ROYAL NAVY. Vol. I., 1217-1688. Vol. II., 1689-1815. Demy 8vo. Each 7s. 6d. net.

Hannay (James O.), M.A. THE SPIRIT AND ORIGIN OF CHRISTIAN MONASTICISM. Cr. 8vo. 6s.
THE WISDOM OF THE DESERT. Fcap. 8vo. 3s. 6d. net.

Hardie (Martin). See Connoisseur's Library.

Hare (A. T.), M.A. THE CONSTRUCTION OF LARGE INDUCTION COILS. With 35 Illustrations. Demy 8vo. 6s.

Harker (Alfred), M.A., F.R.S., Fellow of St. John's College, and Lecturer in Petrology in the University of Cambridge. THE NATURAL HISTORY OF IGNEOUS ROCKS. With 112 Diagrams and 2 Plates. Demy 8vo. 12s. 6d. net.

Harper (Charles G.). THE AUTOCAR ROAD-BOOK. In three Volumes. Crown 8vo. Each 7s. 6d. net.
Vol. I.—SOUTH OF THE THAMES.

Harvey (Alfred), M.B. See Ancient Cities and Antiquary's Books.

Hawthorne (Nathaniel). See Little Library.

*Headley (F. W.). DARWINISM AND MODERN SOCIALISM. Cr. 8vo. 5s. net.

Heath (Frank R.). See Little Guides.

Heath (Dudley). See Connoisseur's Library.

Henderson (B. W.), Fellow of Exeter College, Oxford. THE LIFE AND PRINCIPATE OF THE EMPEROR NERO. Illustrated. New and cheaper issue. Demy 8vo. 7s. 6d. net.
AT INTERVALS. Fcap 8vo. 2s. 6d. net.

Henderson (M. Sturge). GEORGE MEREDITH: NOVELIST, POET, REFORMER. With a Portrait in Photogravure. Second Edition. Crown 8vo. 6s.

Henderson (T. F.). See Little Library and Oxford Biographies.

Henderson (T. F.), and Watt (Francis). SCOTLAND OF TO-DAY. With 20 Illustrations in colour and 24 other Illustrations. Second Edition. Cr. 8vo. 6s.

Henley (W. E.). ENGLISH LYRICS. CHAUCER TO POE, 1340-1849. Second Edition. Cr. 8vo. 2s. 6d. net.

Henley (W. E.) and Whibley (C.) A BOOK OF ENGLISH PROSE, CHARACTER, AND INCIDENT, 1387-1649. Cr. 8vo. 2s. 6d. net.

Herbert (George). See Library of Devotion.

Herbert of Cherbury (Lord). See Miniature Library.

Hett (Walter S.), B.A. A SHORT HISTORY OF GREECE TO THE DEATH OF ALEXANDER THE GREAT. With 3 Maps and 4 Plans. Cr. 8vo. 3s. 6d.

Hewins (W. A. S.), B.A. ENGLISH TRADE AND FINANCE IN THE SEVENTEENTH CENTURY. Cr. 8vo. 2s. 6d.

Hewitt (Ethel M.) A GOLDEN DIAL. A Day Book of Prose and Verse. Fcap. 8vo. 2s. 6d. net.

Hey (H.), Inspector, Surrey Education Committee, and Rose (G. H.), City and Guilds Woodwork Teacher. A WOODWORK CLASS-BOOK. Pt. I. Illustrated. 4to. 2s.

Heywood (W.). See St. Francis of Assisi.

Hill (Clare). See Textbooks of Technology.

*Hill (George Francis). ONE HUNDRED MASTERPIECES OF SCULPTURE. with 101 Illustrations. Demy 8vo. 10s. 6d. net.

Hill (Henry), B.A., Headmaster of the Boy's High School, Worcester, Cape Colony. A SOUTH AFRICAN ARITHMETIC. Cr. 8vo. 3s. 6d.

Hind (C. Lewis). DAYS IN CORNWALL. With 16 Illustrations in Colour by William Pascoe, and 20 other Illustrations and a Map. Second Edition. Cr. 8vo. 6s.

Hirst (F. W.) See Books on Business.

Hobhouse (L. T.), late Fellow of C.C.C., Oxford. THE THEORY OF KNOWLEDGE. Demy 8vo. 10s. 6d. net.

Hobson (J. A.), M.A. INTERNATIONAL TRADE: A Study of Economic Principles. Cr. 8vo. 2s. 6d. net.
PROBLEMS OF POVERTY. An Inquiry

into the Industrial Condition of the Poor. *Seventh Edition. Cr. 8vo.* 2s. 6d.
THE PROBLEM OF THE UNEMPLOYED. *Fourth Edition. Cr. 8vo.* 2s. 6d.
Hodgetts (E. A. Brayley). THE COURT OF RUSSIA IN THE NINETEENTH CENTURY. With 20 Illustrations. *Two Volumes. Demy 8vo.* 24s. net.
Hodgkin (T.), D.C.L. See Leaders of Religion.
Hodgson (Mrs. W.) HOW TO IDENTIFY OLD CHINESE PORCELAIN. With 40 Illustrations. *Second Edition. Post 8vo.* 6s.
Holden-Stone (G. de). See Books on Business.
Holdich (Sir T. H.), K.C.I.E., C.B., F.S.A. THE INDIAN BORDERLAND, 1880-1900. With 22 Illustrations and a Map. *Second Edition. Demy 8vo.* 10s. 6d. net.
Holdsworth (W. S.), D.C.L. A HISTORY OF ENGLISH LAW. *In Four Volumes. Vols. I., II., III. Demy 8vo.* Each 10s. 6d. net.
Holland (Clive). TYROL AND ITS PEOPLE. With 16 Illustrations in Colour by ADRIAN STOKES, and 31 other Illustrations. *Demy 8vo.* 10s. 6d. net.
Holland (H. Scott), Canon of St. Paul's. See Newman (J. H.)
Hollings (M. A.), M.A. See Six Ages of European History.
Hollway-Calthrop (H. C.), late of Balliol College, Oxford; Bursar of Eton College. PETRARCH: HIS LIFE, WORK, AND TIMES. With 24 Illustrations. *Demy 8vo.* 12s. 6d. net.
Holmes (T. Scott). See Ancient Cities.
Holyoake (G. J.). THE CO-OPERATIVE MOVEMENT OF TO-DAY. *Fourth Ed. Cr. 8vo.* 2s. 6d.
Hone (Nathaniel J.). See Antiquary's Books.
Hook (A.) HUMANITY AND ITS PROBLEMS. *Cr. 8vo.* 5s. net.
Hoppner. See Little Galleries.
Horace. See Classical Translations.
Horsburgh (E. L. S.), M.A. LORENZO THE MAGNIFICENT: AND FLORENCE IN HER GOLDEN AGE. With 24 Illustrations and 2 Maps. *Second Edition. Demy 8vo.* 15s. net.
WATERLOO: With Plans. *Second Edition. Cr. 8vo.* 5s.
See also Oxford Biographies.
Horth (A. C.). See Textbooks of Technology.
Horton (R. F.), D.D. See Leaders of Religion.
Hosie (Alexander). MANCHURIA. With 30 Illustrations and a Map. *Second Edition. Demy 8vo.* 7s. 6d. net.
How (F. D.). SIX GREAT SCHOOLMASTERS. With 13 Illustrations. *Second Edition. Demy 8vo.* 7s. 6d.
Howell (A. G. Ferrers). FRANCISCAN DAYS. Being Selections for every day in the year from ancient Franciscan writings. *Cr. 8vo.* 3s. 6d. net.
Howell (G.). TRADE UNIONISM—NEW AND OLD. *Fourth Edition. Cr. 8vo.* 2s. 6d.

Huggins (Sir William), K.C.B., O.M., D.C.L., F.R.S. THE ROYAL SOCIETY; OR, SCIENCE IN THE STATE AND IN THE SCHOOLS. With 25 Illustrations. *Wide Royal 8vo.* 4s. 6d. net.
Hughes (C. E.). THE PRAISE OF SHAKESPEARE. An English Anthology. With a Preface by SIDNEY LEE. *Demy 8vo.* 3s. 6d. net.
Hugo (Victor). See Simplified French Texts.
*****Hulton (Samuel F.).** THE CLERK OF OXFORD IN FICTION. With 12 Illustrations. *Demy 8vo.* 15s. net.
Hume (Martin), M.A. See Romantic History.
Hutchinson (Horace G.) THE NEW FOREST. Illustrated in colour with 50 Pictures by WALTER TYNDALE and 4 by LUCY KEMP-WELCH. *Third Edition. Cr. 8vo.* 6s.
Hutton (A. W.), M.A. See Leaders of Religion and Library of Devotion.
Hutton (Edward). THE CITIES OF UMBRIA. With 20 Illustrations in Colour by A. PISA, and 12 other Illustrations. *Third Edition. Cr. 8vo.* 6s.
THE CITIES OF SPAIN. With 24 Illustrations in Colour, by A. W. RIMINGTON, 20 other Illustrations and a Map. *Third Edition. Cr. 8vo.* 6s.
FLORENCE AND THE CITIES OF NORTHERN TUSCANY, WITH GENOA. With 16 Illustrations in Colour by WILLIAM PARKINSON, and 16 other Illustrations. *Second Edition. Cr. 8vo.* 6s.
ENGLISH LOVE POEMS. Edited with an Introduction. *Fcap. 8vo.* 3s. 6d. net.
COUNTRY WALKS ABOUT FLORENCE. With 32 Drawings by ADELAIDE MARCHI and 20 other Illustrations. *Fcap. 8vo.* 5s. net.
IN UNKNOWN TUSCANY. With an Appendix by WILLIAM HEYWOOD. With 8 Illustrations in Colour and 20 others. *Second Edition. Demy 8vo.* 7s. 6d. net.
*ROME. With 16 Illustrations in Colour by MAXWELL ARMFIELD, and 12 other Illustrations. *Cr. 8vo.* 6s.
Hutton (R. H.). See Leaders of Religion.
Hutton (W. H.), M.A. THE LIFE OF SIR THOMAS MORE. With Portraits after Drawings by HOLBEIN. *Second Edition. Cr. 8vo.* 5s.
See also Leaders of Religion.
Hyde (A. G.) GEORGE HERBERT AND HIS TIMES. With 32 Illustrations. *Demy 8vo.* 10s. 6d. net.
Hyett (F. A.). FLORENCE: HER HISTORY AND ART TO THE FALL OF THE REPUBLIC. *Demy 8vo.* 7s. 6d. net.
Ibsen (Henrik). BRAND. A Drama. Translated by WILLIAM WILSON. *Third Edition. Cr. 8vo.* 3s. 6d.
Inge (W. R.), M.A., Fellow and Tutor of Hertford College, Oxford. CHRISTIAN MYSTICISM. (The Bampton Lectures of 1899.) *Demy 8vo.* 12s. 6d. net.
See also Library of Devotion.

General Literature 13

Innes (A. D.), M.A. A HISTORY OF THE BRITISH IN INDIA. With Maps and Plans. *Cr. 8vo.* 6s.
ENGLAND UNDER THE TUDORS. With Maps. *Second Edition. Demy 8vo.* 10s. 6d. net.
***Innes (Mary).** SCHOOLS OF PAINTING. With 76 Illustrations. *Cr. 8vo.* 5s. net.
Isaiah. See Churchman's Bible.
Jackson (C. E.), B.A. See Textbooks of Science.
Jackson (S.), M.A. See Commercial Series.
Jackson (F. Hamilton). See Little Guides.
Jacob (F.), M.A. See Junior Examination Series.
Jeans (J. Stephen). TRUSTS, POOLS, AND CORNERS AS AFFECTING COMMERCE AND INDUSTRY. *Cr. 8vo.* 2s. 6d.
See also Books on Business.
Jebb (Camilla). A STAR OF THE SALONS: JULIE DE LESPINASSE. With 20 Illustrations. *Demy 8vo.* 10s. 6d. net.
Jeffery (Reginald W.), M.A. THE HISTORY OF THE THIRTEEN COLONIES OF NORTH AMERICA 1497-1763. With 8 Illustrations and a Map. *Demy 8vo.* 7s. 6d. net.
Jeffreys (D. Gwyn). DOLLY'S THEATRICALS. *Super Royal 16mo.* 2s. 6d.
Jenks (E.), M.A., B.C.L. AN OUTLINE OF ENGLISH LOCAL GOVERNMENT. *Second Ed.* Revised by R. C. K. ENSOR, M.A. *Cr. 8vo.* 2s. 6d.
Jenner (Mrs. H.). See Little Books on Art.
Jennings (A. C.), M.A. See Handbooks of English Church History.
Jennings (Oscar), M.D. EARLY WOODCUT INITIALS. *Demy 4to.* 21s. net.
***Jerningham (Charles Edward).** THE MAXIMS OF MARMADUKE. *Crown 8vo.* 5s.
Jessopp (Augustus), D.D. See Leaders of Religion.
Jevons (F. B.), M.A., Litt.D., Principal of Hatfield Hall, Durham. RELIGION IN EVOLUTION. *Cr. 8vo.* 3s. 6d. net.
See also Churchman's Library and Handbooks of Theology.
Johnson (A. H.), M.A. See Six Ages of European History.
Johnston (Sir H. H.), K.C.B. BRITISH CENTRAL AFRICA. With nearly 200 Illustrations and Six Maps. *Third Edition. Cr. 4to.* 18s. net.
Jones (H.). See Commercial Series.
Jones (H. F.). See Textbooks of Science.
Jones (L. A. Atherley), K.C., M.P., and **Bellot (Hugh H. L.)**, M.A., D.C.L. THE MINER'S GUIDE TO THE COAL MINES REGULATION ACTS AND THE LAW OF EMPLOYERS AND WORKMEN. *Cr. 8vo.* 2s. 6d. net.
COMMERCE IN WAR. *Royal 8vo.* 21s. net.
Jones (R. Compton), M.A. POEMS OF THE INNER LIFE. Selected by. *Thirteenth Edition. Fcap. 8vo.* 2s. 6d. net.

Jonson (Ben). See Standard Library.
Julian (Lady) of Norwich. REVELATIONS OF DIVINE LOVE. Ed. by GRACE WARRACK. *Third Ed. Cr. 8vo.* 3s. 6d.
Juvenal. See Classical Translations.
'Kappa.' LET YOUTH BUT KNOW: A Plea for Reason in Education. *Cr. 8vo.* 3s. 6d. net.
Kaufmann (M.), M.A. SOCIALISM AND MODERN THOUGHT. *Second Edition Revised and Enlarged. Cr. 8vo.* 2s. 6d. net.
Keats (John). THE POEMS. Edited with Introduction and Notes by E. de SÉLINCOURT, M.A. With a Frontispiece in Photogravure. *Second Edition Revised. Demy 8vo.* 7s. 6d. net.
REALMS OF GOLD. Selections from the Works of. *Fcap. 8vo.* 3s. 6d. net.
See also Little Library and Standard Library.
Keble (John). THE CHRISTIAN YEAR. With an Introduction and Notes by W. LOCK, D.D., Warden of Keble College. Illustrated by R. ANNING BELL. *Third Edition. Fcap. 8vo.* 3s. 6d.; *padded morocco,* 5s.
See also Library of Devotion.
Kelynack (T. N.), M.D., M.R.C.P. See New Library of Medicine.
Kempis (Thomas à). THE IMITATION OF CHRIST. With an Introduction by DEAN FARRAR. Illustrated by C. M. GERE. *Third Edition. Fcap. 8vo.* 3s. 6d.; *padded morocco,* 5s.
Also Translated by C. BIGG, D.D. *Cr. 8vo.* 3s. 6d.
See also Montmorency (J. E. G. de), Library of Devotion, and Standard Library.
Kennedy (James Houghton), D.D., Assistant Lecturer in Divinity in the University of Dublin. See St. Paul.
Kerr (S. Parnell). GEORGE SELWYN AND THE WITS. With 16 Illustrations. *Demy 8vo.* 12s. 6d. net.
Kimmins (C. W.), M.A. THE CHEMISTRY OF LIFE AND HEALTH. Illustrated. *Cr. 8vo.* 2s. 6d.
Kinglake (A. W.). See Little Library.
Kipling (Rudyard). BARRACK-ROOM BALLADS. 91st *Thousand.* Twenty-sixth *Edition. Cr. 8vo.* 6s. Also *Fcap. 8vo, Leather.* 5s.
THE SEVEN SEAS. 79th *Thousand. Fifteenth Edition. Cr. 8vo.* 6s. Also *Fcap. 8vo, Leather.* 5s.
THE FIVE NATIONS. 66th *Thousand. Fifth Edition. Cr. 8vo.* 6s. Also *Fcap. 8vo, Leather.* 5s.
DEPARTMENTAL DITTIES. *Seventeenth Edition. Cr. 8vo.* 6s. Also *Fcap. 8vo, Leather.* 5s.
Knight (Albert E.). THE COMPLETE CRICKETER. With 50 Illustrations. *Demy 8vo.* 7s. 6d. net.
Knowling (R. J.), M.A., Professor of New Testament Exegesis at King's College, London. See Westminster Commentaries.

MESSRS. METHUEN'S CATALOGUE

Knox (Winifred F.). THE COURT OF A SAINT. With 16 Illustrations. *Demy 8vo.* 10s. 6d. net.
Kropotkin (Prince). THE TERROR IN RUSSIA. Seventh Edition. *Cr. 8vo.* 2d. net.
Laboulaye (Edouard) See Simplified French Texts.
Lamb (Charles and Mary), THE WORKS. Edited by E. V. Lucas. Illustrated. *In Seven Volumes. Demy 8vo.* 7s. 6d. each.
See also Little Library and Lucas (E. V.)
Lambert (F. A. H.). See Little Guides.
Lambros (Professor S. P.). See Byzantine Texts.
Lane-Poole (Stanley). A HISTORY OF EGYPT IN THE MIDDLE AGES. With 101 Illustrations and a Map. *Cr. 8vo.* 6s.
Langbridge (F.), M.A. BALLADS OF THE BRAVE: Poems of Chivalry, Enterprise, Courage, and Constancy. *Third Edition. Cr. 8vo.* 2s. 6d.
Lankester (Sir E. Ray), K.C.B., F.R.S. SCIENCE FROM AN EASY CHAIR. With many Illustrations, of which 2 are in Colour. *Cr. 8vo.* 6s.
Law (William). See Library of Devotion and Standard Library.
Leach (Henry). THE SPIRIT OF THE LINKS. *Cr. 8vo.* 6s.
See also Braid (James).
Le Braz (Anatole). THE LAND OF PARDONS. Translated by Frances M. Gostling. With 12 Illustrations in Colour by T. C. Gotch, and 40 other Illustrations. *Third Edition. Crown 8vo.* 6s.
Lees (Beatrice). See Six Ages of European History.
Lees (Frederick). A SUMMER IN TOURAINE. With 12 Illustrations in Colour by Maxwell Armfield, and 87 from Photographs. Also a Map. *Second Edition. Demy 8vo.* 10s. 6d. net.
Lehmann (R. C.), M.P. THE COMPLETE OARSMAN. With 59 Illustrations. *Demy 8vo.* 10s. 6d. net.
Lewes (V. B.), M.A. AIR AND WATER. Illustrated. *Cr. 8vo.* 2s. 6d.
Lewis (B. M. Gwyn). A CONCISE HANDBOOK OF GARDEN SHRUBS. With 20 Illustrations. *Fcap. 8vo.* 3s. 6d. net.
Lindsay (Lady Mabel). ANNI DOMINI: A Gospel Study. *In Two Volumes. Super Royal 8vo.* 10s. net.
Lindsay (W. M.), Fellow of Jesus College, Oxford. See Plautus.
Lisle (Fortunéede). See Little Books on Art.
Littlehales (H.). See Antiquary's Books.
Llewellyn (Owen) and Raven-Hill (L.). THE SOUTH-BOUND CAR. With 85 Illustrations. *Crown 8vo.* 6s.
Lock (Walter), D.D., Warden of Keble College. ST. PAUL, THE MASTER-BUILDER. *Second Ed. Cr. 8vo.* 3s. 6d.
THE BIBLE AND CHRISTIAN LIFE. *Cr. 8vo.* 6s.
See also Keble (J.) and Leaders of Religion.

Locker (F.). See Little Library.
Lodge (Sir Oliver), F.R.S. THE SUBSTANCE OF FAITH, ALLIED WITH SCIENCE: A Catechism for Parents and Teachers. *Ninth Ed. Cr. 8vo.* 2s. net.
MAN AND THE UNIVERSE: A Study of the Influence of the Advance in Scientific Knowledge upon our Understanding of Christianity. *Sixth Edition. Demy 8vo.* 7s. 6d. net.
*THE SURVIVAL OF MAN: A Study of Unrecognised Human Faculty. *Demy 8vo.* 7s. 6d. net.
Lodge (Eleanor C.). See Six Ages of European History.
Lofthouse (W. F.), M.A. ETHICS AND ATONEMENT. With a Frontispiece. *Demy 8vo.* 5s. net.
Longfellow (H. W.). See Little Library.
Lorimer (George Horace). LETTERS FROM A SELF-MADE MERCHANT TO HIS SON. *Seventeenth Edition. Cr. 8vo.* 3s. 6d.
OLD GORGON GRAHAM. *Second Edition. Cr. 8vo.* 6s.
*Lorimer (Norma).** BY THE WATERS OF EGYPT. With 12 Illustrations in Colour by Benton Fletcher, and other Illustrations. *Demy 8vo.* 16s. net.
Lover (Samuel). See I.P.L.
Lucas (E. V.). THE LIFE OF CHARLES LAMB. With 28 Illustrations. *Fourth and Revised Edition in One Volume. Demy 8vo.* 7s. 6d. net.
A WANDERER IN HOLLAND. With 20 Illustrations in Colour by Herbert Marshall, 34 Illustrations after old Dutch Masters, and a Map. *Ninth Edition. Cr. 8vo.* 6s.
A WANDERER IN LONDON. With 16 Illustrations in Colour by Nelson Dawson, 36 other Illustrations and a Map. *Seventh Edition. Cr. 8vo.* 6s.
A WANDERER IN PARIS. With 16 Illustrations in Colour by Walter Dexter, and 32 from Photographs after Old Masters. *Second Edition. Cr. 8vo.* 6s.
THE OPEN ROAD: a Little Book for Wayfarers. *Fifteenth Edition. Fcap. 8vo.* 5s.; *India Paper,* 7s. 6d.
THE FRIENDLY TOWN: a Little Book for the Urbane. *Fourth Edition. Fcap. 8vo.* 5s.; *India Paper,* 7s. 6d.
FIRESIDE AND SUNSHINE. *Fourth Edition. Fcap. 8vo.* 5s.
CHARACTER AND COMEDY. *Fourth Edition. Fcap. 8vo.* 5s.
THE GENTLEST ART. A Choice of Letters by Entertaining Hands. *Fifth Edition. Fcap. 8vo.* 5s.
A SWAN AND HER FRIENDS. With 24 Illustrations. *Demy 8vo.* 12s. 6d. net.
HER INFINITE VARIETY: A Feminine Portrait Gallery. *Fourth Edition. Fcap. 8vo.* 5s.
LISTENER'S LURE: An Oblique Narration. *Fifth Edition. Fcap. 8vo.* 5s.

General Literature

*GOOD COMPANY: A RALLY OF MEN. *Fcap. 8vo.* 5s.
ONE DAY AND ANOTHER: A VOLUME OF ESSAYS. *Fcap. 8vo.* 5s.
OVER BEMERTON'S: AN EASY-GOING CHRONICLE. *Sixth Edition. Fcap. 8vo.* 5s. net.
   See also Lamb (Charles).
Lucian. See Classical Translations.
Lyde (L. W.), M.A. See Commercial Series.
Lydon (Noel S.). A PRELIMINARY GEOMETRY. With numerous Diagrams. *Cr. 8vo.* 1s.
   See also Junior School Books.
Lyttelton (Hon. Mrs. A.). WOMEN AND THEIR WORK. *Cr. 8vo.* 2s. 6d.
M. (R.). THE THOUGHTS OF LUCIA HALIDAY. With some of her Letters. Edited by R. M. *Fcap. 8vo.* 2s. 6d. net.
Macaulay (Lord). CRITICAL AND HISTORICAL ESSAYS. Edited by F. C. MONTAGUE, M.A. *Three Volumes. Cr. 8vo.* 18s.
M'Allen (J. E. B.), M.A. See Commercial Series.
McCabe (Joseph) (formerly Very Rev. F. ANTONY, O.S.F.). THE DECAY OF THE CHURCH OF ROME. *Demy 8vo.* 7s. 6d. net.
MacCunn (Florence A.). MARY STUART. With 44 Illustrations, including a Frontispiece in Photogravure. *New and Cheaper Edition. Large Cr. 8vo.* 6s.
   See also Leaders of Religion.
McDermott (E. R.). See Books on Business.
McDougall (William), M.A. (Oxon., M.B. (Cantab.). AN INTRODUCTION TO SOCIAL PSYCHOLOGY. *Cr. 8vo.* 5s. net.
M'Dowall (A. S.). See Oxford Biographies.
MacFie (Ronald C.), M.A., M.B. See New Library of Medicine.
Mackay (A. M.), B.A. See Churchman's Library.
Mackenzie (W. Leslie), M.A., M.D., D.P.H., etc. THE HEALTH OF THE SCHOOL CHILD. *Cr. 8vo.* 2s. 6d.
Macklin (Herbert W.), M.A. See Antiquary's Books.
M'Neile (A. H.), B.D. See Westminster Commentaries.
'Mdlle Mori' (Author of). ST. CATHERINE OF SIENA AND HER TIMES. With 28 Illustrations. *Second Edition. Demy 8vo.* 7s. 6d. net.
Maeterlinck (Maurice). THE BLUE BIRD: A FAIRY PLAY IN FIVE ACTS. Translated by ALEXANDER TEIXEIRA DE MATTOS. *Second Edition. Fcap. 8vo. Deckle Edges.* 3s. 6d. net.
Magnus (Laurie), M.A. A PRIMER OF WORDSWORTH. *Cr. 8vo.* 2s. 6d.
Mahaffy (J. P.), Litt.D. A HISTORY OF THE EGYPT OF THE PTOLEMIES. With 79 Illustrations. *Cr. 8vo.* 6s.
Maitland (F. W.), M.A., LL.D. ROMAN CANON LAW IN THE CHURCH OF ENGLAND. *Royal 8vo.* 7s. 6d.
Major (H.), B.A., B.Sc. A HEALTH AND TEMPERANCE READER. *Cr. 8vo.* 1s.
Malden (H. E.), M.A. ENGLISH RECORDS. A Companion to the History of England. *Cr. 8vo.* 3s. 6d.
THE RIGHTS AND DUTIES OF A CITIZEN. *Seventh Edition. Cr. 8vo.* 1s. 6d.
   See also School Histories.
Marchant (E. C.), M.A., Fellow of Peterhouse, Cambridge. A GREEK ANTHOLOGY. *Second Edition. Cr. 8vo.* 3s. 6d.
   See also Cook (A. M.).
Marett (R. R.), M.A., Fellow and Tutor of Exeter College, Oxford. THE THRESHOLD OF RELIGION. *Cr. 8vo.* 3s. 6d net.
Marks (Jeannette), M.A. ENGLISH PASTORAL DRAMA from the Restoration to the date of the publication of the 'Lyrical Ballads' (1660-1798). *Cr. 8vo.* 5s. net.
Marr (J. E.), F.R.S., Fellow of St John's College, Cambridge. THE SCIENTIFIC STUDY OF SCENERY. *Third Edition. Revised. Illustrated. Cr. 8vo.* 6s.
AGRICULTURAL GEOLOGY. Illustrated. *Cr. 8vo.* 6s.
Marriott (Charles). A SPANISH HOLIDAY. With 8 Illustrations by A. M. FOWERAKER, R.B.A., and 22 other Illustrations. *Demy 8vo.* 7s. 6d. net.
Marriott (J. A. R.), M.A. THE LIFE AND TIMES OF LORD FALKLAND. With 23 Illustrations. *Second Edition. Demy 8vo.* 7s. 6d. net.
   See also Six Ages of European History.
Marvell (Andrew). See Little Library.
Masefield (John). SEA LIFE IN NELSON'S TIME. With 16 Illustrations. *Cr. 8vo.* 3s. 6d. net.
ON THE SPANISH MAIN: or, SOME ENGLISH FORAYS IN THE ISTHMUS OF DARIEN. With 22 Illustrations and a Map. *Demy 8vo.* 10s. 6d. net.
A SAILOR'S GARLAND. Selected and Edited by. *Second Ed. Cr. 8vo.* 3s. 6d. net.
AN ENGLISH PROSE MISCELLANY. Selected and Edited by. *Cr. 8vo.* 6s.
Maskell (A.). See Connoisseur's Library.
Mason (A. J.), D.D. See Leaders of Religion.
Masterman (C. F. G.), M.A., M.P. TENNYSON AS A RELIGIOUS TEACHER. *Cr. 8vo.* 6s.
THE CONDITION OF ENGLAND. *Second Edition. Cr. 8vo.* 6s.
Masterman (J. H. B.), M.A. See Six Ages of European History.
Matheson (E. F.). COUNSELS OF LIFE. *Fcap. 8vo.* 2s. 6d. net.
Maude (J. H.), M.A. See Handbooks of English Church History.
May (Phil). THE PHIL MAY ALBUM. *Second Edition. 4to.* 1s. net.
Mayne (Ethel Colburn). ENCHANTERS OF MEN. With 24 Illustrations. *Demy 8vo.* 10s. 6d. net.

MESSRS. METHUEN'S CATALOGUE

Meakin (Annette M. B.), Fellow of the Anthropological Institute. WOMAN IN TRANSITION. *Cr. 8vo.* 6s.
GALICIA: THE SWITZERLAND OF SPAIN. With 105 Illustrations and a Map. *Demy 8vo.* 12s. 6d. *net.*
*Medley (D. J.), M.A., Professor of History in the University of Glasgow. ORIGINAL ILLUSTRATIONS OF ENGLISH CONSTITUTIONAL HISTORY, COMPRISING A SELECTED NUMBER OF THE CHIEF CHARTERS AND STATUTES. *Cr. 8vo.* 7s. 6d. *net.*
Mellows (Emma S.). A SHORT STORY OF ENGLISH LITERATURE. *Cr. 8vo.* 3s. 6d.
Mérimée (P.). See Simplified French Texts.
Methuen (A. M. S.), M.A. THE TRAGEDY OF SOUTH AFRICA. *Cr. 8vo.* 2s. *net.* Also *Cr. 8vo.* 3d. *net.*
ENGLAND'S RUIN: DISCUSSED IN FOURTEEN LETTERS TO A PROTECTIONIST. *Ninth Edition. Cr. 8vo.* 3d. *net.*
Meynell (Everard). COROT AND HIS FRIENDS. With 28 Illustrations. *Demy 8vo* 10s. 6d. *net.*
Miles (Eustace), M.A. LIFE AFTER LIFE: OR, THE THEORY OF REINCARNATION. *Cr. 8vo.* 2s. 6d. *net.*
THE POWER OF CONCENTRATION: How TO ACQUIRE IT. *Third Edition. Cr. 8vo.* 3s. 6d. *net.*
Millais (J. G.). THE LIFE AND LETTERS OF SIR JOHN EVERETT MILLAIS, President of the Royal Academy. With many Illustrations, of which 2 are in Photogravure. *New Edition. Demy 8vo.* 7s. 6d. *net.*
See also Little Galleries.
Millin (G. F.). PICTORIAL GARDENING. With 21 Illustrations. *Crown 8vo.* 3s. 6d. *net.*
Mills (C. T.), M.I.M.E. See Textbooks of Technology.
Milne (J. G.), M.A. A HISTORY OF EGYPT UNDER ROMAN RULE. With 143 Illustrations. *Cr. 8vo.* 6s.
Milton (John). A DAY BOOK OF MILTON. Edited by R. F. TOWNDROW. *Fcap. 8vo.* 2s. 6d. *net.*
See also Little Library and Standard Library.
Minchin (H. C.), M.A. See Peel (R.).
Mitchell (P. Chalmers), M.A. OUTLINES OF BIOLOGY. With 74 Illustrations. *Second Edition. Cr. 8vo.* 6s.
Mitton (G. E.). JANE AUSTEN AND HER TIMES. With 21 Illustrations. *Second and Cheaper Edition. Large Cr. 8vo.* 6s.
Moffat (Mary M.). QUEEN LOUISA OF PRUSSIA. With 20 Illustrations. *Fourth Edition. Crown 8vo.* 6s.
Moll (A.). See Books on Business.
Moir (D. M.). See Little Library.
Molinos (Dr. Michael de). See Library of Devotion.
Money (L. G. Chiozza), M.P. RICHES AND POVERTY. *Eighth Edition. Demy 8vo.* 5s. *net.* Also *Cr. 8vo.* 1s. *net.*
Montagu (Henry), Earl of Manchester. See Library of Devotion.
Montaigne. A DAY BOOK OF. Edited by C. F. POND. *Fcap. 8vo.* 2s. 6d. *net.*
Montgomery (H. B.) THE EMPIRE OF THE EAST. With a Frontispiece in Colour and 18 other Illustrations. *Second Edition. Demy 8vo.* 7s. 6d. *net.*
Montmorency (J. E. G. de), B.A., LL.B. THOMAS À KEMPIS, HIS AGE AND BOOK. With 22 Illustrations. *Second Edition. Demy 8vo.* 7s. 6d. *net.*
Moore (H. E.). BACK TO THE LAND. *Cr. 8vo.* 2s. 6d.
*Moore (T. Sturge). ART AND LIFE. Illustrated *Cr. 8vo.* 5s. *net.*
Moorhouse (E. Hallam). NELSON'S LADY HAMILTON. With 51 Portraits. *Second Edition. Demy 8vo.* 7s. 6d. *net.*
Moran (Clarence G.). See Books on Business.
More (Sir Thomas). See Standard Library.
Morfill (W. R.), Oriel College, Oxford. A HISTORY OF RUSSIA FROM PETER THE GREAT TO ALEXANDER II. With 12 Maps and Plans. *Cr. 8vo.* 3s. 6d.
Morich (R. J.). See School Examination Series.
Morley (Margaret W.), Founded on. THE BEE PEOPLE. With 74 Illustrations. *Sq. Crown 8vo.* 2s. 6d.
LITTLE MITCHELL: THE STORY OF A MOUNTAIN SQUIRREL TOLD BY HIMSELF. With 26 Illustrations. *Sq. Cr. 8vo.* 2s. 6d.
Morris (J.). THE MAKERS OF JAPAN. With 24 Illustrations. *Demy 8vo.* 12s. 6d. *net.*
Morris (Joseph E.). See Little Guides.
Morton (A. Anderson). See Brodrick (M.).
Moule (H. C. G.), D.D., Lord Bishop of Durham. See Leaders of Religion.
Muir (M. M. Pattison), M.A. THE CHEMISTRY OF FIRE. Illustrated. *Cr. 8vo.* 2s. 6d.
Mundella (V. A.), M.A. See Dunn (J. T.).
Munro (R.), M.A., LL.D. See Antiquary's Books.
Musset (Alfred de). See Simplified French Text.
Myers (A. Wallis), THE COMPLETE LAWN TENNIS PLAYER. With 90 Illustrations. *Second Edition. Demy 8vo.* 10s. 6d. *net.*
Naval Officer (A). See I. P. L.
Newman (Ernest). See New Library of Music.
Newman (George), M.D., D.P.H., F.R.S.E. See New Library of Medicine.
Newman (J. H.) and others. See Library of Devotion.
Newsholme (Arthur), M.D., F.R.C.P. See New Library of Medicine.
Nichols (Bowyer). See Little Library.
Nicklin (T.), M.A. EXAMINATION PAPERS IN THUCYDIDES. *Cr. 8vo.* 2s.
Nimrod. See I. P. L.
Norgate (G. Le Grys). THE LIFE OF

GENERAL LITERATURE

SIR WALTER SCOTT. With 53 Illustrations by JENNY WYLIE. *Demy 8vo. 7s. 6d. net.*
Norway (A. H.). NAPLES, PAST AND PRESENT. With 25 Coloured Illustrations by MAURICE GREIFFENHAGEN. *Third Edition. Cr. 8vo. 6s.*
Novalis. THE DISCIPLES AT SAIS AND OTHER FRAGMENTS. Edited by Miss UNA BIRCH. *Fcap. 8vo. 3s. 6d. net.*
Officer (An). See I. P. L.
Oldfield (W. J.), M.A., Prebendary of Lincoln. A PRIMER OF RELIGION. BASED ON THE CATECHISM OF THE CHURCH OF ENGLAND. *Crown 8vo. 2s. 6d.*
Oldham (F. M.), B.A. See Textbooks of Science.
Oliphant (Mrs.). See Leaders of Religion.
Oliver, Thomas, M.D. See New Library of Medicine.
Oman (C. W. C.), M.A., Fellow of All Souls', Oxford. A HISTORY OF THE ART OF WAR IN THE MIDDLE AGES. Illustrated. *Demy 8vo. 10s. 6d. net.*
ENGLAND BEFORE THE CONQUEST. With Maps. *Demy 8vo. 10s. 6d. net.*
Oppé (A. P.). See Classics of Art.
Ottley (R. L.), D.D. See Handbooks of Theology and Leaders of Religion.
Overton (J. H.). See Leaders of Religion.
Owen (Douglas). See Books on Business.
Oxford (M. N.), of Guy's Hospital. A HANDBOOK OF NURSING. *Fifth Edition. Cr. 8vo. 3s. 6d.*
Pakes (W. C. C.). THE SCIENCE OF HYGIENE. Illustrated. *Demy 8vo. 15s.*
Parker (Eric). THE BOOK OF THE ZOO; BY DAY AND NIGHT. With 24 Illustrations from Photographs by HENRY IRVING. *Cr. 8vo. 6s.*
Parker (Gilbert), M.P. A LOVER'S DIARY. *Fcap. 8vo. 5s.*
Parkes (A. K.). SMALL LESSONS ON GREAT TRUTHS. *Fcap. 8vo. 1s. 6d.*
Parkinson (John). PARADISI IN SOLE PARADISUS TERRESTRIS, OR A GARDEN OF ALL SORTS OF PLEASANT FLOWERS. *Folio. £3, 3s. net.*
Parsons (Mrs. C.). GARRICK AND HIS CIRCLE. With 36 Illustrations. *Second Edition. Demy 8vo. 12s. 6d. net.*
THE INCOMPARABLE SIDDONS. With 20 Illustrations. *Demy 8vo. 12s. 6d. net.*
Pascal. See Library of Devotion.
Paston (George). SOCIAL CARICATURE IN THE EIGHTEENTH CENTURY. With 214 Illustrations. *Imperial Quarto. £2, 12s. 6d. net.*
LADY MARY WORTLEY MONTAGU AND HER TIMES. With 24 Illustrations. *Second Edition. Demy 8vo. 15s. net.*
See also Little Books on Art and I.P.L.
Patmore (K. A.). THE COURT OF LOUIS XIII. With 16 Illustrations. *Demy 8vo. 10s. 6d. net.*
Patterson (A. H.). NOTES OF AN EAST COAST NATURALIST. Illustrated in Colour by F. SOUTHGATE, R.B.A. *Second Edition. Cr. 8vo. 6s.*

NATURE IN EASTERN NORFOLK. With 12 Illustrations in Colour by FRANK SOUTHGATE, R.B.A. *Second Edition. Cr. 8vo. 6s.*
WILD LIFE ON A NORFOLK ESTUARY. With 40 Illustrations by the Author, and a Prefatory Note by Her Grace the DUCHESS OF BEDFORD. *Demy 8vo. 10s. 6d. net.*
*MAN AND NATURE ON TIDAL WATERS. With Illustrations by the Author. *Cr. 8vo. 6s.*
Peacock (Netta). See Little Books on Art.
Peake (C. M. A.), F.R.H.S. A CONCISE HANDBOOK OF GARDEN ANNUAL AND BIENNIAL PLANTS. With 24 Illustrations. *Fcap. 8vo. 3s. 6d. net.*
Peel (Robert), and **Minchin (H. C.),** M.A. OXFORD. With 100 Illustrations in Colour. *Cr. 8vo. 6s.*
Peel (Sidney), late Fellow of Trinity College, Oxford, and Secretary to the Royal Commission on the Licensing Laws. PRACTICAL LICENSING REFORM. *Second Edition. Cr. 8vo. 1s. 6d.*
Pentin (Herbert), M.A. See Library of Devotion.
Petrie (W. M. Flinders), D.C.L., LL.D., Professor of Egyptology at University College. A HISTORY OF EGYPT. Fully Illustrated. *In six volumes. Cr. 8vo. 6s. each.*
VOL. I. FROM THE EARLIEST KINGS TO XVIth DYNASTY. *Sixth Edition.*
VOL. II. THE XVIIth AND XVIIIth DYNASTIES. *Fourth Edition.*
VOL. III. XIXth TO XXXth DYNASTIES.
VOL. IV. EGYPT UNDER THE PTOLEMAIC DYNASTY. J. P. MAHAFFY, Litt.D.
VOL. V. EGYPT UNDER ROMAN RULE. J. G. MILNE, M.A.
VOL. VI. EGYPT IN THE MIDDLE AGES. STANLEY LANE-POOLE, M.A.
RELIGION AND CONSCIENCE IN ANCIENT EGYPT. Lectures delivered at University College, London. Illustrated. *Cr. 8vo. 2s. 6d.*
SYRIA AND EGYPT, FROM THE TELL EL AMARNA LETTERS. *Cr. 8vo. 2s. 6d.*
EGYPTIAN TALES. Translated from the Papyri. First Series, IVth to XIIth Dynasty. Edited by W. M. FLINDERS PETRIE. Illustrated by TRISTRAM ELLIS. *Second Edition. Cr. 8vo. 3s. 6d.*
EGYPTIAN TALES. Translated from the Papyri. Second Series. XVIIIth to XIXth Dynasty. Illustrated by TRISTRAM ELLIS. *Crown 8vo. 3s. 6d.*
EGYPTIAN DECORATIVE ART. A Course of Lectures delivered at the Royal Institution. Illustrated. *Cr. 8vo. 3s. 6d.*
Phillips (W. A.). See Oxford Biographies.
Phillpotts (Eden). MY DEVON YEAR. With 38 Illustrations by J. LEY PETHYBRIDGE. *Second and Cheaper Edition. Large Cr. 8vo. 6s.*
UP-ALONG AND DOWN-ALONG. Illustrated by CLAUDE SHEPPERSON. *Cr. 4to. 5s. net.*

A 3

Messrs. Methuen's Catalogue

Phythian (J. Ernest). TREES IN NATURE, MYTH, AND ART. With 24 Illustrations. *Crown 8vo.* 6s.
Plarr (Victor G.). M.A. See School Histories.
Plato. See Standard Library.
Plautus. THE CAPTIVI. Edited, with an Introduction, Textual Notes, and a Commentary, by W. M. LINDSAY, Fellow of Jesus College, Oxford. *Demy 8vo.* 10s. 6d. net.
Plowden-Wardlaw (J. T.), B.A. See School Examination Series.
Podmore (Frank). MODERN SPIRITUALISM. *Two Volumes. Demy 8vo.* 21s. net.
MESMERISM AND CHRISTIAN SCIENCE: A Short History of Mental Healing. *Demy 8vo.* 10s. 6d. net.
Pollard (Alice). See Little Books on Art.
Pollard (Alfred W.). THE SHAKESPEARE'S FOLIOS AND QUARTOS. With numerous Facsimiles. *Folio. One Guinea net.*
Pollard (Eliza F.). See Little Books on Art.
Pollock (David), M.I.N.A. See Books on Business.
Potter (M. C.), M.A., F.L.S. AN ELEMENTARY TEXT-BOOK OF AGRICULTURAL BOTANY. Illustrated. *Third Edition. Cr. 8vo.* 4s. 6d.
Power (J. O'Connor). THE MAKING OF AN ORATOR. *Cr. 8vo.* 6s.
Price (Eleanor C.). A PRINCESS OF THE OLD WORLD. With 21 Illustrations. *Demy 8vo.* 12s. 6d. net.
Price (L. L.), M.A., Fellow of Oriel College, Oxon. A HISTORY OF ENGLISH POLITICAL ECONOMY FROM ADAM SMITH TO ARNOLD TOYNBEE. *Fifth Edition. Cr. 8vo.* 2s. 6d.
Protheroe (Ernest). THE DOMINION OF MAN. GEOGRAPHY IN ITS HUMAN ASPECT. With 32 full-page Illustrations. *Second Edition. Cr. 8vo.* 2s.
Psellus. See Byzantine Texts.
Pullen-Burry (B.). IN A GERMAN COLONY; or, FOUR WEEKS IN NEW BRITAIN. With 8 Illustrations and 2 Maps. *Cr. 8vo.* 5s. net.
Pycraft (W. P.). BIRD LIFE. With 2 Illustrations in Colour by G. E. LODGE, and others from Drawings and Photographs. *Demy 8vo.* 10s. 6d. net.
'Q' (A. T. Quiller Couch). THE GOLDEN POMP. A PROCESSION OF ENGLISH LYRICS FROM SURREY TO SHIRLEY. *Second and Cheaper Edition. Cr. 8vo.* 2s. 6d. net.
G. R. and E. S. MR. WOODHOUSE'S CORRESPONDENCE. *Cr. 8vo.* 6s.
Also published in a Colonial Edition.
Rackham (R. B.), M.A. See Westminster Commentaries.
Ragg (Laura M.). THE WOMEN ARTISTS OF BOLOGNA. With 20 Illustrations. *Demy 8vo.* 7s. 6d. net.
Ragg (Lonsdale). B.D., Oxon. DANTE AND HIS ITALY. With 32 Illustrations. *Demy 8vo.* 12s. 6d. net.
Rahtz (F. J.), M.A., B.Sc. HIGHER ENGLISH. *Fourth Edition. Cr. 8vo.* 3s. 6d.
JUNIOR ENGLISH. *Second Edition. Cr. 8vo.* 1s. 6d.
Randolph (B. W.), D.D. See Library of Devotion.
Rannie (D. W.), M.A. A STUDENT'S HISTORY OF SCOTLAND. *Cr. 8vo.* 3s. 6d.
WORDSWORTH AND HIS CIRCLE. With 20 Illustrations. *Demy 8vo.* 12s. 6d. net.
Rashdall (Hastings), M.A., Fellow and Tutor of New College, Oxford. DOCTRINE AND DEVELOPMENT. *Cr. 8vo.* 6s.
Raven (J. J.), D.D., F.S.A. See Antiquary's Books.
Raven-Hill (L.). See Llewellyn (Owen).
Rawlings (Gertrude Burford). COINS AND HOW TO KNOW THEM. With 206 Illustrations. *Second Edition. Cr. 8vo.* 6s.
Rawstorne (Lawrence, Esq.). See I.P.L.
Raymond (Walter). See School Histories.
Rea (Lilian). THE LIFE AND TIMES OF MARIE MADELEINE COUNTESS OF LA FAYETTE. With 20 Illustrations. *Demy 8vo.* 10s. 6d. net.
Read (C. Stanford), M.B. (Lond.), M.R.C.S., L.R.C.P. FADS AND FEEDING. *Cr. 8vo.* 2s. 6d.
Real Paddy (A). See I.P.L.
Reason (W.), M.A. UNIVERSITY AND SOCIAL SETTLEMENTS. Edited by *Cr. 8vo.* 2s. 6d.
Redpath (H. A.), M.A., D.Litt. See Westminster Commentaries.
Rees (J. D.), C.I.E., M.P. THE REAL INDIA. *Second Edition. Demy 8vo.* 10s. 6d. net.
Reich (Emil), Doctor Juris. WOMAN THROUGH THE AGES. With 36 Illustrations. *Two Volumes. Demy 8vo.* 21s. net.
Reynolds (Sir Joshua). See Little Galleries.
Rhodes (W. E.). See School Histories.
Ricketts (Charles). See Classics of Art.
Richardson (Charles). THE COMPLETE FOXHUNTER. With 46 Illustrations, of which 4 are in Colour. *Second Edition. Demy 8vo.* 12s. 6d. net.
Richmond (Wilfrid), Chaplain of Lincoln's Inn. THE CREED IN THE EPISTLES. *Cr. 8vo.* 2s. 6d. net.
Riebl (W. H.). See Simplified German Texts.
Roberts (M. E.). See Channer (C. C.).
Robertson (A.), D.D., Lord Bishop of Exeter. REGNUM DEI. (The Bampton Lectures of 1901). *A New and Cheaper Edition. Demy 8vo.* 7s. 6d. net.
Robertson (C. Grant). M.A., Fellow of All Souls' College, Oxford. SELECT STATUTES, CASES, AND CONSTITUTIONAL DOCUMENTS, 1660-1832. *Demy 8vo.* 10s. 6d. net.

General Literature 19

Robertson (C. Grant) and Bartholomew (J. G.), F.R.S.E., F.R.G.S. A HISTORICAL AND MODERN ATLAS OF THE BRITISH EMPIRE. *Demy Quarto.* 4s. 6d. net.

Robertson (Sir G. S.), K.C.S.I. CHITRAL: THE STORY OF A MINOR SIEGE. With 8 Illustrations. *Third Edition.* Demy 8vo. 10s. 6d. net.

Robinson (Cecilia). THE MINISTRY OF DEACONESSES. With an Introduction by the late Archbishop of Canterbury. *Cr. 8vo.* 3s. 6d.

Robinson (F. S.). See Connoisseur's Library.

Rochefoucauld (La). See Little Library.

Rodwell (G.), B.A. NEW TESTAMENT GREEK. A Course for Beginners. With a Preface by WALTER LOCK, D.D., Warden of Keble College. *Fcap. 8vo.* 3s. 6d.

Roe (Fred). OLD OAK FURNITURE. With many Illustrations by the Author, including a frontispiece in colour. *Second Edition.* Demy 8vo. 10s. 6d. net.

Rogers (A. G. L.), M.A. See Books on Business.

Roland. See Simplified French Texts.

Romney (George). See Little Galleries.

Roscoe (E. S.). See Little Guides.

Rose (Edward). THE ROSE READER. Illustrated. *Cr. 8vo.* 2s. 6d. *Also in* 4 *Parts. Parts I. and II.* 6d. *each; Part III.* 8d.; *Part IV.* 10d.

Rose (G. H.). See Hey (H.) and Baring-Gould (S).

Rowntree (Joshua). THE IMPERIAL DRUG TRADE. A RE-STATEMENT OF THE OPIUM QUESTION. *Third Edition Revised. Cr. 8vo.* 2s. net.

Royde-Smith (N. G.). THE PILLOW BOOK : A GARNER OF MANY MOODS. Collected by. *Second Edition. Cr. 8vo.* 4s. 6d. net.

POETS OF OUR DAY. Selected, with an Introduction, by. *Fcap. 8vo.* 5s.

Rubie (A. E.), D.D. See Junior School Books.

Rumbold (The Right Hon. Sir Horace). Bart., G. C. B., G. C. M. G. THE AUSTRIAN COURT IN THE NINETEENTH CENTURY. With 16 Illustrations. *Demy 8vo.* 18s. net.

Russell (Archibald G. B.). See Blake (William.)

Russell (W. Clark). THE LIFE OF ADMIRAL LORD COLLINGWOOD. With 12 Illustrations by F. BRANGWYN. *Fourth Edition. Cr. 8vo.* 6s.

Ryley (M. Beresford). QUEENS OF THE RENAISSANCE. With 24 Illustrations. *Demy 8vo.* 10s. 6d. net.

Sainsbury (Harrington), M.D., F.R.C.P. PRINCIPIA THERAPEUTICA. *Demy 8vo.* 7s. 6d. net.
See also New Library of Medicine.

St. Anselm. See Library of Devotion.
St. Augustine. See Library of Devotion.
St. Bernard. See Library of Devotion.

St. Cyres (Viscount) See Oxford Biographies.

St. Francis of Assisi. THE LITTLE FLOWERS OF THE GLORIOUS MESSER, AND OF HIS FRIARS. Done into English, with Notes by WILLIAM HEYWOOD. With 40 Illustrations from Italian Painters. *Demy 8vo.* 5s. net.
See also Library of Devotion and Standard Library.

St. Francis de Sales. See Library of Devotion.

St. James. See Churchman's Bible and Westminster Commentaries.

St. Luke. See Junior School Books.

St. Mark. See Junior School Books and Churchman's Bible.

St. Matthew. See Junior School Books.

St. Paul. SECOND AND THIRD EPISTLES OF PAUL THE APOSTLE TO THE CORINTHIANS. Edited by JAMES HOUGHTON KENNEDY, D.D., Assistant Lecturer in Divinity in the University of Dublin. With Introduction, Dissertations, and Notes by J. SCHMITT. *Cr. 8vo.* 6s. *See also* Churchman's Bible and Westminster Commentaries.

'Saki' (H. Munro). REGINALD. *Second Edition. Fcap. 8vo.* 2s. 6d. net.

Salmon (A. L.). See Little Guides.

Sanders (Lloyd). THE HOLLAND HOUSE CIRCLE. With 24 Illustrations. *Second Edition. Demy 8vo.* 12s. 6d. net.

Sathas (C.). See Byzantine Texts.

Schmitt (John). See Byzantine Texts.

Schofield (A. T.), M.D., Hon. Phys. Freidenham Hospital. See New Library of Medicine.

Scudamore (Cyril). See Little Guides.

Scupoli (Dom. L.). See Library of Devotion.

Ségur (Madame de). See Simplified French Texts.

Sélincourt (E. de.) See Keats (John).

Sélincourt (Hugh de). GREAT RALEGH. With 16 Illustrations. *Demy 8vo.* 10s. 6d. net.

Sells (V. P.), M.A. THE MECHANICS OF DAILY LIFE. Illustrated. *Cr. 8vo.* 2s. 6d.

Selous (Edmund). TOMMY SMITH'S ANIMALS. Illustrated by G. W. ORD. *Eleventh Edition. Fcap. 8vo.* 2s. 6d.
School Edition, 1s. 6d.
TOMMY SMITH'S OTHER ANIMALS. Illustrated by AUGUSTA GUEST. *Fifth Edition. Fcap. 8vo.* 2s. 6d.
School Edition, 1s. 6d.

Senter (George), B.Sc. (Lond.), Ph.D. See Textbooks of Science.

Shakespeare (William).
THE FOUR FOLIOS, 1623; 1632; 1664; 1685. Each £4, 4s. *net*, or a complete set, £12, 12s. *net*.
Folios 2, 3 and 4 are ready.
THE POEMS OF WILLIAM SHAKESPEARE. With an Introduction and Notes

by GEORGE WYNDHAM. *Demy* 8*vo*. *Buckram, gilt top*, 10*s*. 6*d*.
See also Arden Shakespeare, Standard Library and Little Quarto Shakespeare.
Sharp (A.). VICTORIAN POETS. *Cr.* 8*vo*. 2*s*. 6*d*.
Sharp (Cecil). See Baring-Gould (S.).
Sharp (Elizabeth). See Little Books on Art.
Shedlock (J. S.) THE PIANOFORTE SONATA. *Cr.* 8*vo*. 5*s*.
Shelley (Percy B.). See Standard Library.
Sheppard (H. F.), M.A. See Baring-Gould (S.).
Sherwell (Arthur), M.A. LIFE IN WEST LONDON. *Third Edition*. *Cr.* 8*vo*. 2*s*. 6*d*.
Shipley (Mary E.). AN ENGLISH CHURCH HISTORY FOR CHILDREN. With a Preface by the Bishop of Gibraltar. With Maps and Illustrations. *Cr.* 8*vo*. *Each part* 2*s*. 6*d*. *net*.
PART I.—To the Norman Conquest.
PART II.—To the Reformation.
Sichel (Walter). See Oxford Biographies.
Sidgwick (Mrs. Alfred). HOME LIFE IN GERMANY. With 16 Illustrations. *Second Edition*. *Demy* 8*vo*. 10*s*. 6*d*. *net*.
Sime (John). See Little Books on Art.
Simonson (G. A.). FRANCESCO GUARDI. With 41 Plates. *Imperial* 4*to*. £2, 2*s*. *net*.
Sketchley (R. E. D.). See Little Books on Art.
Skipton (H. P. K.). See Little Books on Art.
Sladen (Douglas). SICILY: The New Winter Resort. With over 200 Illustrations. *Second Edition*. *Cr.* 8*vo*. 5*s*. *net*.
Smallwood (M. G.). See Little Books on Art.
Smedley (F. E.). See I.P.L.
Smith (Adam). THE WEALTH OF NATIONS. Edited with an Introduction and numerous Notes by EDWIN CANNAN, M.A. *Two volumes*. *Demy* 8*vo*. 21*s*. *net*.
Smith (H. Bompas), M.A. A NEW JUNIOR ARITHMETIC. *Crown* 8*vo*. Without Answers, 2*s*. With Answers, 2*s*. 6*d*.
Smith (H. Clifford). See Connoisseur's Library.
Smith (Horace and James). See Little Library.
Smith (R. Mudie). THOUGHTS FOR THE DAY. Edited by. *Fcap.* 8*vo*. 3*s*. 6*d*. *net*.
Smith (Nowell C.). See Wordsworth (W).
Smith (John Thomas). A BOOK FOR A RAINY DAY: Or, Recollections of the Events of the Years 1766-1833. Edited by WILFRED WHITTEN. Illustrated. *Wide Demy* 8*vo*. 12*s*. 6*d*. *net*.
Snell (F. J.). A BOOK OF EXMOOR. Illustrated. *Cr.* 8*vo*. 6*s*.
Snowden (C. E.). A HANDY DIGEST OF BRITISH HISTORY. *Demy* 8*vo*. 4*s*. 6*d*.
Sophocles. See Classical Translations.
Sornet (L. A.), and Acatos (M. J.) See Junior School Books.

Southey (R.). ENGLISH SEAMEN Edited by DAVID HANNAY.
Vol. I. (Howard, Clifford, Hawkins, Drake, Cavendish). *Second Edition*. *Cr.* 8*vo*. 6*s*.
Vol. II. (Richard Hawkins, Grenville, Essex, and Raleigh). *Cr.* 8*vo*. 6*s*.
See also Standard Library.
Souvestre (E.). See Simplified French Texts.
Spence (C. H.), M.A. See School Examination Series.
Spicer (A. Dykes), M.A. THE PAPER TRADE. A Descriptive and Historical Survey. With Diagrams and Plans. *Demy* 8*vo*. 12*s*. 6*d*. *net*.
Spooner (W. A.), M.A. See Leaders of Religion.
Spragge (W. Horton), M.A. See Junior School Books.
Staley (Edgcumbe). THE GUILDS OF FLORENCE. Illustrated. *Second Edition*. *Royal* 8*vo*. 16*s*. *net*.
Stanbridge (J. W.), B.D. See Library of Devotion.
'Stancliffe.' GOLF DO'S AND DONT'S. *Second Edition*. *Fcap.* 8*vo*. 1*s*.
Stead (D. W.). See Gallaher (D.).
Stedman (A. M. M.), M.A.
INITIA LATINA: Easy Lessons on Elementary Accidence. *Eleventh Edition*. *Fcap.* 8*vo*. 1*s*.
FIRST LATIN LESSONS. *Eleventh Edition*. *Cr.* 8*vo*. 2*s*.
FIRST LATIN READER. With Notes adapted to the Shorter Latin Primer and Vocabulary. *Seventh Edition*. 18*mo*. 1*s*. 6*d*.
EASY SELECTIONS FROM CÆSAR. The Helvetian War. *Fourth Edition*. 18*mo*. 1*s*.
EASY SELECTIONS FROM LIVY. The Kings of Rome. *Second Edition*. 18*mo*. 1*s*. 6*d*.
EASY LATIN PASSAGES FOR UNSEEN TRANSLATION. *Twelfth Ed*. *Fcap.* 8*vo*. 1*s*. 6*d*.
EXEMPLA LATINA. First Exercises in Latin Accidence. With Vocabulary. *Fourth Edition*. *Cr.* 8*vo*. 1*s*.
EASY LATIN EXERCISES ON THE SYNTAX OF THE SHORTER AND REVISED LATIN PRIMER. With Vocabulary. *Twelfth Edition*. *Cr.* 8*vo*. 1*s*. 6*d*. KEY, 3*s*. *net*.
THE LATIN COMPOUND SENTENCE: Rules and Exercises. *Second Edition*. *Cr.* 8*vo*. 1*s*. 6*d*. With Vocabulary. 2*s*.
NOTANDA QUAEDAM: Miscellaneous Latin Exercises on Common Rules and Idioms. *Fifth Edition*. *Fcap.* 8*vo*. 1*s*. 6*d*. With Vocabulary. 2*s*. KEY, 2*s*. *net*.
LATIN VOCABULARIES FOR REPETITION: Arranged according to Subjects. *Sixteenth Edition*. *Fcap.* 8*vo*. 1*s*. 6*d*.
A VOCABULARY OF LATIN IDIOMS. 18*mo*. *Fourth Edition*. 1*s*.

General Literature

STEPS TO GREEK. *Fourth Edition.* 18mo. 1s.

A SHORTER GREEK PRIMER. *Third Edition. Cr. 8vo.* 1s. 6d.

EASY GREEK PASSAGES FOR UNSEEN TRANSLATION. *Fourth Edition, revised. Fcap. 8vo.* 1s. 6d.

GREEK VOCABULARIES FOR REPETITION. Arranged according to Subjects. *Fourth Edition. Fcap. 8vo.* 1s 6d.

GREEK TESTAMENT SELECTIONS. For the use of Schools. With Introduction, Notes, and Vocabulary. *Fourth Edition. Fcap. 8vo.* 2s. 6d.

STEPS TO FRENCH. *Ninth Edition.* 18mo. 8d.

FIRST FRENCH LESSONS. *Ninth Edition. Cr. 8vo.* 1s.

EASY FRENCH PASSAGES FOR UNSEEN TRANSLATION. *Sixth Edition. Fcap. 8vo.* 1s. 6d.

EASY FRENCH EXERCISES ON ELEMENTARY SYNTAX. With Vocabulary. *Fourth Edition. Cr. 8vo.* 2s. 6d. KEY. 3s. *net.*

FRENCH VOCABULARIES FOR REPETITION: Arranged according to Subjects. *Fourteenth Edition. Fcap. 8vo.* 1s.

See also School Examination Series.

Steel (R. Elliott), M.A., F.C.S. THE WORLD OF SCIENCE. With 147 Illustrations. *Second Edition. Cr. 8vo.* 2s. 6d.

See also School Examination Series.

Stephenson (C.), of the Technical College, Bradford, and **Suddards (F.)** of the Yorkshire College, Leeds. A TEXTBOOK DEALING WITH ORNAMENTAL DESIGN FOR WOVEN FABRICS. With 66 full-page Plates and numerous Diagrams in the Text. *Third Edition. Demy 8vo.* 7s. 6d.

Sterne (Laurence). See Little Library.

Steuart (Katherine). BY ALLAN WATER. *Second Edition. Cr. 8vo.* 6s.

RICHARD KENNOWAY AND HIS FRIENDS. A Sequel to 'By Allan Water.' *Demy 8vo.* 7s. 6d. *net.*

Stevenson (R. L.) THE LETTERS OF ROBERT LOUIS STEVENSON TO HIS FAMILY AND FRIENDS. Selected and Edited by SIDNEY COLVIN. *Eighth Edition.* 2 vols. *Cr. 8vo.* 12s.

VAILIMA LETTERS. With an Etched Portrait by WILLIAM STRANG. *Seventh Edition. Cr. 8vo. Buckram.* 6s.

THE LIFE OF R. L. STEVENSON See Balfour (G.).

Stevenson (M. I.). FROM SARANAC TO THE MARQUESAS. Being Letters written by Mrs. M. I. STEVENSON during 1887-88. *Cr. 8vo.* 6s. *net.*

LETTERS FROM SAMOA, 1891-95. Edited and arranged by M. C. BALFOUR. With many Illustrations. *Second Edition Cr. 8vo.* 6s. *net.*

Stoddart (Anna M.). See Oxford Biographies.

Stokes (F. G.), B.A. HOURS WITH RABELAIS. From the translation of SIR T. URQUHART and P. A. MOTTEUX. With a Portrait in Photogravure. *Cr. 8vo.* 3s. 6d. *net.*

Stone (S. J.). POEMS AND HYMNS. With a Memoir by F. G. ELLERTON, M.A. With Portrait. *Cr. 8vo.* 6s.

Storr (Vernon F.), M.A., Canon of Winchester. DEVELOPMENT AND DIVINE PURPOSE *Cr. 8vo.* 5s. *net.*

Story (Alfred T.). AMERICAN SHRINES IN ENGLAND. With 4 Illustrations in Colour, and 19 other Illustrations. *Crown 8vo.* 6s.

See also Little Guides.

Straker (F.). See Books on Business.

Streane (A. W.), D.D. See Churchman's Bible.

Streatfeild (R. A.). MODERN MUSIC AND MUSICIANS. With 24 Illustrations. *Second Ed. Demy 8vo.* 7s. 6d. *net.*

See also New Library of Music.

Stroud (Henry), D.Sc., M.A. ELEMENTARY PRACTICAL PHYSICS. With 115 Diagrams. *Second Edit., revised. Cr. 8vo.* 4s. 6d.

Sturch (F.), Staff Instructor to the Surrey County Council. MANUAL TRAINING DRAWING (WOODWORK). With Solutions to Examination Questions, Orthographic, Isometric and Oblique Projection. With 50 Plates and 140 Figures. *Foolscap.* 5s. *net.*

Suddards (F.). See Stephenson (C.).

Surtees (R. S.). See I.P.L.

Sutherland (William). OLD AGE PENSIONS IN THEORY AND PRACTICE, WITH SOME FOREIGN EXAMPLES. *Cr. 8vo.* 3s. 6d. *net.*

*****Swanton (E. W.)**, Member of the British Mycological Society. FUNGI AND HOW TO KNOW THEM. With 16 Coloured Plates by M. K. SPITTAL, and 32 Black and White Plates. *Cr. 8vo.* 5s. *net.*

Symes (J. E.), M.A. THE FRENCH REVOLUTION. *Second Edition. Cr. 8vo.* 2s. 6d.

Sympson (E. Mansel), M.A., M.D. See Ancient Cities.

Tabor (Margaret E.). THE SAINTS IN ART. With 20 Illustrations. *Fcap. 8vo.* 3s. 6d. *net.*

Tacitus. AGRICOLA. Edited by R. F. DAVIS, M.A. *Cr. 8vo.* 2s.

GERMANIA. By the same Editor. *Cr. 8vo.* 2s.

See also Classical Translations.

Tallack (W.). HOWARD LETTERS AND MEMORIES. *Demy 8vo.* 10s. 6d. *net.*

Tatham (Frederick). See Blake (William).

Tauler (J.). See Library of Devotion.

Taylor (A. E.). THE ELEMENTS OF METAPHYSICS. *Second Edition. Demy 8vo.* 10s. 6d. *net.*

Taylor (F. G.), M.A. See Commercial Series.

Taylor (I. A.). See Oxford Biographies.

MESSRS. METHUEN'S CATALOGUE

Taylor (John W.). THE COMING OF THE SAINTS. With 26 Illustrations. *Demy 8vo. 7s. 6d. net.*
Taylor (T. M.), M.A., Fellow of Gonville and Caius College, Cambridge. A CONSTITUTIONAL AND POLITICAL HISTORY OF ROME. To the Reign of Domitian. *Cr. 8vo. 7s. 6d.*
Teasdale-Buckell (G. T.). THE COMPLETE SHOT. With 53 Illustrations. *Third Edition. Demy 8vo. 12s. 6d. net.*
Tennyson (Alfred, Lord). EARLY POEMS. Edited, with Notes and an Introduction, by J. CHURTON COLLINS, M.A. *Cr. 8vo. 6s.*
IN MEMORIAM, MAUD, AND THE PRINCESS. Edited by J. CHURTON COLLINS, M.A. *Cr. 8vo. 6s.*
See also Little Library.
Terry (C. S.). See Oxford Biographies.
Terry (F. J.), B.A. ELEMENTARY LATIN. *Cr. 8vo. 2s.*
TEACHER'S HANDBOOK TO ELEMENTARY LATIN. Containing the necessary supplementary matter to Pupil's edition. *Cr. 8vo. 3s. 6d. net.*
Thackeray (W. M.). See Little Library.
Theobald (F. V.), M.A. INSECT LIFE. Illustrated. *Second Edition Revised. Cr. 8vo. 2s. 6d.*
Thibaudeau (A. C.). BONAPARTE AND THE CONSULATE. Translated and Edited by G. K. FORTESQUE, LL.D. With 12 Illustrations. *Demy 8vo. 10s. 6d. net.*
Thompson (A. H.). See Little Guides.
Thompson (Francis). SELECTED POEMS OF FRANCIS THOMPSON. With a Biographical Note by WILFRID MEYNELL. With a Portrait in Photogravure. *Second Edition. Fcap. 8vo. 5s. net.*
Thompson (A. P.). See Textbooks of Technology.
*****Thomson (J. M.),** Fellow and Dean of Divinity of Magdalen College, Oxford. JESUS ACCORDING TO ST. MARK. *Cr. 8vo. 5s.*
Tileston (Mary W.). DAILY STRENGTH FOR DAILY NEEDS. *Sixteenth Edition. Medium 16mo. 2s. 6d. net.* Also an edition in superior binding, 6s.
Tompkins (H. W.), F.R.H.S. See Little Books on Art and Little Guides.
Toynbee (Paget), M.A., D.Litt. IN THE FOOTPRINTS OF DANTE. A Treasury of Verse and Prose from the works of Dante. *Small Cr. 8vo. 4s. 6d. net.*
DANTE IN ENGLISH LITERATURE: FROM CHAUCER TO CARY. Two vols. *Demy 8vo. 21s. net.*
See also Oxford Biographies and Dante.
Tozer (Basil). THE HORSE IN HISTORY. With 25 Illustrations. *Cr. 8vo. 6s.*
Tremayne (Eleanor E.). See Romantic History.
Trench (Herbert). DEIRDRE WEDDED, AND OTHER POEMS. *Second and Revised Edition. Large Post 8vo. 6s.*

NEW POEMS. *Second Edition. Large Post 8vo. 6s.*
APOLLO AND THE SEAMAN. *Large Post 8vo. Paper, 1s. 6d. net; cloth, 2s 6d. net.*
Trevelyan (G. M.), Fellow of Trinity College, Cambridge. ENGLAND UNDER THE STUARTS. With Maps and Plans. *Third Edition. Demy 8vo. 10s. 6d. net.*
ENGLISH LIFE THREE HUNDRED YEARS AGO: Being the first two chapters of *England under the Stuarts.* Edited by J. TURRAL, B.A. *Cr. 8vo. 1s.*
Triggs (Inigo H.), A.R.I.B.A. TOWN PLANNING: PAST, PRESEMT, AND POSSIBLE. With 173 Illustrations. *Wide Royal 8vo. 15s. net.*
Troutbeck (G. E.). See Little Guides.
Tyler (E. A.), B.A., F.C.S. See Junior School Books.
Tyrrell-Gill (Frances). See Little Books on Art.
Unwin (George). See Antiquary's Books.
Vardon (Harry). THE COMPLETE GOLFER. With 63 Illustrations. *Tenth Edition. Demy 8vo. 10s. 6d. net.*
Vaughan (Henry). See Little Library.
Vaughan (Herbert M.), B.A. (Oxon.). THE LAST OF THE ROYAL STUARTS, HENRY STUART, CARDINAL, DUKE OF YORK. With 20 Illustrations. *Second Edition. Demy 8vo. 10s. 6d. net.*
THE MEDICI POPES (LEO X. AND CLEMENT VII. With 20 Illustrations. *Demy 8vo. 15s. net.*
THE NAPLES RIVIERA. With 25 Illustrations in Colour by MAURICE GREIFFENHAGEN. *Second Edition. Cr. 8vo. 6s.*
Vernon (Hon. W. Warren), M.A. READINGS ON THE INFERNO OF DANTE. With an Introduction by the Rev. Dr. MOORE. *In Two Volumes. Second Edition. Cr. 8vo. 15s. net.*
READINGS ON THE PURGATORIO OF DANTE. With an Introduction by the late DEAN CHURCH. *In Two Volumes. Third Edition. Cr. 8vo. 15s. net.*
READINGS ON THE PARADISO OF DANTE. With an Introduction by the BISHOP OF RIPON. *In Two Volumes. Second Edition. Cr. 8vo. 15s. net.*
Vincent (J. E.). THROUGH EAST ANGLIA IN A MOTOR CAR. With 16 Illustrations in Colour by FRANK SOUTHGATE, R.B.A., and a Map. *Cr. 8vo. 6s.*
Voegelin (A.), M.A. See Junior Examination Series.
Waddell (Col. L. A.), LL.D., C.B. LHASA AND ITS MYSTERIES. With a Record of the Expedition of 1903-1904. With 155 Illustrations and Maps. *Third and Cheaper Edition. Medium 8vo. 7s. 6d. net.*
Wade (G. W.), D.D. OLD TESTAMENT HISTORY. With Maps. *Sixth Edition. Cr. 8vo. 6s.*
Wade (G. W.), D.D., and **Wade (J. H.),** M.A. See Little Guides.
Wagner (Richard). RICHARD WAG-

General Literature 23

NER'S MUSIC DRAMAS: Interpretations, embodying Wagner's own explanations. By ALICE LEIGHTON CLEATHER and BASIL CRUMP. *In Three Volumes. Fcap 8vo.* 2s. 6d. each.
VOL. I.—THE RING OF THE NIBELUNG. *Third Edition.*
VOL. II.—PARSIFAL, LOHENGRIN, and THE HOLY GRAIL.
VOL. III.—TRISTAN AND ISOLDE.

Waineman (Paul). A SUMMER TOUR IN FINLAND. With 16 Illustrations in Colour by ALEXANDER FEDERLEY, 16 other Illustrations and a Map. *Demy 8vo.* 10s. 6d. net.

Walkley (A. B.). DRAMA AND LIFE. *Cr. 8vo.* 6s.

Wall (J. C.). See Antiquary's Books.

Wallace-Hadrill (F.), Second Master at Herne Bay College. REVISION NOTES ON ENGLISH HISTORY. *Cr. 8vo.* 1s.

Walters (H. B.). See Little Books on Art and Classics of Art.

Walton (F. W.), M.A. See School Histories.

Walton (Izaak) and **Cotton (Charles).** See I.P.L. and Little Library.

Waterhouse (Elizabeth). WITH THE SIMPLE-HEARTED: Little Homilies to Women in Country Places. *Second Edition. Small Pott 8vo.* 2s. net.
COMPANIONS OF THE WAY. Being Selections for Morning and Evening Reading. Chosen and arranged by ELIZABETH WATERHOUSE. *Large Cr. 8vo.* 5s. net.
THOUGHTS OF A TERTIARY. *Small Pott 8vo.* 1s. net.
See also Little Library.

Watt (Francis). See Henderson (T. F.).

Weatherhead (T. C.), M.A. EXAMINATION PAPERS IN HORACE. *Cr. 8vo.* 2s.
See also Junior Examination Series.

*****Webb (George W.),** B.A. A SYSTEMATIC GEOGRAPHY OF THE BRITISH ISLES. With Maps and Diagrams. *Cr. 8vo.* 1s.

Webber (F. C.). See Textbooks of Technology.

*****Weigall (Arthur E. P.).** A GUIDE TO THE ANTIQUITIES OF UPPER EGYPT: From Abydos to the Sudan Frontier. With 67 Maps, and Plans. *Cr. 8vo.* 7s. 6d. net.

Weir (Archibald), M.A. AN INTRODUCTION TO THE HISTORY OF MODERN EUROPE. *Cr. 8vo.* 6s.

Welch (Catharine). THE LITTLE DAUPHIN. With 16 Illustrations. *Cr. 8vo.* 6s.

Wells (Sidney H.) See Textbooks of Science.

Wells (J.), M.A., Fellow and Tutor of Wadham College. OXFORD AND OXFORD LIFE. *Third Edition. Cr. 8vo.* 3s. 6d.
A SHORT HISTORY OF ROME. *Ninth Edition.* With 3 Maps. *Cr. 8vo.* 3s. 6d.
See also Little Guides.

Wesley (John). See Library of Devotion.

Westell (W. Percival). THE YOUNG NATURALIST. With 8 Coloured Plates by C. F. NEWALL, and many other Illustrations. *Cr. 8vo.* 6s.

Westell (W. Percival), F.L.S., M.B.O.U., and **Cooper (C. S.),** F.R.H.S. THE YOUNG BOTANIST. With 8 Coloured and 63 Black and White Plates drawn from Nature, by C. F. NEWALL. *Cr. 8vo.* 3s. 6d. net.

Whibley (C.). See Henley (W. E.).

Whibley (L.), M.A., Fellow of Pembroke College, Cambridge. GREEK OLIGARCHIES: THEIR ORGANISATION AND CHARACTER. *Cr. 8vo.* 6s.

White (Eustace E.). THE COMPLETE HOCKEY PLAYER. With 32 Illustrations. *Second Edition. Demy 8vo.* 5s. net.

White (George F.), Lieut.-Col. A CENTURY OF SPAIN AND PORTUGAL. *Demy 8vo.* 12s. 6d. net.

White (Gilbert). See Standard Library.

Whitfield (E. E.), M.A. See Commercial Series.

Whitehead (A. W.). GASPARD DE COLIGNY, ADMIRAL OF FRANCE. With 26 Illustrations and 10 Maps and Plans. *Demy 8vo.* 12s. 6d. net.

Whiteley (R. Lloyd), F.I.C., Principal of the Municipal Science School, West Bromwich. AN ELEMENTARY TEXT-BOOK OF INORGANIC CHEMISTRY. *Cr. 8vo.* 2s. 6d.

Whitley (Miss). See Dilke (Lady).

Whitling (Miss L.), late Staff Teacher of the National Training School of Cookery. THE COMPLETE COOK. With 42 Illustrations. *Demy 8vo.* 7s. 6d. net.

Whitten (W.). See Smith (John Thomas).

Whyte (A. G.), B.Sc. See Books on Business.

Wilberforce (Wilfrid). See Little Books on Art.

Wilde (Oscar). DE PROFUNDIS. *Twelfth Edition. Cr. 8vo.* 5s. net.
THE WORKS OF OSCAR WILDE. *In 12 Volumes. Fcap. 8vo.* 5s. net each volume.
I. THE DUCHESS OF PADUA. II. LADY WINDERMERE'S FAN. III. A WOMAN OF NO IMPORTANCE. IV. THE IMPORTANCE OF BEING EARNEST. V. AN IDEAL HUSBAND. VI. DE PROFUNDIS and PRISON LETTERS. VII. INTENTIONS. VIII. ESSAYS. IX. A HOUSE OF POMEGRANATES. X. LORD ARTHUR SAVILE'S CRIME and the PORTRAIT OF MR. W. H. XI. POEMS. XII. SALOMÉ, A FLORENTINE TRAGEDY, and LA SAINTE COURTISANE

Wilkins (W. H.), B.A. THE ALIEN INVASION. *Cr. 8vo.* 2s. 6d.

Williams (H. Noel). THE WOMEN BONAPARTES. The Mother and three Sisters of Napoleon. With 36 Illustrations. *In Two Volumes Demy 8vo.* 24s net.
A ROSE OF SAVOY: MARIE ADELÉIDE OF SAVOY, DUCHESSE DE BOURGOGNE, MOTHER OF LOUIS XV. With a Frontispiece in Photogtavure and 16 other Illustrations. *Demy 8vo.* 15s. net.

Williams (A.). PETROL PETER: or Pretty Stories and Funny Pictures. Illustrated in Colour by A. W. MILLS. *Demy 4to. 3s. 6d. net.*

Williamson (M. G.), M.A. See Ancient Cities.

Williamson (W.), B.A. See Junior Examination Series, Junior School Books, and Beginner's Books.

Wilmot-Buxton (E. M.), F. R. Hist. S. MAKERS OF EUROPE. Outlines of European History for the Middle Forms of Schools. With 12 Maps. *Tenth Edition. Cr. 8vo. 3s. 6d.*

THE ANCIENT WORLD. With Maps and Illustrations. *Cr. 8vo. 3s. 6d.*

A BOOK OF NOBLE WOMEN. With 16 Illustrations. *Cr. 8vo. 3s. 6d.*

A HISTORY OF GREAT BRITAIN: FROM THE COMING OF THE ANGLES TO THE YEAR 1870. With 20 Maps. *Cr. 8vo. 3s. 6d.* See also Beginner's Books and New Historical Series.

Wilson (Bishop.). See Library of Devotion.

Wilson (A. J.). See Books on Business.

Wilson (H. A.). See Books on Business.

Wilton (Richard), M.A. LYRA PASTORALIS: Songs of Nature, Church, and Home. *Pott 8vo. 2s. 6d.*

Winbolt (S. E.), M.A. EXERCISES IN LATIN ACCIDENCE. *Cr. 8vo. 1s. 6d.*

LATIN HEXAMETER VERSE: An Aid to Composition. *Cr. 8vo. 3s. 6d.* KEY, *5s. net.*

Windle (B. C. A.), D.Sc., F.R.S., F.S.A. See Antiquary's Books, Little Guides, Ancient Cities, and School Histories.

Wood (Sir Evelyn), F. M., V.C., G.C.B., G.C.M.G. FROM MIDSHIPMAN TO FIELD-MARSHAL. With Illustrations, and 29 Maps. *Fifth and Cheaper Edition. Demy 8vo. 7s. 6d. net.*

THE REVOLT IN HINDUSTAN. 1857-59. With 8 Illustrations and 5 Maps. *Second Edition. Cr. 8vo. 6s.*

Wood (J. A. E.). See Textbooks of Technology.

Wood (J. Hickory). DAN LENO. Illustrated. *Third Edition. Cr. 8vo. 6s.*

Wood (W. Birkbeck), M.A., late Scholar of Worcester College, Oxford, and **Edmonds (Major J. E.),** R.E., D.A.Q.-M.G. A HISTORY OF THE CIVIL WAR IN THE UNITED STATES. With an Introduction by H. SPENSER WILKINSON. With 24 Maps and Plans. *Second Edition. Demy 8vo. 12s. 6d. net.*

Wordsworth (Christopher), M.A. See Antiquary's Books.

Wordsworth (W.). THE POEMS OF. With an Introduction and Notes by NOWELL C. SMITH, late Fellow of New College, Oxford. *In Three Volumes. Demy 8vo. 15s. net.*

POEMS BY WILLIAM WORDSWORTH. Selected with an Introduction by STOPFORD A. BROOKE. With 40 Illustrations by E. H. NEW, including a Frontispiece in Photogravure. *Cr. 8vo. 7s. 6d. net.*
See also Little Library.

Wordsworth (W.) and Coleridge (S. T.). See Little Library.

Wright (Arthur), D.D., Fellow of Queen's College, Cambridge. See Churchman's Library.

Wright (C. Gordon). See Dante.

Wright (J. C.). TO-DAY. Thoughts on Life for every day. *Demy 16mo. 1s. 6d. net.*

Wright (Sophie). GERMAN VOCABULARIES FOR REPETITION. *Fcap. 8vo. 1s. 6d.*

Wyatt (Kate M.). See Gloag (M. R.).

Wylde (A. B.). MODERN ABYSSINIA. With a Map and a Portrait. *Demy 8vo. 15s. net.*

Wyllie (M. A.). NORWAY AND ITS FJORDS. With 16 Illustrations, in Colour by W. L. WYLLIE, R.A., and 17 other Illustrations. *Crown 8vo. 6s.*

Wyndham (George). See Shakespeare (William).

Yeats (W. B.). A BOOK OF IRISH VERSE. *Revised and Enlarged Edition. Cr. 8vo. 3s. 6d.*

Young (Filson). THE COMPLETE MOTORIST. With 138 Illustrations. *New Edition (Seventh), with many additions. Demy 8vo. 12s. 6d. net.*

THE JOY OF THE ROAD: An Appreciation of the Motor Car. With a Frontispiece in Photogravure. *Small Demy 8vo. 5s. net.*

Zachariah of Mitylene. See Byzantine Texts.

Zimmern (Antonia). WHAT DO WE KNOW CONCERNING ELECTRICITY? *Fcap. 8vo. 1s. 6d. net.*

Ancient Cities
General Editor, B. C. A. WINDLE, D.Sc., F.R.S.

Cr. 8vo. 4s. 6d. net.

BRISTOL. By Alfred Harvey, M.B. Illustrated by E. H. New.
CANTERBURY. By J. C. Cox, LL.D., F.S.A. Illustrated by B. C. Boulter.
CHESTER. By B. C. A. Windle, D.Sc. F.R.S. Illustrated by E. H. New.
DUBLIN. By S. A. O. Fitzpatrick. Illustrated by W. C. Green.

EDINBURGH. By M. G. Williamson, M.A. Illustrated by Herbert Railton.
LINCOLN. By E. Mansel Sympson, M.A., M.D. Illustrated by E. H. New.
SHREWSBURY. By T. Auden, M.A., F.S.A. Illustrated by Katharine M. Roberts.
WELLS and GLASTONBURY. By T. S. Holmes. Illustrated by E. H. New.

The Antiquary's Books

General Editor, J. CHARLES COX, LL.D., F.S.A

Demy 8vo.   7s. 6d. net.

ARCHÆOLOGY AND FALSE ANTIQUITIES. By R. Munro, LL.D. With 81 Illustrations.

BELLS OF ENGLAND, THE. By Canon J. J. Raven, D.D., F.S.A. With 60 Illustrations. *Second Edition.*

BRASSES OF ENGLAND, THE. By Herbert W. Macklin, M.A. With 85 Illustrations. *Second Edition.*

CELTIC ART IN PAGAN AND CHRISTIAN TIMES. By J. Romilly Allen, F.S.A. With 44 Plates and numerous Illustrations.

DOMESDAY INQUEST, THE. By Adolphus Ballard, B.A., LL.B. With 27 Illustrations.

ENGLISH CHURCH FURNITURE. By J. C. Cox, LL.D., F.S.A., and A. Harvey, M.B. With 121 Illustrations. *Second Edition.*

ENGLISH COSTUME. From Prehistoric Times to the End of the Eighteenth Century. By George Clinch, F.G.S. With 131 Illustrations.

ENGLISH MONASTIC LIFE. By the Right Rev. Abbot Gasquet, O.S.B. With 30 Illustrations, Maps and Plans. *Third Edition.*

ENGLISH SEALS. By J. Harvey Bloom. With 93 Illustrations.

FOLK-LORE AS AN HISTORICAL SCIENCE. By G. L. Gomme. With 28 Illustrations.

GILDS AND COMPANIES OF LONDON, THE. By George Unwin. With 37 Illustrations.

MANOR AND MANORIAL RECORDS, THE. By Nathaniel J. Hone. With 54 Illustrations.

MEDIÆVAL HOSPITALS OF ENGLAND, THE. By Rotha Mary Clay. With many Illustrations.

OLD SERVICE BOOKS OF THE ENGLISH CHURCH. By Christopher Wordsworth, M.A., and Henry Littlehales. With 38 Coloured and other Illustrations.

PARISH LIFE IN MEDIÆVAL ENGLAND. By the Right Rev. Abbott Gasquet, O.S.B. With 39 Illustrations. *Second Edition.*

REMAINS OF THE PREHISTORIC AGE IN ENGLAND. By B. C. A. Windle, D.Sc., F.R.S. With 94 Illustrations. *Second Edition.*

ROYAL FORESTS OF ENGLAND, THE. By J. C. Cox, LL.D., F.S.A. With 25 Plates and 23 other Illustrations.

SHRINES OF BRITISH SAINTS. By J. C. Wall. With 28 Plates and 50 other Illustrations.

The Arden Shakespeare

Demy 8vo.   2s. 6d. net each volume.

An edition of Shakespeare in single Plays. Edited with a full Introduction, Textual Notes, and a Commentary at the foot of the page.

ALL'S WELL THAT ENDS WELL. Edited by W. O. Brigstocke.

ANTONY AND CLEOPATRA. Edited by R. H. Case.

CYMBELINE. Edited by E. Dowden.

COMEDY OF ERRORS, THE. Edited by Henry Cuningham.

HAMLET. Edited by E. Dowden. *Second Edition.*

JULIUS CAESAR. Edited by M. Macmillan.

KING HENRY V. Edited by H. A. Evans.

KING HENRY VI. PT. I. Edited by H. C. Hart.

KING HENRY VI. PT. II. Edited by H. C. Hart and C. K. Pooler.

KING LEAR. Edited by W. J. Craig.

KING RICHARD III. Edited by A. H. Thompson.

LIFE AND DEATH OF KING JOHN, THE. Edited by Ivor B. John.

LOVE'S LABOUR'S LOST. Edited by H. C. Hart.

*MACBETH. Edited by H. Cuningham.

MEASURE FOR MEASURE. Edited by H. C. Hart.

MERCHANT OF VENICE, THE. Edited by C. K. Pooler.

MERRY WIVES OF WINDSOR, THE. Edited by H. C. Hart.

A MIDSUMMER NIGHT'S DREAM. Edited by H. Cuningham.

OTHELLO. Edited by H. C. Hart.

PERICLES. Edited by K. Deighton.

ROMEO AND JULIET. Edited by Edward Dowden.

TAMING OF THE SHREW, THE. Edited by R. Warwick Bond.

TEMPEST, THE. Edited by M. Luce.

TIMON OF ATHENS. Edited by K. Deighton.

TITUS ANDRONICUS. Edited by H. B. Baildon.

TROILUS AND CRESSIDA. Edited by K. Deighton.

TWO GENTLEMEN OF VERONA, THE. Edited by R. W. Bond.

TWELFTH NIGHT. Edited by M. Luce.

The Beginner's Books

Edited by W. WILLIAMSON, B.A.

EASY DICTATION AND SPELLING. By W. Williamson, B.A. *Seventh Ed. Fcap. 8vo.* 1s.

EASY EXERCISES IN ARITHMETIC. Arranged by W. S. Beard. *Third Edition. Fcap. 8vo.* Without Answers, 1s. With Answers. 1s. 3d.

EASY FRENCH RHYMES. By Henri Blouet. *Second Edition.* Illustrated. *Fcap. 8vo.* 1s.

AN EASY POETRY BOOK. Selected and arranged by W. Williamson, B.A. *Second Edition. Cr. 8vo.* 1s.

EASY STORIES FROM ENGLISH HISTORY. By E. M. Wilmot-Buxton, F.R.Hist.S. *Fifth Edition. Cr. 8vo.* 1s.

A FIRST HISTORY OF GREECE. By E. E. Firth. With 7 Maps. *Cr. 8vo.* 1s. 6d.

STORIES FROM ROMAN HISTORY. By E. M. Wilmot-Buxton. *Second Edition. Cr. 8vo.* 1s. 6d.

STORIES FROM THE OLD TESTAMENT. By E. Wilmot-Buxton. *Cr. 8vo.* 1s. 6d.

Books on Business

Cr. 8vo. 2s. 6d. net.

AUTOMOBILE INDUSTRY, THE. G. Holden-Stone.

BREWING INDUSTRY, THE. J. L. Baker, F.I.C., F.C.S. With 28 Illustrations.

BUSINESS OF ADVERTISING, THE. C. G. Moran. With 11 Illustrations.

BUSINESS SIDE OF AGRICULTURE, THE. A. G. L. Rogers.

BUSINESS OF INSURANCE, THE. A. J. Wilson.

CIVIL ENGINEERING. C. T. Fidler. With 15 Illustrations.

COTTON INDUSTRY AND TRADE, THE. S. J. Chapman. With 8 Illustrations.

THE ELECTRICAL INDUSTRY: LIGHTING, TRACTION, AND POWER. A. G. Whyte.

IRON TRADE OF GREAT BRITAIN, THE. J. S. Jeans. With 12 Illustrations.

LAW IN BUSINESS. H. A. Wilson.

MINING AND MINING INVESTMENTS. A. Moil.

MONEY MARKET, THE. F. Straker.

MONOPOLIES, TRUSTS, AND KARTELLS. F. W. Hirst.

PORTS AND DOCKS. Douglas Owen.

RAILWAYS. E. R. McDermott.

SHIPBUILDING INDUSTRY THE: Its History, Practice, Science, and Finance. David Pollock, M.I.N.A.

STOCK EXCHANGE, THE. C. Duguid. *Second Edition.*

TRADE UNIONS. G. Drage.

Byzantine Texts

Edited by J. B. BURY, M.A., Litt.D.

THE SYRIAC CHRONICLE KNOWN AS THAT OF ZACHARIAH OF MITYLENE. Translated by F. J. Hamilton, D.D., and E. W. Brooks. *Demy 8vo.* 12s. 6d. net.

EVAGRIUS. Edited by L. Bidez and Léon Parmentier. *Demy 8vo.* 10s. 6d. net.

THE HISTORY OF PSELLUS. Edited by C. Sathas. *Demy 8vo.* 15s. net.

ECTHESIS CHRONICA AND CHRONICON ATHENARUM. Edited by Professor S. P. Lambros. *Demy 8vo.* 7s. 6d. net.

THE CHRONICLE OF MOREA. Edited by John Schmitt. *Demy 8vo.* 15s. net.

The Churchman's Bible

General Editor, J. H. BURN, B.D., F.R.S.E.

Fcap. 8vo. 1s. 6d. net each.

THE EPISTLE OF ST. PAUL THE APOSTLE TO THE GALATIANS. Explained by A. W. Robinson, M.A. *Second Edition.*

ECCLESIASTES. Explained by A. W. Streane, D.D.

THE EPISTLE OF ST. PAUL THE APOSTLE TO THE PHILIPPIANS. Explained by C. R. D. Biggs, D.D. *Second Edition.*

THE EPISTLE OF ST. JAMES. Explained by H. W. Fulford M.A.

ISAIAH. Explained by W. E. Barnes, D.D. *Two Volumes.* With Map. 2s. net each.

THE EPISTLE OF ST. PAUL THE APOSTLE TO THE EPHESIANS. Explained by G. H. Whitaker, M.A.

THE GOSPEL ACCORDING TO ST. MARK. Explained by J. C. Du Buisson, M.A. 2s. 6d. net.

THE EPISTLE OF PAUL THE APOSTLE TO THE COLOSSIANS AND PHILEMON. Explained by H. J. C. Knight. 2s. net.

General Literature

The Churchman's Library

General Editor, J. H. BURN, B.D., F.R.S.E.

Crown 8vo. 3s. 6d. each.

THE BEGINNINGS OF ENGLISH CHRISTIANITY. By W. E. Collins, M.A. With Map.

THE CHURCHMAN'S INTRODUCTION TO THE OLD TESTAMENT. By A. M. Mackay, B.A. *Second Edition.*

EVOLUTION. By F. B. Jevons, M.A., Litt.D.

SOME NEW TESTAMENT PROBLEMS. By Arthur Wright, D.D. 6s.

THE WORKMANSHIP OF THE PRAYER BOOK: Its Literary and Liturgical Aspects. By J. Dowden, D.D. *Second Edition, Revised and Enlarged.*

Classical Translations

Crown 8vo.

AESCHYLUS—The Oresteian Trilogy (Agamemnon, Choëphoroe, Eumenides). Translated by Lewis Campbell, LL.D. 5s.

CICERO—De Oratore I. Translated by E. N. P. Moor, M.A. *Second Edition.* 3s. 6d.

CICERO—The Speeches against Cataline and Antony and for Murena and Milo. Translated by H. E. D. Blakiston, M.A. 5s.

CICERO—De Natura Deorum. Translated by F. Brooks, M.A. 3s. 6d.

CICERO—De Officiis. Translated by G. B. Gardiner, M.A. 2s. 6d.

HORACE—The Odes and Epodes. Translated by A. D. Godley, M.A. 2s.

LUCIAN—Six Dialogues Translated by S. T. Irwin, M.A. 3s. 6d.

SOPHOCLES—Ajax and Electra. Translated by E. D. Morshead, M.A. 2s. 6d.

TACITUS—Agricola and Germania. Translated by R. B. Townshend. 2s. 6d.

JUVENAL—Thirteen Satires. Translated by S. G. Owen, M.A. 2s. 6d.

Classics of Art

Edited by DR. J. H. W. LAING

Wide Royal 8vo. Gilt top.

THE ART OF THE GREEKS. By H. B. Walters. With 112 Plates and 18 Illustrations in the Text. 12s. 6d. net.

FLORENTINE SCULPTORS OF THE RENNAISANCE. Wilhelm Bode, Ph.D. Translated by Jessie Haynes. With 94 Plates. 12s. 6d. net.

GHIRLANDAIO. Gerald S. Davies, Master of the Charterhouse. With 50 Plates. *Second Edition.* 10s. 6d.

*MICHELANGELO. Gerald S. Davies, Master of the Charterhouse. With 126 Plates. 12s. 6d. net.

RUBENS. Edward Dillon, M.A. With a Frontispiece in Photogravure and 483 Plates. 25s. net.

RAPHAEL. A. P. Oppé. With a Frontispiece in Photogravure and 200 Illustrations. 12s. 6d. net.

TITIAN. Charles Ricketts. With about 220 Illustrations. 12s. 6d. net.

VELAZQUEZ. By A. de Beruete. With 94 Plates. 10s. 6d. net.

Commercial Series

Crown 8vo.

BRITISH COMMERCE AND COLONIES FROM ELIZABETH TO VICTORIA. By H. de B. Gibbins, Litt.D., M.A. *Fourth Edition.* 2s.

COMMERCIAL EXAMINATION PAPERS. By H. de B. Gibbins, Litt.D., M.A. 1s. 6d.

THE ECONOMICS OF COMMERCE, By H. de B. Gibbins, Litt.D., M.A. *Second Edition.* 1s. 6d.

A GERMAN COMMERCIAL READER. By S. E. Bally. With Vocabulary. 2s.

A COMMERCIAL GEOGRAPHY OF THE BRITISH EMPIRE. By L. W. Lyde, M.A. *Seventh Edition.* 2s.

A COMMERCIAL GEOGRAPHY OF FOREIGN NATIONS. By F. C. Boon, B.A. 2s.

A PRIMER OF BUSINESS. By S. Jackson, M.A. *Fourth Edition.* 1s. 6d.

A SHORT COMMERCIAL ARITHMETIC. By F. G. Taylor, M.A. *Fourth Edition.* 1s. 6d.

FRENCH COMMERCIAL CORRESPONDENCE. By S. E. Bally. With Vocabulary. *Fourth Edition.* 2s.

GERMAN COMMERCIAL CORRESPONDENCE. By S. E. Bally. With Vocabulary. *Second Edition.* 2s. 6d.

A FRENCH COMMERCIAL READER. By S. E. Bally. With Vocabulary. *Second Edition.* 2s.

PRECIS WRITING AND OFFICE CORRESPONDENCE. By E. E. Whitfield, M.A. *Second Edition.* 2s.

AN ENTRANCE GUIDE TO PROFESSIONS AND BUSINESS. By H. Jones. 1s. 6d.

THE PRINCIPLES OF BOOK-KEEPING BY DOUBLE ENTRY. By J. E. B. M'Allen, M.A. 2s.

COMMERCIAL LAW. By W. Douglas Edwards. *Second Edition.* 2s.

The Connoisseur's Library

Wide Royal 8vo. 25s. net.

MEZZOTINTS. By Cyril Davenport. With 40 Plates in Photogravure.

PORCELAIN. By Edward Dillon. With 19 Plates in Colour, 20 in Collotype, and 5 in Photogravure.

MINIATURES. By Dudley Heath. With 9 Plates in Colour, 15 in Collotype, and 15 in Photogravure.

IVORIES. By A. Maskell. With 80 Plates in Collotype and Photogravure.

ENGLISH FURNITURE. By F. S. Robinson. With 160 Plates in Collotype and one in Photogravure. *Second Edition.*

ENGLISH COLOURED BOOKS. By Martin Hardie. With 28 Illustrations in Colour and Collotype.

EUROPEAN ENAMELS. By Henry H. Cunynghame, C.B. With 54 Plates in Collotype and Half-tone and 4 Plates in Colour.

GOLDSMITHS' AND SILVERSMITHS' WORK. By Nelson Dawson. With 51 Plates in Collotype and a Frontispiece in Photogravure. *Second Edition.*

GLASS. By Edward Dillon. With 37 Illustrations in Collotype and 12 in Colour.

SEALS. By Walter de Gray Birch. With 52 Illustrations in Collotype and a Frontispiece in Photogravure.

JEWELLERY. By H. Clifford Smith. With 50 Illustrations in Collotype, and 4 in Colour. *Second Edition.*

Handbooks of English Church History

Edited by J. H. BURN, B.D. *Crown 8vo. 2s. 6d. net.*

THE FOUNDATIONS OF THE ENGLISH CHURCH. J. H. Maude.

THE SAXON CHURCH AND THE NORMAN CONQUEST. C. T. Cruttwell.

THE MEDIÆVAL CHURCH AND THE PAPACY. A. C. Jennings.

*THE REFORMATION PERIOD. By Henry Gee.

The Illustrated Pocket Library of Plain and Coloured Books

Fcap 8vo. 3s. 6d. net each volume.

COLOURED BOOKS

OLD COLOURED BOOKS. By George Paston. With 16 Coloured Plates. *Fcap. 8vo. 2s. net.*

THE LIFE AND DEATH OF JOHN MYTTON, ESQ. By Nimrod. With 18 Coloured Plates by Henry Alken and T. J. Rawlins. *Fourth Edition.*

THE LIFE OF A SPORTSMAN. By Nimrod. With 35 Coloured Plates by Henry Alken.

HANDLEY CROSS. By R. S. Surtees. With 17 Coloured Plates and 100 Woodcuts in the Text by John Leech. *Second Edition.*

MR. SPONGE'S SPORTING TOUR. By R. S. Surtees. With 13 Coloured Plates and 90 Woodcuts in the Text by John Leech.

JORROCKS' JAUNTS AND JOLLITIES. By R. S. Surtees. With 15 Coloured Plates by H. Alken. *Second Edition.*

ASK MAMMA. By R. S. Surtees. With 13 Coloured Plates and 70 Woodcuts in the Text by John Leech.

THE ANALYSIS OF THE HUNTING FIELD. By R. S. Surtees. With 7 Coloured Plates by Henry Alken, and 43 Illustrations on Wood.

THE TOUR OF DR. SYNTAX IN SEARCH OF THE PICTURESQUE. By William Combe. With 30 Coloured Plates by T. Rowlandson.

THE TOUR OF DOCTOR SYNTAX IN SEARCH OF CONSOLATION. By William Combe. With 24 Coloured Plates by T. Rowlandson.

THE THIRD TOUR OF DOCTOR SYNTAX IN SEARCH OF A WIFE. By William Combe. With 24 Coloured Plates by T. Rowlandson.

THE HISTORY OF JOHNNY QUAE GENUS: the Little Foundling of the late Dr. Syntax. By the Author of 'The Three Tours.' With 24 Coloured Plates by Rowlandson.

THE ENGLISH DANCE OF DEATH, from the Designs of T. Rowlandson, with Metrical Illustrations by the Author of 'Doctor Syntax.' *Two Volumes.*
This book contains 76 Coloured Plates.

THE DANCE OF LIFE: A Poem. By the Author of 'Doctor Syntax.' Illustrated with 26 Coloured Engravings by T. Rowlandson.

LIFE IN LONDON: or, the Day and Night Scenes of Jerry Hawthorn, Esq., and his Elegant Friend, Corinthian Tom. By Pierce Egan. With 36 Coloured Plates by I. R. and G. Cruikshank. With numerous Designs on Wood.

REAL LIFE IN LONDON: or, the Rambles and Adventures of Bob Tallyho, Esq., and his Cousin, The Hon. Tom Dashall. By an Amateur (Pierce Egan). With 31 Coloured Plates by Alken and Rowlandson, etc. *Two Volumes.*

THE LIFE OF AN ACTOR. By Pierce Egan. With 27 Coloured Plates by Theodore Lane, and several Designs on Wood.

THE VICAR OF WAKEFIELD. By Oliver Goldsmith. With 24 Coloured Plates by T. Rowlandson.

THE MILITARY ADVENTURES OF JOHNNY NEWCOME. By an Officer. With 15 Coloured Plates by T. Rowlandson.

General Literature

ILLUSTRATED POCKET LIBRARY OF PLAIN AND COLOURED BOOKS—*continued*.

THE NATIONAL SPORTS OF GREAT BRITAIN. With Descriptions and 50 Coloured Plates by Henry Alken.

THE ADVENTURES OF A POST CAPTAIN. By A Naval Officer. With 24 Coloured Plates by Mr. Williams.

GAMONIA : or, the Art of Preserving Game ; and an Improved Method of making Plantations and Covers, explained and illustrated by Lawrence Rawstorne, Esq. With 15 Coloured Plates by T. Rawlins.

AN ACADEMY FOR GROWN HORSEMEN : Containing the completest Instructions for Walking, Trotting, Cantering, Galloping, Stumbling, and Tumbling. Illustrated with 27 Coloured Plates, and adorned with a Portrait of the Author. By Geoffrey Gambado, Esq.

REAL LIFE IN IRELAND, or, the Day and Night Scenes of Brian Boru, Esq., and his Elegant Friend, Sir Shawn O'Dogherty. By a Real Paddy. With 19 Coloured Plates by Heath, Marks, etc.

THE ADVENTURES OF JOHNNY NEWCOME IN THE NAVY. By Alfred Burton. With 16 Coloured Plates by T. Rowlandson.

THE OLD ENGLISH SQUIRE : A Poem. By John Careless, Esq. With 20 Coloured Plates after the style of T. Rowlandson.

THE ENGLISH SPY. By Bernard Blackmantle. An original Work, Characteristic, Satirical, Humorous, comprising scenes and sketches in every Rank of Society, being Portraits of the Illustrious, Eminent, Eccentric, and Notorious. With 72 Coloured Plates by R. CRUIKSHANK, and many Illustrations on wood. *Two Volumes. 7s. net.*

PLAIN BOOKS

THE GRAVE : A Poem. By Robert Blair. Illustrated by 12 Etchings executed by Louis Schiavonetti from the original Inventions of William Blake. With an Engraved Title Page and a Portrait of Blake by T. Phillips, R.A. The illustrations are reproduced in photogravure.

ILLUSTRATIONS OF THE BOOK OF JOB. Invented and engraved by William Blake. These famous Illustrations—21 in number—are reproduced in photogravure.

WINDSOR CASTLE By W. Harrison Ainsworth. With 22 Plates and 87 Woodcuts in the Text by George Cruikshank.

THE TOWER OF LONDON. By W. Harrison Ainsworth. With 40 Plates and 58 Woodcuts in the Text by George Cruikshank.

FRANK FAIRLEGH. By F. E. Smedley. With 30 Plates by George Cruikshank.

HANDY ANDY. By Samuel Lover. With 24 Illustrations by the Author.

THE COMPLEAT ANGLER. By Izaak Walton and Charles Cotton. With 14 Plates and 77 Woodcuts in the Text.

THE PICKWICK PAPERS. By Charles Dickens. With the 43 Illustrations by Seymour and Phiz, the two Buss Plates, and the 32 Contemporary Onwhyn Plates.

Junior Examination Series

Edited by A. M. M. STEDMAN, M.A. *Fcap. 8vo. 1s.*

JUNIOR ALGEBRA EXAMINATION PAPERS. By S. W. Finn, M.A.

JUNIOR ARITHMETIC EXAMINATION PAPERS. By W. S. Beard. *Fifth Edition.*

JUNIOR ENGLISH EXAMINATION PAPERS. By W. Williamson, B.A. *Second Edition.*

JUNIOR FRENCH EXAMINATION PAPERS. By F. Jacob, M.A. *Second Edition.*

JUNIOR GENERAL INFORMATION EXAMINATION PAPERS. By W. S. Beard. KEY, 3s. 6d. net.

JUNIOR GEOGRAPHY EXAMINATION PAPERS. By W. G. Baker, M.A.

JUNIOR GERMAN EXAMINATION PAPERS. By A. Voegelin, M.A.

JUNIOR GREEK EXAMINATION PAPERS. By T. C. Weatherhead, M.A. KEY, 3s. 6d. net.

JUNIOR LATIN EXAMINATION PAPERS. By C. G. Botting, B.A. *Sixth Edition.* KEY, 3s. 6d. net.

*JUNIOR HISTORY EXAMINATION PAPERS. By W. O. P. Davis.

Methuen's Junior School-Books

Edited by O. D. INSKIP, LL.D., and W. WILLIAMSON, B.A.

A CLASS-BOOK OF DICTATION PASSAGES. By W. Williamson, B.A. *Fourteenth Edition. Cr. 8vo.* 1s. 6d.

THE GOSPEL ACCORDING TO ST. MATTHEW. Edited by E. Wilton South, M.A. With Three Maps. *Cr. 8vo.* 1s. 6d.

THE GOSPEL ACCORDING TO ST. MARK. Edited by A. E. Rubie, D.D. With Three Maps. *Cr. 8vo.* 1s. 6d.

A JUNIOR ENGLISH GRAMMAR. By W. Williamson, B.A. With numerous passages for parsing and analysis, and a chapter on Essay Writing. *Fourth Edition. Cr. 8vo.* 2s.

A JUNIOR CHEMISTRY. By E. A. Tyler, B.A., F.C.S. With 78 Illustrations. *Fourth Edition. Cr. 8vo.* 2s. 6d.

THE ACTS OF THE APOSTLES. Edited by A. E. Rubie, D.D. *Cr. 8vo.* 2s.

MESSRS. METHUEN'S CATALOGUE

METHUEN'S JUNIOR SCHOOL BOOKS—*continued.*

A JUNIOR FRENCH GRAMMAR. By L. A. Sornet and M. J. Acatos. *Third Edition.* Cr. 8vo. 2s.

ELEMENTARY EXPERIMENTAL SCIENCE. PHYSICS by W. T. Clough, A.R.C.Sc. (Lond.), F.C.S. CHEMISTRY by A. E. Dunstan, B.Sc. (Lond.), F.C.S. With 2 Plates and 154 Diagrams. *Seventh Edition.* Cr. 8vo. 2s. 6d.

A JUNIOR GEOMETRY. By Noel S. Lydon. With 276 Diagrams. *Seventh Edition.* Cr. 8vo. 2s.

ELEMENTARY EXPERIMENTAL CHEMISTRY. By A. E. Dunstan, B.Sc. (Lond.), F.C.S. With 4 Plates and 109 Diagrams. *Third Edition.* Cr. 8vo. 2s.

A JUNIOR FRENCH PROSE. By R. R. N. Baron, M.A. *Third Edition.* Cr. 8vo. 2s.

THE GOSPEL ACCORDING TO ST. LUKE. With an Introduction and Notes by William Williamson, B.A. With Three Maps. Cr. 8vo. 2s.

THE FIRST BOOK OF KINGS. Edited by A. E. RUBIE, D.D. With 4 Maps. Cr. 8vo. 2s.

A JUNIOR GREEK HISTORY. By W. H. Spragge, M.A. With 4 Illustrations and 5 Maps. Cr. 8vo. 2s. 6d.

A SCHOOL LATIN GRAMMAR. By H. G. Ford, M.A. Cr. 8vo. 2s. 6d.

A JUNIOR LATIN PROSE. By H. N. Asman, M.A., B.D. Cr. 8vo. 2s. 6d.

*ELEMENTARY EXPERIMENTAL ELECTRICITY AND MAGNETISM. By W. T. Clough, A.R.C.Sc. (Lond.), F.C.S. With 200 Illustrations and Diagrams. Cr. 8vo. 2s. 6d.

ENGLISH LITERATURE FOR SCHOOLS. By Edith E. Firth. Cr. 8vo. 2s. 6d.

Leaders of Religion

Edited by H. C. BEECHING, M.A., Canon of Westminster. *With Portraits.* Cr. 8vo. 2s. net.

CARDINAL NEWMAN. By R. H. Hutton.
JOHN WESLEY. By J. H. Overton, M.A.
BISHOP WILBERFORCE. By G. W. Daniell, M.A.
CARDINAL MANNING. By A. W. Hutton, M.A.
CHARLES SIMEON. By H. C. G. Moule, D.D.
JOHN KNOX. By F. MacCunn. *Second Edition.*
JOHN HOWE. By R. F. Horton, D.D.
THOMAS KEN. By F. A. Clarke, M.A.
GEORGE FOX, THE QUAKER. By T. Hodgkin, D.C.L. *Third Edition.*
JOHN KEBLE. By Walter Lock, D.D.

THOMAS CHALMERS. By Mrs. Oliphant.
LANCELOT ANDREWES. By R. L. Ottley, D.D. *Second Edition.*
AUGUSTINE OF CANTERBURY. By E. L. Cutts, D.D.
WILLIAM LAUD. By W. H. Hutton, M.A. *Third Edition.*
JOHN DONNE. By Augustus Jessopp, D.D.
THOMAS CRANMER. By A. J. Mason, D.D.
BISHOP LATIMER. By R. M. Carlyle and A. J. Carlyle, M.A.
BISHOP BUTLER. By W. A. Spooner, M.A.

The Library of Devotion

With Introductions and (where necessary) Notes.

Small Pott 8vo, cloth, 2s.; leather, 2s. 6d. net.

THE CONFESSIONS OF ST. AUGUSTINE. Edited by C. Bigg, D.D. *Sixth Edition.*
THE IMITATION OF CHRIST: called also the Ecclesiastical Music. Edited by C. Bigg, D.D. *Fifth Edition.*
THE CHRISTIAN YEAR. Edited by Walter Lock, D.D. *Fourth Edition.*
LYRA INNOCENTIUM. Edited by Walter Lock, D.D. *Second Edition.*
THE TEMPLE. Edited by E. C. S. Gibson, D.D. *Second Edition.*
A BOOK OF DEVOTIONS. Edited by J. W. Stanbridge. B.D. *Second Edition.*
A SERIOUS CALL TO A DEVOUT AND HOLY LIFE. Edited by C. Bigg, D.D. *Fourth Ed.*
A GUIDE TO ETERNITY. Edited by J. W. Stanbridge, B.D.
THE INNER WAY. By J. Tauler. Edited by A. W. Hutton, M.A.

ON THE LOVE OF GOD. By St. Francis de Sales. Edited by W. J. Knox-Little, M.A.
THE PSALMS OF DAVID. Edited by B. W. Randolph, D.D.
LYRA APOSTOLICA. By Cardinal Newman and others. Edited by Canon Scott Holland, M.A., and Canon H. C. Beeching, M.A.
THE SONG OF SONGS. Edited by B. Blaxland, M.A.
THE THOUGHTS OF PASCAL. Edited by C. S. Jerram, M.A.
A MANUAL OF CONSOLATION FROM THE SAINTS AND FATHERS. Edited by J. H. Burn, B.D.
*DEVOTIONS FROM THE APOCRYPHA. Edited, with an Introduction, by Herbert Pentin, M.A.

General Literature

The Library of Devotion—*continued.*

*The Spiritual Combat. By Dom Lorenzo Scupoli. Newly translated, with an Introduction and Notes, by Thomas Barns, M.A.
The Devotions of St. Anselm. Edited by C. C. J. Webb, M.A.
Grace Abounding to the Chief of Sinners. By John Bunyan. Edited by S. C. Freer, M.A.
Bishop Wilson's Sacra Privata. Edited by A. E. Burn, B.D.
Lyra Sacra: A Book of Sacred Verse. Edited by Canon H. C. Beeching, M.A. *Second Edition, revised.*
A Day Book from the Saints and Fathers. Edited by J. H. Burn, B.D.
A Little Book of Heavenly Wisdom. A Selection from the English Mystics. Edited by E. C. Gregory.
Light, Life, and Love. A Selection from the German Mystics. Edited by W. R. Inge, M.A.
An Introduction to The Devout Life. By St. Francis de Sales. Translated and Edited by T. Barns, M.A.
The Little Flowers of the Glorious Messer St. Francis and of his Friars. Done into English by W. Heywood. With an Introduction by A. G. Ferrers Howell.

Manchester al Mondo: a Contemplation of Death and Immortality. By Henry Montagu, Earl of Manchester. With an Introduction by Elizabeth Waterhouse, Editor of 'A Little Book of Life and Death.'
The Spiritual Guide, which Disentangles the Soul and brings it by the Inward Way to the Fruition of Perfect Contemplation, and the Rich Treasure of Internal Peace. Written by Dr. Michael de Molinos, Priest. Translated from the Italian copy, printed at Venice, 1685. Edited with an Introduction by Kathleen Lyttelton. And a Note by Canon Scott Holland.
Devotions for Every Day of the Week and the Great Festivals. By John Wesley. Edited, with an Introduction by Canon C. Bodington.
Preces Privatae. By Lancelot Andrewes, Bishop of Winchester. Selections from the Translation by Canon F. E. Brightman. Edited, with an Introduction, by A. E. Burn, D.D.
Horae Mysticae: A Day Book from the Writings of Mystics of Many Nations. Edited by E. C. Gregory.

Little Books on Art

With many Illustrations. Demy 16mo. 2s. 6d. net.

Each volume consists of about 200 pages, and contains from 30 to 40 Illustrations, including a Frontispiece in Photogravure.

Albrecht Dürer. J. Allen.
Arts of Japan, The. E. Dillon.
Bookplates. E. Almack.
Botticelli. Mary L. Bonnor.
Burne-Jones. F. de Lisle.
Christ in Art. Mrs. H. Jenner.
Claude. E. Dillon.
Constable. H. W. Tompkins.
Corot. A. Pollard and E. Birnstingl.
Enamels. Mrs. N. Dawson.
Frederic Leighton. A. Corkran.
George Romney. G. Paston.
Greek Art. H. B. Walters.
Greuze and Boucher. E. F. Pollard.
Holbein. Mrs. G. Fortescue.
Illuminated Manuscripts. J. W. Bradley.
Jewellery. C. Davenport.
John Hoppner. H. P. K. Skipton.
Sir Joshua Reynolds. J. Sime.
Millet. N. Peacock.
Miniatures. C. Davenport.
Our Lady in Art. Mrs. H. Jenner.
Raphael. A. R. Dryhurst. *Second Edition.*
Rembrandt. Mrs. E. A. Sharp.
Turner. F. Tyrrell-Gill.
Vandyck. M. G. Smallwood.
Velasquez. W. Wilberforce and A. R. Gilbert.
Watts. R. E. D. Sketchley.

The Little Galleries

Demy 16mo. 2s. 6d. net.

Each volume contains 20 plates in Photogravure, together with a short outline of the life and work of the master to whom the book is devoted.

A Little Gallery of Reynolds.
A Little Gallery of Romney.
A Little Gallery of Hoppner.
A Little Gallery of Millais.
A Little Gallery of English Poets.

The Little Guides

With many Illustrations by E. H. NEW and other artists, and from photographs.

Small Pott 8vo, cloth, 2s. 6d. net.; leather, 3s. 6d. net.

The main features of these Guides are (1) a handy and charming form; (2) illustrations from photographs and by well-known artists; (3) good plans and maps; (4) an adequate but compact presentation of everything that is interesting in the natural features, history, archæology, and architecture of the town or district treated.

CAMBRIDGE AND ITS COLLEGES. A. H. Thompson. *Second Edition.*
ENGLISH LAKES, THE. F. G. Brabant.
ISLE OF WIGHT, THE. G. Clinch.
MALVERN COUNTRY, THE. B. C. A. Windle.
NORTH WALES. A. T. Story.
OXFORD AND ITS COLLEGES. J. Wells. *Eighth Edition.*
SHAKESPEARE'S COUNTRY. B. C. A. Windle. *Third Edition.*
ST. PAUL'S CATHEDRAL. G. Clinch.
WESTMINSTER ABBEY. G. E. Troutbeck. *Second Edition.*

BUCKINGHAMSHIRE. E. S. Roscoe.
CHESHIRE. W. M. Gallichan.
CORNWALL. A. L. Salmon.
DERBYSHIRE. J. C. Cox.
DEVON. S. Baring-Gould.
DORSET. F. R. Heath. *Second Edition.*
ESSEX. J. C. Cox.
HAMPSHIRE. J. C. Cox.

HERTFORDSHIRE. H. W. Tompkins.
KENT. G. Clinch.
KERRY. C. P. Crane.
MIDDLESEX. J. B. Firth.
MONMOUTHSHIRE. G. W. Wade and J. H. Wade.
NORFOLK. W. A. Dutt.
NORTHAMPTONSHIRE. W. Dry.
OXFORDSHIRE. F. G. Brabant.
SOMERSET. G. W. and J. H. Wade.
SUFFOLK. W. A. Dutt.
SURREY. F. A. H. Lambert.
SUSSEX. F. G. Brabant. *Second Edition.*
YORKSHIRE, THE EAST RIDING. J. E. Morris.
YORKSHIRE, THE NORTH RIDING. J. E. Morris.

BRITTANY. S. Baring-Gould.
NORMANDY. C. Scudamore.
ROME. C. G. Ellaby.
SICILY. F. H. Jackson.

The Little Library

With Introductions, Notes, and Photogravure Frontispieces.

Small Pott 8vo. Each Volume, cloth, 1s. 6d. net; leather, 2s. 6d. net.

Anon. A LITTLE BOOK OF ENGLISH LYRICS. *Second Edition.*
Austen (Jane). PRIDE AND PREJUDICE. Edited by E. V. LUCAS. *Two Vols.*
NORTHANGER ABBEY. Edited by E. V. LUCAS.
Bacon (Francis). THE ESSAYS OF LORD BACON. Edited by EDWARD WRIGHT.
Barham (R. H.). THE INGOLDSBY LEGENDS. Edited by J. B. ATLAY. *Two Volumes.*
Barnett (Mrs. P. A.). A LITTLE BOOK OF ENGLISH PROSE. *Second Edition.*
Beckford (William). THE HISTORY OF THE CALIPH VATHEK. Edited by E. DENISON ROSS.
Blake (William). SELECTIONS FROM WILLIAM BLAKE. Edited by M. PERUGINI.
Borrow (George). LAVENGRO. Edited by F. HINDES GROOME. *Two Volumes.*
THE ROMANY RYE. Edited by JOHN SAMPSON.
Browning (Robert). SELECTIONS FROM THE EARLY POEMS OF ROBERT BROWNING. Edited by W. HALL GRIFFIN, M.A.

Canning (George). SELECTIONS FROM THE ANTI-JACOBIN: with GEORGE CANNING'S additional Poems. Edited by LLOYD SANDERS.
Cowley (Abraham). THE ESSAYS OF ABRAHAM COWLEY. Edited by H. C. MINCHIN.
Crabbe (George). SELECTIONS FROM GEORGE CRABBE. Edited by A. C. DEANE.
Craik (Mrs.). JOHN HALIFAX, GENTLEMAN. Edited by ANNIE MATHESON. *Two Volumes.*
Crashaw (Richard). THE ENGLISH POEMS OF RICHARD CRASHAW. Edited by EDWARD HUTTON.
Dante (Alighieri). THE INFERNO OF DANTE. Translated by H. F. CARY. Edited by PAGET TOYNBEE, M.A., D.Litt.
THE PURGATORIO OF DANTE. Translated by H. F. CARY. Edited by PAGET TOYNBEE, M.A., D.Litt.
THE PARADISO OF DANTE. Translated by H. F. CARY. Edited by PAGET TOYNBEE, M.A., D.Litt.
Darley (George). SELECTIONS FROM THE POEMS OF GEORGE DARLEY. Edited by R. A. STREATFEILD.

General Literature

The Little Library—*continued.*

Deane (A. C.). A LITTLE BOOK OF LIGHT VERSE.
Dickens (Charles). CHRISTMAS BOOKS. *Two Volumes.*
Ferrier (Susan). MARRIAGE. Edited by A. Goodrich - Freer and Lord Iddesleigh. *Two Volumes.*
THE INHERITANCE. *Two Volumes.*
Gaskell (Mrs.). CRANFORD. Edited by E. V. Lucas. *Second Edition.*
Hawthorne (Nathaniel). THE SCARLET LETTER. Edited by Percy Dearmer.
Henderson (T. F.). A LITTLE BOOK OF SCOTTISH VERSE.
Keats (John). POEMS. With an Introduction by L. Binyon, and Notes by J. Masefield.
Kinglake (A. W.). EOTHEN. With an Introduction and Notes. *Second Edition.*
Lamb (Charles). ELIA, AND THE LAST ESSAYS OF ELIA. Edited by E. V. Lucas.
Locker (F.). LONDON LYRICS. Edited by A. D. Godley, M.A. A reprint of the First Edition.
Longfellow (H. W.). SELECTIONS FROM LONGFELLOW. Edited by L. M. Faithfull.
Marvell (Andrew). THE POEMS OF ANDREW MARVELL. Edited by E. Wright.
Milton (John). THE MINOR POEMS OF JOHN MILTON. Edited by H. C. Beeching, M.A.
Moir (D. M.). MANSIE WAUCH. Edited by T. F. Henderson.
Nichols (J. B. B.). A LITTLE BOOK OF ENGLISH SONNETS.

Rochefoucauld (La). THE MAXIMS OF LA ROCHEFOUCAULD. Translated by Dean Stanhope. Edited by G. H. Powell.
Smith (Horace and James). REJECTED ADDRESSES. Edited by A. D. Godley, M.A.
Sterne (Laurence). A SENTIMENTAL JOURNEY. Edited by H. W. Paul.
Tennyson (Alfred, Lord). THE EARLY POEMS OF ALFRED, LORD TENNYSON. Edited by J. Churton Collins, M.A.
IN MEMORIAM. Edited by H. C. Beeching, M.A.
THE PRINCESS. Edited by Elizabeth Wordsworth.
MAUD. Edited by Elizabeth Wordsworth.
Thackeray (W. M.). VANITY FAIR. Edited by S. Gwynn. *Three Volumes.*
PENDENNIS. Edited by S. Gwynn. *Three Volumes.*
ESMOND. Edited by S. Gwynn.
CHRISTMAS BOOKS. Edited by S. Gwynn.
Vaughan (Henry). THE POEMS OF HENRY VAUGHAN. Edited by Edward Hutton.
Walton (Izaak). THE COMPLEAT ANGLER. Edited by J. Buchan.
Waterhouse (Elizabeth). A LITTLE BOOK OF LIFE AND DEATH. Edited by. *Twelfth Edition.*
Wordsworth (W.). SELECTIONS FROM WORDSWORTH. Edited by Nowell C. Smith.
Wordsworth (W.) and **Coleridge (S. T.).** LYRICAL BALLADS. Edited by George Sampson.

The Little Quarto Shakespeare

Edited by W. J. CRAIG. With Introductions and Notes.

Pott 16*mo. In* 40 *Volumes. Leather, price* 1s. *net each volume.*

Mahogany Revolving Book Case. 10s. *net.*

Miniature Library

Reprints in miniature of a few interesting books which have qualities of humanity, devotion, or literary genius.

Euphranor: A Dialogue on Youth. By Edward FitzGerald. From the edition published by W. Pickering in 1851. *Demy* 32*mo. Leather,* 2s. *net.*

The Life of Edward, Lord Herbert of Cherbury. Written by himself. From the edition printed at Strawberry Hill in the year 1764. *Demy* 32*mo. Leather,* 2s. *net.*

Polonius: or Wise Saws and Modern Instances. By Edward FitzGerald. From the edition published by W. Pickering in 1852. *Demy* 32*mo. Leather,* 2s. *net.*

The Rubáiyát of Omar Khayyám. By Edward FitzGerald. From the 1st edition of 1859, *Fourth Edition. Leather,* 1s. *net.*

34   MESSRS. METHUEN'S CATALOGUE

A New Historical Series
Edited by the Rev. H. N. ASMAN, M.A., B.D.

*STORIES FROM ANCIENT HISTORY. By E. Bower, B.A. *Cr. 8vo.* 1s. 6d.

*STORIES FROM MODERN HISTORY. By E. M. Wilmot-Buxton, F.R.Hist.S. *Cr. 8vo.* 1s.6d.

The New Library of Medicine
Edited by C. W. SALEEBY, M.D., F.R.S. Edin. *Demy 8vo.*

CARE OF THE BODY, THE. F. Cavanagh. Second Edition. 7s. 6d. net.
CHILDREN OF THE NATION, THE. Right Hon. Sir John Gorst. 7s. 6d. net.
CONTROL OF A SCOURGE, THE: or, How Cancer is Curable. Chas. P. Childe. 7s. 6d. net.
DISEASES OF OCCUPATION. Sir Thomas Oliver. 10s. 6d. net.
DRINK PROBLEM, THE, in its Medico-Sociological Aspects. Edited by T. N. Kelynack. 7s. 6d. net.

DRUGS AND THE DRUG HABIT. H. Sainsbury.
FUNCTIONAL NERVE DISEASES. A. T. Schofield. 7s. 6d. net.
HYGIENE OF MIND, THE. T. S. Clouston. Fifth Edition. 7s. 6d. net.
INFANT MORTALITY. George Newman. 7s. 6d. net.
PREVENTION OF TUBERCULOSIS (CONSUMPTION), THE. Arthur Newsholme. 10s. 6d. net.
*AIR AND HEALTH. Ronald C. Macfie, M.A., M.B. 7s. 6d. net.

The New Library of Music
Edited by ERNEST NEWMAN. *Demy 8vo.* 7s. 6d. net.

HUGO WOLF. By Ernest Newman. With 13 Illustrations.

HANDEL. By R. A. Streatfeild. With 12 Illustrations.

Oxford Biographies
Fcap. 8vo. Each volume, cloth, 2s. 6d. net; leather, 3s. 6d. net.

DANTE ALIGHIERI. By Paget Toynbee, M.A., D.Litt. With 12 Illustrations. *Third Edition.*
GIROLAMO SAVONAROLA. By E. L. S. Horsburgh, M.A. With 12 Illustrations. *Second Edition.*
JOHN HOWARD. By E. C. S. Gibson, D.D., Bishop of Gloucester. With 12 Illustrations.
ALFRED TENNYSON. By A. C. Benson, M.A. With 9 Illustrations. *Second Edition.*
SIR WALTER RALEIGH. By I. A. Taylor. With 12 Illustrations.
ERASMUS. By E. F. H. Capey. With 12 Illustrations.
THE YOUNG PRETENDER. By C. S. Terry. With 12 Illustrations.

ROBERT BURNS. By T. F. Henderson. With 12 Illustrations.
CHATHAM. By A. S. M'Dowall. With 12 Illustrations.
FRANCIS OF ASSISI. By Anna M. Stoddart. With 16 Illustrations.
CANNING. By W. Alison Phillips. With 12 Illustrations.
BEACONSFIELD. By Walter Sichel. With 12 Illustrations.
JOHANN WOLFGANG GOETHE. By H. G. Atkins. With 16 Illustrations.
FRANÇOIS FENELON. By Viscount St Cyres. With 12 Illustrations.

Romantic History
Edited by MARTIN HUME, M.A. *With Illustrations. Demy 8vo.*

A series of attractive volumes in which the periods and personalities selected are such as afford romantic human interest, in addition to their historical importance.

THE FIRST GOVERNESS OF THE NETHERLANDS, MARGARET OF AUSTRIA. Eleanor E. Tremayne. 10s. 6d. net.
TWO ENGLISH QUEENS AND PHILIP. Martin Hume, M.A. 15s. net.
THE NINE DAYS' QUEEN. Richard Davey. With a Preface by Martin Hume, M.A. With 12 Illustrations. 10s. 6d. net.

General Literature

School Examination Series

Edited by A. M. M. STEDMAN, M.A.   Crown 8vo.   2s. 6d.

EXAMINATION PAPERS IN ENGLISH HISTORY. By J. Tait Plowden-Wardlaw, B.A.
FRENCH EXAMINATION PAPERS. By A. M. M. Stedman, M.A. *Fifteenth Edition.*
KEY. *Sixth Edition.* 6s. net.
GENERAL KNOWLEDGE EXAMINATION PAPERS. By A. M. M. Stedman, M.A. *Sixth Edition.*
KEY. *Fourth Edition.* 7s. net.
GERMAN EXAMINATION PAPERS. By R. J. Morich. *Seventh Edition.*
KEY. *Third Edition.* 6s. net.

GREEK EXAMINATION PAPERS. By A. M. M. Stedman, M.A. *Ninth Edition.*
KEY. *Fourth Edition.* 6s. net.
HISTORY AND GEOGRAPHY EXAMINATION PAPERS. By C. H. Spence, M.A. *Third Edition.*
LATIN EXAMINATION PAPERS. By A. M. M. Stedman, M.A. *Fourteenth Edition.*
KEY. *Seventh Edition.* 6s. net.
PHYSICS EXAMINATION PAPERS. By R. E. Steel, M.A., F.C.S.

School Histories

Illustrated.   Crown 8vo.   1s. 6d.

A SCHOOL HISTORY OF WARWICKSHIRE. By B. C. A. Windle, D.Sc., F.R.S.
A SCHOOL HISTORY OF SOMERSET. By Walter Raymond. *Second Edition.*
A SCHOOL HISTORY OF LANCASHIRE. By W. E. Rhodes, M.A.

A SCHOOL HISTORY OF SURREY. By H. E Malden, M.A.
A SCHOOL HISTORY OF MIDDLESEX. By V. G. Plarr, M.A., and F. W. Walton, M.A.

Simplified French Texts

Edited by T. R. N. CROFTS, M.A.

Fcap 8vo.   1s.

ABDALLAH. By Edouard Laboulaye. Adapted by J. A. Wilson.
*DEUX CONTES. By P. Mérimée. Adapted by J. F. Rhoades.
*EDMOND DANTÈS. By A. Dumas. Adapted by M. Ceppi.
JEAN VALJEAN. By Victor Hugo. Adapted by F. W. M. Draper, M.A.
LA BATAILLE DE WATERLOO. By Erckmann-Chatrian. Adapted by G. H. Evans.
LA BOUILLIE AU MIEL. By A. Dumas. Adapted by P. B. Ingham, M.A.
LA CHANSON DE ROLAND. Adapted by H. Rieu, M.A. *Second Edition.*
LE CONSCRIT DE 1813. By Erckmann-Chatrian. Adapted by H. Rieu.

LE DOCTEUR MATHÉUS. By Erckmann-Chatrian. Adapted by W. P. Fuller, M.A.
*LE DUC DE BEAUFORT. By A. Dumas. Adapted by P. B. Ingham, M.A.
L'EQUIPAGE DE LA BELLE-NIVERNAISE. By Alphonse Daudet. Adapted by T. R. N. Crofts, M.A.
L'HISTOIRE D'UNE TULIPE. By A. Dumas. Adapted by T. R. N. Crofts, M.A. *Second Edition.*
L'HISTOIRE DE PIERRE ET CAMILLE. By A. de Musset. Adapted by J. B. Patterson, M.A.
MÉMOIRES DE CADICHON. By Madam de Ségur. Adapted by J. F. Rhoades.
*D'AJACCIO À SAINT HÉLÈNE. By A. Dumas. Adapted by F. W. M. DRAFER, M.A.
REMY LE CHEVRIER. By E. Souvestre. Adapted by E. E. Chottin, B-es-L.

Simplified German Texts

Edited by T. R. G. CROFTS, M.A.   Fcap. 8vo.   1s.

DER MULLER AM RHEIN. By C. Brentano. Adapted by Florence A. Ryan.
DIE GESCHICHTE VON PETER SCHLEMIHL. By A. v. Chamisso. Adapted by R. C. Perry.

DIE NOTHELFER. By W. H. Riehl. Adapted by P. B. Ingham, M.A.
UNDINE UND HULDBRAND. By La Motte Fouqué. Adapted by T. R. N. Crofts, M.A.

36   MESSRS. METHUEN'S CATALOGUE

Six Ages of European History

Edited by A. H. JOHNSON, M.A. With Maps. *Crown 8vo. 2s. 6d.*

AGE OF THE ENLIGHTENED DESPOT, THE, 1660-1789. A. H. Johnson.
CENTRAL PERIOD OF THE MIDDLE AGE, THE, 918-1273. Beatrice A. Lees.
DAWN OF MEDIÆVAL EUROPE, THE, 476-918. J. H. B. Masterman.
END OF THE MIDDLE AGE, THE, 1273-1453. E. C. Lodge.
EUROPE IN RENAISSANCE AND REFORMATION, 1453-1659. M. A. Hollings.
REMAKING OF MODERN EUROPE, THE, 1789-1878. J. A. R. Marriott.

Methuen's Standard Library

Cloth, 1s. net; double volumes, 1s. 6d. net.   Paper, 6d. net; double volume, 1s. net.

THE MEDITATIONS OF MARCUS AURELIUS. Translated by R. Graves.
SENSE AND SENSIBILITY. Jane Austen.
ESSAYS AND COUNSELS and THE NEW ATLANTIS. Francis Bacon, Lord Verulam.
RELIGIO MEDICI and URN BURIAL. Sir Thomas Browne. The text collated by A. R. Waller.
THE PILGRIM'S PROGRESS. John Bunyan.
REFLECTIONS ON THE FRENCH REVOLUTION. Edmund Burke.
THE POEMS AND SONGS OF ROBERT BURNS. Double Volume.
THE ANALOGY OF RELIGION, NATURAL AND REVEALED. Joseph Butler.
MISCELLANEOUS POEMS. T. CHATTERTON.
THE ROWLEY POEMS. T. Chatterton.
TOM JONES. Henry Fielding. Treble Vol.
CRANFORD. Mrs. Gaskell.
THE POEMS AND PLAYS OF OLIVER GOLDSMITH.
THE CASE IS ALTERED. EVERY MAN IN HIS HUMOUR. EVERY MAN OUT OF HIS HUMOUR. Ben Jonson.
CYNTHIA'S REVELS. POETASTER. Ben Jonson.
THE POEMS OF JOHN KEATS. Double volume. The Text has been collated by E. de Sélincourt.
ON THE IMITATION OF CHRIST. By Thomas à Kempis. Translation by C. Bigg.
A SERIOUS CALL TO A DEVOUT AND HOLY LIFE. W. Law.
PARADISE LOST. John Milton.
EIKONOKLASTES AND THE TENURE OF KINGS AND MAGISTRATES. John Milton.
UTOPIA AND POEMS. Sir Thomas More.
THE REPUBLIC OF PLATO. Translated by Sydenham and Taylor. Double Volume. Translation revised by W. H. D. Rouse.
THE LITTLE FLOWERS OF ST. FRANCIS. Translated by W. Heywood.
THE WORKS OF WILLIAM SHAKESPEARE. In 10 volumes.
THE POEMS OF PERCY BYSSHE SHELLEY. In 4 volumes. With Introductions by C. D. Locock.
THE LIFE OF NELSON. Robert Southey.
THE NATURAL HISTORY AND ANTIQUITIES OF SELBORNE. Gilbert White.

Textbooks of Science

Edited by G. F. GOODCHILD, M.A., B.Sc., and G. R. MILLS, M.A.

Fully Illustrated.

COMPLETE SCHOOL CHEMISTRY, THE. By F. M. Oldham, B.A. With 126 Illustrations. *Third Edition. Cr. 8vo.* 4s. 6d.
ELEMENTARY SCIENCE FOR PUPIL TEACHERS. PHYSICS SECTION. By W. T. Clough, A.R.C.Sc. (Lond.), F.C.S. CHEMISTRY SECTION. By A. E. Dunstan, B.Sc. (Lond.), F.C.S. With 2 Plates and 10 Diagrams. *Cr. 8vo.* 2s.
EXAMPLES IN ELEMENTARY MECHANICS, Practical, Graphical, and Theoretical. By W. J. Dobbs, M.A. With 52 Diagrams. *Cr. 8vo.* 5s.
EXAMPLES IN PHYSICS. By C. E. Jackson, M.A. *Cr. 8vo.* 2s. 6d.
FIRST YEAR PHYSICS. By C. E. Jackson, M.A. With 51 Diagrams. *Cr. 8vo.* 1s. 6d.
OUTLINES OF PHYSICAL CHEMISTRY. By George Senter, B.Sc. (Lond.), Ph.D. With many Diagrams. *Cr. 8vo.* 3s. 6d.
ORGANIC CHEMISTRY, AN, FOR SCHOOLS AND TECHNICAL INSTITUTES. By A. E. Dunstan, B.Sc. (Lond.), F.C.S. With many Illustrations. *Cr. 8vo.* 2s. 6d.
PLANT LIFE, Studies in Garden and School. By Horace F. Jones, F.C.S. With 320 Illustrations. *Cr. 8vo.* 3s. 6d.
PRACTICAL CHEMISTRY. Part I. W. French, M.A. *Fifth Edition. Cr. 8vo.* 1s. 6d.
PRACTICAL CHEMISTRY. Part II. W. French, M.A., and T. H. Boardman, M.A. *Cr. 8vo.* 1s. 6d.
*PRACTICAL CHEMISTRY FOR SCHOOLS AND TECHNICAL INSTITUTES, A. By A. E. Dunstan, B.Sc. (Lond.), F.C.S. *Cr. 8vo.* 3s. 6d.
PRACTICAL MECHANICS. S. H. Wells. *Fourth Edition. Cr. 8vo.* 3s. 6d.
TECHNICAL ARITHMETIC AND GEOMETRY. By C. T. Millis, M.I.M.E. *Cr. 8vo.* 3s. 6d.

General Literature

Textbooks of Technology
Fully Illustrated.

BUILDERS' QUANTITIES. By H. C. Grubb. *Cr. 8vo. 4s. 6d.*
CARPENTRY AND JOINERY. By F. C. Webber. *Fifth Edition. Cr. 8vo. 3s. 6d.*
ELECTRIC LIGHT AND POWER: An Introduction to the Study of Electrical Engineering. By E. E. Brooks, B.Sc. (Lond.), and W. H. N. James, A.M.I.E.E., A.R.C.Sc. *Cr. 8vo. 4s. 6d.*
ENGINEERING WORKSHOP PRACTICE. By C. C. Allen. *Cr. 8vo. 3s. 6d.*
HOW TO MAKE A DRESS. By J. A. E. Wood. *Fourth Edition. Cr. 8vo. 1s. 6d.*
INSTRUCTION IN COOKERY. A. P. Thomson. *Cr. 8vo. 2s. 6d.*
INTRODUCTION TO THE STUDY OF TEXTILE DESIGN, AN. By Aldred F. Barker. *Demy 8vo. 7s. 6d.*
MILLINERY, THEORETICAL AND PRACTICAL. By Clare Hill. *Fourth Edition. Cr. 8vo. 2s.*
REPOUSSÉ METAL WORK. By A. C. Horth. *Cr. 8vo. 2s. 6d.*

Handbooks of Theology

THE DOCTRINE OF THE INCARNATION. By R. L. Ottley, D.D. *Fourth Edition revised. Demy 8vo. 12s. 6d.*
A HISTORY OF EARLY CHRISTIAN DOCTRINE. By J. F. Bethune-Baker, M.A. *Demy 8vo. 10s. 6d.*
AN INTRODUCTION TO THE HISTORY OF RELIGION. By F. B. Jevons. M.A., Litt.D. *Fourth Edition. Demy 8vo. 10s. 6d.*
AN INTRODUCTION TO THE HISTORY OF THE CREEDS. By A. E. Burn, D.D. *Demy 8vo. 10s. 6d.*
THE PHILOSOPHY OF RELIGION IN ENGLAND AND AMERICA. By Alfred Caldecott, D.D. *Demy 8vo. 10s. 6d.*
THE XXXIX. ARTICLES OF THE CHURCH OF ENGLAND. Edited by E. C. S. Gibson, D.D. *Sixth Edition. Demy 8vo. 12s. 6d.*

The Westminster Commentaries

General Editor, WALTER LOCK, D.D., Warden of Keble College, Dean Ireland's Professor of Exegesis in the University of Oxford.

THE ACTS OF THE APOSTLES. Edited by R. B. Rackham, M.A. *Demy 8vo. Fourth Edition. 10s. 6d.*
THE FIRST EPISTLE OF PAUL THE APOSTLE TO THE CORINTHIANS. Edited by H. L. Goudge, M.A. *Second Ed. Demy 8vo. 6s.*
A COMMENTARY ON EXODUS. By A. H. M'Neile, B.D. With a Map and 3 Plans. *Demy 8vo. 10s. 6d.*
THE BOOK OF EZEKIEL. Edited H. A. Redpath, M.A., D.Litt. *Demy 8vo. 10s. 6d.*
THE BOOK OF GENESIS. Edited with Introduction and Notes by S. R. Driver, D.D. *Seventh Edition Demy 8vo. 10s. 6d.*
THE BOOK OF JOB. Edited by E. C. S. Gibson, D.D. *Second Edition. Demy 8vo. 6s.*
THE EPISTLE OF ST. JAMES. Edited with Introduction and Notes by R. J. Knowling, D.D. *Demy 8vo. 6s.*

Part II.—Fiction

Albanesi (E. Maria). SUSANNAH AND ONE OTHER. *Fourth Edition. Cr. 8vo. 6s.*
THE BLUNDER OF AN INNOCENT. *Second Edition. Cr. 8vo. 6s.*
CAPRICIOUS CAROLINE. *Second Edition. Cr. 8vo. 6s.*
LOVE AND LOUISA. *Second Edition. Cr. 8vo. 6s.* Also *Medium 8vo. 6d.*
PETER, A PARASITE. *Cr. 8vo. 6s.*
THE BROWN EYES OF MARY. *Third Edition. Cr. 8vo. 6s.*
I KNOW A MAIDEN. *Third Edition. Cr. 8vo. 6s.* Also *Medium 8vo. 6d.*
THE INVINCIBLE AMELIA: OR, THE POLITE ADVENTURESS. *Third Edition. Cr. 8vo. 3s. 6d.*
Annesley (Maude). THIS DAY'S MADNESS. *Cr. 8vo. 6s.*
Anstey (F.). A BAYARD FROM BENGAL. *Medium 8vo. 6d.*
Austen (Jane). PRIDE AND PREJUDICE. *Medium 8vo. 6d.*
Aveling (Francis). ARNOUL THE ENGLISHMAN. *Cr. 8vo. 6s.*
Bagot (Richard). A ROMAN MYSTERY. *Third Edition. Cr. 8vo. 6s.* Also *Medium 8vo. 6d.*

THE PASSPORT. *Fourth Edition. Cr. 8vo.* 6s.
TEMPTATION. *Fifth Edition. Cr. 8vo.* 6s.
ANTHONY CUTHBERT. *Fourth Edition Cr. 8vo.* 6s.
LOVE'S PROXY. *A New Edition. Cr. 8vo.* 6s.
DONNA DIANA. *Second Edition. Cr. 8vo.* 6s. Also *Medium 8vo.* 6d.
CASTING OF NETS. *Twelfth Edition. Cr. 8vo.* 6s. Also *Medium 8vo.* 6d.
Balfour (Andrew). BY STROKE OF SWORD. *Medium 8vo.* 6d.
Ball (Oona H.) (Barbara Burke). THEIR OXFORD YEAR. With 16 Illustrations *Cr. 8vo.* 6s.
BARBARA GOES TO OXFORD. With 16 Illustrations. *Third Edition. Cr. 8vo.* 6s.
Baring-Gould (S.). ARMINELL. *Fifth Edition. Cr. 8vo.* 6s. Also *Medium 8vo.* 6d.
URITH. *Fifth Edition. Cr. 8vo.* 6s. Also *Medium 8vo.* 6d.
IN THE ROAR OF THE SEA. *Seventh Edition. Cr. 8vo.* 6s. Also *Medium 8vo.* 6d.
CHEAP JACK ZITA. *Medium 8vo.* 6d.
MARGERY OF QUETHER. *Third Edition. Cr. 8vo.* 6s.
THE QUEEN OF LOVE. *Fifth Edition. Cr. 8vo.* 6s. Also *Medium 8vo.* 6d.
JACQUETTA. *Third Edition. Cr. 8vo.* 6s.
KITTY ALONE. *Fifth Edition. Cr. 8vo.* 6s. Also *Medium 8vo.* 6d.
NOÉMI. Illustrated. *Fourth Edition. Cr. 8vo.* 6s. Also *Medium 8vo.* 6d.
THE BROOM-SQUIRE. Illustrated. *Fifth Edition. Cr. 8vo.* 6s. Also *Medium 8vo.* 6d.
DARTMOOR IDYLLS. *Cr. 8vo.* 6s.
GUAVAS THE TINNER. Illustrated. *Second Edition. Cr. 8vo.* 6s.
BLADYS OF THE STEWPONEY. Illustrated. *Second Edition. Cr. 8vo.* 6s.
PABO THE PRIEST. *Cr. 8vo.* 6s.
WINEFRED. Illustrated. *Second Edition. Cr. 8vo.* 6s. Also *Medium 8vo.* 6d.
ROYAL GEORGIE. Illustrated. *Cr. 8vo.* 6s.
CHRIS OF ALL SORTS. *Cr. 8vo.* 6s.
IN DEWISLAND. *Second Edition. Cr. 8vo.* 6s.
THE FROBISHERS. *Crown 8vo.* 6s. Also *Medium 8vo.* 6d.
DOMITIA. Illus. *Second Ed. Cr. 8vo.* 6s.
MRS. CURGENVEN OF CURGENVEN. *Crown 8vo.* 6s.
LITTLE TU'PENNY. *Medium 8vo.* 6d.
FURZE BLOOM. *Medium 8vo.* 6d.
Barnett (Edith A.). A WILDERNESS WINNER. *Second Edition. Cr. 8vo.* 6s.

Barr (James). LAUGHING THROUGH A WILDERNESS. *Cr. 8vo.* 6s.
Barr (Robert). IN THE MIDST OF ALARMS. *Third Edition. Cr. 8vo.* 6s. Also *Medium 8vo.* 6d.
THE COUNTESS TEKLA. *Fourth Edition. Cr. 8vo.* 6s. Also *Medium 8vo.* 6d.
THE MUTABLE MANY. *Third Edition. Cr. 8vo.* 6s. Also *Medium 8vo.* 6d.
THE TEMPESTUOUS PETTICOAT. Illustrated. *Third Edition. Cr. 8vo.* 6s.
JENNIE BAXTER JOURNALIST. *Medium 8vo.* 6d.
Begbie (Harold). THE CURIOUS AND DIVERTING ADVENTURES OF SIR JOHN SPARROW; or, THE PROGRESS OF AN OPEN MIND. With a Frontispiece. *Second Edition. Cr. 8vo.* 6s.
Belloc (H.), EMMANUEL BURDEN, MERCHANT. With 36 Illustrations by G. K. CHESTERTON. *Second Ed. Cr. 8vo.* 6s.
A CHANGE IN THE CABINET. *Second Edition. Cr. 8vo.* 6s.
Benson (E. F.) DODO: A DETAIL OF THE DAY. *Fifteenth Edition. Cr. 8vo.* 6s. Also *Medium 8vo.* 6d.
THE VINTAGE. *Medium 8vo.* 6d.
Benson (Margaret). SUBJECT TO VANITY. *Cr. 8vo.* 3s. 6d.
Birmingham (George A.). THE BAD TIMES. *Second Edition. Cr. 8vo.* 6s.
SPANISH GOLD. *Fourth Edition. Cr. 8vo.* 6s.
THE SEARCH PARTY. *Cr. 8vo.* 6s.
Bowles (G. Stewart). A GUN-ROOM DITTY BOX. *Second Ed. Cr. 8vo.* 1s. 6d.
Bretherton (Ralph Harold). THE MILL. *Cr. 8vo.* 6s.
AN HONEST MAN. *Second Edition. Cr. 8vo.* 6s.
Brontë (Charlotte). SHIRLEY. *Medium 8vo.* 6d.
Burton (J. Bloundelle). ACROSS THE SALT SEAS. *Medium 8vo.* 6d.
Caffyn (Mrs.) ('Iota'). ANNE MAULE-VERER. *Medium 8vo.* 6d.
Campbell (Mrs. Vere). FERRIBY. *Second Edition. Cr. 8vo.* 6s.
Capes (Bernard). THE EXTRAORDINARY CONFESSIONS OF DIANA PLEASE. *Third Edition. Cr. 8vo.* 6s.
A JAY OF ITALY. *Fourth Ed. Cr. 8vo.* 6s.
LOAVES AND FISHES. *Second Edition. Cr. 8vo.* 6s.
A ROGUE'S TRAGEDY. *Second Edition. Cr. 8vo.* 6s.
THE GREAT SKENE MYSTERY. *Second Edition. Cr. 8vo.* 6s.
THE LOVE STORY OF ST. BEL. *Second Edition. Cr. 8vo.* 6s.

Fiction

THE LAKE OF WINE. *Medium 8vo. 6d.*
Carey (Wymond). LOVE THE JUDGE. *Second Edition. Cr. 8vo. 6s.*
Castle (Agnes and Egerton). FLOWER O' THE ORANGE, and Other Tales. With a Frontispiece in Colour by A. H. Buckland. *Third Edition. Cr. 8vo. 6s.*
Charlton (Randal). M A V E. *Second Edition. Cr. 8vo. 6s.*
THE VIRGIN WIDOW. *Cr. 8vo. 6s.*
Chesney (Weatherby). THE MYSTERY OF A BUNGALOW. *Second Edition. Cr. 8vo. 6s.*
Clifford (Mrs. W. K.). THE GETTING WELL OF DOROTHY. Illustrated by GORDON BROWNE. *Second Edition. Cr. 8vo. 3s. 6d.*
A FLASH OF SUMMER. *Medium 8vo. 6d.*
MRS. KEITH'S CRIME. *Medium 8vo. 6d.*
Conrad (Joseph). THE SECRET AGENT: A Simple Tale. *Fourth Ed. Cr. 8vo. 6s.*
A SET OF SIX. *Fourth Edition. Cr. 8vo. 6s.*
Corbett (Julian). A BUSINESS IN GREAT WATERS. *Third Edition. Cr. 8vo. 6s.* Also *Medium 8vo. 6d.*
Corelli (Marie). A ROMANCE OF TWO WORLDS. *Twenty-Ninth Ed. Cr. 8vo. 6s.*
VENDETTA. *Twenty-Seventh Edition. Cr. 8vo. 6s.*
THELMA. *Thirty-Ninth Ed. Cr. 8vo. 6s.*
ARDATH: THE STORY OF A DEAD SELF. *Nineteenth Edition. Cr. 8vo. 6s.*
THE SOUL OF LILITH. *Sixteenth Edition. Cr. 8vo. 6s.*
WORMWOOD. *Sixteenth Ed. Cr. 8vo. 6s.*
BARABBAS: A DREAM OF THE WORLD'S TRAGEDY. *Forty-Fourth Edition. Cr. 8vo. 6s.*
THE SORROWS OF SATAN. *Fifty-Fifth Edition. Cr. 8vo. 6s.*
THE MASTER CHRISTIAN. *Twelfth Edition. 177th Thousand. Cr. 8vo. 6s.*
TEMPORAL POWER: A STUDY IN SUPREMACY. *Second Edition. 150th Thousand. Cr. 8vo. 6s.*
GOD'S GOOD MAN: A SIMPLE LOVE STORY. *Thirteenth Edition. 150th Thousand. Cr. 8vo. 6s.*
HOLY ORDERS: THE TRAGEDY OF A QUIET LIFE. *Second Edition. 120th Thousand. Crown 8vo. 6s.*
THE MIGHTY ATOM. *Twenty-seventh Edition. Cr. 8vo. 6s.*
BOY: a Sketch. *Eleventh Edition. Cr. 8vo. 6s.*
CAMEOS. *Thirteenth Edition. Cr. 8vo. 6s.*
Cotes (Mrs. Everard). See Duncan (Sara Jeanette).
Cotterell (Constance). THE VIRGIN AND THE SCALES. Illustrated. *Second Edition. Cr. 8vo. 6s.*

Crockett (S. R.), LOCHINVAR. Illustrated. *Third Edition. Cr. 8vo. 6s.* Also *Medium 8vo. 6d.*
THE STANDARD BEARER. *Cr. 8vo. 6s.*
Croker (Mrs. B. M.). THE OLD CANTONMENT. *Cr. 8vo. 6s.*
JOHANNA. *Second Edition. Cr. 8vo. 6s.* Also *Medium 8vo. 6d.*
THE HAPPY VALLEY. *Fourth Edition. Cr. 8vo. 6s.*
A NINE DAYS' WONDER. *Third Edition. Cr. 8vo. 6s.*
PEGGY OF THE BARTONS. *Seventh Ed. Cr. 8vo. 6s.* Also *Medium 8vo. 6d.*
ANGEL. *Fifth Edition. Cr. 8vo. 6s.* Also *Medium 8vo. 6d.*
A STATE SECRET. *Third Edition. Cr. 8vo. 3s. 6d.* Also *Medium 8vo. 6d.*
KATHERINE THE ARROGANT. *Fifth Edition. Cr. 8vo. 6s.*
Crosbie (Mary). DISCIPLES. *Second Ed. Cr. 8vo. 6s.*
Cuthell (Edith E.). ONLY A GUARD-ROOM DOG. Illustrated by W. PARKINSON. *Crown 8vo. 3s. 6d.*
Dawson (Warrington). THE SCAR. *Second Edition. Cr. 8vo. 6s.*
THE SCOURGE *Cr. 8vo. 6s.*
Deakin (Dorothea). THE YOUNG COLUMBINE. With a Frontispiece by LEWIS BAUMER. *Cr. 8vo. 6s.*
Deane (Mary). THE OTHER PAWN. *Cr. 8vo. 6s.*
Doyle (A. Conan). ROUND THE RED LAMP. *Eleventh Edition. Cr. 8vo. 6s.* Also *Medium 8vo. 6d.*
Dumas (Alexandre). See page 46.
Duncan (Sara Jeannette) (Mrs. Everard Cotes). THOSE DELIGHTFUL AMERICANS. *Medium 8vo. 6d.*
A VOYAGE OF CONSOLATION. Illustrated. *Third Edition. Cr. 8vo. 6s.* Also *Medium 8vo. 6d.*
COUSIN CINDERELLA. *Second Edition. Cr. 8vo. 6s.*
THE BURNT OFFERING. *Cr. 8vo. 6s.*
Eldridge (George D.). IN THE POTTER'S HOUSE. *Cr. 8vo. 6s.*
Eliot (George). THE MILL ON THE FLOSS. *Medium 8vo. 6d.*
Erskine (Mrs. Steuart). THE MAGIC PLUMES. *Cr. 8vo. 6s.*
Fenn (G. Manville). SYD BELTON; or, The Boy who would not go to Sea. Illustrated by GORDON BROWNE. *Second Ed. Cr. 8vo. 3s. 6d.*
Findlater (J. H.). THE GREEN GRAVES OF BALGOWRIE. *Fifth Edition. Cr. 8vo. 6s.* Also *Medium 8vo. 6d.*
THE LADDER TO THE STARS. *Second Edition. Cr. 8vo. 6s.*

Findlater (Mary). A NARROW WAY. *Third Edition. Cr. 8vo. 6s.*
OVER THE HILLS. *Second Edition. Cr. 8vo. 6s.*
THE ROSE OF JOY. *Third Edition. Cr. 8vo. 6s.*
A BLIND BIRD'S NEST. With 8 Illustrations. *Second Edition. Cr. 8vo. 6s.*
Fitzpatrick (K.) THE WEANS AT ROWALLAN. Illustrated. *Second Edition. Cr. 8vo. 6s.*
Francis (M. E.). (Mrs. Francis Blundell). 'STEPPING WESTWARD. *Second Edition. Cr. 8vo. 6s.*
MARGERY O' THE MILL. *Third Edition. Cr. 8vo. 6s.*
HARDY-ON-THE-HILL. *Third Edition. Cr. 8vo. 6s.*
GALATEA OF THE WHEATFIELD. *Second Edition. Cr. 8vo. 6s.*
Fraser (Mrs. Hugh). THE SLAKING OF THE SWORD. *Second Edition. Cr. 8vo. 6s.*
GIANNELLA. *Cr. 8vo. 6s.*
IN THE SHADOW OF THE LORD. *Third Edition. Crown 8vo. 6s.*
Fry (B. and C. B.). A MOTHER'S SON. *Fifth Edition. Cr. 8vo. 6s.*
Fuller-Maitland (Ella). BLANCHE ESMEAD. *Second Edition. Cr. 8vo. 6s.*
Gallon (Tom). RICKERBY'S FOLLY. *Medium 8vo. 6d.*
Gaskell (Mrs.). CRANFORD. *Medium 8vo. 6d.*
MARY BARTON. *Medium 8vo. 6d.*
NORTH AND SOUTH. *Medium 8vo. 6d.*
Gates (Eleanor). THE PLOW-WOMAN. *Cr. 8vo. 6s.*
Gerard (Dorothea). HOLY MATRIMONY. *Medium 8vo. 6d.*
MADE OF MONEY. *Medium 8vo. 6d.*
THE IMPROBABLE IDYL. *Third Edition. Cr. 8vo. 6s.*
THE BRIDGE OF LIFE. *Cr. 8vo. 6s.*
THE CONQUEST OF LONDON. *Medium 8vo. 6d.*
Gibbs (Philip). THE SPIRIT OF REVOLT. *Second Edition. Cr. 8vo. 6s.*
Gissing (George). THE TOWN TRAVELLER. *Medium 8vo. 6d.*
THE CROWN OF LIFE. *Cr. 8vo. 6s.* Also *Medium 8vo. 6d.*
Glanville (Ernest). THE INCA'S TREASURE. Illustrated. *Cr. 8vo. 3s. 6d.* Also *Medium 8vo. 6d.*
THE KLOOF BRIDE. *Medium 8vo. 6d.*
Gleig (Charles). BUNTER'S CRUISE. Illustrated. *Cr. 8vo. 3s. 6d.* Also *Medium 8vo. 6d.*
Grimm (The Brothers). GRIMM'S FAIRY TALES. Illustrated. *Medium 8vo. 6d.*

Haig (J. C.). IN THE GRIP OF THE TRUSTS: A STORY OF 1914. *Cr. 8vo. 1s. net.*
Hamilton (M.). THE FIRST CLAIM. *Second Edition. Cr. 8vo. 6s.*
Harraden (Beatrice). IN VARYING MOODS. *Fourteenth Edition. Cr. 8vo. 6s.*
THE SCHOLAR'S DAUGHTER. *Fourth Edition. Cr. 8vo. 6s.*
HILDA STRAFFORD and THE REMITTANCE MAN. *Twelfth Ed. Cr. 8vo. 6s.*
INTERPLAY. *Fifth Edition. Cr. 8vo. 6s.*
Harrod (F.) (Frances Forbes Robertson). THE TAMING OF THE BRUTE. *Cr. 8vo. 6s.*
Hart (Mabel). SISTER K. *Cr. 8vo. 6s.*
Hichens (Robert). THE PROPHET OF BERKELEY SQUARE. *Second Edition. Cr. 8vo. 6s.*
TONGUES OF CONSCIENCE. *Third Edition. Cr. 8vo. 6s.*
FELIX. *Sixth Edition. Cr. 8vo. 6s.*
THE WOMAN WITH THE FAN. *Seventh Edition. Cr. 8vo. 6s.*
BYEWAYS. *Cr. 8vo. 6s.*
THE GARDEN OF ALLAH. *Eighteenth Edition. Cr. 8vo. 6s.*
THE BLACK SPANIEL. *Cr. 8vo. 6s.*
THE CALL OF THE BLOOD. *Seventh Edition. Cr. 8vo. 6s.*
BARBARY SHEEP. *Second Edition. Cr. 8vo. 3s. 6d.*
Hope (Anthony). THE GOD IN THE CAR. *Eleventh Edition. Cr. 8vo. 6s.*
A CHANGE OF AIR. *Sixth Ed. Cr. 8vo. 6s.* Also *Medium 8vo. 6d.*
A MAN OF MARK. *Sixth Ed. Cr. 8vo. 6s.* Also *Medium 8vo. 6d.*
THE CHRONICLES OF COUNT ANTONIO. *Sixth Edition. Cr. 8vo. 6s.* Also *Medium 8vo. 6d.*
PHROSO.' Illustrated by H. R. MILLAR. *Eighth Edition. Cr. 8vo. 6s.* Also *Medium 8vo. 6d.*
SIMON DALE. Illustrated. *Eighth Edition. Cr. 8vo. 6s.*
THE KING'S MIRROR. *Fourth Edition. Cr. 8vo. 6s.*
QUISANTE. *Fourth Edition. Cr. 8vo. 6s.*
THE DOLLY DIALOGUES. *Cr. 8vo. 6s.* Also *Medium 8vo. 6d.*
A SERVANT OF THE PUBLIC. Illustrated. *Fourth Edition. Cr. 8vo. 6s.*
TALES OF TWO PEOPLE. With a Frontispiece by A. H. BUCKLAND. *Third Ed. Cr. 8vo. 6s.*
THE GREAT MISS DRIVER. With a Frontispiece by A. H. BUCKLAND. *Fourth Edition. Cr. 8vo. 6s.*

Fiction

Hornung (E. W.). DEAD MEN TELL NO TALES. *Medium 8vo. 6d.*
Housman (Clemence). THE LIFE OF SIR AGLOVALE DE GALIS. *Cr. 8vo. 6s.*
Hueffer (Ford Madox). AN ENGLISH GIRL: A ROMANCE. *Second Edition. Cr. 8vo. 6s.*
MR. APOLLO: A JUST POSSIBLE STORY. *Second Edition. Cr. 8vo. 6s.*
Hutten (Baroness von). THE HALO. *Fifth Edition. Cr. 8vo. 6s.*
Hyne (C. J. Cutcliffe). MR. HORROCKS, PURSER. *Fourth Edition. Cr. 8vo. 6s.*
PRINCE RUPERT, THE BUCCANEER. Illustrated. *Third Edition. Cr. 8vo. 6s.*
Ingraham (J. H.). THE THRONE OF DAVID. *Medium 8vo. 6d.*
Jacobs (W. W.). MANY CARGOES. *Thirty-first Edition. Cr. 8vo. 3s. 6d.*
SEA URCHINS. *Fifteenth Edition. Cr. 8vo. 3s. 6d.*
A MASTER OF CRAFT. Illustrated by WILL OWEN. *Eighth Edition. Cr. 8vo. 3s. 6d.*
LIGHT FREIGHTS. Illustrated by WILL OWEN and Others. *Seventh Edition. Cr. 8vo. 3s. 6d.*
THE SKIPPER'S WOOING. *Ninth Edition. Cr. 8vo. 3s. 6d.*
AT SUNWICH PORT. Illustrated by WILL OWEN. *Ninth Edition. Cr. 8vo. 3s. 6d.*
DIALSTONE LANE. Illustrated by WILL OWEN. *Seventh Edition. Cr. 8vo. 3s. 6d.*
ODD CRAFT. Illustrated by WILL OWEN. *Third Edition. Cr. 8vo. 3s. 6d.*
THE LADY OF THE BARGE. Illustrated. *Eighth Edition. Cr. 8vo. 3s. 6d.*
SALTHAVEN. Illustrated by WILL OWEN. *Second Edition. Cr. 8vo. 3s. 6d.*
SAILORS' KNOTS. *Cr. 8vo. 3s. 6d.*
James (Henry). THE SOFT SIDE. *Second Edition. Cr. 8vo. 6s.*
THE BETTER SORT. *Cr. 8vo. 6s.*
THE GOLDEN BOWL. *Third Edition. Cr. 8vo. 6s.*
Keays (H. A. Mitchell). HE THAT EATETH BREAD WITH ME. *Cr. 8vo. 6s.*
Kester (Vaughan). THE FORTUNES OF THE LANDRAYS. *Cr. 8vo. 6s.*
Lawless (Hon. Emily). WITH ESSEX IN IRELAND. *Cr. 8vo. 6s.*
Le Queux (William). THE HUNCHBACK OF WESTMINSTER. *Third Ed. Cr. 8vo. 6s. Also Medium 8vo. 6d.*
THE CLOSED BOOK. *Third Edition. Cr. 8vo. 6s.*
THE VALLEY OF THE SHADOW. Illustrated. *Third Edition. Cr. 8vo. 6s.*
BEHIND THE THRONE. *Third Edition. Cr. 8vo. 6s.*

THE CROOKED WAY. *Second Edition. Cr. 8vo. 6s.*
Levett-Yeats (S. K.). ORRAIN. *Second Edition. Cr. 8vo. 6s. Also Medium 8vo. 6d.*
THE TRAITOR'S WAY. *Medium 8vo. 6d.*
Linton (E. Lynn). THE TRUE HISTORY OF JOSHUA DAVIDSON. *Medium 8vo. 6d.*
London (Jack). WHITE FANG. With a Frontispiece by CHARLES RIVINGSTON BULL. *Sixth Edition. Cr. 8vo. 6s.*
Lubbock (Basil). DEEP SEA WARRIORS. Illustrated. *Second Edition. Cr. 8vo. 6s.*
*****Lucas (St. John).** THE FIRST ROUND. *Cr. 8vo. 6s.*
Lyall (Edna). DERRICK VAUGHAN, NOVELIST. *43rd Thousand, Cr. 8vo. 3s. 6d. Also Medium 8vo. 6d.*
Maartens (Maarten). THE NEW RELIGION: A MODERN NOVEL. *Third Edition. Cr. 8vo. 6s.*
BROTHERS ALL; MORE STORIES OF DUTCH PEASANT LIFE. *Third Edition. Cr. 8vo. 6s.*
THE PRICE OF LIS DORIS. *Cr. 8vo. 6s.*
M'Carthy (Justin H.). THE LADY OF LOYALTY HOUSE. Illustrated. *Third Edition. Cr. 8vo. 6s.*
THE DRYAD. *Second Edition. Cr. 8vo. 6s.*
THE DUKE'S MOTTO. *Third Edition. Cr. 8vo. 6s.*
Macdonald (Ronald). A HUMAN TRINITY. *Second Edition. Cr. 8vo. 6s.*
Macnaughtan (S.). THE FORTUNE OF CHRISTINA M'NAB. *Fourth Edition. Cr. 8vo. 6s.*
Malet (Lucas). COLONEL ENDERBY'S WIFE. *Fourth Edition. Cr. 8vo. 6s.*
A COUNSEL OF PERFECTION. *Second Edition. Cr. 8vo. 6s. Also Medium 8vo. 6d.*
THE WAGES OF SIN. *Sixteenth Edition. Cr. 8vo. 6s.*
THE CARISSIMA. *Fifth Ed. Cr. 8vo. 6s. Also Medium 8vo. 6d.*
THE GATELESS BARRIER. *Fifth Edition. Cr. 8vo. 6s.*
THE HISTORY OF SIR RICHARD CALMADY. *Seventh Edition. Cr. 8vo. 6s.*
Mann (Mrs. M. E.). OLIVIA'S SUMMER. *Second Edition. Cr. 8vo. 6s.*
A LOST ESTATE. *A New Ed. Cr. 8vo. 6s. Also Medium 8vo. 6d.*
THE PARISH OF HILBY. *A New Edition. Cr. 8vo. 6s.*
THE PARISH NURSE. *Fourth Edition. Cr. 8vo. 6s.*
GRAN'MA'S JANE. *Cr. 8vo. 6s.*

42   Messrs. Methuen's Catalogue

MRS. PETER HOWARD. *Second Edition.* *Cr.* 8*vo.* 6*s.* Also *Medium* 8*vo.* 6*d.*
A WINTER'S TALE. *A New Edition.* *Cr.* 8*vo.* 6*s.* Also *Medium* 8*vo.* 6*d.*
ONE ANOTHER'S BURDENS. *A New Edition. Cr.* 8*vo.* 6*s.* Also *Medium* 8*vo.* 6*d.*
ROSE AT HONEYPOT. *Third Ed. Cr.* 8*vo.* 6*s.*
THERE WAS ONCE A PRINCE. Illustrated by M. B. MANN. *Cr.* 8*vo.* 3*s.* 6*d.*
WHEN ARNOLD COMES HOME. Illustrated by M. B. MANN. *Cr.* 8*vo.* 3*s.* 6*d.*
THE EGLAMORE PORTRAITS. *Third Edition. Cr.* 8*vo.* 6*s.*
THE MEMORIES OF RONALD LOVE. *Cr.* 8*vo.* 6*s.*
THE SHEEP AND THE GOATS. *Third Edition. Cr.* 8*vo.* 6*s.*
A SHEAF OF CORN. *Second Edition. Cr.* 8*vo.* 6*s.*
THE HEART-SMITER. *Second Edition. Cr.* 8*vo.* 6*s.*
AVENGING CHILDREN. *Cr.* 8*vo.* 6*s.*
THE PATTEN EXPERIMENT. *Medium* 8*vo.* 6*d.*
THE CEDAR STAR. *Medium* 8*vo.* 6*d.*
Marchmont (A. W.). MISER HOADLEY'S SECRET. *Medium* 8*vo.* 6*d.*
A MOMENT'S ERROR. *Medium* 8*vo.* 6*d.*
Marriott (Charles). GENEVRA. *Second Edition. Cr.* 8*vo.* 6*s.*
Marryat (Captain). PETER SIMPLE *Medium* 8*vo.* 6*d.*
JACOB FAITHFUL. *Medium* 8*vo.* 6*d.*
Marsh (Richard). THE TWICKENHAM PEERAGE. *Second Edition. Cr.* 8*vo.* 6*s.* Also *Medium* 8*vo.* 6*d.*
THE MARQUIS OF PUTNEY. *Second Edition. Cr.* 8*vo.* 6*s.*
IN THE SERVICE OF LOVE. *Third Edition. Cr.* 8*vo.* 6*s.*
THE GIRL AND THE MIRACLE. *Third Edition. Cr.* 8*vo.* 6*s.*
THE COWARD BEHIND THE CURTAIN. *Cr.* 8*vo.* 6*s.*
THE SURPRISING HUSBAND. *Second Edition. Cr.* 8*vo.* 6*s.*
A ROYAL INDISCRETION. *Cr.* 8*vo.* 6*s.*
A METAMORPHOSIS. *Medium* 8*vo.* 6*d.*
THE GODDESS. *Medium* 8*vo.* 6*d.*
THE JOSS. *Medium* 8*vo.* 6*d.*
Marshall (Archibald). MANY JUNES. *Second Edition. Cr.* 8*vo.* 6*s.*
THE SQUIRE'S DAUGHTER. *Cr.* 8*vo.* 6*s.*
Mason (A. E. W.). CLEMENTINA. Illustrated. *Third Edition. Cr.* 8*vo.* 6*s.* Also *Medium* 8*vo.* 6*d.*
Mathers (Helen). HONEY. *Fourth Ed. Cr.* 8*vo.* 6*s.* Also *Medium* 8*vo.* 6*d.*

GRIFF OF GRIFFITHSCOURT. *Second Edition. Cr.* 8*vo.* 6*s.* Also *Medium* 8*vo.* 6*d.*
THE FERRYMAN *Second Edition. Cr.* 8*vo.* 6*s.*
TALLY-HO! *Fourth Edition. Cr.* 8*vo.* 6*s.*
SAM'S SWEETHEART. *Medium* 8*vo.* 6*d.*
Maud (Constance). A DAUGHTER OF FRANCE. With a Frontispiece. *Second Edition. Cr.* 8*vo.* 6*s.*
Maxwell (W. B.). VIVIEN. *Ninth Edition. Cr.* 8*vo.* 6*s.*
THE RAGGED MESSENGER. *Third Edition. Cr.* 8*vo.* 6*s.*
FABULOUS FANCIES. *Cr.* 8*vo.* 6*s.*
THE GUARDED FLAME. *Seventh Edition. Cr.* 8*vo.* 6*s.*
ODD LENGTHS. *Second Ed. Cr.* 8*vo.* 6*s.*
HILL RISE. *Fourth Edition. Cr.* 8*vo.* 6*s.*
THE COUNTESS OF MAYBURY: BETWEEN YOU AND I. *Fourth Edition. Cr.* 8*vo.* 6*s.*
Meade (L. T.). DRIFT. *Second Edition. Cr.* 8*vo.* 6*s.* Also *Medium* 8*vo.* 6*d.*
RESURGAM. *Second Edition. Cr.* 8*vo.* 6*s.*
VICTORY. *Cr.* 8*vo.* 6*s.*
A GIRL OF THE PEOPLE. Illustrated. *Fourth Edition. Cr.* 8*vo.* 3*s.* 6*d.*
HEPSY GIPSY. Illustrated. *Cr.* 8*vo.* 2*s.* 6*d.*
THE HONOURABLE MISS: A STORY OF AN OLD-FASHIONED TOWN. Illustrated. *Second Edition. Cr.* 8*vo.* 3*s.* 6*d.*
Melton (R.). CÆSAR'S WIFE. *Second Edition. Cr.* 8*vo.* 6*s.*
Meredith (Ellis). HEART OF MY HEART. *Cr.* 8*vo.* 6*s.*
Miller (Esther). LIVING LIES. *Third Edition. Cr.* 8*vo.* 6*s.* Also *Medium* 8*vo.* 6*d.*
Mitford (Bertram). THE SIGN OF THE SPIDER. Illustrated. *Sixth Edition. Cr.* 8*vo.* 3*s.* 6*d.* Also *Medium* 8*vo.* 6*d.*
IN THE WHIRL OF THE RISING. *Third Edition. Cr.* 8*vo.* 6*s.*
THE RED DERELICT. *Second Edition. Cr.* 8*vo.* 6*s.*
Molesworth (Mrs.). THE RED GRANGE. Illustrated. *Second Edition. Cr.* 8*vo.* 3*s.* 6*d.*
Montgomery (K. L.). COLONEL KATE. *Second Edition. Cr.* 8*vo.* 6*s.*
Montresor (F. F.). THE ALIEN. *Third Edition. Cr.* 8*vo.* 6*s.* Also *Medium* 8*vo.* 6*d.*
Morrison (Arthur). TALES OF MEAN STREETS. *Seventh Edition. Cr.* 8*vo.* 6*s.*
A CHILD OF THE JAGO. *Fifth Edition. Cr.* 8*vo.* 6*s.*
THE HOLE IN THE WALL. *Fourth Edition. Cr.* 8*vo.* 6*s.* Also *Medium* 8*vo.* 6*d.*

Fiction

TO LONDON TOWN. *Second Ed. Cr. 8vo. 6s.*
DIVERS VANITIES. *Cr. 8vo. 6s.*
Nesbit (E.). (Mrs. H. Bland). THE RED HOUSE. Illustrated. *Fourth Edition. Cr. 8vo. 6s.* Also *Medium 8vo. 6d.*
Noble (Edward). LORDS OF THE SEA. *Second Edition. Cr. 8vo. 6s.*
Norris (W. E.). HARRY AND URSULA: A STORY WITH TWO SIDES TO IT. *Second Edition. Cr. 8vo. 6s.*
HIS GRACE. *Medium 8vo. 6d.*
GILES INGILBY. *Medium 8vo. 6d.*
THE CREDIT OF THE COUNTY. *Medium 8vo. 6d.*
LORD LEONARD THE LUCKLESS. *Medium 8vo. 6d.*
MATTHEW AUSTIN. *Medium 8vo. 6d.*
CLARISSA FURIOSA. *Medium 8vo. 6d.*
Oliphant (Mrs.). THE LADY'S WALK. *Medium 8vo. 6d.*
SIR ROBERT'S FORTUNE. *Medium 8vo. 6d.*
THE PRODIGALS. *Medium 8vo. 6d.*
THE TWO MARYS. *Medium 8vo. 6d.*
Ollivant (Alfred). OWD BOB, THE GREY DOG OF KENMUIR. With a Frontispiece. *Eleventh Ed. Cr. 8vo. 6s.*
Oppenheim (E. Phillips). MASTER OF MEN. *Fourth Edition. Cr. 8vo. 6s.* Also *Medium 8vo. 6d.*
Oxenham (John). A WEAVER OF WEBS. With 8 Illustrations by MAURICE GREIFFENHAGEN. *Fourth Edition. Cr. 8vo. 6s.*
THE GATE OF THE DESERT. With a Frontispiece in Photogravure by HAROLD COPPING. *Fifth Edition. Cr. 8vo. 6s.*
PROFIT AND LOSS. With a Frontispiece in photogravure by HAROLD COPPING. *Fourth Edition. Cr. 8vo. 6s.*
THE LONG ROAD. With a Frontispiece in Photogravure by HAROLD COPPING. *Fourth Edition. Cr. 8vo. 6s.*
THE SONG OF HYACINTH, AND OTHER STORIES. *Second Edition. Cr. 8vo. 6s.*
MY LADY OF SHADOWS. *Fourth Edition. Cr. 8vo. 6s.*
Pain (Barry). LINDLEY KAYS. *Third Edition. Cr. 8vo. 6s.*
Parker (Gilbert). PIERRE AND HIS PEOPLE. *Sixth Edition. Cr. 8vo. 6s.*
MRS. FALCHION. *Fifth Edition. Cr. 8vo. 6s.*
THE TRANSLATION OF A SAVAGE. *Third Edition. Cr. 8vo. 6s.*
THE TRAIL OF THE SWORD. Illustrated. *Tenth Edition. Cr. 8vo. 6s.* Also *Medium 8vo. 6d.*

WHEN VALMOND CAME TO PONTIAC: The Story of a Lost Napoleon. *Sixth Edition. Cr. 8vo. 6s.* Also *Medium 8vo. 6d.*
AN ADVENTURER OF THE NORTH. The Last Adventures of 'Pretty Pierre.' *Fourth Edition. Cr. 8vo. 6s.*
THE SEATS OF THE MIGHTY. Illustrated. *Sixteenth Edition. Cr. 8vo. 6s.*
THE BATTLE OF THE STRONG: a Romance of Two Kingdoms. Illustrated. *Sixth Edition. Cr. 8vo. 6s.*
THE POMP OF THE LAVILETTES. *Third Edition. Cr. 8vo. 3s. 6d.* Also *Medium 8vo. 6d.*
NORTHERN LIGHTS. *Cr. 8vo. 6s.*
*****Pasture (Mrs. Henry de la).** THE TYRANT. *Cr. 8vo. 6s.*
Patterson (J. E.). WATCHERS BY THE SHORE. *Second Edition. Cr. 8vo. 6s.*
Pemberton (Max). THE FOOTSTEPS OF A THRONE. Illustrated. *Third Edition. Cr. 8vo. 6s.* Also *Medium 8vo. 6d.*
I CROWN THEE KING. With Illustrations by Frank Dadd and A. Forrestier. *Cr. 8vo. 6s.* Also *Medium 8vo. 6d.*
LOVE THE HARVESTER: A STORY OF THE SHIRES. Illustrated. *Third Edition. Cr. 8vo. 3s. 6d.*
Phillpotts (Eden). LYING PROPHETS. *Third Edition. Cr. 8vo. 6s.*
CHILDREN OF THE MIST *Fifth Edition. Cr. 8vo. 6s.* Also *Medium 8vo. 6d.*
THE HUMAN BOY. With a Frontispiece *Sixth Edition. Cr. 8vo. 6s.* Also *Medium 8vo. 6d.*
SONS OF THE MORNING. *Second Edition. Cr. 8vo. 6s.*
THE RIVER. *Third Edition. Cr. 8vo. 6s.* Also *Medium 8vo. 6d.*
THE AMERICAN PRISONER. *Fourth Edition. Cr. 8vo. 6s.*
THE SECRET WOMAN. *Fourth Edition. Cr. 8vo. 6s.*
KNOCK AT A VENTURE. With a Frontispiece. *Third Edition. Cr. 8vo. 6s.*
THE PORTREEVE. *Fourth Ed. Cr. 8vo. 6s.*
THE POACHER'S WIFE. *Second Edition. Cr. 8vo. 6s.* Also *Medium 8vo. 6d.*
THE STRIKING HOURS. *Second Edition. Crown 8vo. 6s.*
THE FOLK AFIELD. *Crown 8vo. 6s.*
Pickthall (Marmaduke). SAÏD THE FISHERMAN. *Seventh Ed. Cr. 8vo. 6s.*
BRENDLE. *Second Edition. Cr. 8vo. 6s.*
THE HOUSE OF ISLAM. *Third Edition. Cr. 8vo. 6s.*

'Q' (A. T. Quiller Couch). THE WHITE WOLF. *Second Edition. Cr. 8vo. 6s.* Also *Medium 8vo. 6d.*

THE MAYOR OF TROY. *Fourth Edition. Cr. 8vo. 6s.*

MERRY-GARDEN, AND OTHER STORIES. *Cr. 8vo. 6s.*

MAJOR VIGOUREUX. *Third Edition. Cr. 8vo. 6s.*

Querida (Israel). TOIL OF MEN. Translated by F. S. ARNOLD. *Cr. 8vo. 6s.*

Rawson (Maud Stepney). THE ENCHANTED GARDEN. *Fourth Edition. Cr. 8vo. 6s.*

THE EASY GO LUCKIES: OR, ONE WAY OF LIVING. *Second Edition. Cr. 8vo. 6s.*

HAPPINESS. *Cr. 8vo. 6s.*

Rhys (Grace). THE WOOING OF SHEILA. *Second Edition. Cr. 8vo. 6s.*

THE BRIDE. *Cr. 8vo. 6s.*

Ridge W. Pett). LOST PROPERTY. *Second Edition. Cr. 8vo. 6s.* Also *Medium 8vo. 6d.*

ERB. *Second Edition. Cr. 8vo. 6s.* Also *Medium 8vo. 6d.*

A SON OF THE STATE. *Second Edition. Cr. 8vo. 3s. 6d.* Also *Medium 8vo. 6d.*

A BREAKER OF LAWS. *A New Edition. Cr. 8vo. 3s. 6d.*

MRS. GALER'S BUSINESS. Illustrated. *Second Edition. Cr. 8vo. 6s.*

THE WICKHAMSES. *Fourth Edition. Cr. 8vo. 6s.*

NAME OF GARLAND. *Third Edition. Cr. 8vo. 6s.*

SPLENDID BROTHER. *Second Edition. Cr. 8vo. 6s.*

GEORGE and THE GENERAL. *Medium 8vo. 6d.*

Ritchie (Mrs. David G.). MAN AND THE CASSOCK. *Second Edition. Cr. 8vo. 6s.*

Roberts (C. G. D.). THE HEART OF THE ANCIENT WOOD. *Cr. 8vo. 3s. 6d.*

Robins (Elizabeth). THE CONVERT. *Third Edition. Cr. 8vo. 6s.*

Rosenkrantz (Baron Palle). THE MAGISTRATE'S OWN CASE. *Cr. 8vo. 6s.*

Russell (W. Clark). MY DANISH SWEETHEART. Illustrated. *Fifth Edition. Cr. 8vo. 6s.* Also *Medium 8vo. 6d.*

HIS ISLAND PRINCESS. Illustrated. *Second Edition. Cr. 8vo. 6s.* Also *Medium 8vo. 6d.*

ABANDONED. *Second Edition. Cr. 8vo. 6s.* Also *Medium 8vo. 6d.*

MASTER ROCKAFELLAR'S VOYAGE. Illustrated by GORDON BROWNE. *Fourth Edition. Cr. 8vo. 3s. 6d.*

A MARRIAGE AT SEA. *Medium 8vo. 6d.*

Ryan (Marah Ellis). FOR THE SOUL OF RAFAEL. *Cr. 8vo. 6s.*

Sandys (Sydney). JACK CARSTAIRS OF THE POWER HOUSE. With 4 Illustrations by STANLEY L. WOOD. *Cr. 8vo. 6s.*

Sergeant (Adeline). THE PASSION OF PAUL MARILLIER. *Crown 8vo. 6s.*

THE QUEST OF GEOFFREY DARRELL. *Cr. 8vo. 6s.*

THE COMING OF THE RANDOLPHS. *Cr. 8vo. 6s.*

THE PROGRESS OF RACHAEL. *Cr. 8vo. 6s.*

BARBARA'S MONEY. *Medium 8vo. 6d.*

THE MASTER OF BEECHWOOD. *Medium 8vo. 6d.*

THE YELLOW DIAMOND. *Second Ed. Cr. 8vo. 6s.* Also *Medium 8vo. 6d.*

THE LOVE THAT OVERCAME. *Medium 8vo. 6d.*

Shelley (Bertha). ENDERBY. *Third Ed. Cr. 8vo. 6s.*

Sidgwick (Mrs. Alfred). THE KINSMAN. With 8 Illustrations by C. E. BROCK. *Third Edition. Cr. 8vo. 6s.*

THE SEVERINS. *Cr. 8vo. 6s.*

Smith (Dorothy V. Horace). MISS MONA. *Cr. 8vo. 3s. 6d.*

Sonnichsen (Albert). DEEP-SEA VAGABONDS. *Cr. 8vo. 6s.*

Stewart (Newton V.). A SON OF THE EMPEROR: BEING PASSAGES FROM THE LIFE OF ENZIO, KING OF SARDINIA AND CORSICA. *Cr. 8vo. 6s.*

Sunbury (George). THE HA'PENNY MILLIONAIRE. *Cr. 8vo. 3s. 6d.*

Surtees (R. S.). HANDLEY CROSS. Illustrated. *Medium 8vo. 6d.*

MR. SPONGE'S SPORTING TOUR. Illustrated. *Medium 8vo. 6d.*

ASK MAMMA. Illus. *Medium 8vo. 6d.*

Swayne (Martin Lutrell). THE BISHOP AND THE LADY. *Second Edition. Cr. 8vo. 6s.*

Thurston (E. Temple). MIRAGE. *Fourth Edition. Cr. 8vo. 6s.*

Underhill (Evelyn). THE COLUMN OF DUST. *Cr. 8vo. 6s.*

Urquhart (M.). A TRAGEDY IN COMMONPLACE. *Second Ed. Cr. 8vo. 6s.*

Vorst (Marie Van). THE SENTIMENTAL ADVENTURES OF JIMMY BULSTRODE. *Cr. 8vo. 6s.*

IN AMBUSH. *Cr. 8vo. 6s.*

Waineman (Paul). THE BAY OF LILACS: A Romance from Finland. *Second Edition. Cr. 8vo. 6s.*

THE SONG OF THE FOREST. *Cr. 8vo. 6s.*

FICTION

Walford (Mrs. L. B.). MR SMITH. *Medium 8vo. 6d.*
THE BABY'S GRANDMOTHER. *Medium 8vo. 6d.*
COUSINS. *Medium 8vo. 6d.*
TROUBLESOME DAUGHTERS. *Medium 8vo. 6d.*
Wallace (General Lew). BEN-HUR. *Medium 8vo. 6d.*
THE FAIR GOD. *Medium 8vo. 6d.*
Waltz (Elizabeth C.). THE ANCIENT LANDMARK: A KENTUCKY ROMANCE. *Cr. 8vo. 6s.*
Watson (H. B. Marriott). TWISTED EGLANTINE Illustrated. *Third Edition. Cr. 8vo. 6s.*
THE HIGH TOBY: Being further Chapters in the Life and Fortunes of Dick Ryder, otherwise Galloping Dick. With a Frontispiece. *Third Edition. Cr. 8vo. 6s.*
A MIDSUMMER DAY'S DREAM. *Third Edition. Crown 8vo. 6s.*
THE CASTLE BY THE SEA. *Second Edition. Cr. 8vo. 6s.*
THE PRIVATEERS. Illustrated. *Second Edition. Cr. 8vo. 6s.*
A POPPY SHOW: BEING DIVERS AND DIVERSE TALES. *Cr. 8vo. 6s.*
THE FLOWER OF THE HEART. *Third Edition. Cr. 8vo. 6s.*
THE ADVENTURERS. *Medium 8vo. 6d.*
Webling (Peggy). THE STORY OF VIRGINIA PERFECT. *Third Edition. Cr. 8vo. 6s.*
Weekes (A. B.). THE PRISONERS OF WAR. *Medium 8vo. 6d.*
Wells (H. G.). THE SEA LADY. *Cr. 8vo. 6s.* Also *Medium 8vo. 6d.*
Weyman (Stanley). UNDER THE RED ROBE. With Illustrations by R. C. Woodville. *Twenty-Second Ed. Cr. 8vo. 6s.*
Whitby (Beatrice). THE RESULT OF AN ACCIDENT. *Second Edition. Cr. 8vo. 6s.*
White (Percy). THE SYSTEM. *Third Edition. Cr. 8vo. 6s.*

A PASSIONATE PILGRIM. *Medium 8vo. 6d.*
LOVE AND THE WISE MEN. *Cr. 8vo. 6s.*
Williams (Margery). THE BAR. *Cr. 8vo. 6s.*
Williamson (Mrs. C. N.). THE ADVENTURE OF PRINCESS SYLVIA. *Second Edition. Cr. 8vo. 6s.*
THE WOMAN WHO DARED. *Cr. 8vo. 6s.*
THE SEA COULD TELL. *Second Edition. Cr. 8vo. 6s.*
THE CASTLE OF THE SHADOWS. *Third Edition. Cr. 8vo. 6s.*
PAPA. *Cr. 8vo. 6s.*
Williamson (C. N. and A. M.). THE LIGHTNING CONDUCTOR: The Strange Adventures of a Motor Car. With 16 Illustrations. *Seventeenth Edition. Cr. 8vo. 6s.* Also *Cr. 8vo. 1s. net.*
THE PRINCESS PASSES: A Romance of a Motor. With 16 Illustrations. *Ninth Edition. Cr. 8vo. 6s.*
MY FRIEND THE CHAUFFEUR. With 16 Illustrations. *Tenth Edit. Cr. 8vo. 6s.*
LADY BETTY ACROSS THE WATER. *Tenth Edition. Cr. 8vo. 6s.*
THE CAR OF DESTINY AND ITS ERRAND IN SPAIN. With 17 Illustrations. *Fourth Edition. Cr. 8vo. 6s.*
THE BOTOR CHAPERON. With a Frontispiece in Colour by A. H. BUCKLAND, 16 other Illustrations, and a Map. *Fifth Edition. Cr. 8vo. 6s.*
SCARLET RUNNER. With a Frontispiece in Colour by A. H. BUCKLAND, and 8 other Illustrations. *Third Ed. Cr. 8vo. 6s.*
SET IN SILVER. With a Frontispiece. *Second Edition. Cr. 8vo. 6s.*
Wyllarde (Dolf). THE PATHWAY OF THE PIONEER (Nous Autres). *Fourth Edition. Cr. 8vo. 6s.*
Yeldham (C. C.). DURHAM'S FARM. *Cr. 8vo. 6s.*

Books for Boys and Girls

Illustrated. Crown 8vo. 3s. 6d.

THE GETTING WELL OF DOROTHY. By Mrs. W. K. Clifford. *Second Edition.*
ONLY A GUARD-ROOM DOG. By Edith E. Cuthell.
MASTER ROCKAFELLAR'S VOYAGE. By W. Clark Russell. *Fourth Edition.*
SYD BELTON: Or, the Boy who would not go to Sea. By G. Manville Fenn. *Second Ed.*

THE RED GRANGE. By Mrs. Molesworth.
A GIRL OF THE PEOPLE. By L. T. Meade. *Fourth Edition.*
HEPSY GIPSY. By L. T. Meade. 2s. 6d.
THE HONOURABLE MISS. By L. T. Meade. *Second Edition.*
THERE WAS ONCE A PRINCE. By Mrs. M. E. Mann.
WHEN ARNOLD COMES HOME. By Mrs. M. E. Mann.

The Novels of Alexandre Dumas

Medium 8vo. Price 6d. Double Volumes, 1s.

Acté.
The Adventures of Captain Pamphile.
Amaury.
The Bird of Fate.
The Black Tulip.
The Castle of Eppstein.
Catherine Blum.
Cecile.
The Chevalier D'Harmental. (Double volume.) 1s.
Chicot the Jester.
Conscience.
The Convict's Son.
The Corsican Brothers; and Otho the Archer.
Crop-Eared Jacquot.
Dom Gorenflot.
The Fatal Combat.
The Fencing Master.
Fernande.
Gabriel Lambert.
Georges.
The Great Massacre.
Henri de Navarre.
Hélène de Chaverny.
The Horoscope.
Louise de la Vallière. (Double volume.) 1s.
The Man in the Iron Mask. (Double volume.) 1s.
Maître Adam.
The Mouth of Hell.
Nanon. (Double volume.) 1s.
Pauline; Pascal Bruno; and Bontekoe.
Père la Ruine.
The Prince of Thieves.
The Reminiscences of Antony.
Robin Hood.
The Snowball and Sultanetta.
Sylvandire.
Tales of the Supernatural.
Tales of Strange Adventure.
The Three Musketeers. (Double volume.) 1s.
The Tragedy of Nantes.
Twenty Years After. (Double volume.) 1s.
The Wild-Duck Shooter.
The Wolf-Leader.

Methuen's Sixpenny Books

Medium 8vo.

Albanesi (E. Maria). LOVE AND LOUISA.
I KNOW A MAIDEN.
Anstey (F.). A BAYARD OF BENGAL.
Austen (J.). PRIDE AND PREJUDICE.
Bagot (Richard). A ROMAN MYSTERY.
CASTING OF NETS.
DONNA DIANA.
Balfour (Andrew). BY STROKE OF SWORD.
Baring-Gould (S.). FURZE BLOOM.
CHEAP JACK ZITA.
KITTY ALONE.
URITH.
THE BROOM SQUIRE.
IN THE ROAR OF THE SEA.
NOÉMI.
A BOOK OF FAIRY TALES. Illustrated.
LITTLE TU'PENNY.
WINEFRED.
THE FROBISHERS.
THE QUEEN OF LOVE.
ARMINELL.
Barr (Robert). JENNIE BAXTER.
IN THE MIDST OF ALARMS.
THE COUNTESS TEKLA.
THE MUTABLE MANY.
Benson (E. F.). DODO.
THE VINTAGE.
Brontë (Charlotte). SHIRLEY.
Brownell (C. L.). THE HEART OF JAPAN.
Burton (J. Bloundelle). ACROSS THE SALT SEAS.
Caffyn (Mrs.). ANNE MAULEVERER.
Capes (Bernard). THE LAKE OF WINE.
Clifford (Mrs. W. K.). A FLASH OF SUMMER.
MRS. KEITH'S CRIME.
Corbett (Julian). A BUSINESS IN GREAT WATERS.
Croker (Mrs. B. M.). ANGEL.
A STATE SECRET.
PEGGY OF THE BARTONS.
JOHANNA.
Dante (Alighieri). THE DIVINE COMEDY (Cary).
Doyle (A. Conan). ROUND THE RED LAMP.
Duncan (Sara Jeannette). A VOYAGE OF CONSOLATION.
THOSE DELIGHTFUL AMERICANS.
Eliot (George). THE MILL ON THE FLOSS.
Findlater (Jane H.). THE GREEN GRAVES OF BALGOWRIE.
Gallon (Tom). RICKERBY'S FOLLY.
Gaskell (Mrs.). CRANFORD.
MARY BARTON.
NORTH AND SOUTH.

Fiction

Gerard (Dorothea). HOLY MATRIMONY.
THE CONQUEST OF LONDON.
MADE OF MONEY.

Gissing (G). THE TOWN TRAVELLER.
THE CROWN OF LIFE.

Glanville (Ernest). THE INCA'S TREASURE.
THE KLOOF BRIDE.

Gleig (Charles). BUNTER'S CRUISE.

Grimm (The Brothers). GRIMM'S FAIRY TALES.

Hope (Anthony). A MAN OF MARK.
A CHANGE OF AIR.
THE CHRONICLES OF COUNT ANTONIO.
PHROSO.
THE DOLLY DIALOGUES.

Hornung (E. W.). DEAD MEN TELL NO TALES.

Ingraham (J. H.). THE THRONE OF DAVID.

Le Queux (W.). THE HUNCHBACK OF WESTMINSTER.

Levett-Yeats (S. K.). THE TRAITOR'S WAY.
ORRAIN.

Linton (E. Lynn). THE TRUE HISTORY OF JOSHUA DAVIDSON.

Lyall (Edna). DERRICK VAUGHAN.

Malet (Lucas). THE CARISSIMA.
A COUNSEL OF PERFECTION.

Mann (Mrs. M. E.). MRS. PETER HOWARD.
A LOST ESTATE.
THE CEDAR STAR.
ONE ANOTHER'S BURDENS.
THE PATTEN EXPERIMENT.
A WINTER'S TALE.

Marchmont (A. W.). MISER HOADLEY'S SECRET.
A MOMENT'S ERROR.

Marryat (Captain). PETER SIMPLE.
JACOB FAITHFUL.

Marsh (Richard). A METAMORPHOSIS.
THE TWICKENHAM PEERAGE.
THE GODDESS.
THE JOSS.

Mason (A. E. W.). CLEMENTINA.

Mathers (Helen). HONEY.
GRIFF OF GRIFFITHSCOURT.
SAM'S SWEETHEART.

Meade (Mrs. L. T.). DRIFT.

Miller (Esther). LIVING LIES.

Mitford (Bertram). THE SIGN OF THE SPIDER.

Montresor (F. F.). THE ALIEN.

Morrison (Arthur). THE HOLE IN THE WALL.

Nesbit (E.) THE RED HOUSE.

Norris (W. E.). HIS GRACE.
GILES INGILBY.
THE CREDIT OF THE COUNTY.
LORD LEONARD THE LUCKLESS.
MATTHEW AUSTIN.
CLARISSA FURIOSA.

Oliphant (Mrs.). THE LADY'S WALK.
SIR ROBERT'S FORTUNE.
THE PRODIGALS.
THE TWO MARYS.

Oppenheim (E. P.). MASTER OF MEN.

Parker (Gilbert). THE POMP OF THE LAVILETTES.
WHEN VALMOND CAME TO PONTIAC.
THE TRAIL OF THE SWORD.

Pemberton (Max). THE FOOTSTEPS OF A THRONE.
I CROWN THEE KING.

Phillpotts (Eden). THE HUMAN BOY.
CHILDREN OF THE MIST.
THE POACHER'S WIFE.
THE RIVER.

'Q' (A. T. Quiller Couch). THE WHITE WOLF.

Ridge (W. Pett). A SON OF THE STATE.
LOST PROPERTY.
GEORGE and THE GENERAL.
ERB.

Russell (W. Clark). ABANDONED.
A MARRIAGE AT SEA.
MY DANISH SWEETHEART.
HIS ISLAND PRINCESS.

Sergeant (Adeline). THE MASTER OF BEECHWOOD.
BARBARA'S MONEY.
THE YELLOW DIAMOND.
THE LOVE THAT OVERCAME.

Sidgwick (Mrs. Alfred). THE KINSMAN.

Surtees (R. S.). HANDLEY CROSS.
MR. SPONGE'S SPORTING TOUR.
ASK MAMMA.

Walford (Mrs. L. B.). MR. SMITH.
COUSINS.
THE BABY'S GRANDMOTHER.
TROUBLESOME DAUGHTERS.

Wallace (General Lew). BEN-HUR.
THE FAIR GOD.

Watson (H. B. Marriott). THE ADVENTURERS.

Weekes (A. B.). PRISONERS OF WAR.

Wells (H. G.). THE SEA LADY.

White (Percy). A PASSIONATE PILGRIM.

ImTheStory.com

Personalized Classic Books in many genre's

Unique gift for kids, partners, friends, colleagues

Customize:
- Character Names
- Upload your own front/back cover images (optional)
- Inscribe a personal message/dedication on the inside page (optional)

Customize many titles Including
- Alice in Wonderland
- Romeo and Juliet
- The Wizard of Oz
- A Christmas Carol
- Dracula
- Dr. Jekyll & Mr. Hyde
- And more...

Lightning Source UK Ltd.
Milton Keynes UK
UKOW06f1844080615

253117UK00008B/105/P